MIDDLE STATE

BY

Mike Miller

authorHOUSE®

AuthorHouse™
1663 Liberty Drive
Bloomington, IN 47403
www.authorhouse.com
Phone: 1-800-839-8640

First published by AuthorHouse 8/25/2011

ISBN: 978-1-4567-3900-3 (ebk)
ISBN: 978-1-4567-3901-0 (sc)
ISBN: 978-1-4567-3902-7 (hc)

Library of Congress Control Number: 2011901796

Printed in the United States of America

Any people depicted in stock imagery provided by Thinkstock are models,
and such images are being used for illustrative purposes only.
Certain stock imagery © Thinkstock.

This book is printed on acid-free paper.

....unless constrained by the moral vision of the persons in them, institutions move in the direction of power and self-preservation, not high principle.

Wendell Berry
"Discipline and Hope"
A Continuous Harmony

Students who are passionate about learning, or could become so, do exist. Faculty members who love their subjects passionately and are eager to teach what they know and to plumb its depths further also exist. But institutions devoted to respecting and fulfilling these needs as their first purposes have become rare. . . .

Jane Jacobs
Dark Age Ahead

TABLE OF CONTENTS

I

II

I

one
WARREN

I'll never get out, Chris Warren thought as he stared dejectedly at Middle State's updated Schedule of Fall Classes for his senior year. Down the hall from the shabby dorm-floor study lounge where he was temporarily exiled, his roommate Plumb Bob was still in a rowdy if muffled morning study session with his woman-of-the-week, and Warren had to wait until the well-exercised pupil had been dismissed and gone slowly past him to the elevator before rushing down to announce that coming to college was the dumbest thing he had ever done.

"It's the same courses as they listed last spring," he said to Plumb Bob's attempt at comprehension from the pile of bedclothes, part of which were on the floor. "There's only two required upper division courses offered this fall that I haven't had, and I need eight to graduate. That means there'll have to be six scheduled next spring, and you know they won't have that many or anything close to it. I'll have to stay another semester at least. I can't afford it, my folks can't."

"That can't be a problem," Plumb Bob said, plucking weakly at the covers. "Change majors. It's easy, just a little paperwork. And I'll guarantee that whatever you change it to, they'll be glad to have you. When I switched from Animal Husbandry to Telecommunications they gave me $100. Or maybe it was from Wildlife Management to Animal Husbandry. But anyway I got $100. I hear if you change to Physics they give you a car, on condition that you graduate. I'd definitely change majors. Changing majors is the way to go."

"I don't want to change majors. And anyway, that wouldn't do me any good," Warren said, noticing that Plumb Bob's coal black hair, in spite of the devastation of the bed, was in perfect place. "I'm running

1

out of money. If I change majors, it'll take at least another year to get out, maybe two. Even if I stick with English it's going to take an extra semester, at least. Either way I've got to come up with the money for tuition, and room and board, and books. I can't afford it."

"Borrow the money," Plumb Bob said, strength returning to his voice.

"No way," Warren said. "I already owe six thousand in student loans. And my folks have helped me out, all they could. I'd like someday to pay them back. Everything I saved from summer work went for the next year's expenses. I can't borrow any more money. I don't want to."

Both his parents did actual work for a living and were therefore in a low income bracket. In addition there were two younger children whom they were convinced they must send to college or else be failures as parents and human beings.

"Borrow the money and then take bankruptcy as soon as you get out. Everybody does it."

Warren looked at the floor. He knew many did but was shocked at Plumb Bob, whose advice as a venerable sage of twenty-six, with women literally lined up for him, Warren generally respected.

"Wait, listen," Plumb Bob said, trying to sort out the sheets, which appeared to have been braided and then stirred, "what about an independent study course, you know about them? When I was in Family Planning I took one one summer. Tammie–Dr. Russo–offered it. She was writing a book and all I had to do for credit was read it and meet her at her house for a couple of times a week and write a book report on it. I never wrote the report," he mused. "I never really read the book. In fact, I'm not sure she ever wrote it. But I got an A. You ought to get an independent study courses, or several if you can. Did you know about them?"

"Yes, but, I don't know, I just want to be able to take the courses I'm supposed to take. If they require certain courses for graduation, they ought to offer them. Hoh's got the same problem in Instrument Design."

Hoh, who roomed with Jeeks across the hall from Warren and Plumb Bob, had known his plight for several days. Warren suspected that even more of the mix of juniors and seniors that made up the dorm floor might be in the same boat, or were going to be. Only the obsessively organized Sola was likely exempt from the problem, and, of course, Bolinger, who was above such concerns.

"I've followed the model schedule every semester. I've taken the courses they said to. What I don't get is that they're offering 500-level courses, but they're stuff like"–he looked at the Schedule of Classes–"Teaching Teachers Teaching. Advanced Haiku Writing. Pro-active Rhetoric in the World of Work. My area is literature and there's only three lit courses listed and I've had one of them."

"What about your advisor" Plumb Bob asked, "have you talked to your advisor? I think he's the first person above you in the Managerial Hierarchy. You ought to start there. Maybe he can get some courses added."

An advisor. Warren could remember how deeply reassuring that term was when as a freshman he saw it, along with his first faculty advisor's name, on his Middle State registration packet. Yes, an advisor–a wise, kindly mentor who would gauge his needs, spread the map of his education before him, counsel him on his journey, and be his friend and guide into a higher world that Warren sensed was to come. He never met his first one, primarily because he had been denied tenure at Middle State three years earlier, his departure evidently unregistered by the university computer. Since then Warren had been assigned four different advisors, two of whom gave him bad advice and two, because he could never find them in their offices, no advice at all. His lofty concept of an advisor had gradually slipped out of his mind, but the previous spring semester, when his grim situation first became apparent, Warren had determined to contact whoever this elusive personage might at present be and appeal for justice.

It took him two days, pounding across campus from one administrative office to another, to discover with some certainty who this advisor was, and when he went to his office in Humanities Hall, a curled and yellowing note taped askew to the door informed him that Prof. Appleby, as Director of Supervisors for International Studies, was out of the country for the year. Which year, the note didn't specify, but both the note and the sealed office itself, as decisively closed as a pharaoh's tomb, gave the sense that for epochs to come, the escaped and vagabond spirit of Prof. Appleby would be disporting abroad.

Not enough 'revenue person hours' generated. Revenue–from Middle French, I believe, revenir, to come again, which is what they want you to do–not that they know the derivation of revenue, or for that matter that it has a derivation. But they actually use phrases like 'revenue person hours,'" he said sorrowfully before coming back to Warren's concern. "Now there is a way to get credit for some of these courses, but I never found it satisfactory. Independent study courses. Even when I gave in myself and agreed to offer one to a student, I never felt much was accomplished."

He looked closely at Warren for a moment. "You do know," he said, "that it's still possible to get a good education here? Sometimes that's better than job training. You never know what you'll need to know. Or want to know. I suppose you'll want a good job when you get out?"

"I'd like to have a job, yes sir," Warren said. Paying off his loans and repaying his parents were settled obligations to him, but he rarely thought about his studies preparing him just to hold down some job. While he felt it best to keep his feelings to himself, he actually loved his courses, most of them. He was an oddball who was curious and liked to know things.

"It's not all job training," Dr. Hobart said, "although that's all it's sold on anymore. That's all they think young people care about. They think they're all like them."

He was silent for a moment, and Warren, in spite of the uneasiness he felt over Dr Hobart's strange confidings, hoped he would go on.

"Well," Dr. Hobart said suddenly, coming to himself, "all this won't help you any. You need to go to the Job Office or whatever they call it–I'm sure they don't call it the Job Office–and see if that brochure on job possibilities has anything to it. It's unbelievable what they can do with the future over there. Their offices are in Wilmore Hall, or they used to be."

Warren thanked him, and after finding Dr. Brumley, who had tried to help him the previous spring still at lunch, taped a note on his office door and to avoid the crowded elevators took the stairs down. He wanted to hear more from Dr. Hobart, who clearly thought what was happening to him was wrong and that more was at fault than an isolated oversight in scheduling or simple indifference on the part of the department. He even criticized the way offices named themselves, and Warren had hardly ever heard an instructor criticize anything, other than various kinds of discrimination against minorities. And the remarks about those who believed job training was all there was—who were *they*, thinking all young people were like them? Warren wasn't sure what Dr. Hobart was getting at, but he thought he would like to hear more, especially after a long wait in the outer offices of the Director of Employment Placement and Career Counseling.

"Another job seeker," Eigleman, the Director, trumpeted as Warren, nearly an hour later, was called into his roomy office. "Please come in. Ah, would you mind sitting over here?" He directed Warren away from the two heavily padded, wing-backed leather chairs at the side of his large desk toward a folding metal chair in front of it.

"I like to talk to students head-on, so to speak," and he swiveled his high-back, plush chair toward a computer that nestled in an elaborate console to the side and rolled to it.

"What was that name again?"

"Chris—Christopher—Warren."

Eigleman typed furiously, punched several buttons, looked, punched another button.

"Goddamnit," he said. "This piece of shit. Pardon my French. It must not have any capacity. How do they think I can keep up with. . . . Ah, there," he said, still typing, pushing buttons, manipulating the pointer. The computer erupted in a series of flashes and messages.

"No, wait . . . goddamn this son of a bitch!"

He swiveled disgustedly and rolled to a bank of file cabinets flanking the other side of the desk.

"Let's see. Watson, you said?"

"Warren. Christopher Warren."

"Christopher Warren," Eigleman muttered. Christopher Warren, Warren—Carmen, Cecil—here we are, Warren, Christopher." He pulled the thin file folder out, wheeled back to his desk and opened it.

"Now. What can I do for you?"

"My advisor said I should see you about the brochure I got with my registration packet that said anyone with my major. . . ."

"What's your major?" Eigleman asked.

"Humanities, English, with teaching. Teaching writing."

Eigleman smiled suddenly at the folder and held it toward Warren.

"Yes," he said, "yes, Humanities, right here—this pink marker on the file indicates a Humanities major." He proudly pointed to the pink marker.

"I came up with the idea to color code these folders just before I was made director," he said with satisfaction. "Bill Compton had this job then. Didn't like the idea. Said any idiot could open the folder and read the major on the info sheet. But we didn't have just any idiot in this office. I mean, I wanted people to see we had a system, an innovative system, not just ordinary file folders with a name on the tag. You open these drawers—which, by the way, we don't do enough of these days with this"—he pointed at the computer—"piece of shit—pardon my French—we've got to use. No color coding with that thing. Einstein couldn't make any innovations with that thing; it's all innovations to start with. And innovation is all there is. You better remember that when you get a job. Innovation."

Eigleman had hoped that by continuing to perform as innovatively as Director as he had as Assistant Director he could draw the Department of Student Affairs under his purview with a raise in salary commensurate with his expanded power. Then, perhaps, a vice-presidency, though he wasn't sure which one of the vice-presidents he would like to be. Presently his department was under the Vice-president for Outreach and Intake, although when he was assistant director, before his color-coding coup had driven Compton into the Student Affairs office, he had been under the Vice-president for University and Public Services. But any vice-presidency would do, and he was confident he could handle whichever one he could attain—Vice-president for Student Services, for University and Public Affairs, for Academics, for Football, for Public Information, for Basketball—these or any of the several others would suit him fine, and with his talent for innovation and his friendly, dignified style, he would prosper.

"No, Mr. Christopher, there's no innovation in computers. Now, where were we? What were you saying.?"

Warren was unable to reply for that moment too long that Eigleman took for criticism.

"You're here to talk about yourself," Eigleman said coldly, his friendly, dignified style forgotten. "What do you want?"

"I got this brochure the other day. It says I don't have much of a chance for a job when I get out. When I started school, there were plenty of jobs in teaching, all kinds of teaching. Now I owe six thousand dollars in student loans and except for what I made in summer work I haven't even started making a living. My folks co-signed my loans. If I don't pay the loans back, they'll have to. And they don't have the money." He wanted to say more, but knew he'd already said too much.

"Market saturation," said Eigleman, now with great contentment. "We call it market saturation. For a period of time there will be a great demand for certain talents, for certain training—stock brokers during the 1920's, nuclear workers before Three Mile Island and Chernobyl—that sort of thing. First there will be a big demand for a position, people go to school to get a certificate that says they can fill that position—and then there are too many of the position fillers and not enough positions. Market saturation. You see?"

"Yes," Warren replied. It was all so obvious.

"By the way," Eigleman asked, "where did you get the idea there were plenty of jobs in teaching English?"

"From a brochure Middle State sent me when I was in high school. I'd asked about going to school here and they sent it. Along with other stuff."

"A brochure saying there were jobs in teaching? From here?" Eigleman smiled in disbelief. "I don't know about that—you sure it wasn't some other school?"

"No, sir," Warren said. "I didn't apply to any other school. Middle State was near home, and all your advertisements said what a good school it was"—and, he thought, it was cheap. "In fact," he said, reaching for his backpack and withdrawing from it a slick-paged brochure, "I still have it. The information is on page three, in this table of Career Fields, Job Prospects of—right here."

Eigleman, who had rolled nimbly around to the metal chair, carefully took the brochure and eyed it dubiously.

"Hmmm," he said. "Now where did this come from?"

He turned to the last page, where Prepared and Edited by Alfred Eigleman, Asst. Dir. of Employment Placement and Career Counseling

9

and by the Office of Public Information was spelled out in bold lettering.

"Oh, yes, I see now," he said, glancing quickly up at Warren. "This is a preliminary career survey bulletin–hardly a brochure–that we prepare for the Office of Public Information every year. We supply the information, though it's their responsibility to see that it's up-to-date and arrange it properly. I can certainly understand how you might have had your expectations raised, but you can see while it did look as though there would be a thousand more teaching positions available five years down the road than there would be position fillers for them, you can also see that nursing home associates and fast-food chefs would have a surplus of a hundred thousand positions. So really, the number of teacher positions was quite small, easily within the margin of error of no positions or even negative positions of the survey techniques. I hear what you're saying about your hopes, but frankly, I don't think this bulletin is at fault. Do you see?"

Warren did not.

"Yes," he said.

"And anyway," Eigleman went on, evidently relieved, "this was not a scientifically documented job opening survey, not legally binding. The Public Information office asked us for what we thought the market might look like in five years, and you know Public Information–we gave them what we thought and they knew what would sound best and made this pretty bulletin."

He held it toward Warren. The color picture on the front showed a young, handsome couple, diplomas in hand and still wearing their graduation caps and gowns, walking toward what was clearly their future in the form of a large house of some vaguely European provincial design with many roofs and gables. Two large vehicles sat in its driveway, and neighbors standing in the yards of small houses on each side regarded with admiration and envy these educated darlings of fortune.

"Public Information knows how to handle these things. Over here," he pointed to the very small print at the extreme bottom of the last page of text, "they make it pretty clear that the nature of this information is projective."

The print was so fine Warren couldn't read it until Eigleman helpfully indicated the leather chair nearer the light from his office's two large windows. There, buoyed on the expensive cushioning under the cold hide, Warren read:

"The material in this brochure, while based on the best information presently available, is speculative only. Market conditions outside the control of these offices may negate certain indicated trends. Prospective position seekers should keep such unanticipated variables in mind."

"I didn't see that," he said. "It's in pretty fine print."

"I remember telling those shitheads in PI we shouldn't send these out," Eigleman said, shaking his head. "If enough students got together and said we were misleading them about their education guaranteeing them money, my career would be seriously threatened. I might be stuck in this goddamned office from now on–look at this," he gestured broadly at what Warren thought was an office both spacious and expensively appointed, certainly more so than that of Dr. Hobart or any other instructor and particularly roomy and lavish compared to his and Plumb Bob's concrete block cubicle of a dorm room.

"You know, you hear me belly-aching about computers," Eigleman went on, gripped by the subject. "If I'd had the idea to put computers everywhere on this campus but in the toilet stalls, I'd have been out of this flea bag of an office long ago. Darby–hell, he was one of those humanities guys, wasn't he?–he saw the wave of the future, that unless you fuck with these things, you're fucked. And I'm fucked and he's head of Computer Services, gave away all his books and is damn near a Vice-president. There are rumors that he'll be made Vice-president of Computer Affairs any day. Goddamnit."

Warren, who had slid out of the seat and was edging toward the door, was almost free when Eigleman became aware of him again.

"Wait, look, your situation isn't hopeless, not by any means," he said, seizing a pile of papers on his desk and sorting through it until he found another colorful brochure, this one with a letter affixed to it.

"Come here a minute, here's an offer for a teaching job–teaching writing even, and some other things. From Los Angeles–you like sunny California?–one of 1400 mailings their school system sent to colleges all over the country. Here, look at this."

He handed it to Warren after removing the letter. The front of the brochure showed a happy teenage foursome of a Latino in a serape, a white, a black and an Asian-American striding toward the entrance of a left his office and found Barnes conferring by the open hood of her car with a distraught janitor, late to pick up her child from day care. He had maneuvered his car over, helped connect his jumper cables to the weak battery, and along with Barnes pushed the car, its near-treadless tires singing, onto cleared pavement. Warmed by the exertion, he and Barnes had talked for a few minutes until the cold seeped back in. Ever since, Barnes always hailed Brumley, stopping to chat with him when they both had time, and only once over the years had he given him a ticket, for which he was deeply apologetic but, as he explained, he had no choice since Brumley had parked his then new car, the only one he'd ever purchased, with one tire touching the parking line. Barnes was an institutional institution, over forty years on the force, and hardly a year went by without an inaccurate and dully-written feature on him appearing in the student-run *Middle State News*. Typically, it missed the real story. When he was first hired, it was told, he had ticketed the large, costly car supplied by the Reigning Board to then-President Walls that had been arrogantly parked in a handicap space. Who had parked it was never clearly established, though an assistant in the President's office quickly offered to pay the fine, which was as quickly canceled by the Director of Security. In the nearly forty years since, Barnes was assigned patrol duties only in areas where no one of any importance was likely to park, and he had never been promoted from his lowly duties.

He did not care, having a higher duty to fulfill. It was to see that the rich did their part and then some, and that the arrogant got their due. Revenue from parking tickets paid the upkeep of the parking lots, including the salaries of the needy student-workers who picked up trash, painted the parking space lines and trimmed the lots' grass borders. Since Barnes gave out the tickets, he was in a position to see justice done that few ever attained. And because he did not ticket excessively or without cause, the fact that he cited in great disproportion the owners of the newest, gaudiest and most expensive vehicles went undetected. In fact and predictably, in almost as great disproportion, they actually did violate parking regulations.

Brumley, now fully alert, watched Barns pause on the grassy border separating faculty and staff parking from the student section, which stretched away like a rolling asphalt field up and over the crest of a small hill and out of Barnes' sight. Cars were still pulling in, the starting time for classes a full three minutes away, giving students plenty of time to be only five minutes late. This was Barnes' favorite stalking hour. Not only was it the first day of the term that parking regulations were enforced–students were given almost two weeks to learn to distinguish signs reading Students from those reading Faculty and Staff–but it was early morning and students with affluent parents were even less likely than usual to comply with anything that might cause them the slightest inconvenience. Brumley saw turn into the area a huge pickup, bejeweled with multiple headlights, a great chrome bar diademed above the cab, and gleaming rails necklaced around the truck bed. The dealer's price sticker was still displayed in the passenger-side window, which like all the other windows was tinted to a shade dark enough that no commoner's eyes could defile whatever royalty rode within. It pranced and bucked on its tight clutch around section D, and finding no empty slot pulled at an angle to the yellow curb at the entrance and stopped, just in front of a No Parking sign.

Brumley leaned forward and tried to clear away some of the film of dirt on the window, which like all the others had not been washed, inside or out, since the building was built. Although the truck was surely out of sight to Barnes, Brumley saw him lift his head, as if scenting the wind, and begin to quarter methodically across lots A and B, checking vehicles as he went but being pulled inexorably toward the crown jewel of a truck, whose driver had leapt from it, punched for a moment at some electronic device to lock the vehicle and activate its security system, and then sauntered off, empty handed, toward Humanities Hall and the academic rigors of the day. On the way, he passed Barnes without a glance.

In lot C, Barnes ticketed two late-model cars and then paused like an aged but canny hawk on the wing, looking past what might have been an entire section of permitless and illegally parked vehicles to lock implacably on the fat, bespangled truck lolling insolently under the No Parking sign. He approached warily, circled the truck with slow deliberation, paused to unsheath his pen and flip back the metal cover of his ticket book and then pounced. No Permit, undoubtedly– Improperly Parked, Illegally Parked. Barnes, Brumley knew, would extract the maximum. When he lifted the windshield wiper to place the ticket, the vehicle's security alarm began to shriek in outrage. Barnes and he was already a legend–that's legend, from Medieval Latin, associated with sainthood."

Hobart was right; Old Cadoon was a legend among those of the faculty who longed for legends, and Hobart, huge, slipshod, and an incorrigible etymologist, was determined to keep the name of Old Cadoon alive. Along with Greenman, and Norens, Hobart was Brumley's other kindred spirit in the department. By virtue of his nearly thirty long years at Middle State Hobart had a greater store of memories than was good for him and had contacts from broom closets to President Curtis's office.

"Remember Old Cadoon," he intoned. "That's re-member, an unrecognized antonym of dis-member. We re-member, re-collect, re-call–in fact, re-cognize–all by putting together patterned fragments from all parts of the mind, re-assembling them. Re-member. Get it?"

Brumley got it and was worried that President Curtis, inscrutably silent in response to his intemperate letter, would remember him as a troublemaker. And he knew there were many ways of handling troublemakers, beginning with identifying them by encouraging open discussion, and Brumley, ready to discuss Chris Warren's quandary openly, understood how easily his discussion could be taken as criticism, which hardly differed from insubordination or even sedition.

But just as likely, President Curtis had never been given his letter, or, if he had, hadn't bothered to consider or even read it, and Brumley decided to try to stop worrying. He had other concerns at the moment, and first was preparing for today's two sections of the General Humanities course required of all Middle State students. He had two hours to do so; luckily the main humanities office was empty, which meant he wouldn't have to see or speak to Huckston, the truckling Director of Creative Writing; or Davis, the Director of the Literature of the Oppressed, Marginalized and Disempowered; or Stephens, for-now directorless; or any of the other operators or lunatics who were slowly taking over not just the humanities, though they seemed largely attracted there, but the whole university. Checking his empty mail box, he headed for his cramped office on the other side, weaving around the stacks of pipes and materials for the new sprinkler system intended to protect from fire the scores of computers now invading classrooms, and also to protect the building from fires that might originate in computers.

He tried imagining Officer Barnes out on the parking lot, directing the tow truck into position, and then, even more consoling, the fury of the offending pickup's owner when sprinting for his glittering coach to get the hell out of there he found his means of conveyance gone and noticed for the first time, his fury redoubling, the No Parking sign.

Cheered by the thought, Brumley walked down the narrow corridor to his office, avoiding stepping on the faint remnants of white stripes at ten-yard intervals on the bright green carpet. Previous to its installation in the office areas of Humanities Hall, the carpet had graced the football field before slight wear had required its replacement with an even more expensive material, which already was showing signs of excessive cleating and whose replacement was being urged by Coach Seighel and the full might of the football Booster Club. Taped to his office door was a note that Brumley carefully pulled loose. *Dr. Brumley*, it read, *I'm still trying to get the courses I need to graduate next spring. I'll stop by later to tell you how it's going. Hope you had a good summer break.* It was signed *Chris Warren*.

Brumley felt a rush of sympathy and guilt. Warren, no doubt, still believed he could graduate on time and that he, Brumley, in spite of his fruitless attempts to help him the previous spring, could somehow see to it. That meant Warren had faith in him. Warren liked his classes, Brumley was sure: as a sophomore and junior he had taken two classes under him, and this semester he was taking two more, a second Humanities class and British Literature. Somehow—through youth and innocence, Brumley supposed—Warren misconstrued an instructor's semblance of knowledge as signifying influence or power.

Brumley unlocked his office, flipped on the light switch and sat down at his desk in the twenty-year-old chair that now fit him, with only a few sags and rough seams, like a glove. Out his window he could see the smokestacks of the Transuranic Department and the Center for Life Form Enhancement that towered over Middle State. He had time to grade, from a stack of sixty-two short essays, the last five that he'd been unable to face after a weekend of struggling through the first fifty-seven. Those five he could do in an hour, then have time to review Plato's *Apology*, which he had read with care and his usual admiration the previous evening. His office was small, the walls lined with crammed book shelves, his desk facing the door and a filing cabinet to its left. Brumley opened his briefcase, took out the two rubber-band bound sheaves of papers and extracted from one sheaf the five ungraded essays.

The first two went smoothly. The topic dealt with the class's first reading of the semester, selections from the *Odyssey*, and while both papers showed no enthusiasm for the topic or the work itself and were written without insight, wit, or as far as possible even style, Brumley could see they were more or less on the topic and were not plagiarized. Along with suggestions for improvement that he doubted would be considered or even read, he gave each a C.

When machines write, he reflected, *it will be like this.* A part of him had long ago understood that the great majority of his students never read anything for pleasure and therefore could not write anything that gave pleasure. But he could never fully accept their refusal to read. On the other hand, he realized, he had never had the distractions from reading that they had: the video games, the ever-growing lure of the Internet, the nascent rise of the cell phone and the resultant death of reflective solitude.

He went to the next paper: "And then this woman tried to turn Odysseus into a pig," read Kimee Deneen Garland's second breathless paragraph of pointless plot summary, "but Odysseus said 'No way, Sursee!'"

What can you say, he thought. What can you possibly say that Kimee Deneen could understand and that wouldn't offend? Inappropriate style? Would that even be accurate in characterizing the horror? Would she have the slightest idea what that meant or even care? He poised his red-ink pen over the spacious margin beside the sentence from the void. Sighing with near despair he finally wrote:

"KD–would Odysseus have spoken as you have him speak? Is your version of his response true to the way Homer has him speak–or represents him as a person–through the rest of the poem? Does it really reflect what O. does when Circe (the usual transcription of Circe's name into English) tries to harm him? And is it"—he searched fruitlessly for the truly proper word—"right to refer to Circe, the immortal enchantress, as 'this woman'?"

He groaned inwardly when he considered Kimee Deneen's uncomprehending or indifferent reaction to what he'd written. Kimee

Deneen, as blooming a piece of ass as ever bewitched his classroom, had the first day worn a dress so short that every shift of her long and perfect legs flashed the silken white crotch of her panties at him, a Morse code of unintentional temptation, the key to whose deciphering he knew he would never possess. Even with the effort that was habitual with him he could not put her secret, unconscious dispatch out of his mind. That she would go far and do well he felt certain, and formal education would have nothing to do with her journey. And yet, he had realized, she clearly listened in class and often responded intelligently to his questions. He recalled their first class meeting of the semester, when preliminary to their readings from the *Odyssey* he had given them some background to the Trojan War.

"So Hera–Athena–Aphrodite," he had said as he wrote the names on the board, "each made a separate bribe to Paris, the young prince of Troy." He wrote Power, Knowledge and, lamely, Most Beautiful Woman under the proffering deities.

"Which do you think this young, virile prince chose?"

Kimee Deneen raised her hand, her eyes, Brumley fancied, burning.

"Knowledge," she said firmly, certain, Brumley imagined, that a middle-aged bookworm like himself would have only 'knowledge' at the head of any list he might make or present—knowledge that could only be boring or useless.

"Well, certainly knowledge is going to be important in the *Odyssey*, but it's not what Paris chose. Think about it, he's been out of town on this lonely mountainside" *–though he had lots of sheep available* he almost said but caught himself— "and has these offers. What would most young men choose? What would most here at Middle State choose?"

Please, he thought, please, no one say power.

"Was it Power?" asked Colson, the leader of a group of fraternity boys who sat together in snobbish indifference just behind Kimee Deneen. Their fashionable baseball-style caps were emblazoned with the symbol π, which when he had first come to Middle State Brumley had assumed designated a math club member before he realized that there was no math club at Middle State and that the symbol stood for the Pi Iota fraternity, the largest, costliest and most despicable one on campus. Some of its more unbearable members, Brumley had heard,

But Warren, Brumley knew, wasn't a bone-crushing defensive tackle, or even a sub or benchwarmer or towel carrier. On the other hand, neither was he physically or mentally handicapped. He wasn't from a foreign country or a member of a once-oppressed minority. There were no advocates or laws or special offices for the likes of Warren. He could put two and two together and get four. He could remember in a class what had taken place the previous meeting and tried to learn from his course materials and not just learn about them; he even saw relationships between materials from different courses. He belonged to no social organization and did not try to get elected to any student government position. He studied hard, never cheated, worked summers, spent little on himself and tried to stay out of debt.

He did not, Brumley was afraid, have a chance.

Warren was not the only one. Later that morning, when re-checking his mail, Brumley found a memo in his box from Vice president of Academic Affairs Staull. He had been assigned to a sub-committee of the Asteroid Preparedness Committee under Vice president of Emergency Preparedness Hays. It was the Sub-committee on Signage.

three
THE SKY IS FALLING

Some two weeks before classes had begun for the fall, Vice president Hays of Emergency Preparedness had spent his morning reading through the several newspapers his office subscribed to in hopes that overnight there had been an earthquake in China or a typhoon in the Bay of Bengal or a flood almost anywhere, preferably in an area of dense human habitation. Nothing, he knew, could spice up the report that he would not be asked to give that afternoon at the Vice presidents Council like a recent newsworthy calamity with much destruction and death. President Curtis would preside at the Council, and should grace descend and Hays at last be called on to present the state of preparedness of the Office of Emergency Preparedness, he wanted to be prepared. But there had been no fortunate calamities, and he was losing hope.

Hays had been hired two years earlier when President Curtis, reading through the *Journal of State University Presidents,* had come upon an article outlining the dangers to state university presidents should they not foresee and prepare for a disaster that resulted in student property damage, injury or loss of life. The dangers were truly career threatening and President Curtis resolved to act at once.

"Judy," he called to his secretary. "Get Larson down here."

Larson, his Administrative Assistant for Planning, appeared quickly before his desk with a heaped plate of warm oatmeal cookies she had baked that morning and which Curtis impatiently waved aside.

"We've got to hire somebody to look into disasters."

He waited while Larson, bewildered, stood clutching the dismissed cookies.

"Yes, sir. Could I ask what kind of disasters, sir?" She sat the cookies down.

"You know, disasters like tornados and hurricanes, earthquakes, tidal waves."

"Yes, sir," Larson replied, producing her notepad. "How should they look into them?"

"What?"

"How should they look into them? The disasters."

"They should find out about them."

"Is there anything particular they should find out?"

"How the hell should I know? If I knew, I wouldn't be hiring anybody to find out. Look, it's all in this article, which you ought to read by the way. It says that--" and he held the open journal toward Larson to keep her from getting too close "--it says here that disasters can occur unexpectedly. They can happen anywhere, at any time. If one happens here and we're not ready for it, it could be my ass. They talk a lot about earthquakes. One could hit and the dorms and classroom buildings all collapse, and if it was shown we weren't ready for it, I'd be open to more lawsuits than a tobacco company. The finger would point at me. We've got to do something."

"Sir, I don't see how you could be held accountable for an earthquake. That doesn't make sense. Isn't an earthquake what they call in legal parlance an Act of God?"

"What the lawyers call it is one thing; what the parents and board members call it is something else. No, Larson, an Act of God is when there's an earthquake and you leave the building just before it collapses and kills everyone in it. You were saved–that's an Act of God. The earthquake and the ones killed are just one of those things. So forget pinning it on God. If an earthquake hits, or a tornado, and we aren't ready, I'm the fall guy. I'm out. I might even have to go back to the classroom."

Such an emergency could be met only by decisive managerial action, and President Curtis at once created a new administrative unit to address any and all potential disasters. A costly national search to find a vice president for the unit turned up Hays, an assistant director at a nearby junior college who was the son-in-law of a prominent member of Middle State's Reigning Board. He was an earnest young man, on his way up and being whipped smartly along the rising path by a well-educated wife who apparently owned every book that examined and condemned the spiritual emptiness of materialism, status consciousness and consumerism. She enjoyed purchasing and possessing these books and displaying them on her coffee table, and she read them as guides to perfecting the practices they condemned. She drove Hays savagely in hopes of someday having enough money to buy anything she wanted, and Hays, who believed as she did that having material commodities to display gave meaning to life, was a willingly mount. His flaw was a naive misunderstanding of the true nature of his new job. He stumbled almost from the starting gate.

A month after being hired, at his second meeting with the thirteen other Vice presidents at the Vice presidents Council, he stood and presented his elaborate plan to insure Middle State's readiness for any disaster, natural or otherwise. It required the hiring of two medical doctors and a staff of nurses, technicians and emergency personnel, along with eighteen trained firefighters. Also the purchase of four fire-trucks, one with ladders capable of reaching the roofs of the tallest dorms, and the construction of a fire-, tornado-, and earthquake-proof Emergency Preparedness building to house communications and control, the medical staff and fire-fighting equipment and his own administrative offices. He proposed that the building be named Curtis Hall.

There was silence around the table when he sat down.

"How much?" President Curtis asked grimly.

"I don't have a figure yet—an absolutely accurate figure," Hays said, calculating rapidly, wildly. He had assumed that protecting students was so important that cost was of little account. "It should be around three million dollars a year, for the next ten years, at least. About the same as the new Wellness Center."

President Curtis moved on to the Vice president of Institutional Effectiveness who sensing Curtis's disgust prudently curtailed his report and took his seat. The Vice presidents of Basketball and Football having already given their reports, Curtis dismissed the group, who avoided Hays, pretending to arrange and straighten his papers as the rest of the vice presidents filed wordlessly out.

Hays understood it was pointless to submit his plan formally and had never again been asked about his office's affairs or progress at any subsequent meeting of the Vice presidents Council. In fact, he had not been asked for any information of any kind by anyone. There was no help even from Shank, the founder-consultant from Shank Educational Consulting, whose large fee had been included in the first year's budget for the Office of Emergency Preparedness.

"Odds are," he told a dismayed Hays at their first meeting over salad, lobster thermidor and a dry white wine at Middle State Alumni House, where Shank insisted they lunch. "Odds are your purpose is to be window dressing. So really there's not much for me to tell you other than come to the office most days, keep a large file on disasters along with some comments on what could have been done to prevent too much death and destruction from each. But in general--" he laughed and winked conspiratorially at Hays, "--don't make waves. I'm pretty sure there are other budgetary areas that require more attention than student safety, though I don't think anyone would want to say as much. A new Business Building, for example, or just some asphalt to spread around. Or a need for funds to expand faculty and administrative travel abroad–to increase 'institutional visibility'."

He paused appreciatively, a spoonful of his succulent lobster dish half-way to his mouth.

"*Institutional visibility,*" he said sensuously. "It rolls off the tongue like lobster thermidor. And this, by the way, is delicious. The quality of food I get has certainly gone up since these state schools have seen the need to suck up to rich alumni by building posh Alumni Clubs. This one, I believe"–he glanced around the large atrium where luncheon tables had been set out for the few administrators who had come to eat—"was built with a large contribution from one of your more successful graduates, Thompson, I think it was, invented—ironic, isn't it–the square hamburger. When I first got in the consulting profession and was taken out to eat, it was those same square hamburgers at dorm cafeterias. Then Salisbury steak at Faculty Clubs. But now the really important people are being stroked, I eat pretty well, well enough to have to join a health club to keep the old abs in shape. As a consultant, my best advice is to get in with the rich."

"But about my duties," a distraught Hays cut in. "I'm not sure what you mean by keeping a file–how? And how do I get my agenda before President Curtis?"

Shank dabbed at his mouth with his linen napkin embossed with a graceful MS and leaned forward in his expensive, well-tailored suit, beckoning Hays to do likewise.

"Like I say," he spoke confidentially, "your job is essentially of an ass-covering nature. I wouldn't try to get my agenda before the Chief here. In fact, I wouldn't even have an agenda."

"For God's sake, I've got to do something," Hays cried, appalled. "I can't just sit in an office."

Shanks looked at him with wonder.

"All right. If you've got to do *something*," he said finally, "try this—you'll see it's a good idea. About once or twice a year declare an Emergency Preparedness Week or some such thing. Take a strictly non-binding proclamation to your president along with a photographer. The chief will sign it and look concerned; you'll have a little publicity and a chance to kiss some ass, and that will be *something*. Jesus, son, you've got it made and can't see it."

Shank genuinely wanted to help Hays; he wanted to help all the poor academic chumps he was called in to show the ropes. But sometimes their lack of understanding of which side their bread was buttered on dumbfounded him.

"I can see what you mean, all right," Hays said. "It's just that unless I do something visible, something innovative, my career is stymied. I can't go anywhere sitting still."

Hays' substantial salary had already become inadequate, and his wife's tastes were rendering it more so quickly.

"I can't promise anything about your getting ahead," Shanks submitted, "but at least you'll get a little visibility, and visibility and innovativeness are what count. Unfortunately, I don't see much hope for innovativeness in your position. Not that you're incapable of innovativeness and at a very high level. It's just that innovativeness costs money and it doesn't look like there is going to be an increase in your budget for the foreseeable future. Now, as for how to keep a file on disasters, one thing you can do is watch TV."

He extracted from his rich leather brief case beside his chair a sheet of paper and handed it to Hays. It was headed *Watch TV.*

"You keep a list of really good disasters and then come up with pro-active steps to be prepared for them and send the whole package to the president's office the first chance you get. If you can come by some video tapes or stills from the disaster scene showing bodies or weeping relatives of whoever's body it is, you might just possibly get the kind of recognition and budget you deserve, though I very much doubt it will work. I suggest a volcano–you know, restless bowels of the earth, unappeasable forces, that kind of thing."

"Yes, I understand that," Hays agreed. "It gets attention. But what can you do about a volcano? How do you prepare for a volcano, not that there's a one in a billion chance of there being a volcano here,"

"Okay," Shanks said, pleased that Hays' attitude now allowed him to come decisively to the point. "Here's the real heart of the matter. Of course you can't do anything about a volcano. But you're not supposed to *do* anything about it. All you've got to do is *be prepared* for it. Now, how would you get prepared for a volcano?"

"I guess I'd be prepared by figuring out how to get as far from it as fast as I could."

"Now you've got it," the sleek consultant vigorously agreed. "All you need to do next is elaborate on that–find out which roads go away from here, or if any ships or airplanes leave from here and so on. Busses, taxis."

"But my God, everybody knows which roads go away from here and surely if a volcano popped up they'd be on the nearest one in a flash. Or they'd go cross-country. It's too obvious."

"Nobody said it wasn't," Shanks agreed, rising to leave. "But if you've got it written down, then you're prepared. You've done your job. Oh, and you can read the newspapers, too," and he handed Hays another sheet of paper, this one headed *Read Newspapers* over a list of local and national newspapers and tabloids.

The meeting left Hays depressed, but not entirely without hope. While a lackey, he was not wholly a fool, and he knew his job was of no real importance and would continue to be ignored. But he also knew it was extremely important in the indispensable area of convincing fronts. And while if single he would have been content to live out his life collecting a large salary for doing nothing in an important position of no consequence, there were in his present state of matrimonial stress new wardrobes to be bought each season, a new and fancier car each year, a bigger house each decade. His proclaiming Tornado Awareness

Week did nothing to achieve a much desired jump in salary. Ozone Hole Awareness Month hardly caused an eye to turn heavenward, and Top Soil Loss Awareness Week was predictably the subject of a heckling and almost literate editorial in the student newspaper. But the fact of the matter was that Middle State lay outside Tornado Alley, too far inland for hurricanes, not in an earthquake zone, and situated on high ground. Hays' future appeared stagnant.

And then, out of the August sky, his fortune came orbiting.

"Would you look at this," Hays said to Cutter, his assistant. "Did you see this?"

Cutter never read the paper. He turned away from his computer and looked at his boss.

"See what?"

"This article. It's about the asteroid that hit the earth million of years ago and killed all the dinosaurs."

"Killed the dinosaurs? How did it kill all the dinosaurs?"

Hays looked at him. "It squashed them. All of them had got together for a meeting and it fell on them and squashed them."

"Aw, come on. How did it kill them?"

"When it hit, it was going so fast that it vaporized everything like an atomic bomb. There was a shock wave and so much smoke and dust that it covered the earth and shut out the sun for two years. Everything got cold and the dinosaurs froze to death."

"No kidding?" Cutter reflected. "Couldn't they migrate or something?"

"I said the dust cloud covered the earth; it was everywhere. When it covers the earth, there's no place to migrate to."

"Oh."

Hays went back to the article.

"And listen to this. There's a possibility that another asteroid could hit again any time. 'Scientists say that at least four hundred objects as big as the asteroid that wiped out the dinosaurs orbit the sun in the same plane as the earth'."

"You know," Cutter said, his interest finally aroused, "there's a movie coming out about that. I saw an ad for on TV–*Killer Asteroid* or something like that. And it said that Notre Dameus or somebody predicted the other day that something was going to hit the earth within the next five years."

As Cutter spoke, Hays had been gazing with growing absorption into the distance, his eyes slowly widening. He rose carefully to his feet.

"Cutter," he said, controlling his excitement, his face shining. "Do you know what an asteroid about to hit the earth would be?"

Cutter did not.

"Think, Cutter."

Cutter thought.

"Cutter, it would be an emergency, the emergency of all emergencies. This is it, this is what we've been waiting for. Get away from that computer," he said, his eyes now wild. "I've got a report to write."

At the Vice presidents Council that afternoon, Hays did something so rash that ordinarily it would have cost him his vice presidency. The meeting had proceeded smoothly. The Vice presidents of Basketball and Football reported that dribbling and tackling were doing well and that only misdemeanor criminal charges had been brought against any team members that week. The Vice president of Outreach and Intake said that plenty of both were going on; the Vice president of Student Services proclaimed they were serving plenty; the Vice president for University and Public Services and the Vice president of University and Public Affairs reported that affairs were in order and service was with a smile. President Curtis, who had heard enough, ignored the doleful looks of the rest of the Vice presidents down the table and was about to declare the council adjourned when Vice president Hays, at the very far end, said clearly:

"I have something else."

No one had ever prolonged a meeting of the Vice presidents Council by having something to say, not even the Vice presidents of Basketball and Football. Almost before his fellow Vice presidents could swing looks of wonderment at him, before President Curtis could glare to see who was darkening council in opposition to his clear indications that he wanted to get the hell out of there, Vice president Hays uttered the words that launched the great Asteroid Preparedness Program.

"The sky is falling."

The Vice presidents looked at each other in astonishment.

"What?" Said the Vice president for Outreach and Intake.

"The sky is falling."

"Who says so?" Vice president Drane of Football growled.

"The newspaper says so," Hays replied coolly, and began passing out copies of the article he had come across that morning. "Of course it may not fall completely today, but it's definitely going to fall. One of the major TV networks is doing a program on it next week and depending on the ratings, which almost certainly will be high, I'm sure the other networks will follow suit shortly. The program will start with Nostradamus's prophecy and move up to today's scientific calculations that an asteroid definitely could hit the earth in the next five years."

Even President Curtis was reading Hays' handout. "Huh!" he said. "What are the odds this is going to happen? This one that killed the dinosaurs was millions of years ago. Once in millions of years doesn't seem much to be worried about. What's the problem?"

"That's precisely it," Hays said. "The longer we go without one hitting us, the more likely one will. It's something like an earthquake. When you haven't had one for a long time, it's like the forces are building up and then you're going to have one, a big one. Asteroids are very much like that. We haven't had an asteroid hit us for millions of years, and one is getting closer all the time. The odds are building up that it will hit. I wouldn't be surprised if one hit any time now, even before the end of this semester."

"Wait a minute," the Vice president for Institutional Effectiveness objected, sensing a potential shift in attention away from present budgeting priorities. "What the hell can we do about it anyway? This article says the asteroid that killed the dinosaurs was five miles in diameter. How are you going to dodge that?"

Hays had given some brief thought before the meeting to the possibilities of shooting a missile with a nuclear warhead, or several missiles with many nuclear warheads, whatever it took to destroy the asteroid. Or else having a large number of rocket engines aligned along half the equator to slow or to speed the earth's revolution around the sun and cause the asteroid to miss. He felt there might be difficulties with either method, but since developing them would require great effort and still not necessarily help keep his career path ascending, he had dismissed them. "I'm not sure you can dodge it," Hays answered with calm affability. "But you can *be prepared*." He waited a moment until certain that the clear, commonsensical need to be prepared registered with them and its connection to the purpose–to the very name–of his department grew in their minds.

"And gentlemen, the Office of Emergency Preparedness is about to make preparations. I have here a preliminary report–really not more than a work sheet–that I'd like you all to be thinking about in preparation for a fuller report I'll be circulating next week and then for a survey I'll distribute in a month to see if your area is in any compliance with the guidelines I'll be sending out after the report. With final assessive follow-ups after that, of course. We'll need to have an Asteroid Preparedness Week with drills and a dance and some posters and things like that–all this is just preliminary, but my assistant Cutter and I, along with the new permanent staff we'll need, will be working on it day and night until we're satisfied we have a plan to be proud of. And there's another consideration," he added, his voice growing ominous. "Not only will parents want to know that the safety of their sons and daughters is of highest priority here at Middle State, which it goes without saying it is, but even more that in the event of an asteroid collision, those sons and daughters have a much better chance of surviving than those at an unprepared university. At Middle State, our students are not helpless dinosaurs. We're thinking about them day and night, and if it's the last thing we do, we should see they're not made extinct."

Even President Curtis had to admire Hays' coup and knew there was little to do but increase his staff, budget and salary. Within the next month all the TV networks had done a ninety second in-depth segment on their evening news dealing with the threat of asteroids, and at home Hays was putting in a swimming pool, his married life approaching ecstasy.

"What do you think of this?" Hays called to Cutter through the open door into his assistant's large, new office, which was a mere annex to Hays' capacious quarters. "We have a floor captain for each floor of offices and one for each dorm floor. They get a kit with emergency preparedness supplies that they can use if–I should say when–an asteroid hits. We could also have a lieutenant appointed to each captain in case the captain wasn't around when needed. Maybe badges or caps or something that indicated who they were."

"What about contests," Cutter happily shot back, "could there be contests between floors? You know, see which floor could get out of the building the fastest with the fewest injuries, things like that?"

"I don't see why not. That way, we'd have a kind of control over everybody at Middle State. And there would have to be monitors for each floor to see how quickly they got out. Cutter, how many dorm and office floors are there here? Great god, we may have to have a hundred new staff to handle it all."

It was coming too fast. Hays for a fleeting moment saw himself displacing Vice president Drane of Football and seated at President Curtis's right hand, the other Vice President impotently exiled to the far end of the Council table. He knew pride goeth before a fall, but he also knew it cometh after a well deserved triumph, and only with difficulty could he rein in his visions of ascendancy.

"Wait," he cautioned, thinking it through. "Do we really want people to evacuate the buildings? I mean, the scientists would know an asteroid was coming a week in advance, wouldn't they? They made that clear on TV. If everyone knew a week in advance, they'd leave anyway and have plenty of time to get out. We wouldn't need to practice rapid evacuation. I guess that particular increase in staff isn't in the cards after all."

"Yeah," Cutter mused. "Even if we had only ten minutes warning and everybody got outside all right, what difference would it make? If a rock five miles across hits you, it won't matter if you're inside or out, although if it doesn't hit here and there's a dust cloud that blocks out the sun, they might could make it to classes if they were already outside. It's hard to tell."

"We'll revisit that later," Hays decided. "For now I've got to get ready to see Curtis this afternoon about my Signage Subcommittee to the Asteroid Preparedness Committee. Something's come up. By the way, what did you find on the Asteroid Preparedness Kit? Anything in the literature?"

Cutter had been entrusted to survey the internet to find if back issues of *Emergency Preparedness Directors' Newsletter* were reproduced there and to comb them for any articles on emergency preparedness kits for any type of emergency.

"I couldn't find anything," he admitted, "I don't think. I mean, there was some stuff about having personal flotation devices on boats and on airplanes that fly over water. But I didn't see anything about a kit anywhere."

Hays considered the difficulty of getting good help, began to reflect on some possible items for the kit, and then stopped.

"Cutter, come in here," he called. He heard Cutter ease out of his chair and make the long walk across his thick carpet to their connecting door.

"Why don't you handle this? Yes," he went on, pleased to be delegating authority and getting some else to do his work, "give some thought to what we could put in these kits and have me a couple of alternatives for the contents by, say, Friday."

He saw Cutter's eyes fill with dismay.

"Me?"

"Why not?"

"Well, I guess I could try. You'd check what I come up with before we made up the kits, wouldn't you?"

"Goes without saying. Just make sure you find out if every item you include is available, how much it costs, and how soon we can get it after we order."

Two days later, Cutter submitted his lists. Hays checked the first one.

"Rope, crowbar, Bible, playing cards, bandages, iodine, blankets, condoms–condoms?–flashlight, hard hat, candles, matches, video games, Morse code chart, whistle–goddamn, Cutter," he began, but seeing Cutter cringe he tried to soften his response. "I don't see the need for condoms. Or a whistle. And what's this Morse code?"

"I wasn't sure about the condoms either, but when we had Sexually Transmitted Disease Week we encouraged the use of condoms, and if the asteroid hits and everything gets dark. . . .you know how the students are. When there was that black-out in New York there was a big increase in births nine months after that night. If we put condoms in the kit, no one can say we weren't prepared. We can get all we need from Vice president Timmons over in Student Affairs. I think parents would be glad we kept their daughters from getting knocked up, or AIDS. Or their sons. From getting AIDS. Parents would think we're on the ball."

"No, Cutter, parents would think we promote fucking. Condoms are out. Now what about the hard hat? What's it for?"

"Well, you know. It's for protection."

"From the asteroid?"

"Sort of."

"A rock five miles across going at seven miles a second. You said the other day it wouldn't matter if you were inside or outside when it hit. And you want a hard hat for protection. Cutter, God's hard hat would be useless. Let's forget the hard hat."

"Okay. Now the whistle," Cutter continued, this time with more confidence, "the whistle will let people signal to other people where they are if–when–everything gets dark."

"But they'll have flashlights. And candles, you've got flashlights and candles on the list. Why can't they use them?"

"I thought the flashlight batteries would finally go bad and the candles burn down. But you can blow a whistle by yourself."

Hays, who thought candles burned indefinitely, was impressed.

"But you can just get some more batteries and put them in. I do it all the time."

"I guess you're right," Cutter admitted, disappointed. "But if it's dark all over, how can they find the store? Then, if the candles were gone too, they could blow the whistles and. . . ."

"And what? That won't help them find the store."

"Wait!" Joy flooded Cutter's face. "We could also give a whistle to store owners. That way they could blow them and the students could find the store and get batteries. Then they could find their way back with their flashlights."

"I don't know, Hays reflected. "It may be against the law for a state institution to give anything to private individuals. Other than money, of course. But if not, I don't see why we couldn't do it. That sounds like a fine idea, Cutter. I'll see you get credit for it if President Curtis gives us the go-ahead. Now, what about the Morse code?"

"I thought that if everything is dark and all, the students could use the Morse code charts and signal with the flashlights from one dorm to the other. Or if the flashlight batteries run down, then they could use their whistles to send Morse code. Or if the asteroid hits and the dorms collapse, students could tap out a message, like 'I'm trapped' or something like that. They could even use the charts for entertainment, like two roommates could use their flashlights and talk in Morse code."

Hays decided to evaluate Cutter's second list later, though he noticed that the first item on it was peanut butter.

"Let's hold off on these for the time being," he said to a disappointed Cutter. "I'll check this other one tomorrow when I get through with our questionnaire. Why don't you go through this morning's papers and see if there's anything about asteroid dangers. I've got to get ready to see Curtis about his thinking on our Signage Sub-committee. I hope he wants some of Middle State's more important personnel aboard and doesn't see this as a revenge committee, like the Faculty Committee on Garbage Collection was. After all, placing the names of buildings and structures in a consistent and aesthetically pleasing format in easily visible locations is very important, according to the *Emergency Preparedness Directors Newsletter*. In case of a disaster, it helps emergency personnel know which pile of rubble is which. I think Curtis is on the same page with us this time."

four

THE AMERICAN DREAM

Brumley's renewal of Warren's cause went nowhere. Calls and visits to various administrative offices, one to the madhouse cell of Eigleman, resulted in either a mildly sympathetic run-around or indifference—or, in Eigleman's case, a long diatribe against the promise and treachery of computers. But nowhere was there help. Hobart, when he found out what Brumley was doing, went immediately to Vice president Staull's office to demand a meeting on the issue, but found Staull had departed that morning for a quick jaunt to China, where Middle State was trying to establish a beachhead in one of the more rural provinces prior to a full-scale invasion by a studies-abroad division. When it was clear that Warren's cause was irrevocably lost, Brumley, at the close of the humanities class the next week, motioned to Warren to wait for him.

"Chris, I'm sorry, but the courses you need can't be added this semester. Won't be added," Brumley said, trying to be accurate.

"I didn't think they would," Warren replied. He had given up days ago. "I guess I'll just have to go another semester or two. Maybe the job market will be unsaturated by then. Or I can take some courses in Spanish or Vietnamese and go to California," he laughed. "Not that I'd go. In fact, I'd kind of like to stay around here, around my home."

Brumley set the piece of chalk he'd been fiddling with back in the chalk tray, the room being one of the few as yet uninvaded by computers, which would not tolerate chalk dust.

"Dr. Hobart went to see Vice president Staull. And of course a number of faculty members are upset about it. But. . . ," he trailed off.

"It's okay," Warren reassured him. "I didn't have much hope. But I'd

39

still like to try writing a letter to President Curtis. I know it probably won't do much good, but I still may try."

"It might, it might," Brumley said, not wishing to involve Warren in what would almost certainly be a futile and possibly a harmful course of action. "But I told you, I didn't have much luck with my letter. You never can tell, though," he said, seeing Warren's expression of helplessness deepen. "You might as well give it a try. And if that draws a blank, don't stop with Curtis. There's the Reigning Board. The Governor, even."

"I don't know about the Governor," Warren said, almost alarmed. "I don't want to cause any trouble. But I will write President Curtis. Do you think the student newspaper would be interested? I'm not the only one who's not able to get enough courses to graduate. They might do a story on it or print a letter."

"Chris, that's an excellent idea," Brumley exclaimed. Since the end of the Vietnam war about the only protest appearing in the student newspaper had been over insufficient parking within one hundred feet of any building the students had class in. Hobart had claimed that the only possible student uprising at present would be to demand driving their cars into classes, which would then be conducted like drive-in movies of old. But maybe a letter in the student newspaper would give Warren's grievance some attention, who knew?

"I'd definitely give the newspaper a try. Doing anything is better than nothing," he said, without real conviction. He couldn't just give up on Warren. As for himself, he still could try to stir up a little action, however self-endangering it might be. Maybe he could write a letter-to-the-editor about the situation, but to a newspaper with a little larger readership than the *Middle State News*. "Keep me posted on how it goes."

What is he, twenty? Brumley thought, beginning again to assess Warren after he left. Twenty years old. He can't yet believe that playing straight will get you nowhere. And what a good kid. He follows the rules, is honest. He tries to learn, *likes* to learn, doesn't try to get by through glad-handing or buttering up authority or networking. He knew Warren's merits well and only hoped the boy wasn't coming to believe that they put him at a great disadvantage.

Brumley was right on most counts. Warren didn't like to be bilked.

He did play it on the level, and above all he didn't cheat. But he resented those who did.

"I study my ass off," he said to Plumb Bob, who was shaving in preparation for the short, voluptuous little mermaid who had surfaced up against him during his swimming class that afternoon. "Those guys in Pi fraternity cheat and make passing grades and never learn anything. They don't want to learn anything; they think it's a disgrace or something. Last week Sean Johns had his math book on his desk before Brumley's class and that prick Colson saw it and asked him what in the name of god was he doing taking partial differential equations. Johns said he wanted to learn how to solve them, and Colson and his bunch fell out laughing at him. They think people who want to learn and who don't cheat are dorks."

"And they're right," Plumb Bob said cheerily, his electric razor buzzing with anticipation. "Colson and his buddies are learning how to get ahead. I mean, they don't make the high grades you do, but they don't have to put out any effort to do about as good. The night before a test you're sitting here—or down at the study lounge," he added sheepishly, "and they're drinking and dancing at The Mug. But they're definitely learning. They're just learning that honesty and responsibility and all that don't pay. It's the best thing they could learn for the jobs with big companies they hope to get when they graduate. God, will they ever laugh their ass off at you, out teaching kids for peanuts—or at Shepherd, wanting to farm. You and Shepherd will be working—they'll be living the American Dream. They'll be kicking ass from a swivel chair."

"Come on," Warren said, laughing, "kicking ass from a swivel chair is the American Dream?"

He trusted Plumb Bob's oracular insights, because Plumb Bob uttered them without rancor, even the most outrageously pessimistic ones, and also because Plumb Bob's opinions were informed by experience much more varied and extensive than Warren knew he would ever have. And again, if Plumb Bob could get as many women as he did, then his views had to be worth something.

"I'm telling you, that's the American dream," Plumb Bob said, working the razor along his jaw line. "You get to be a boss, though they call it a leader now, and you kick ass from a swivel chair."

"But you've got to work to be a boss," Warren objected. "You've got to know something about what you're in charge of, don't you? You can't just be a 'boss'. There's not a major in bossing, is there?"

"To kick ass from a swivel chair," Plumb Bob said, feeling above his upper lip, "all you've got to know is the basics of ass kicking. That comes naturally to all shit-heads. Then you've got to get a swivel chair. And there is a major that will get you one. It's called Management. They teach you how to manage to get a swivel chair. I majored in it for a year-and-a-half, and that's where you can learn how to fulfill the American dream, which is kicking ass and so on."

"What do you mean?" Warren asked. He knew of a major called Management, but had considered it some nullity like Communications or Education. "How does it teach you to be a boss?"

"You'd think a person gets to be a boss by knowing all about what's done where he works," Plumb Bob said reflectively. "And knows better than anybody else. Plus, can get along pretty good with people he's boss of. But if you're in Management, at least according to the management theory they taught us, you don't have to know anything about work to be a boss. You just have to know about managing. First, except for show, you don't have anything to do with the people that work there except for those directly under you in what they call the Management Hierarchy. Say you're president of something, or the CEO–then once a month all the vice-presidents come in to your office, and you let them know in a polite way that you've got a grip on their balls, and they tell you how everything is going. Usually they'll say it's going good. That's about it. Say you're the boss of a company that makes pins. You don't have to know which end of a pin is sharp or even what a pin is used for. All you have to know is how to give orders down the chain of command–the Management Hierarchy–and scare them into making more pins for less pay."

Plumb Bob turned away from the mirror to see if Warren was following him, and saw that as usual he was.

"As far as I could figure out, " he went on, "the main thing to do to get that swivel chair and keep it was to start off being a team player, which means you begin by kissing ass–in a dignified way of course–but then you let it be known that what you'd really like to do is kick ass. And to have others kiss yours. But to have others kiss yours, you generally had to kick theirs every now and then. Look, I never did really figure it all out; the management profs never just came out and said that it was all about kicking ass from a swivel chair. In fact, they aren't exactly in swivel chairs themselves, at least not very fancy ones. But they sure kicked my ass over that paper I wrote for Pomerene's class. He wanted a paper about the greatest manager we'd ever heard of. Fulson in his history class had had us reading about Hitler, his hero, so I picked Hitler—Der Manager, I called him—and showed you could manage a house painting concern, a political party or a concentration camp as long as you knew management theory. They kicked my ass out of that major. I believe I'm the only person ever kicked out of a major at Middle State."

"How can they kick you out of a major?" Warren asked, urged by a slight premonition of what might happen to him if he made trouble about required courses that weren't offered. "Can they do that, I mean, if your grades are all right?"

"They can if they know something about Management Theory. I got my walking papers later that semester when they announced a special test that would be given to all sophomores in the major. It was an essay test that asked you to describe the best manager you knew of, based on what you'd learned so far about what it took to be a successful manager. I wrote roughly the same thing I did on Pomerene's paper. Two people out of 250 failed it, me and a student from Bangladesh who couldn't speak, read, write or understand English, though I heard he was reinstated the next term by the Cultural Justice Committee. You see how it is. They can't just tell you they don't like the way you think. They've got to come up with an official golden toilet to flush you away with. If kicking ass from a swivel chair is your dream, and it's definitely theirs, then they won't have much trouble finding a commode you'll fit in. So I was out of Management. Switched to Wildlife Management. Thought it was about the same thing but it wasn't. Turned out to be one of my best moves. More women in it than you'd think. Outdoors types, like to hike out in the woods. But I couldn't see any sense in taking care of animals so people could shoot them, so I got out. You know, I think that's when I got that $100, to go into Animal Husbandry, but that wasn't what I thought it was either."

"Listen," he said, having put up his razor and splashing his lightly scented after-shave into his hand, "Megan will be here any minute. Could you give me the room for about an hour? I believe the Galileo Club is in session in Hoh's room. Or, if you've still pulled out of it, there's nobody down at the study area."

"Sure," Warren said brightly to cover the pang he always felt when surrendering the room to Plumb Bob. Plumb Bob never had to surrender it to him, though neither did he ever, in any way, indicate an awareness that Warren and the others never seemed to get any women. But Warren knew he knew.

"It's all yours. Just don't kick my ass from your swivel chair as I leave," Warren said.

Most of Warren's fellow students at Middle State were unreflective and well-behaved. They hoped to lead, now and in the future, comfortable and proper lives with everything self-evident and, above all, not boring, which to them meant free from sustained effort, mental or physical.

Except, at present, for cheating. In this area, they expended great effort, which had it been applied to study and deliberation would have resulted in the same end as the cheating, namely, higher grades. Higher grades, they believed, meant eventually a better–that is to say, a higher paying–job, which they were sure would permit them lives of comfort, propriety and fun. All this was self-evident. And since studying was neither comfortable nor fun, and was becoming unfashionable, they cheated.

Either they stole tests by first stealing keys to university offices and then entering them to copy computer files containing an instructor's tests, or stole them by gaining access to an instructor's computer through other computers to which it was connected. Or, refusing such low thievery, they bought tests someone else had stolen, or they joined fraternities and sororities and had access to these organizations' files of tests stolen over the years by their bogus brothers or pseudo-sisters.

As for written essays still required in a few, ever-dwindling courses, now that the Internet had become a fixture in academia there was no assignable topic for which an appropriate paper was not available in several ranks of complexity, length and style. In his sophomore year, Warren had watched with fascination as Sean Johns, a computer obsessed fanatic, searched scores of Internet sites with their tens of thousands of topics, from which the owners of these sites, for various sums from twenty to two hundred dollars, would provide a custom-made paper for some enterprising student. "Methods of Dating Rocks" was one topic he recalled Johns locating for a frantic junior, though that transaction had turned out badly when the eager purchaser, enraptured at finding precisely this title, had overlooked its Premarital Courting classification and turned in the paper unread to his Geology class. Warren had seen such titles as "Effects of the 1848 Tariff on Molasses Production," "Penis Envy in Adrianne Rich," "Evolution: A Text," "Quasar Distribution and Theory," "History: A Survey," "Deconstructing the Pyramids," "Strength of Plywoods," and "Folly to Be Wise." Thousands of others were available at the touch of a download button. As low a quality as many were, they were much better than what most of the students would have written on their own, and consequently many of the instructors who had to grade them were reluctant to confront their students on even the most obvious plagiarism.

"I don't care if they cheat," Fulson of History announced loudly to Brumley who unavoidably found himself on a student-packed elevator with him. "I got a paper last week on 'Hume, Condorcet and Rationality in the 18th Century.' It was discriminating, wide-ranging, stylistically excellent and virtually error free. A week earlier the dolt had written on a test, 'The Inlitement was when thought and reason began.'"

He brayed raucously, oblivious both to the perplexed but embarrassed students and to Brumley's discomfort.

"You think I'm going to spend hours finding where he got the paper? If I found out and flunked him, he could still drag me through four levels of university appeals, and there's no guarantee he'd be found guilty even if I had a signed and witnessed confession from him. If he were judged guilty, at best I'd have to write a report justifying whatever action I chose to take against him; at worst he or his parents would sue me. I'm no fool. I read the paper, complimented him on the miraculous improvement in insight and writing style he'd undergone in a week's time, and gave him a C. I don't imagine he read the comment; if he did, he probably thought it was sincere and was smugly delighted at the success of his deception and confirmed in believing that sloth and dishonesty pay big."

Hand-held calculators, that for twenty years had relieved students of the burden of learning arithmetic and had therefore now become a necessity in all courses requiring the use of numbers, had been developed to such complexity and capacity that they could be programmed to display on their screens large amounts of formulas, information and even pictures. These in turn could be used to cheat on tests in a stunning number of courses from calculus to accounting to statistics to art history, and if an instructor grew suspicious during an examination and approached a student, the press of a button could erase the screen and lock the information from retrieval by anyone without the proper code. And not far down the road, the new, constantly refined cell phones promised yet another instrument for thwarting thought and effort.

There were more traditional, less technologically sophisticated ways to cheat. Boys could coerce their girlfriends, or, much less often, girls their boyfriends into writing their papers for them. Or they could in many ways conceal notes to take into tests—the venerable cheat-sheet—or could copy off others' tests, or could devise and memorize elaborate signals to send surreptitiously across a room. If an instructor had two sections of the same course, which many in the service areas—primarily the humanities—did have, then students could find willing fellow students in the earlier section who could tell them test contents, provided they could remember the questions by the time they had handed in their test and left the room. A very few instructors forestalled this ploy by making up two separate tests, but doing so took work.

Outside the classroom, some students from out-of-state were lying about their residency by giving as their home address that of a complicit in-state relative or acquaintance to avoid paying the much higher rates of tuition charged to non-residents. Some freshmen and sophomores, especially those from affluent families, claimed they were commuting from near-by areas so they could live in posh apartments off campus rather than having to live, as required, in the drab, Bedlamitic dorms.

A few happily discovered that they had an officially approved learning disability.

These highly coveted disabilities could be conferred on a shrewd, robust student by his paying for a stolen evaluative test that he studied for days in order to fail in such a way that rather than appearing academically to be his customary slow-witted, uncaring, imperceptive and unretentive self, he was revealed to have a government approved, professionally sanctioned learning disorder. Far from being slow-witted, he instead suffered from DC, or Dilatory Cognizance. He was not rude and uncaring, but was revealed to have IVD, or Impulsive Vocalization Disorder. If his self-esteem were dimmed by his being labeled imperceptive, it was brightened by the discovery that he had in fact DI, or Discernment Impedance. And his unretentiveness was forgotten when testing showed in fact he was a victim of MDS, or Memory Dissipation Syndrome. Failing the test meant he had passed it splendidly with a reward of compulsory special treatment in all courses in the form of free tutoring, extra time to take tests and a freely-provided note taker for his classes, along with numerous watchdog advocates, each of whom championed a particular disability and was milking it for all it was worth by piously advocating the rights of those who had it or faked having it.

Some students were accepting student loans that they had no sense they would ever have to pay back and ultimately no intentions of doing so. They would later blame drugs for their dereliction or claim they were too young to know what they were doing when they signed for the loans. A considerable number, although they would never admit it openly, quite clearly believed that while accepting loans and spending the money was a pleasant thing, paying it back was just some obscure part of the agreement that, because it was demanding and disagreeable, hardly applied to them. And nearly all were cheating themselves or their parents by pretending to an education that cost a great deal of money but in which they had no real interest and stoutly refused to acquire. Higher education at schools like Middle State was becoming an economic transaction in which all the buyer wanted was a bill of sale.

five
THE GALILEO CLUB

Warren's dorm section for upperclassmen-only had almost the same occupants as the previous year. Gone was Sitwell, who after three years of teetering on the edge of a 2.0 grade point average had finally wearied and fallen into a month long, ruinous debauch the previous spring; gone too was Cantrell, a closet idealist who had actually joined the Marines over the summer in search of adventure but, according to a near-incoherent letter, was finding none in cleaning out grease traps at Parris Island. Since only a few upperclassmen chose to live in the dorms, the Sitwell and Cantrell vacancies were unfilled, and the group, largely congenial, was intact. Due to the purported maturity of upperclassmen and in hopes of attracting more of them to live in the dorms, Middle State's administration had assigned the floor no resident advisor–a combination counselor, warden and informant–to oversee them. This meant that three of the group who had undertaken to build a telescope for an astronomy class project the previous year could continue refining the device to provide ever better clarity and magnification of the windows of Susan B. Anthony Hall, the women's dormitory some hundred yards away. Plumb Bob, who whenever he wished could gaze with warm compliance and actually touch the heavenly bodies the others could only worship from afar, never attended the gatherings of what had come to be called the Galileo Club..

"It is my turn," Mohamed, the corrupted Moroccan insisted, trying to wedge between Bolinger and Jeek to dislodge at the telescope the transfixed Hoh. "Let me look."

"Quiet, quiet," Hoh hissed illogically, "I'm trying to see." And

Bolinger, off-balance, lurched against him, throwing the telescope off target.

"Goddamnit," Hoh cried, elbowing Bolinger back and frantically trying to relocate the right window. "Okay, I've got it. There she is. . .No! No! She's put a T-shirt on."

He remained bent over the eye-piece for a few moments, then straightened up with a sigh.

"That's it. She must have sat down at the desk. I think I can see part of her head. Thanks. Thanks a lot," he said to the others. "It was a near perfect view. You should have seen them–oh God," and he lifted his hands in mock worship.

"I've told you, we've got to restrict it to three in the room at any one time," Sola said, who had come in in time to catch the general drift of things. "And we need to have a schedule. Otherwise all we do is wrestle for a turn and screw up everybody's view."

"No schedule," Hoh said. "It's my room and my telescope–or mine and Mohamed's and Jeek's. I did most of the work."

"Fine," Sola said, "fine. Then it'll be like tonight every time. Look, there's no problem in working up a schedule that gives you three priority and that makes you the big Galileo. We've just got to have some kind of order, that's all."

"Tell you what I want," Jeeks said slyly. "Friday and Saturday nights."

There were immediate protests from everyone, including Demumbers and Shepherd, who, unable to study for the provocative exclamations from the observatory, had drifted down in hopes of getting in some viewing time. Hoh went home every weekend, but all knew that Friday and Saturday nights were most likely to produce spectacular, near nova-like sights. Enough of the girls came in tipsy to insure that blinds were frequently left open, lights kept bright and a general heedlessness displayed. In fact, before he had quietly ceased attending the gatherings, Warren had begun to believe that some of the females knowingly revealed themselves, in modes from blatant disport to a modest but lazily mindful unveiling that drove him almost mad.

"Okay Jeeks, you can have Friday and Saturday," Sola agreed. "Mo, you can't have Saturday because that's a holy day for you, right?"

"I don't give a damn whether it's holy or not," Mohamed said.

"Living with you degenerates, I can't even remember where is Mecca's direction any more. The West has corrupted me. Hoh, you are worst of all. Buddhists don't even feel guilt for lust."

"I don't feel any guilt for lust," Bolinger announced, sitting down on Hoh's bed. "I'd like to indulge it almost without limit. The trouble is, I can't find a woman to indulge with, even with lots of limits. Like our Welcome Back party last winter. Nobody came, or almost nobody, no girls, anyway."

They were all uncomfortably silent for a moment, remembering the floor's sparsely-attended party the previous January. While it had been conceived with great enthusiasm, no one thought to publicize it other than telling a few friends, and most took the disappointing turn-out as an unusually evident and humiliating proof of their lowly position in the unjust scheme of things.

"No, we're screwed," Bolinger went on. "Women are all looking for somebody like Plumb Bob. Or maybe even somebody like me but who's not shaped like a bowling pin and is rich. I didn't ask for a sex drive, or a world where only a few get satisfied at anything like the level they'd like. Why should I feel guilty about having one? I should gratify it however I can and whenever I can. I'll take any night but Sunday."

On Sunday nights, serious purpose and responsibility reasserted themselves in Susan B. Anthony Hall, and many of its inmates sat fully dressed at their desks, preparing for the coming week and trying to catch up on all they had missed the previous one. Overhead lights were out and blinds usually closed to prevent any distraction.

"Okay, I'll make up a schedule," Sola said. "Only three in the room at once, per night. . . . ."

"Wait, now wait," Jeeks protested. "What if something happens? Remember those two that stripped and wrestled? Or that one at the window rubbing her nipples? We ought to have an alert or something. So everybody can see."

"All right, all right, we have to agree that if there's something really awesome happening, whoever sees it proclaims, say, a red alert. . . ."

"A pink alert," Bolinger suggested.

". . .a pink alert, right, and the other two in the room have to get out the word. Yes, one goes to Plumb Bob and Warren's and to Mohamed and my room, the other to Linton and Well's and to. . . ."

"Why not stick head out of door and yell the Pink Alert?" Mohamed asked.

"That's okay, I guess," Sola agreed. "But if nobody responds, like they've got on headphones or are asleep, then the two who aren't on the scope go in different directions, up the hall and down the hall and alert each room. That way nobody gets left out."

"Come on," Warren said, appearing at the door in time to hear most of the plan. "If there's another nipple flipping show, whoever is in here will be so busy fighting over the scope that the girl will have the lights out and be asleep before anyone is alerted. We ought to give this stuff up, all of it."

"Aw, Warren," Sola said, his great scheme of order dissolving as usual before it ever had a chance. "That's the whole idea of the plan, so everybody gets an equal chance at the scope, and if there's really something to see, everybody gets a look."

"I'm afraid Warren is right, in part," Bolinger observed. "Why should it be any different with us than it is in the larger world? Maybe we can keep to the three-in-the-room part of the plan and the schedule—maybe. But you don't see Plumb Bob or that asshole Colson giving anybody equal time with the dozens of women they get. When they run up on a smoking hot one—and they're all smoking hot for them—they sure don't issue an alert so everybody else has a chance. Colson may brag about his triumphs, but never to us, of course—he doesn't even talk to us—and certainly never with the idea of letting us in on any. It doesn't work that way. Alpha wolves or alpha walruses don't share. I don't know about the rest of you, but if I'm on the scope and see a celestial body, I'm not even going to tell the ones in the room, let alone alert everyone else."

Bolinger was right, in part. The next Friday night Jeeks was the Big Picture man watching the entire side of the dorm for an uncurtained window, while Mohamed was on the binoculars looking for more particular action. Bolinger was staring dully through the scope at an occupied room well below their level where a short, luscious brunette was occasionally in sight when he suddenly tensed and bent purposely to the scope.

"What?' Jeeks asked, and Mohamed, lowering the binoculars and seeing Bolinger's concentration, raised them and scanned quickly across the dorm's facade.

"Where? What are the coordinates?"

Sola had designed a lettered and numbered grid that identified each window in a Cartesian coordinate system that facilitated the records he kept and urged unsuccessfully for everyone else to make entries in. If D4, the fourth window from the left on the fourth floor, had a good display on Tuesday night and did so the next Tuesday also, he argued that the club, instead of fruitlessly sweeping the many other rooms the next Tuesday could concentrate mainly on D4. Before long, he hoped, they would have a schedule so tested and proven that they would never miss anything.

"Over on the right, about three floors up. She's got. . .I believe it's a dildo."

Bolinger had never seen a dildo, but they were easily identifiable. Neither had Mohamed, though Jeeks had seen several.

"She's lying down. Oh my god."

"Her clothes off?" Mohamed urgently asked. "Let me see."

"No, but she's taking—wait, she just got up and checked the door. She's turned off the overhead but the desk light is still on. She's back on the bed. Oh my god, oh my god. Stop pushing, goddamnit," and he fended off a maddened Jeeks.

Mohamed, who with the binoculars could get a seven power view of the wholly absorbed performer, proclaimed there was no god but Allah, and Jeeks after a few frenzied moments displaced the still resisting Bolinger.

"I don't believe it, I don't believe it. Look at her," he crooned and then fell into an utterly absorbed silence, breathing shallowly.

"For the love of Allah," Mohamed shouted. "My turn."

All got clear and almost equitable views of the prolonged and unmistakably satisfying procedure, but no alert was sounded.

"Should we tell what we've seen?" Mohamed asked.

They did, to Sola's indictment of their not sounding the Pink Alert, but the sighting was so inconceivable, so staggering, that Hoh began immediately grinding a larger mirror and promoting the purchase of a camcorder so another miracle, should it be vouchsafed them, could be documented for posterity but especially for their own repeated viewing.

"You're losing it, Hoh," Warren said, and Demumbers and Shepherd agreed. "It's bad enough what we're doing. If you taped anything, sooner or later it would get out. Think about it. How would you like to be the girl?"

"Who would sue our asses, with good cause," Bolinger pointed out. "We're all poor enough as it is. Of course, if we had money or Plumb Bob's looks, sex wouldn't be a spectator sport with us in the first place. If you've got money and good looks and don't have leprosy, you'll get women and won't have to do anything insulting or invasive to get sued for. Otherwise, you can't be too careful. If you're not one of the chosen, even watching from a distance will get you humiliated or even prosecuted. But Warren objects on other grounds, I believe."

They all looked at Warren. Not long after they had begun the Galileo Club, his enthusiasm had suddenly disappeared, and it was clear that he put in an occasional appearance during viewing nights only for show.

"Well," he said. "It's not right. I mean, we could get in trouble, but, I don't know, it makes me see. . .I just don't think we should do it. I love to look, but we probably shouldn't do it."

Warren's reluctant refusal of their voyeurism was not for fear of legal repercussions, and not, as he would have considered it, for moral reasons. One Monday night, two weeks after Hoh had his telescope in place and the Galileo Club had been formed, Jeeks poked his head into Warren's room.

"Want to go climb the smokestack?" he asked unenthusiastically. "I got a joint."

"No. I think I'll stay here and read. Is Hoh down there?"

"He's got a night class."

You mind if I use the scope for awhile? Would Hoh?"

"Naw," Jeeks said. "But nothing's happening. Not but one or two rooms you can see into. But help yourself. I don't care; Hoh won't."

In their darkened room, Warren slowly scanned the face of the Susan B. Anthony Hall until he saw a girl reading at her desk. He watched for awhile, wondering what she was reading and was about to give it up when he saw her lift her head and stare blankly out the window. She bowed her head, and Warren suddenly saw she was crying, only a few tears at first that she brushed absently away, then, her face contorted, sobbing openly. He watched, embarrassed. He felt he should comfort her, wanted to comfort her, but the impossibility of doing so complicated his feelings. He didn't know who she was or how to reach her, and if he found out, he would have to reveal how he had come to know of her sorrow and in doing so would immediately be despised and rebuffed. Why was she crying? Was it something so insignificant as the material she was studying being too difficult to master before a test tomorrow? Or had someone she loved died, a grandparent or friend? Were her parents indifferent to her, or divorcing? Was she pregnant, or maybe not pregnant? Most likely she had been dumped by some boy to whom she had given her heart, someone Warren could never replace. Or maybe she was simply lonely, as lonely as Warren was, or like him saw no future for herself she could understand or wish for. Behind those tears could be causes without number, and Warren, seeing her put her face in her hands, turned his head away from the eyepiece. He swiveled the scope upright and placed the cover over its end. Looking toward the lighted window, he could vaguely see the girl, her head bent, and he watched over her until she seemed to recover. No one else was on his floor, or else they were asleep or studying. He sat in the dark for awhile. After that night, he avoided the gatherings in Hoh and Jeek's room.

But after the night of the dildo, neither Warren's unspecified disapproval nor fear of the law stopped the Galileos, and Hoh missed three days of classes grinding his new, fourteen inch mirror and the rest of the week prevailed on the others to grind in his absence. When the mirror was polished and mounted in its tube and the new eyepiece installed, everyone–including Warren, who wanted to honor the effort–crammed into the room for the christening. Hoh was on the binoculars and Mohamed, muttering imprecations in Arabic at the lack of action, was in momentary command of the Hoh II, whose light-gathering power and magnification was a stunning advance over the now-obsolescent eight-inch peewee that Sola had offered to station in his room and devise an elaborate auxiliary viewing schedule for that everyone ignored.

"Moh, try, let's see, G6," Demumbers said. "There's something going on. It looks like there were five or six in there and then the lights went off."

Hoh, with the more maneuverable binoculars, was first to lock on. "Yeah," he said. "The lights are off, but there's still something. . .it's like there's a shade or something on a lamp. Yeah, they're still in there. I can't tell what's going on."

"You'd better look with this," Mohamed said from the telescope, and he moved quickly away from the scope and back toward the door. Hoh, as the most seasoned observer of the club, took the chair.

"Yes, they're in there all right. It looks like they're gathered at the window."

"Look with care," Mohamed said.

"I don't know. I can't tell for sure."

"Let me," Warren said, curiosity overcoming his aversion, and took over from Hoh. There was definitely something going on in the darkened room. He could make out several dim forms, which moved occasionally, and sensed behind him the rest of the club focused on the distant window, Demumbers now beside him with the binoculars, resting his elbows on the window sill for a steadier view.

"It looks like there might be two by the window and some more back in the room," Demumbers said. "Have you got that thing focused for your eyes?"

Warren delicately turned the focusing knob and a slight fuzziness in the field of view coalesced into a sharp image.

"Much better," he said. "Okay, there's definitely one at the window looking out, and another one, her head anyway, beside the first one and some more back in the room that are hard to see."

Suddenly, he had the eerie feeling that he was looking in a mirror. He gently turned the focus knob again and then turned it back. He looked up, to find Mohamed regarding him.

"Is it what I think?"

Warren moved wordlessly away from the scope and over against the wall. Hoh slid back into position.

"What? What is it?" he said, readjusting the focus. He sat hunched over the eyepiece.

"It can't be," he said to himself.

"What?" Sola demanded. "What?"

"They've got a scope," Warren said. "And binoculars. One's looking through the binoculars and one's on the scope."

"It looks like a refractor, about a four inch," Hoh said with professional assessment. "I can't make out any details but the one on it is facing out instead of sitting sideways like at ours. Probably was too much magnification for their aperture. . . ."

"Goddamnit, Hoh, that doesn't matter. They're looking at *us*, they're doing what we are. Are they looking here, at this window. Can you tell?" Bolinger asked.

"I don't think so," Hoh said after a long, careful survey. The group behind him was quiet, most sitting down or moved back to be out of sight of their counterparts across the way. "I think they're doing what we are, two spotters, one on the scope. It looks like they're checking out the windows. I don't think they've spotted us. We'd better close the blinds, though."

"They're looking, too, just like us," Jeeks chortled. "I'm going to whip it out and stand up here with a spotlight on it." But he made no move to do so. The rest were silent, trying to comprehend.

"Women looking for lustful views of men," Mohamed said sorrowfully. "It must have been like this in Rome, before its fall. I am in the land of the wicked, surely."

"Fuck you, Mo. You're doing your part for the great Satan, I notice," Demumbers said. "But think of it. Maybe they're as horny as we are."

"Wonders will never cease on this earth," Bolinger said. "But what do we do? Do we turn on the light, stand unmistakably at the window— Jeeks with his prick out–and make ourselves known to them? How would they respond, knowing they were being watched and their watching known to the watchers? Would they come streaming down and meet us for a mad orgy half-way between the dorms? I don't think so. These things never happen like they should. But what would happen is interesting speculation."

Warren, like the rest, sat in reverent but impotent silence. From childhood, almost daily, he and the others had been bombarded by their world's most effective entertainer and teacher with endless story lines, casual remarks and heart stopping images, all portraying the most honeyed and ubiquitous female sexuality. Even Mohamed, in a mud house in Marrakesh, had not escaped them. But in reality, the entire Galileo Club had experienced very little. Their understanding was like their grasp of conditions on Venus. The temperature may have been white-hot, mighty winds of exotic elements might rage, the ground forever be rocked by seismic convulsions–somewhere, someone was near these facts. The members of the Galileo Club were not. Venus was still the bright star of twilight, a distant promise that remained inaccessible and gave no warmth. Their fate was to have dangled before them forever the lip-licking, willowy beauty, on fire for a certain brand of car or cola or credit card, sliding with sultry looks into the seat beside an implausibly handsome male who possessed the goods. Warren was beginning to see that whatever the goods were, he and his friends would likely never have them. The seat beside them would remain empty or, perhaps worse, be filled by a near-stranger, barely compliant, as lost as they were.

And across the way, in the Susan B. Anthony dorm, the comely girls were equally tempted and betrayed, perhaps more so. Even more than Warren and his friends, they were taught by the same instructor, subtly and persistently, that they must fear never finding a desirable mate. Or even more despairingly, a desirable self.

six

HUMANITIES HALL

No word had come from the Signage Committee about meetings or anything else, and Brumley began to hope he had been forgotten or the committee itself dissolved, its purpose and especially its vile name recognized by some sane, relict administrator for the execrations they were. His hope held until he walked into the main Humanities office one morning to see Huckston, replacing a memo and a package in Brumley's slot in the departmental mail center. The director of the two-person creative writing program, Huckston regularly and openly read unsealed letters, memos, brochures and checked the return addresses on the mail of all departmental faculty. Brumley suspected that he took sealed letters with interesting return addresses to his office and steamed them open.

"You're going to love that top memo," Huckston gloated, his long blonde hair falling artistically across his eyes. "Signage Committee. Somebody up there must have it in for you. When the Service component for merit raises comes out, Signage Committee work will get you rated about a four-and-a half, with a five being the bottom, of course."

Huckston was a member of the departmental-insiders poker group, where all departmental business was decided before the spurious official departmental meetings were called to rubber stamp the poker group's decisions. Brumley did not need any insider information to tell him the Signage Committee was more a sentence than a service.

"Been reading my mail again?" Brumley asked indifferently. "Are you still stealing money out of the coffee fund? Or shaking down students for grades? Oh, I forgot, you don't need the money now that your man Cole is chair."

When the chairmanship had last become vacant, Huckston had campaigned, written letters of support and spoken boldly to Dean Wainwright during one of their fishing trips about Cole's vast qualifications for the job as chair of the English Department. When Cole got the position, Huckston had immediately been named director of creative writing, a position Cole created that carried with it a reduced teaching load and a pay raise retroactive to the previous semester, when Huckston had begun his duties with the kissing of Cole's ass. As director, Huckston quickly directed himself to do as little as possible. The poet who made up the other half of the creative writers Huckston avoided since she actually wrote poetry, worked hard, and read a great deal.

"If you knew which side your bread was buttered on," he told Brumley loftily, "you might be a director, though of what I don't know. How about Director of Hopeless Causes, that would be about right. Writing a letter for that Warren kid. How noble. That kind of stuff can get you a bad rep upstairs."

"I've already got a bad rep upstairs; farther up, though, I believe I've got a good one. How many directors do we have now—eight? nine? For twenty-two people. Fifteen years ago there were three. We've got more people in the Director category than any other category in the department, including literature teachers. Listen, Huckston, if you can suck up to Cole delicately enough, maybe you can be named Director of Directors. For a great talent like yourself who believes in the transforming power of language, a title like that might transform you out of the toad-eater category."

"All right, Brumely," Huckston said as Brumely went out, "no need to get personal." He checked the return address of a letter in Hobart's mailbox, then turned to Miss Pam, the middle-aged, utterly non-committal and invaluable department secretary who had paid no attention to the exchange. In the unending scrimmage between high ideals and scheming ambitions that embroiled the department, Miss Pam, gray, plump and serene, refused to be other than friendly and helpful to any of the shifting alliances. Her bipartite classification of department members she kept to herself: Nice Guys and Shit Heads.

Huckston, she knew, was a Shit Head who read other people's mail, bullied whomever he could, and shamelessly played up to anyone he thought could get him more money and less work. He also grew his thick, blonde hair in a careless, bohemian cut that he had styled twice a month, and prior to meeting his creative writing classes he undid the top buttons of his shirt to reveal a simple, gold-plated chain on a carefully shaved chest.

"I'll need these by 10:30," he said to her, indicating a stack of papers he had placed in the copy tray on her desk and heading for the door. "Six copies of each, collated and stapled."

"Ah, Mr. Huckston, I don't think I can get to them this morning," Miss Pam said with perfect ease as Huckston breezed out, only to whip back in when her words registered. "The student worker called in sick, and I've got to fill out these forms for Dr. Cole. They're due in the Dean's office by noon."

Huckston looked at her in disbelief. "I've got to have these by 10:30," he said, "or we won't have anything to critique." Huckston was teaching a prose creative writing course in which students wrote things that he copied, distributed to the other students to read, and then discussed in class. Brumely, hearing the exchange and sensing conflict, came back and sauntered to Miss Pam's desk. He glanced at the stack of papers in the tray. The one on top was evidently a short story whose author's computer spell-check had once again betrayed her. It was entitled "Brent and Ashley Meet and Become Aquatinted."

"I'd get this one to the presses quick," he said to a barely listening Huckston. "Could you make an extra copy for me? Brent and Ashley sound like a fetching pair to become acquainted. Or maybe it *is* aquatinted, some kinky body painting. Oh, yes, I'd like to take it home and read it, over and over. I'll put it in my mailbox when I'm through so you'll be sure to get it back."

Huckston, whose opinion of his students' abilities was low but who was shrewd enough never to voice it, looked wildly for a moment at Brumley and turned on Miss Pam.

"But I've got to have these by 10:30," he reiterated, as though clarifying the situation.

"I wish I could help you, but you know how these forms are—they've got to get done. I don't believe anyone is using the copier," she suggested.

Huckston, his will collapsing, swayed about before scooping up the stack of papers and darting in desperation toward the copy room.

Brumley glanced at Miss Pam for some sign of disgust, but as usual she met his conspiratorial look with a bland smile of greeting.

"It's demeaning for artistic faculty members to make their own copies," he explained with mock concern, but Miss Pam, still smiling, turned to the urgent forms she was filling out and resumed typing. But he was sure what she thought of Huckston.

'Today Officer Barnes," he thought vaguely as he started again toward his office. "Tomorrow, maybe, Miss Pam."

As much as he hoped Tomorrow Miss Pam, Brumley had to admit how unlikely that was. In fact, he was unsure what it was that he hoped tomorrow Miss Pam would do or transform or convert to. And what was Officer Barnes doing today that one might take hope from? Out in the heat–and the snow in winter–Officer Barnes was trying to set something right, or appeared to be. Maybe Miss Pam could find some way to curb the Huckstons of the world who could have made her life miserable if she let them. Maybe her unflappable approach was the key–*resist not evil*. But could Huckston be called evil? Evil ought to have some grandeur, some stature, a mighty will. It ought to be a worthy adversary. But Huckston and his kind? Maybe in the aggregate they were evil, but taken singly they were so little, so insignificant, as to be merely embarrassing in their commitment never to let principle stand in the way of their upward mobility. Considered one by one, they were hardly even incremental evil. Most of the time they went about their lives as harmlessly as everyone else did, until they became a part of some organization or institution on which they depended for their economic existence. That, Brumley thought, may explain it all. He wasn't sure. Only one thing was for certain. However vain his resistance to them and their ways might be, he had to resist.

Carrying the Signage memo like a flat, venomous reptile, the package containing what he assumed was a book under his arm, Brumley set out again for his office. Because of a new stack of sprinkler pipes, he had to detour through the coffee room to reach the suite where his office was located at the far end of the long, concrete block corridor, along which were spaced his colleagues' offices. Most of them were still unoccupied this early in the morning. Golfing had recently become a rage among many of the faculty, and Brumley had a vision of several morning foursomes, all preparatorily declaiming their afternoon lectures to the spacious fairways of the university golf course. Professor Appleby's office, unopened now for over a year-and-a-half, reminded him of what had become possible in college teaching. Appleby had leapt early into the cockpit of the jumbo jet called International Programs and had subsequently spent almost all of his career at Middle State abroad, finding interesting cultural sites for the few affluent students whose parents could afford to send their offspring across the seas to study economics or calculus or American history, evidently the European varieties. His was a grueling quest for bars in Barcelona, cafes in Cannes, discos in Danzig, nightclubs in Nice, gigolos in Giglio and whorehouses in The Hague, and he had finally reached an incredible pinnacle of academic success by being named Director of Supervisors for International Studies for West-central Europe and having to teach no courses at all. The rest of Europe had been Balkanized among other far-sighted professors, and everything had gone prosperously until a failure of volunteers for a backwater district undergoing a violent civil war led to a glut of International Directors and Assistant International Directors that not even the most hardened supporter of junketeering and featherbedding could ignore. Three of the seventeen directors and assistant directors had to be returned, virtually in strait-jackets, to the Middle State classroom.

One of them, Skipworth of Economics, Brumley knew and was overjoyed to see his gray, blighted face at the university-wide faculty meeting at the beginning of the academic year of his disgrace. That Christmas break, facing the second straight semester of full-time teaching of large, introductory courses—the other two former internationalists had been found part-time administrative duties on campus—Skipworth shot himself, which, since he had no family, turned out to be a good thing for everybody. The vacancy of his position meant a new, young, even more malleable faculty member could now be hired to replace him at a much lower salary than Skipworth's. Consequently, the money saved could go into the Dean of Business's slush fund as discretionary money to allow the dean to slip some of it with discretion to his favorites, or to himself. As for poor Skipworth, who saw only the demands of the classroom before him, he must have realized the benefits in suicide or he wouldn't have pulled the trigger. As far as Brumley could find out, no scholarship fund had been established in Skipworth's name.

Once in his office Brumley decided to save the worst until last and lay aside the memo to open the package. It was a book, but rather than a collection of short stories or poems for teaching or a much-needed philosophy reader with copious explanatory material, it was a text on the regulation of air moisture content—somewhere several years ago, almost certainly in a computer, Brumley's Professorship of Humanities had been misidentified as a Professorship of Humidities, one of the few such in the world. As a result, he regularly received information from various scientific publishing companies, professional humidity organizations, and once an offer from NASA to be a consultant on a Mars Rover project. He had toyed with accepting. The repercussions from the inevitable exposure, as well as the dishonesty, restrained him, even though the two year's consulting fee would have been the equivalent of four years of his regular salary. In fact, he was fairly certain there would be no inevitable exposure, that he could fake it. A suggestion forwarded to NASA every month or so, first for a packet of silicon gel stuck in the guts of the robot somewhere, then a box of baking soda, then a basement dehumidifier, or a humidifier if the dehumidifier turned out to be the wrong guess. Even if the fraud did become apparent, he was legally guiltless, and no bureaucracy like NASA would want the embarrassment of such a revelation of utter incompetence on their part. Better a box of Arm and Hammer winging to the red planet at a million dollars an ounce than their racket put in jeopardy. Who could know how many geographers had been hired as geologists, mechanics as mechanical engineers, physicians as physicists, physicists as physicians, proctors as doctors, or astrologers as astronomers? No, Brumley would have been safe. After all, what else, other than dedicated bureaucratic self-preservation, could explain the worldwide fireworks show that extinguished the seven well-trained lives of the Challenger astronauts? But the launch was scrubbed for Brumley. He couldn't bring himself to bend with the angles or leap through the loopholes. While Huckston and his like blasted to the heavens, Brumley's mission was grounded.

He set the book aside and picked up the Signage memo. The committee was jointly under the Office of Emergency Preparedness, Vice president Hays in charge, and the Office of Public Relations, headed by Vice president Dodson. There was no hint of the committee's purpose or its mystifying relationship to the crack-brained Asteroid

Preparedness Program, only the dread affirmation that he, Brumley, was doomed shortly to spend an indefinite period of his life on what was likely the most needless, boring committee ever formed at Middle State. If what he assumed was correct–that the only possible reason for such a committee was to design and place signs–then why have a committee? President Curtis would make the final decision anyway, either choosing one of the four alternatives the committee would be asked to provide him or, more likely, ignoring all four and picking something totally different he had wanted to begin with. The whole thing reeked of yet another time- and money-wasting ruse to give the appearance of what management called shared governance. Unionization, which was unlikely to occur at Middle State even if management proclaimed the faculty galley slaves and issued heavy oars, was outlawed in state institutions if the workers involved could be shown to have a part in the running of that institution. So an intricate network of permanent and de facto committees, all of an advisory nature, were in place at Middle State to relieve management of work and give the appearance that power was shared. Brumley didn't mind so much that it wasn't shared as that no one pointed out the fraud, or even seemed to notice it.

At the bottom of the memo were the names of the committee members. Brumley had just begun to scan them when he looked up to see Warren standing in his open door, a sheet of paper in his hand. Warren's usually open face was worried, perplexed.

"Chris," he said, "come in. What's up?"

"Dr. Brumley," Warren said apologetically, "I'm sorry to bother you again, but I wonder if you could tell me about this." He handed Brumley the sheet of paper he was holding. It was a Signage Committee memo, similar to Brumley's except addressed to Warren. "It's this committee. I'm on it. I wondered if you know anything about it? I saw that you were on it, too."

"I don't know much," Brumley said, not wishing to disillusion Warren should he believe with the generous naivete of youth that being named to consider signage was an honor. "Anything specific you don't understand?"

"I guess everything. What's it about? I'm not sure why I was put on it. I don't know anything about signs. Or signage."

"At least you know it's about signs. Hobart said it may be about post-nasal drip. But other than it's about signs–probably what they'll look like and where they'll be placed–I don't know."

"You mean we design signs?"

"I'm not sure," Brumley said. He did not want to be evasive, but what could he say? It was true that he didn't know exactly what fabricated duties the committee would be given. What he did know was that very likely a job that could be done by a single, relatively competent person was being foisted on a large, inefficient group to sustain the shared-governance illusion. Or–and Brumley was struck by the thought–there was some hot potato of an issue involved that management wanted to avoid.

"Why do they have students on it?" Warren asked.

"Shared governance," Brumley couldn't help saying. "Whatever that may be. But listen, I wouldn't take the appointment too seriously," he said, regretting his words when he saw Warren's blank look, which seemed a bit constrained and may have indicated that he did feel, against his better judgment, that being named to the committee was a recognition of some sort. Brumley tried to find the right words. How did one speak to the uncorrupted young who were about to be drug into the cesspool? *He who shall teach the Child to Doubt, The rotting grave shall ne'er get out*, Blake had said, though Brumley never understood why the child shouldn't be taught to doubt, at least doubt the present order of things. Surely there was an obligation to encourage a little incredulity there. But the Signage Committee was only one tiny strut of a multitude of braces, connections and alignments that made up the present order of things and was perhaps too inconsequential to matter. Alerting Warren to the danger was likely not worth risking an eternal stay in Blake's rotting grave. But mainly Brumely didn't want to hurt Warren's feelings or alarm him by disclosing that almost certainly both of them had been named to the Signage Committee by Dean Wainwright or Vice president Staull or, provided he had been given or had read Warren's letter, even by President Curtis, all in revenge for pressing the issue of Too Few Courses. He decided to straddle the fence.

"What I mean is, you should feel good about being named, but like most things, I wouldn't take the committee too seriously," he said. "Don't go out and do research on signs. Come to the meetings, unless you see they're a waste of time. And trust your instincts; don't let the

presence of committee rituals or people in suits or people who like to
be addressed by their titles make you doubt your feelings. Whether you
show up or not isn't going to make much difference even a month from
now, for you or the signs."

Warren still seemed uncertain, and Brumley was afraid he had
played down the non-existent importance of the Signage Committee too
much. Real students like Warren were never recognized or appreciated
in any official way at Middle State, though they hungered for a good
word as much as anyone. Why starve a deserving student of what he
might believe was a crumb of acknowledgment?

"Listen, you'll do fine on this committee. Just pay attention during
the first meeting or two to find out what's going on"–*what they want
us to do*, he wanted to say–"and you'll see there won't be much pressure
on you. You should be pleased that you've been recommended to serve.
Somebody thinks you're worth something–somebody besides your
instructors."

Brumley again considered Warren's virtues. It wasn't just himself,
but Greenman and Hobart and Mulholland of Psychology and Talbot
of Biology had all had taught Warren, and all valued him. None would
have sentenced him, contrary to Warren's every impulse of his youth
and life, to involvement with a subject as manufactured and nugatory
as signage. If left up to him, Brumley would have done all he could to
prevent Warren, or for that matter any student–or any human–from
ever serving on a such a committee or study group or task force, or
attending a workshop or retreat or administrative seminar, or revisiting
an issue or chairing a session or having a micro-problem or setting
parameters. But all he could do to save them was to teach them to give
a little thought to the assumptions, practices and direction of a world
that invented and revered such things; that and, Blake to the contrary,
teach them also, if only occasionally, to doubt.

After Warren had left–unsatisfied, Brumley was afraid–he leaned
back in his creaking chair and began perusing the memo again. He
was right; there was no hint of the committee's purpose, just the dread
announcement that all in the list of names at the bottom had been
chosen to serve, that Franco Weebles of Criminal Justice and Penology
was chairman, and that the committee, oddly, reported to two vice
presidents. Brumley scanned the list of committee members, whose

department or office was listed after each name. There were twenty-five names, one fourth the membership of the U.S. Senate he reflected. Eight were low-level administrators, none of whom Brumley recognized but who, he was confident, could be counted on already to know what the administration wanted and vote accordingly. Only one or two would ever attend, until the meeting when some decisive vote was to be taken. Then all would appear. Following them were the names of eight faculty members, and Brumley felt a thrill of satisfaction when he saw the name of Nancy Bohannon of Theater, a svelte, dark-haired beauty who was a welcome distraction at any meeting. She would fit voluptuously into his Seven Veils fantasy that would likely begin shortly after each meeting had started. Wyandotte of Agribusiness, Poultry Division, was listed, though he had such prestige at Middle State that Brumley could not imagine his private secretary bothering to call the memo to his attention. Wyandotte's specialty was concentration camps for raising animals, especially chickens in the Leo Lear Poultry Complex, and his success at getting grants from all possible sources to perfect his methods was so great that he was seldom seen by other faculty members or students. But a large part of the other faculty members named as members, at least the ones he knew, confirmed Brumley's general assessment of why he was on the committee. Talbot of Biology, Mulholland of Psychology, and Conners of Chemistry were all troublemakers, and Brumley assumed that like him they had been appointed to the Signage Committee by administrators as a reminder that sooner or later, one way or another, vengeance was theirs.

Strangely, two local businessmen, identified as Chamber of Commerce members, were listed, though as it turned out neither attended any meetings. There was an unknown student in addition to Warren, and then four staff members, all undoubtedly overworked and underpaid, who would be grateful for the break in their jobs that each two-hour committee meeting of bewildering and insignificant blather would offer them. One of their names caught Brumley's attention. Junior White. White had once worked in Security; then, Brumely faintly recalled, he had transferred to Electronics. Was there more he had heard about White, or was there something about his demeanor or bearing that made him memorable? Maybe Officer Barnes would know the score. White might be a valuable ally on the committee should Brumley need a second to his motion to adjourn or a deciding vote to do the same. He reached for the phone. Officer Barnes might be on break and could fill him in; Barnes, a sympathetic soul, might give him a little hope.

He got, of course, a recorded message.

"This is the Campus Security Office of Middle State University," the pleasant, even sultry, female voice began. "Our office hours are 7:30 a.m. to 4:30 p.m. If you know the extension of the party you are calling, press One now. If you wish to discuss a traffic or parking ticket, press Two now. If you wish to purchase a parking sticker and need directions to do so, press Three now. If you wish to report a fire, please hang up and dial the city fire department, whose number is in your local phone directory. If you wish to report an emergency other than a fire, press Five now. If you wish to speak to the Director of Security, press Six now. If you are calling from a rotary phone, please hold while we transfer your call to an administrative associate."

Brumley refused ever to use the options but held on grimly until a human, an actual living being, spoke to him. At times, though, there was no such possibility—to "wait until a representative was available." In those cases, he either took his business elsewhere or, if possible, visited in person the place he had called. He knew his position, like many others he held, would soon be untenable. Even Hobart—who when recorded messages began to defile the world would initially enter into one-sided, profane discourse with the soulless voices—had come to tolerate them. But how Brumley wished the recorded voice at the Security office would be a Middle State employee. It was soft, a little low, with none of the practiced enunciation and inflections of the trained voice-recording expert, all dialect erased, purged of all sincere emotion, nothing left but efficiency and sham cordiality. This one was a voice with a tongue, a voice that touched you in your ear. But likely it came from some outfit with a name like Campus Security Voice Recording Inc., headquartered in California with even the unpolished nature of the voice carefully rehearsed and electronically shaped to modify it professionally into a non-professional sound.

"Hello, Campus Security," the same voice spoke miraculously, carressingly, into his ear. "This is Kaneesha Morris. Can I help you?"

Stock phone answer, Brumley thought, but the voice would always be new.

"Yes," he said, "is Barnes there?"

"Just a moment," said Kaneesha, and for only a moment Brumley was put on hold.

"No," the voice returned, "he's away from his desk at the moment. Could I take a message?"

"Is he still out in the parking lot?" Brumley said, deciding to show he was an insider and could see through all the misrepresentations she had to parrot. Barnes had no desk; he and most of the other campus cops, when they had a break, shared a table in their coffee room.

"I think he is," the voice said, immediately relaxed, friendly, and Brumley felt that at least for once he had struck a right note, had not offended by confronting too bluntly a conventional charade or had not appeared too dismissible by weakly acceding to it

"Ann," the voice murmured, "has Officer Barnes come in yet?" Then to Brumley: "He's still out, Dr. Brumley. Do you want me to have him call you?"

Brumley froze—she knows me. For an instant his mind ran wild: she was a former student he had lusted for some ten years ago who had secretly desired him and had never forgotten him and heard his voice in her dreams. Or perhaps recently, while walking through Humanities Hall, she had passed by his classroom, had heard him lecturing and had stopped, spellbound by his knowledge and eloquence.

"I'll get back to him later," Brumley said, knowing it was unofficially frowned upon if hourly employees like Barnes used campus phones for personal reasons. And then, deciding to be direct but also just curious, he asked: "How did you know it was me?"

"We have Caller ID," Keneesha set the inevitable dagger. "Sometimes people who call us are so excited they hang up without saying who they are or what their number is. And sometimes we get crank calls."

"I see," Brumley said with whatever cheer he could muster. Which category did he fit in, panicked or pervert? Both, he decided. "Listen," he went on, "thanks a lot. Maybe I'll stop by over there on his break. What time does he usually get in?"

"Just a moment," Keneesha purred, putting him again on hold but returning quickly. "Usually around 9:30," she said, "but he stays out later a lot. I can have him call you. It's all right."

"Thanks, "Brumley said, now determined to go over. She evidently knew Barnes would be out longer in the heat than the other Security Associates, who used the weather as an excuse to spend as much time as possible around their table. She also knew to reassure him that Barnes wouldn't get in trouble for using the phone.

"Thanks for your offer, but I'll drop by. Maybe not today, but I'll be there. It's nothing important. Thanks again."

"Thank you," said the warm voice of Keneesha. "I'll tell him you called." Brumley hung up the phone. He wanted to think more of Keneesha, but the Signage memo caught his eye again. There was no word of when the first meeting would be, but it couldn't be far away.

seven

THINGS ARE GETTING OUT

The Signage Committee was the least of Warren's problems. The deadline for his adding new courses was long past, Brumley's renewed efforts to help him had failed, and it was clear that without a miracle he would not graduate with most of the his fellow seniors. Of those on his dorm floor, Hoh, Shepherd and Jeeks were similarly shafted, Hoh due to an administrative oversight, Jeeks mainly to improvidence and indifference, and Shepherd to a scarcity of courses in farming and an excess of courses in agribusiness. Bolinger, who took twenty credit hours each semester and made A's in all those that interested him, would graduate with two majors, physics and philosophy, while Sola, as organized as a clock, would punctiliously cross the stage, be given a handshake and diploma, and then be forgotten by Middle State for five years, by which time he might be assumed to have a little money and would be contacted on alumni fund-raising week. Even Plumb Bob, who still had over ten thousand dollars from his Air Force college fund to draw on, was skirting dangerously close to graduation and had stopped going to two classes in late September when it became evident that unless he slacked off considerably or once more changed majors he might find himself before he was thirty flung into the heartless world of the free market. None could help Warren; neither could anyone on the faculty. After his encounter with Eigleman, he avoided the administration.

There was a greater concern. Even if he could graduate, what was there for him to do? Would becoming a teacher, even supposing he could find a job as such, ensnare him in the same kind of binding web that he began to sense was spun throughout Middle State? In many of his favorite instructors, in spite of their enthusiasm for the material they taught, he felt an undercurrent of anger and frustration–that and a pall of resignation. He had read enough to know–even Eisenhower, the last general of the Republic, had known–to fear and mistrust the military-industrial complex. While Warren wasn't sure what exactly the military-industrial complex was, he was beginning to believe it might be everything and that one way or another everybody worked for it.

Meanwhile, there was his required General Science class. Both he and Bolinger had delayed taking the class until this year, hoping the requirement would be dropped or that they would have learned by then which of the many graduate students who taught the course might be informed or interesting. Both were disappointed. The course requirement endured, and their instructor Half-life Anderson, a recent graduate of Middle State now working on his Master's degree in science, seemed confused.

"So half-life," said Anderson, in a final muddling of the topic that had given him his nickname, "is the life of what you have left when half of what you started with is gone. It's how long it takes for half of what you started with, when it's radioactive, to decay–to not be there. Or for half of it not to be there."

"What if you start out with some and then put some more with it later–will that make the half-life longer or shorter?" Bolinger asked with feigned innocence.

"Put more with it?"

"Yes."

"Let's see, anyone got any ideas here?" Anderson stalled, wishing he had scheduled a field trip or computer exercise for the day's class.

"Longer?" one student ventured.

Anderson, trying to think, showed no sign.

"No," another student offered, "it's got to be shorter. It's like you'd dilute it, wouldn't you?"

"What about how much you added?" Anderson asked, buying time in hopes of illumination. "Would that make a difference?" It was clear by his tone that adding more was supposedly significant, but no one saw how. Warren, who had been surreptitiously reading *Lady Chatterley's Lover*, sensed Anderson's entanglement and looked up.

"If you put in more of the stuff so that you have more than you started with," Anderson said decisively, then weakened, "what would that do to the half-life?"

There was no response.

"Okay, here's how it is. If you take the half-life of what you had and add more to it, it would obviously increase the half-life," he said conclusively. "But if you add *less* to it than you had, or if you take away some. . ." his voice trailed off as the black waters of illogic he was wading into begin to deepen, ". . .then what? Let's hear what you have to say."

"I don't see why we have to know anything about half-lifes anyway," a student whined. "We never use it in real life."

Anderson, who wasn't sure why anyone had to either, did feel he should defend what he taught but was uncertain how to do so. To conceal his growing discomfort, he scanned the class with amused anticipation as though expecting some other lover of learning to put the scoffer back in her bird cage.

"It's so we can make bombs that will blow up other countries who have learned about the atom and half-lifes before they blow us up. Or so we can threaten to blow up anybody who doesn't give us what we want," Warren ventured, grasping the opportunity for an interesting drift away from the abstract physical sciences, whose cold-bloodedness he felt but whose bloodstains he was only beginning to see.

"There's something to that, all right," Anderson said gratefully, though he felt there should be some less remote reason for mastering the concept of half-life. "If the Communists had discovered the atom bomb before we did, we'd all be Communists by now."

"They did," Bolinger announced. "We only developed it because we had spies that stole the plans for one from them."

There was a general stir in the class, and Anderson, whose command of history was even less than his mastery of half-lifes, was again at a loss.

"I don't know about that," he said. "It sounds like not everybody agrees."

"They didn't have the bomb first," said a student behind Bolinger with great disdain. "We did and they stole it from us. We dropped the first bomb. Not the Communists."

"Bill sounds pretty certain, Bolinger. What about it?"

"The Communists had the bomb first," Bolinger repeated matter-of-factly. "It's all coming out in documents the Kremlin is releasing now that the Communists aren't Communists but our friends like in WW II. They had the bomb and we stole their plans, and then one of their spies who didn't know it had been stolen stole our plans and sent them back to the Communists. We just act like we had it first for the prestige. Killing eighty thousand people in a second is in the book of world records," he said, too guilelessly even for Anderson to miss.

"Well, there's one thing for sure," Anderson said, taking a stand now that the enemy was clear. "If there hadn't been an atomic bomb, we might have lost the war. And if we didn't have one, whether it was the first one or not, we'd all be Communists by now."

"Japanese by now," Bolinger pointed out. "It was the Japanese we dropped the bomb on."

"Okay, Japanese Communists. But whatever, we wouldn't be Americans and be free."

"Would we have to know about half-lifes then?" the whining student asked plaintively, and amid the appreciative murmur that followed, Half-life Anderson turned again to his obfuscation of the concept and Warren back to *Lady Chatterley's Lover*.

In the deep understructure of the Science Building, far beneath the room where Warren's class met, there were problems in Middle State's Transuranic Department. Plutonium kept getting out. It was either tracked out or vented out or diffused out or carried out or pumped out—no one knew for sure. It was just getting out.

"How much plute does inventory say we ought to have?" Professor Jenkins, the Director of the Transuranic Department asked at the end of the first month of that year's fall term.

"I think, Dr. Jenkins, about fifteen pounds, more or less," Narwala Niyak, his graduate assistant replied, shrewdly eyeing the beaker into which he was managing to pour most of a green, fluorescing liquid from a large flask etched on its side with a black skull and crossbones.

"Narwala," Jenkins looked up tiredly from the huge computer printout sheet he was studying. "It's kilograms, not pounds. Not that it makes a damn if the best you can do is 'think' we've got 'more or less' seven kilograms. Goddamnit Narwala, this is serious. We need to know how much we have down to a thousandths of a gram. And it's grams—grams, kilograms, meters, hectares. This is science, not the world. This dumb-Indian crap has got to stop. Don't they use the metric system in India? It ought to be natural to you. Use it. Jesus!"

"Oh my," Narwala twittered. "Again I am forgetting," and he sloshed out even more of the evil green liquid into the drain basin of the partly closed ventilation hood where he stood. "So difficult was it for me to learn the hated British system of measuring—those pounds, quarts, the dreadful foot that was the distance from Prince Albert's heel to his left big toe. Once the evil colonial imperialists have taken away your culture, their ways are not easily rejected. But I will try to remember and employ only the natural and ancient metric system of my land and people."

"Narwala," Jenkins said. "No more. Play the Hollywood Indian routine elsewhere. I want to know within prescribed Commission accuracy how much plutonium we have and if it agrees with Inventory . By tomorrow. You know more about decay rate theory than I do. If you'll just stop pouring stuff before you hurt yourself and get to work, maybe we can get in the clear."

Given theoretical whizzes like the maladroit Narwala, there was little wonder plutonium was disappearing, but Narwala's presence was indispensable to the Transuranic Department. Middle State could never hope to attract first-rate graduate students, and most of those they did had done their undemanding undergraduate work there. All of these, it could be said in their favor, could boil water. But other than it got real hot, they didn't know why. To get sufficient graduate students to justify a graduate program, and of these to have a few with a theoretical understanding of the boiling of water, it was necessary to accept ever larger numbers of foreign students. They swelled the enrollment numbers and paid very high tuition. Most could not boil water. They also taught many of the sections of General Science 101, a hodgepodge of material required of all Middle State undergraduates. All of this meant that the undergraduates either got an instructor like Anderson, who wasn't clear on a lot of things, or, as had fallen Plumb Bob's lot the previous year, someone like Narwala. In fact, his instructor had been Narwala, who, while well-meaning and intelligent and able to speak a kind of English, had almost daily revealed his shortcomings.

"We are displaying an experiment today," Narwala had announced to Plumb Bob's class one afternoon, at which all the students near the front rose and made for seats further back. Narwala's favorite technical operation, occasionally successful, was a carefully scrutinized pouring of a liquid from one container into another. His first demonstration that semester, to show the generation of thermal energy when acid was mixed with water, had consisted of just such a transfer–of a small amount of concentrated sulfuric acid from one test tube into another containing water and a thermometer. The details, however, had proved overly complex from the very beginning. Narwala placed the thermometer in the test tube containing the acid, then decanted the water into the acid, a process which immediately produced a sharp pop and the disappearance of both acid and thermometer. Over the next few hours, students who had been sitting on the front rows found numerous small holes appearing in their clothing and tiny pustulate blisters on exposed skin. The thermometer was never found. Neutralizing an acid by a base, Narwala's next demonstration, had won him a pain-filled night in the infirmary.

"Our experiment today," Narwala went on, " will have the application of thermal energy to liquid dihydrogen oxide to produce through molecular excitation and phase shift the gaseous form of the compound."

Before class began Narwala had readied his apparatus on the large counter in the front of the room. A 500-milliliter beaker sat on a stand, a Bunsen burner beneath it with its flexible hose attached to one of the several color-coded but otherwise similar nozzles that jutted above the counter's top. With a proud flourish, Narwala sloshed the beaker half-full of dihydrogen oxide and stepped aside so his accomplishment could be better seen.

"First I apply the heat," Narwala happily proclaimed as he lit a match and turned on the nozzle, only to have a great jet of water blast out of the burner, extinguishing the match and blowing the beaker of dihydrogen oxide off into the floor and showering students to the back row.

"Goodness gracious," he cried, "again I have connected the wrong nozzle tit and out has come water!"

Hastily he sat the beaker stand upright and clattered another beaker onto it, while with one sandaled foot he tried to rake the larger pieces of broken beaker under the counter.

"Let me now get the hose properly connected," he said, with an inflection mixing avowal with prayer, and bent over to smell what each nozzle tit would emit as he tried it, immediately turning on the nozzle he had just disconnected and administering himself a quick jet of water in the left nostril.

"Wrong one again," he said, smiling piteously, his eyes rapidly blinking at the deep sting inside his head. "Let us try —agh, stink--" he cried at the renewed pain, looking up with a quick apologetic grimace "--this one, the gas one we need," and he manfully worked the burner hose over it and turned it on. After some preliminary coughs of residual water from the hose, the gas began to hiss from the burner and Narwala lit and thrust another match to it, whereon a diaphanous ball of eyebrow-singeing flame promptly whoofed from the maladjusted burner and settled to a two-foot high, roaring yellow flare that engulfed the beaker. Bravely lunging for the valve at the burner's base, Narwala managed to reduce the billowing flame to a large, hissing cone of blue and yellow that enclosed a smaller cone of solid, intense bright blue.

"Now," he said with relieved finality as the odor of singed hair filled the room, "we will overlook the transformation of liquid dihydrogen oxide into its gaseous form," and he stepped back from the counter, beaming nervously at his well-tuned apparatus.

The bright blue cone bore steadily against the bottom of the beaker, which began at first almost imperceptibly to glow an increasingly vivid pink. Even to the students now packed against the back wall a malformation of the beaker began to appear. Suddenly, in a sickeningly, accelerating sag, the sides tilted in as the bottom melted and ballooned downward.

"Agh," Narwala cried, leaping forward to shut off the gas, "what has happened? Oh, now I see, there is no dihydrogen oxide in the beaker; it was forgotten. But we did see," he raised his voice to be heard over the bell ending the class and to reach the majority of students hurrying out the door, "the transformation of silicon dioxide from one liquid phase to one more recognizably liquid. Did everyone see it?"

Plumb Bob had kept Warren abreast of the more flagrant of Narwala's ineptitudes, and Warren wished he had at least Narwala's

MIKE MILLER

comic element in his General Science class, an element the plodding, uncertain Anderson could rarely provide. But Warren was more directly acquainted with Narwala's struggles against the recalcitrant things of the world, struggles not always entirely comic. Three years ago, during his Summer Orientation at Middle State just prior to his freshman year, Warren had seen Narwala in his full aspect.

Summer O, as the program had been fetchingly abbreviated, allowed high school applicants for admission to Middle State to spend two precious summer days of their seventeenth year being misleadingly oriented to the school, accomplished through a series of embarrassingly contrived meetings and tours around the campus. The program was of course without cost, the considerable bill being footed by taxpayers. Its effectiveness in luring students to enroll at Middle State was never evaluated, but since the state's other state universities had such a program, an evaluation was hardly necessary. The program's slogan was Higher Education: A Fun Thing, and the prospective students were separated into small groups that the Assistant Vice President for Student Services and the Vice president of Public Relations had decided to name crews. Each crew was coxswained by a smooth and acceptable senior to sites and information that the Assistant Vice president and the Director thought would entice the students to choose Middle State as the institution where for the next four to six years they would spend their money. On the second day of Warren's visit, after his crew had left the sullen, pot-bellied faculty softball game, ordered and harshly umpired by President Curtis himself, they had been shepherded down the quadrangle, passing on the way a scattering of smocked and beret-wearing assistant administrators posing as artists, ordered there by another of President Curtis's inspirations, which had them costumed roughly as Salvador Dali, slashing away at easel-mounted butcher paper in a show of Middle State's commitment to excellence in art and such. The crew's destination was the Science Building, for a brief tour of the impressive facilities of the Transuranic Department.

"This is the Trans-uranic Department, I think that's how you say it," said their crew's coxswain Vickie, a bronzed, beautiful senior in tight white shorts and T-shirt who with bubbling cheer and enthusiasm led their tour. "This is where they do science and all."

"Do you know exactly what they do here?" asked one crew member,

78

who Warren noticed had grown more and more withdrawn throughout the two day period.

"Well, science stuff, but no, I don't know exactly," Vickie said, slightly flustered at a question that her two-weeks' training period had not prepared her for. "I think they study half-lifes and that kind of thing. Elements, things like that."

The inquisitive crew member nodded, and after that day Warren never saw her again.

"But I do have some stuff about it," Vickie brightened, and then with furrowed concentration began to read haltingly, syllable by syllable, from a notebook that all the coxswains were issued.

"'The Transuranic Department houses Middle State's plutonium applications laboratories. Positioned as the bedrock of the Science Building, this department is funded by an ongoing grant from the Department of Defense and the Fund for the Development of Nuclear Energy, and another from Middle State's College of Business. Its purpose is to find ways of incorporating plutonium–a transuranic element–into our daily lives. Forged in the heat of nuclear reactors, plutonium is a man-made element with potentially thousands of useful applications, and Middle State's Transuranic Department is dedicated to excellence in plutonium usage.'"

With a frown she looked up for sympathy for having to read such difficult material. Warren, who like all the other male crew members had attended more to the sweet perk of her breasts than her spiel, was quick to respond with a concerned and understanding shake of his head.

"Well, that's what it says," she pouted with mock exasperation, assuming that like her, no one other than the weirdo who'd asked the question could find the slightest interest in the answer. She smiled at Warren's complicity and returned to the notebook.

"'Because plutonium is somewhat radioactive, the exit from the Transuranic Department is equipped with a radiation detector that all those leaving the area must walk over. This insures that no radioactivity can be tracked out on a visitor's or lab worker's shoes. Safety here is of the highest concern, and Middle State's Transuranic Department is dedicated to excellence in safety.'"

"This is that thing, I think." She pointed to a rubber mat with a metal grid over it on the exit side of the doorway to the department, and the group filed by it directly into a long hall that stretched away to the left and right.

"'To further insure the safety of the operation'," Vickie continued to read as they passed in, "'the department's facilities are separated into two sections: a central *hot side* where all plutonium in bulk form is kept and where all the processing and application work is done; and, separated from the hot side by a framing hallway (that you have just entered), a *cold side* that houses the low-level radioactivity labs and the department's offices. One enters the hot side from the cold side through one of two *change-and-decontamination rooms*, usually shortened to *change room*, containing lockers, showers and radiation detectors, where all scientists and technicians who work on the hot side must dress in appropriate protective clothing before entering their work place.'"

Warren had moved within the group to obtain a better view of Vickie, fantasizing *hot side in appropriate clothing*, and noticed behind her beautiful profile the decal of a purple and yellow radiation warning triskelion on the glassed upper portion of a hot-side doorway.

"Is that the hot side?" he asked, pointing to the door.

"Yes," Vickie said slowly, referring to her notebook. "I think so."

"I noticed the radiation warning behind you?"

"Where?"

"There, on the window. That big yellow and purple decal."

"Oh," Vickie jumped back. "Is that what that is?" She looked around uncertainly. "Do you think we should leave? Maybe we should leave."

"I don't think so," Warren said. "People work here all the time, and I don't guess they cover the sign while they're here. There's somebody in that other lab now."

Down the hall, just ahead of the group, he had seen another door to the hot side quickly closing.

"Well," Vickie pouted irresistibly again and then brightened, "I guess we'll be okay. Let's move on then."

The door Warren had seen close, like most of the others from the hot side into the hallway, had in its upper half a large, wire-mesh reinforced window with a radiation warning decal near the top. Beneath the window were signs that read DANGER: OPEN FROM INSIDE ONLY, and KEEP CLOSED EXCEPT IN CASE OF EMERGENCY, and NO FOOD OR SMOKING. In the lab visible through this door's window a group of men in white coveralls and white bonnets, their shoes covered in white cloth galoshes, were converging toward a fiercely beckoning co-worker at the door. Warren at first thought some dire emergency was at hand, but he realized that their crew had been spotted and the only crisis was whether the scientists would get to enjoy ogling some nice young ass.

Vickie halted the group in front of the door and turned back to her notebook.

"'The laboratories on the hot side each contains a "hood line." These hood lines are like a line of elevated cabinets but are made of stainless steel with a Plexiglass front. In each Plexiglass front are located two round ports with long reinforced rubber gloves that project into the hoods and allow scientists to handle objects inside. You may be able to see scientists at work with plutonium in the hoods, many of which are filled with argon, an inert gas, for safety purposes.'"

"I don't know if these scientists are working or not," Vickie said doubtfully as she looked up from her text.

Three of the white clad figures were pretending to talk with one another but were clearly interested only in Vickie's voluptuous presence beyond the glass of the door. Warren saw a small calculator fall from the hand of one when Vickie, brushing back her long blond hair, elevated her breasts slightly. The other two scientists stood unabashedly at the window, one with his nose actually flattened against it, and eyed Vickie as though she were part of some erotic film.

"Let's go down here," Vickie suggested and began walking further down the hall to where it turned to the right. Warren saw one of the scientists sprint toward a telephone while the others, with Vickie turned away, jammed the window until she was nearly out of their angle of vision.

Looking back from the tail end of the group, Warren saw the door open a few inches again, with four foreheads and pairs of eyes stacked vertically up and down it, oblivious to a faint alarm that began to sound inside the lab. Only when the crew member who wanted to know what work was done there had stopped and given the scientists an unladylike finger did they jerk back from the door and allow it to close.

At most of the hot side doors that Warren's crew passed on their circuit, similar white-suited groups of scientists converged. In some labs they wore respirators and some also yellow rubberized protective suits and hoods. All jostled for a place to drink in the ripe figure of Vickie and the lesser nymphs in the group, the more heavily suited scientists reminding Warren of grotesque idols come alive to ravish the nubile maiden paraded before them. He recalled too a made-for-TV movie he'd once seen about the first female prison guard at a maximum security prison for violent sex offenders. The guard was played by a twenty-three-year-old movie star with flawless features, shining hair and perfect body, the norm, apparently, for such an occupation. On the first day on the job she had walked, like Vickie down the hall, along the cells of the fully alerted and aroused sex maniacs of death row.

But at the final lab door they passed before returning to the entrance, no band of jostling, lecherous scientists awaited. Instead, as the crew came abreast of it, blinds that were closed over the windowed section were slowly opened by a smiling, white-suited technician sitting like a sideshow barker on a stool, revealing at a hood against the far wall a foreign student—it was Narwala himself—his hands inside the thick rubber gloves, clearly holding a demonstration for the group. He was pouring inside the hood a reeking brown bromidic liquid from a beaker into a graduated cylinder, while beside this operation, between two vertical, foot-long wires, a series of sizzling electrical arcs followed one another from the base upward to their tips. The crew jammed around the door, and Narwala looked beaming from his experiment to the group, whereon the unattended stream of liquid wandered from the graduated cylinder onto the electrical apparatus, smoldered for a moment, then flashed up into a ghostly white flame, so startling him that he dropped the half-full beaker. Great clouds of brown fumes began to boil from the spillage, illuminated through its billows by flashes of light. Evidently shouting in great alarm, though he could not be heard by the spellbound students, Narwala wrenched his arms from the long gauntlets and frantically began placing large metal discs over the glove ports. The cheerful stage manager at the door, so mesmerized by Vickie that he was oblivious to the developing difficulties until the growing cries of Narwala alerted him, rushed first to help seal the hood, then, as an afterthought, rushed back to the door and pulled the blinds shut. This time a much louder alarm began to sound.

"Wasn't that interesting," Vickie beamed. "But, you know, we should probably get back now," she said with no sense of urgency, checking her watch. She had likely been assured that nothing could go wrong. "Let's walk across the radiation detector to see if we've got any half-lifes on us"

No one had picked up any half-lifes, though Warren noticed the detector's On light was not lit. As they cleared the building, in the far distance they could hear the wail of fire engines, and the crew member who Warren never saw again looked at him, her eyes wide with incredulity and fear. Nothing, as far as Warren knew, ever came of Narwala's failed demonstration, but three years later, in some mysterious, unpredictable and so far undetectable manner, plutonium was still getting out.

Over in Humanities things were also getting out. Following her time-tested approach, Davis of English was unleashing her bold and opportune study on "The Ballad of Columbo," and doing so in a cutting-edge manner sure to win her a two or even a one rating on the research component of merit raise assessment rumored to be under development by Middle State's management.

Davis had long ago discovered that success as a free-thinking academic required following the herd, not just in employing computer gadgetry in her inquiries but also in artfully choosing the subject of her investigations. From her days as a graduate student she had dauntlessly embraced every variation of feminism, but not before each had become established and fortified in universities throughout the country. She had published a book and several articles that reviewers said "shed new light" and "gave new perspectives" on narrow and arcane topics that these reviewers also wrote books and articles about. Davis in turn wrote reviews of their books and articles and found that they too shed new light and gave new perspectives on the same topics. No one else cared about these topics. Davis cared about their advancing her career.

More recently, once she had seen the ground was safe, she had begun denouncing the ill- treatment of various groups who she discovered were ill-treated—lesbians, homosexuals, people of color other than pinkish-white, the handicapped, native Americans. Man's inhumanity to man—or as she would have swiftly uglified and largely falsified it, humanity's inhumanity to humanity—being almost limitless, there would be forever a steady supply of victims, and for the foreseeable future she could advance steadily in the academic world by championing any acceptable category of them. She also could subtly threaten Middle State's administration with high-profile federal lawsuits for discrimination or denial of freedom of speech if her yearly salary raises were not among the highest in the department. They always were. She was also elevated to the Directorship of Literature of the Oppressed, Marginalized and Disempowered, with an increase in salary and time off from teaching.

"Is there any way you could vacuum in here more than once every two weeks?" Davis asked Carla, the overworked and underpaid janitor who cleaned all the English Department offices.

"How often do you think I should?" Carla asked, hoisting Davis's wastebasket.

"Once a week would be fine," Davis said generously, always aware that the lower orders should be treated with respect.

"I can try, but I barely have enough time to get them every two weeks."

She emptied the wastebasket into the large garbage bin on the cart containing all her cleaning supplies, and with a folded cloth began dusting the bookshelves.

"You know," Davis observed helpfully, "instead of taking those cigarette breaks in the afternoon, you could come up here at least once a week and vacuum. It would be good for you to give up those things anyway."

"I guess I could," Carla said wearily. "You wouldn't want to pay me a quarter hour's wages for doing it, would you?"

"What?" Davis swivelled around quickly from her computer screen. "Me pay you? Why should I pay you? You're being paid, I assume."

"Breaks are part of our handbook policy. If I work during my break, I want to be paid."

"Well," Davis said, nearly speechless. "Well, if you could manage to vacuum this office once a week, I'd be grateful. And I'm sure your supervisor would be as well."

"Ask him if he would," Carla said, still dusting.

"I will," Davis said decisively, knowing she wouldn't and furious at the realization. Just because she was a woman and had been ill-nurtured in such a way as to make her passive and non-assertive, she knew she would be taken advantage of in everything she did. Carla would not have dared to speak to a male professor with such a disdainful assumption of equality. The entire burden of being a member of an oppressed minority descended agreeably upon Davis, and it was several minutes after Carla left before she could return to her computer, where she was preparing the first portions of her Columbo project, which combined a popular culture topic–pop culture being a very marketable item in the study of literature–with her ever-dependable feminism. She was sending over the computer network to her Middle State colleagues the successive installments of her reflections. They were waiting.

"Brumley, get over here. It's started," Greenman called to him before rushing down the hall to alert Norens and see if Hobart could heave himself out of his chair and join them. Davis had announced the previous week her general prospectus for the study, which was not only a reading of "The Ballad of Columbo" but also "an attempt to identify the strategy and suggest authorship of this surprisingly neglected work." Brumley and Greenman had immediately tried to recall from their early teens as many of the scatalogical, polymorphously perverse verses of "Columbo" as they could and had been waiting eagerly for Davis's first foray. Hobart, who claimed he had never heard of the masterpiece, and Norens, who despised Davis and quietly believed her a disgrace to the cause of women's rights, had initially pretended indifference. Both she and Hobart rushed to Greenman's office. Greenman cautiously shut his door before resuming his seat before the computer.

"You will see," Davis' computer message read, "that the following is a series of provocations only and do no more than point toward the final argument or form of this study. I intend now simply to examine selected verses of 'The Ballad of Columbo' and interpret them to the end of discovering the sub-text of each and of the entire work. Doing so, I hope, will lead to an overall statement of the poem's intent and also tentatively to identify the author."

"Get to Colombo," Hobart growled. "Move it up, Greenman, *scroll* it up or whatever the hell you do to it. Let's have some action."

Greenman, flanked by Norens and Brumley, with Hobart standing behind him, scrolled the message up and Davis' study began.

"First, the first verse of what Samuelson's *Suppressed American Poetry* titles 'The Ballad of Columbo,' or, alternately, 'The Ballad of

Christopher Columbo.' Although there may be some confusion with the immensely popular television program whose protagonist has the same name, context should assure there will be no difficulties when for ease of reference I refer to the poem throughout simply as 'Columbo.' The first verse:

> In fourteen hundred and ninety-two
> A Dago from I-taly
> Sailed up and down the streets of Spain
> And shit in every alley.

Line one simply sets the well-known date of Columbo's voyage to enslave and/or destroy the natives of America North and South. True, while he was in Spain before this date, grounding the action on this date is accurate, thus establishing a base of realism from the beginning and also providing a system of temporal reference that the reader (or listener, more likely, given the usual and often melodic transmission–about which more later–of this poem)–but also providing, as I say, a temporal reference that the reader immediately realizes is patriarchically determined. So from the initiating line, and underscoring the ghastly event the poem treats, the ascendancy of the male is made crystal clear. There will, however, be surprises, for the second line quickly undercuts the first. The ethnic slur of *Dago* may, on first reading, indicate that the author has little sympathy for Columbo, and the forced pronunciation and inflection of *I-taly* to conform to the rhyme with *alley* may be a further belittlement of him through ridicule of his place of ethnic origin. Yet it is entirely possible that the use of *Dago* is meant to defuse the usual solemn respect paid Columbo and to imbue him with a playful patina. In other words, it is the cultural enshrinement of Columbo, not Columbo himself or his persona that is undercut.

Switching to the present action in line three, the author provides another dimension to Columbo. He does not *walk* up and down the streets of Spain, which would emphasize the plodding, pedestrian (so to speak) nature of his seeking a sponsor for his imperialistic intentions, but rather *sails* up and down, etc. Not only is this a brilliant foreshadowing of the voyage itself, but injects a light-hearted note into Columbo's seeking of preferment. He becomes, as it were, the trickster, and not, perhaps, the hard-eyed conquistador history shows us he was. It is well to keep this in mind.

Then '[He] shit in every alley.' Few public restrooms were present in Spain in 1492—indeed, few private ones. Columbo's need to evacuate himself in alleys stresses his lack of property--"

"He didn't have a pot to shit in!" Hobart observed gleefully.

"--and also reinforces the playful nature of the protagonist, the street-sailing, alley-beshitting Dago.

Next, and I wish to pay very close attention to this feature, comes the chorus, which is, of course (of chorus!), repeated after each verse but which I will treat fully here and refer to where apposite throughout the rest of my study. Preliminarily, the chorus will be seen to bolster and expand on the prefatorial interpretation suggested above, viz., that the poem subverts its surface meaning by undercutting the imperialistic, paternalistic, racist and sexist events it ostensibly commends, even if only by mentioning them. Or, more significantly, by not mentioning them. The chorus goes:

> His balls they were so round-o,
> They hung down to the ground-o.
> That navigating, masturbating,
> Son-of-a-bitch Columbo.

On first reading, all references here appear imbued with testosteronic assertiveness and commendation. But while the sphericity of our protagonist's testicles subtly anticipates (as does 'sail' in the first verse) the truly great revelation of the voyage—the corresponding sphericity of the earth—it can also be seen as part of the scallawaggery assigned to our hero (for it is now becoming more apparent that the Columbo of the poem is not to be the villain he truly was), which is re-enforced by use of the frolicsome *round-o* rather than the commonplace *round*. (I am aware that round-o-ness can apply to diminutive objects such as marbles and BB's and can not in itself account for Columbo's prolongate scrotum. But lines one and two do not necessarily relate as cause and effect; rather, they are cumulative description—his balls are round-o *and* they hang down to the ground-o. Likely the reader supplies the impressive size and mass—cf. Columbo to a mature bull—after the extent of scrotal elongation is revealed. But also contributing to the retrospectively established causal linkage of lines one and two is the intensifier *so* of line one, which likely, again in retrospect, will be taken as applying more to big rather than perfect round-o-ness.) So. Columbo's balls are big and round, but rather than treating them as formidable items of masculine display, such as a rack of antlers or a set of tusks, our author invites us to see the comic side of such organs: the unfashionably large pants legs; the lugubrious, spraddle-legged walk; the painful yet risible possibilities of a misstep.

If the chorus's first two lines are descriptive in nature, lines three and four are expository. Naturally Columbo can be described as 'navigating,' which he blunderingly was (and the adroit sailor imagery of *sail* and *round-o* is here continued), but why *masturbating*? Initially, with such gonads as attributed to him in the opening two lines, masturbating within the larger context of the poem is wholly realistic and consistent. Too, one might assume that when onanistically engaged he would be supine, thus counteracting the gravitational inconvenience of his genitalic prodigality and enforcing further the realistic element of the poem even. (Historistically speaking, it has been well established that there was masturbation in Columbo's culture.) These lines also give full play to word play (fulness!) with *masturbating* following *navigating*, thus suggesting a master navigator and lending more qualities to admire in our trickster protagonist.

Finally, Columbo is not merely that navigating, masturbating Columbo, but that navigating, masturbating, *son-of-a-bitch* Columbo. It is now apparent that the author of this work will have none of the usual assumptions about exclusively male dominance enter the poem. For Columbo, unmistakably if somewhat indirectly, is seen to spring from woman, the fountainhead within this poem of the character and of the action that flows from that character. Verse two contains this reversal of domination and is as follows:

> Columbo went to the Queen of Spain
> To ask for ship and cargo;
> And in return he promised her
> A whorehouse in Chicago.

I intend to address this verse and others in succeeding installments."

There was silence in Greenman's office.

"Top that," Hobart finally said. "Just try to top that."

"I couldn't," Norens admitted and began to laugh.

"Oh god," Greenman joined in. "She's serious. It's not a joke, is it?"

"No, it's for real," Brumley assured him.

"No, not a joke," Hobart concluded. "You couldn't make up a joke that good."

eight
TEACHING

At the top of the stairwell that opened onto the floor of the Humanities offices, Brumley, who almost always took the stairs up in the morning, paused as usual to gather himself. Since he regularly checked his mail each morning before heading to his office, he needed preparation to parry or outright repulse the attentions of Huckston or Stephens, both of whom had mid-morning classes and who often hung around the main office to flirt with the student helpers or any acceptable female who happened in. Calona, too, bug-eyed and glib, the new composition expert who already was angling for a directorship, might be around, or Davis, who was sure to ask his opinion of her cutting-edge treatment of "Colombo." None were in sight when Brumley went quickly to the mail boxes and removed the few items in his slot, spoke to Miss Pam, and started toward the door.

"Hey, Big Brumley, let's not be too hasty here," Huckston's well-modulated voice called from down the hall. "You don't want to discuss another important communique you just got? There's a memo there from the Faculty Excellence Evaluation Committee. Everyone got one. It'll tell you what counts in the Service component for merit raises."

Brumley unwillingly stopped.

"You know, Huckston, that's news I've been waiting for all my life. My lucky day has come round at last. The Service component for merit raises. I can tell you what it says without even looking at it. It says I'm screwed." Brumley said, wishing he had said nothing.

"Oh, I wouldn't go so far as to say that," Huckston said maliciously, slouching against the wall by Chairman Cole's closed office door in what he envisioned as his James Agee pose. "But it does tell you that being on the Signage Committee won't give you a raise big enough to Bondo that rust hole in your car's fender. By the way, there's a Signage Committee memo in there, too; looks like the meetings get underway soon. Sure wish I could join you when you get down to letterings and colors, but I'll be in Europe next summer and they'll want someone who'll stay around this hicksville and give Signage full attention. Wait, wait a minute. I didn't get to read the whole thing. Come back and let me finish it."

Threading his way through the now-diminishing piles of sprinkler pipes and fixtures, Brumley paused at Greenman's office, where Greenman lifted a stricken face from his copy of the Faculty Excellence Evaluation Committee memo. Brumley didn't dare to speak and hurried down to own office, sat down and began to read. The subject of the memo, he saw, was indeed Service.

"Among the various areas of service that the faculty may choose to be evaluated on (subject to the approval of their Dean, the Vice-president for Academic Affairs and the President), the first are Recruitment, Retainment, and Fund Raising. Activity in these areas helps guarantee the growth and viability of Middle State and can take many forms. Under Recruitment, for example, faculty members may choose to visit high schools within a 300 mile radius (in and out of state) to speak with guidance counselors, principals and classes about the opportunities at Middle State for prospective students. Many students at these schools have never seen a college instructor, and the mere presence, let alone the prestige, of our faculty at these secondary educational facilities should do much to enhance our enrollment."

Brumley winced as he recalled such a trip he had volunteered for several years back when the administration was just beginning to see that the faculty could be coerced into doing almost any work that the administrators themselves should have been doing. It was to an inner-city school at the state's largest city. Anne Wellesley of Social Work, a plump and strapping blond, and Malcolm Stoat of Industrial Technology had accompanied him in a university car. At their first stop for gas, Stoat had charged the gas and a case of beer on the university credit card in the glove compartment and by the time they arrived at Stoakley Carmichael High both he and Wellesley were too drunk to leave the vehicle. Brumley, not completely sober, had nodded as prestigiously as he could to a group of staring students on the school's front steps and made for the principal's office, where he discovered that Middle State's Office of Recruitment and Retainment had failed to inform the principal that three illustrious faculty members from Middle State were to grace their school that day. Brumley was passed to an assistant principal who miraculously turned out to understand and sympathize with his situation because of—and in spite of—having it even worse than he did.

"You think you've got to put up with shit," the assistant principal said, gratefully accepting her third by-now warm beer from Brumley. Stoat and Wellesley snored together in the back seat. "You don't know what shit is—you don't know. I think we could teach these kids and I know they can learn, at least some of them. But all the usual roadblocks at a school like Carmichael are nothing compared to the administrative bullshit that's heaped on teachers. And on the students. Everything's against them, including each other. You don't want to recruit here. Our good students go to college about where they want— you know the federal requirements for minority enrollment at any school that gets federal funds. And our bad students are like all bad students: they're a clog or worse in class. At—where you from?—Middle State, they'd never feel at home. I'll tell you something else, when they do go to college, they may use their minority status for all it's worth, but they know damned well they're welcome mainly as a statistic or as an advocacy cause for some university bureaucracy. You know the problem. The general problem. I don't know if it will ever go away."

At lunch time she had to return to the fray and Brumley drove his inebriated load to their cheap motel. Returning to Middle State the next day, Stoat and Wellesley were full of questions about what they called his contact time, presumably so they could coordinate their falsified travel vouchers and activity reports. They affably included Brumley in their plans, but, while having no objections to using administration money for faculty betterment, including beer, he demurred. A year later he realized he had forgotten to write informing the Dean of his trip, and therefore had forfeited all claims for reward.

"You get the memo?" Greenman asked, appearing glumly in Brumley's doorway and breaking his reverie.

"I got two. One for the Signage Committee."

"Did you read the Service memo? The Retainment section?"

"I haven't got past Recruitment."

"Read Retainment. Don't read Fund Raising. Your heart couldn't stand it. But read Retainment, out loud."

Brumley sat down and surveyed the document. It was four pages long.

"'Retainment can take many forms,'" he read to Greenman. "'Participation in the Summer O Faculty softball, volleyball, basketball and horseshoe games is one such form. Helping students move into the dorms on opening day could be another, as could helping those move out on closing day who intend to return to Middle State the following year. Possibly helping them move from one room or dorm to another during the school year could be seen as retainment oriented. Serving as game facilitator at dorm recreation rooms will show students a side of their instructors not seen in the classroom and could be another retainment tool. Actual participation in the games with losing at them a high-priority option could be another. Attending dorm or various student organization picnics, pep rallies, intramural sports events and camp-outs could be yet another. Also, if the faculty member is classroom assigned, the failure rate in his/her courses would naturally be an important consideration in retainment and will be a major consideration in Service evaluation.'"

Brumley put the memo down, unable to go on.

"See! See what I told you," Greenman exclaimed. "Pass them all. You're screwed if you don't pass them all. Hobart will even have to pass Flytrap Jackson."

Flytrap Jackson, whom Hobart in the short time since the semester opened had elevated to the status of legend, was in one of Hobart's freshman composition class and was lacking in certain skills.

"Look at this!" Hobart had said to a group in the foyer of their office section the first week of classes. "In a three hundred word theme he misspelled twenty-four words, twenty-six if you count misspelling the same word two different ways. Look at it." He held up Flytrap's paper, his thick thumb covering Flytrap's name. The first paragraph was almost obliterated by Hobbart's markings and his suggestions in the margins. Thereafter he had marked only the errors.

"Pretty heavy marking," Calona the yakking, on-the-make new

Assistant Professor of Rhetoric, Persuasion, Argument and Dialectic said. "Do you think he can read it all?"

"Probably not," Hobart responded. "But I think I sense a subtle rhetorical import to your words. What you mean is that I've marked his paper too heavily, is that correct?"

Calona, who could recognize and respond to all forms of discourse but the direct truth, was taken aback.

"Well, you know, you don't want to overwhelm the student with his shortcomings on the first paper."

"Why not?"

"It's obvious," Calona said with an expert's certainty. "They won't be motivated to improve. You can't discourage students."

"Oh, I don't want to discourage him," Hobart announced to the room. "I want to encourage him—encourage him to drop out of school immediately and find something he can do well and, I hope, that he likes doing. Your assumption is that 'everyone can learn, and at a high level'. Am I right? You do believe that, don't you?"

"Yes, I do," Calona said proudly.

"Do you mean anyone can learn anything and at a high level, or only certain things, depending on how much brains they've got?"

"I don't think brains have anything to do with it."

"With whether you can learn or not? With what you're capable of learning?"

"Yes."

"Listen," Hobart said, "I want to predict that you have a glorious future in higher education, and I salute you at the beginning of a great career. Maybe sometimes you can show me which writing errors students make that I shouldn't mark. Which is to say, where does it not matter that they make mistakes when they write?"

Calona said nothing.

"I'm sure the same approach applies to engineers and medical doctors. Do you want an engineer building a bridge to be ignorant of strength of materials or of static forces? In fact, you ought to go to the nearest medical school and let them know that this careful screening of med students—not that it always works—has got to stop because the prospective young doctor-gods won't be properly motivated."

"It's not the same at all. You're making a false analogy," Calona the rhetorician triumphantly observed.

"You're right again," Hobart said. "The way you see it, I'm comparing something important like doctoring and technology with something inconsequential like writing well. Which makes me wonder why you got a doctorate degree in writing or whatever they call it these days. Why did you go into this discipline—I'm sorry, I mean career field—that supposedly teaches people to write well if it doesn't matter whether they write well or not? And by the way, I can't help but observe that the less you mark on a student's paper, the less work you're doing. Does that unconsciously influence this trendy new doctrine?"

Calona, of course, hated Hobart from that day on and used all his rhetorical skills to discredit and vilify him whenever possible.

"He thinks students improve by an instructor showing them their mistakes," he would hiss to a group of faculty at the Faculty Club, most of whom thought he was crazy. "Everyone knows you can't evaluate them by what they can do, by some standard—you've got to consider how far they've come in the class, by how hard they've tried. And I'm pretty sure the administration doesn't want us in an anti-retainment mode, flunking students out. And he still uses red ink to mark papers and tests. Hobart's a disgrace to his profession."

Hobart considered his profession a disgrace to himself, or that it had become one. His theory of the modern university, one that Brumley particularly admired of several circulating among the critically minded at Middle State, proclaimed it the modern-day counterpart of the Medieval church. Not only, Hobart maintained, was it the repository of truth and the purveyor of salvation in their present material form, but it also had sunk into a corruption that begged for a hammer- and theses-wielding Luther. But for now the secular monk-instructors—at least the ones who knew which side their wafer was buttered on—were rolling in indulgences. Hobart had no illusions about the courage of comfortable academicians—or uncomfortable ones—to blow any whistles or ring any alarm bells. Nothing would change, not until the Great Change came along to change everything. But meanwhile, there was Flytrap Jackson.

"Not only is he unfamiliar with English usage," Hobart fumed, "he can't organize, he can only accidentally write a complete or sensible sentence, and he's unaware of any punctuation mark except the period. Who convinced this guy he should go to college? *What dickhead let him in?* That's dick," he said, calming down, "generic application of the common name. Around 1890."

Hobart knew who convinced Flytrap to come to college and who let him in; Brumley and Greenman did too. In fact, a large number of faculty knew, though they hardly ever admitted it. Virtually everyone and everything convinced Flytrap to come to college. And everyone and everything let him in. His parents likely loved him and wanted him to do well, as they understood doing well. The administrators of the grade and high school industry cherished their self-assumed infallibility and so, year after year, passed him on. Higher education, in the form of Universities Inc., could enroll him, take his money, and wring more from the state simply because he was there. Corporate America didn't want to invest in his training and so let the public universities take care of it. Nowhere, from anyone, was there a sense that he could be useful and worthy other than by becoming a professional or a 'leader.' Finally, to help Flytrap on his road of life, he had endlessly been told that he could be anything he wanted, with the unspoken corollary that prestige, money, and kicking ass from a swivel chair were naturally what anyone would want. College became the sole means of reaching these goals. And if he failed there, Hobart knew, then Flytrap could only feel there was something terribly wrong–*with himself*! It was a splendid racket that had worked in innumerable venues for over 200 years and was likely to be good for 200 more, unless, again and more likely, the Great Change came first.

"They'll leave it up to us to handle the Flytraps," Brumley told Hobart. "Either we have standards and humiliate the innocent and maybe break their hearts, or we pass everyone and join the racket. Except we don't even get a cut."

During the semester Hobart met regularly with Jackson, and from next door Brumley listened sadly to his patient and repeated suggestions as to how Jackson could improve so he might at least pass the course. Jackson understood that he couldn't write and was trying.

"I never did read much," Brumley heard him tell Hobart during one of the conferences.

"That's probably a big reason why you need to work so hard on your writing now," Hobart said. "It's good that you realize you need to read more."

Brumley was sure that Hobart, like himself, knew it was too late for Jackson and half the student body at Middle State. When to the lack of reading were added seventeen years of television or computer play for five hours per day—or was the average now up to seven?—it was a wonder any of them knew the alphabet.

"But meanwhile," Hobart continued to instruct Jackson, "remember to have a general point in mind that you want your paper to make—it's called a thesis—and write it out clearly pretty near the beginning of your theme. Make it the first sentence. Then see how many supporting points you have and start a new paragraph for each one. And don't forget the old spelling check trick."

Jackson couldn't afford a computer that would dispense with any need to learn to spell and was reluctant to ask to use someone else's since he could not get to know anyone well enough to ask. He worked nights at Global Engines and was unable to use Middle State's growing number of what were called computer labs.

"When you're writing your paper and want to use a word you don't know how to spell, just leave a blank space. Then when you're finished go back and use your dictionary, or, hell, ask somebody, and then write the word in spelled correctly. That ought to help."

Jackson, fly-trapping mouth agape as usual, nodded in dim agreement.

"Yeah, I'll try that," he said, and after thanking Hobart with his usual sincerity trudged away.

The next week Brumley heard a muffled groan from Hobart's office and found him with his great, disheveled head in his arms over a spread-out theme he had been grading.

"You okay?" Brumley asked and Hobart slowly raised his head and held out the unmarked theme for Brumley to scan.

"There are three reasons," the paper began, "why I am not for   punishment. The first reason is that it doesn't do any good. The second reason is that   people could be killed and then what. The third reason is that when   kills somebody for killing somebody is   any better than they are I don't think so."

"He forgot to go back and put in the words," Hobart said. "He left them blank and he forgot to go back." He looked expressionlessly out the window.

"What are you going to do?" Brumley asked.

"A rampage—that's from ramm, Middle English, ramming machine, and page, Middle French, page—which means I'm going to stick this theme up somebody's ass. But what I've really got to do—what else can I do?" he gestured hopelessly toward Flytraps's effort—is grade this theme and flunk Jackson. But I won't make many marks or comments. And I'll even use green ink."

He turned to look at Brumley.

"The bastards," he said.

Flytrap Jackson's abilities were not in academics, though had they been, willingly would he have learned. You had to respect him for that, Brumley thought. But as Warren had concluded, how could you respect those who refused not just to learn but refused to think, and not through laziness or indifference but consciously, determinedly?

"What I believe Sartre is trying to do in this essay," Brumley announced to his Humanities class on the day Sartre's 'Existentialism' was to be discussed, "is to look directly at the consequences of the position that, in effect, there is no God."

Why "I believe"? he thought. And why "trying to do" and "in effect"? He felt his cowardice in the conditionals. Since the recent and growing revival of Christian fundamentalism at Middle State, complete with its fatuous sanctimony and mistrust of thought, Brumley found himself dreading lessons that contained religious content or even implications. He didn't want to offend anyone's beliefs, however unexamined or intolerant. But neither did he wish to show such students as Warren or Bolinger or, he had decided, Kimee Deneen, that he feared confrontations.

"I should say," he corrected himself, "Sartre is facing the inner consequences of being an atheist," and felt somewhat better. "Before we look at the essay in detail, do any of you recall, in general, what any of those consequences are?"

"You'll go to hell," Jenny McDaniel said flatly, smug in her Jesus-Is-the-One T-shirt and prepared for marching as to war.

"Can you find where he says that," Brumley said as kindly as his flash of irritation would allow.

"I don't know. You'll go to hell."

"Is that what Sartre says or what you believe?"

"It's what will happen."

"That may be, but what do you base that on? Is it a part of our reading today?"

Jenny simply looked at him coldly. He decided to persevere, knowing he would lose.

"So those who don't believe in God will go to hell—that means all the Jews and Christians and Moslems are safe?"

"The Christians are."

"So it's not just the atheists who will go to hell, but everyone who isn't Christian, even if they believe in a higher power?"

"If they don't believe in God they will."

"What about Kononai?" Brumley asked knowing he was wrong to do this. Kononai was Muslim from Kenya, who sat with dignified impassiveness as most of the class turned to look at him. "He's a Muslim, as he said last week. Can you honestly look at him and tell him he's going to spend all eternity in endless torment after he's dead just because of where he was born and what his family believed?"

"Yes," Jenny testified, without looking at the doomed infidel.

"But evidently God—the real god, according to you the Christian god—caused Kononai to be born where he was. Let's think a minute. Why would he send him to hell because He—god—created him as he did?"

"I don't know," Jenny said flatly, clearly meaning I don't care.

It was like Pavlov's dog, Brumley thought: the word *atheist* triggered a flood of shocked intolerance. Even the word *think* triggered a flood of shocked intolerance.

"Let's go to the opening paragraph," he relented. "There's a crucial point here that is contained in the phrase "existence precedes essence'—what does Sartre mean by this, how did you understand this phrase?"

"That there's no god," Mark Ogden proclaimed from behind the affronted form of Jenny McDaniel. He daily wore on a chain around his neck an enormous gold cross so large that Brumley wondered why he didn't bear it on his shoulders.

"Wait a minute," Brumley protested in mock alarm. "Let's be a little more precise. Sartre *bases* his statement that existence precedes essence on the assumption that there is no god, or at least one that created humanity with a definite sense of what human essence–or human nature–was to be. But he doesn't mean by 'existence precedes essence' that 'there is no god'. It's important that we make careful distinctions. Do you see the difference?"

Mark may have been trying but didn't see. Jenny and several others in the room did not wish even to try but sat starring before them in tight-lipped silence. There were enough willing but bewildered faces that Brumley decided to plunge on.

"*If* there is no god that determined human nature–or essence–before he created humans–or brought them into existence–then we first exist, or are born, and then gradually our essence or nature or what humans are like is determined–how?"

"We do it," Warren said, a bit more tentatively than the defenders of the faith. "We determine our essence by what we do in our lives."

"That's it," Brumley agreed. "Do you see that? It's not too radical an idea is it? That what each of us is, our essence, is determined by what we do, how we've acted?"

Even Jenny, suspiciously, seemed to agree.

"Now, if one accepts the position that there is no god and therefore no preordained human nature; and also, since there is no god, no truly authoritative moral code or guide such as the Bible is to believers, what are the consequences to a person's accepting this argument?"

"They'll go to hell," Jenny announced, as certain as death.

"Dr. Brumley?" The awful arm of Bolinger that had been in the air since Ogden weighed into the struggle could no longer be ignored.

"Do you know about the lost book of the Bible that they found in a cave near Jerusalem?"

"I don't think I do," Brumley answered, trying to decide if Bolinger was thinking of the Dead Sea Scrolls or perhaps the Gnostic Gospels.

"It's called the Book of Jeroboam. It says you can ignore everything in the rest of the Bible and drink up and have a good time because there is no god."

The room erupted in an uproar of shocked and outraged voices, some addressed to Brumley but most aimed at an inscrutably composed

Bolinger. Only Warren and a few other students were laughing, while the beatific Kimee Deneen sat mildly, surveying them all.

"There is no lost book of the Bible," Jennifer shouted. "The Bible is what the apostles wrote and it's all there. There wasn't any that was lost."

"The apostles didn't write the Bible," Bolinger answered calmly through the dying hubbub. "There's no absolute certainty about the authorship of the books of either the Old or New Testaments, but no one who's studied it thinks the apostles wrote any. It's pretty interesting, how they've figured out so much about it. But I think if you don't know anything about it, you probably shouldn't believe the Bible as literal truth."

Brumley could never tell about Bolinger, and neither could the other instructors Brumley had spoken to about him. His remarks in class at times were so informed and insightful that Brumley, unused to such, was stunned. At other times, while his observations were preposterously exaggerated or far-fetched, they seemed to offer a disturbing comment on the thinking of other students, or even faculty, that could only be by design. And then sometimes he just said dumb things that didn't seem to bother him at all.

"I believe it's the truth!" Jenny loudly asserted and several of the other lay clerics nodded and muttered vigorously in anticipant agreement. "I believe it because the Bible is the word of god."

"Ok, ok," Brumley jumped in, trying to snuff out the racing fuse before it zipped into the magazine. "This is all interesting, but we need to get back to the reading itself. Remember, that's what will be on the test."

In such circumstances, he had long since discovered, threat was the most effective form of persuasion.

"Can you imagine," Bolinger cut in so smoothly that there was no hint of discourtesy, as though he had been so absorbed in his own reflections that he didn't hear Brumley's attempt to restore civility. "Can you imagine what Sartre would think of that non-argument? Or Jesus, what he would think of people who are terrified of any idea they haven't heard daily for twenty years."

"Jesus would think they believed in the word of the Lord," Jenny overrode him with a shriek, producing her Bible, which she held aloft and waved about. "I'm proud to be a believer, I'm proud to serve the Lord," and to Brumley's incredulity she began thumping it powerfully.

Two other students had also unsheathed Bibles from their backpacks and lifting them above their heads, their faces turned ecstatically upward, began thumping them in rhythm with Jenny. Bolinger sat impassively, as though considering a learned disquisition on some fine theological point, and waited for the hail of thumps to abate. Except for Warren, most of the rest of the students sat stricken, by what exactly, Brumley was unsure. Was it the fanaticism of the zealots or Bolinger's calm heresy? Brumley saw Warren speak to Bolinger, who did not look at him, but smiled slightly. Jenny, her face flushed and her arm fatigued, gave her good book one last heavy thump and, to Brumley's relief, desisted. The other disciples, leaderless, quickly lost rhythm and fell silent also.

"I agree with thumps four and twelve," Bolinger observed, "but the rest suffer from various logical fallacies. The last, especially, I thought heavily argumentum ad hominem."

"Enough," Brumley said, trying not to laugh. "That's enough. I don't think the question before us—and we're hopelessly off the track of our reading—is going to be resolved by emotional outbursts or sarcasm. But you ought to realize that a very great deal of energy has gone into this question of the existence of a deity. The library is full of material on this matter. You all would benefit from reading up on it."

He was speaking mostly to Jenny and the other true believers, trying, futilely he knew, to pry open their minds a little—at least to leaven their rock-hard orthodoxy with some knowledge other than the received. Jenny's hand twitched on the black cover of her Bible while Bolinger, who likely had read more than Brumley on the subject, looked absently out the window.

"Now, let's get back to Sartre, and it looks like we'll have to give a few minutes of our next meeting to wrapping his essay up—so here's your chance to clear up on Wednesday what isn't clear to you today. But for now, according to Sartre, there are three states of mind or mental consequences that are inevitable if one accepts that there is no god who predetermined human nature or who gave infallible commandments as to what constitutes proper human conduct. They are anxiety, forlornness and despair," Brumley hurriedly enumerated, feeling at the moment all three. "Let's consider them and what he means by each. First, why would such a position result in anxiety?"

"You'd be anxious because you were going to hell," Jenny McDaniel proclaimed, and Bolinger's laugh of disbelief and delight united with the bell to signal the end of it all.

nine
COMPUTERS

"We're going down to the computer lab today," Ringle of Medieval Literature announced to Warren's Chaucer class, the other required course Warren was taking besides Brumley's. Waiting for them outside the computer lab door was Dean Wainwright.

Several years earlier, educationalist had anointed computers as the greatest teaching instrument since television. College administrations everywhere had then been led into teaching computer use as a central part of a university education. Dean Wainwright, realizing money would be involved, saw he might as well control it and had worked clandestinely with a few gadget-enthralled members of the Humanities department to announce one day that beginning the next year, the first semester of freshman composition would be taught using computers. A large amount of money to purchase, maintain and operate the machines was budgeted to Wainwright to use at his discretion, and the teaching of writing at Middle State thereafter became in large part a class in elementary computer usage; it promised to remain such until the devices were promoted to the point of seeming to be necessities and everyone operated them virtually from birth. Since fooling with computers was much easier than fooling with writing, most of the faculty were quick converts, and Wainwright encouraged them to use computers in all courses.

"Ordinarily I don't 'log on' to the classroom," Wainwright admitted with roguish pride as he led the class, with Ringle following, into the computer lab and mounted to the control booth. He had now limited his teaching to every other spring semester when he met with around

ten students in an honors course in world history, a labor he intended
to drop soon.

Warren, along with Ringle and the rest of the class, took seats behind
the thirty computer consoles that had replaced the classroom's desks and
turned on their computers. The control booth at the front surrounded
Wainwright with various keyboards, control panels, computer screens,
and switchboards, allowing him to view what students might write
to him on their thousand dollar computers and then in turn type his
reply to their message and transmit it back to that computer or to
other computers for that student or other students to ponder. He could
also raise and lower the large projection screens that had displaced
blackboards around the walls and then write or draw on a screen in
the control booth and have his efforts projected on any or all of the
larger screens. Or, he could wing from the confining classroom and
speed throughout the world to see what anyone was writing about
anything and respond to it with something of his own, or he could route
what anyone in the world was writing about anything to the student
computers, where they could respond as they saw fit. The lab was used
mostly by composition classes, but Dean Wainwright, who wished to
deploy its computers on a broader educational front, had slipped Ringle
a grant to reconnoiter computer application in all humanities courses
and to begin the foray in his Medieval Literature class.

"Let's get this show on the 'information highway'," Dean Wainwright
said brightly and began inserting discs, pushing buttons and throwing
switches. Warren and the rest of the class sat expectantly before their
screens, which, except for an occasional convulsive blink, remained
empty. After several fruitless minutes, uninstructed, they began pushing
buttons on their own keyboards in a vain attempt to get something
going. Looking around, Warren saw Kimee Deneen lightly cuff the
side of her console, and when glancing up she saw him watching, gave
him a smile and flicked her eyes upward. He risked smiling back and
shaking his head, but no more.

Wainwright, braced and pulling mightily in the control booth
on a lever large enough to switch locomotives, managed to activate
the projection screens that one after another began to roll up and
down in a stiff, syncopated rhythm, one occasionally freezing while the
others continued their stately dance, then joining them while another

froze, each as if waiting for the correct moment in the quadrille to join back in. Then the text of the speech Wainwright intended to make if all had gone well began to flash on the screens in a bewildering, psychedelic reel that transfixed every heavy pot smoker in the class until Wainwright inadvertently but mercifully hit a kill switch at which the speech faded away, never to be recovered, and the projection screens, fully unrolled and lolling like the tongues of exhausted dogs, fell still. Undaunted, Wainwright launched again into a series of button-pushings, while Ringle, not wanting to appear wholly irrelevant but fearful of underscoring Wainwright's incompetence, discreetly eased to the control booth to help, inserting other discs, pressing other buttons, or the same buttons in different sequences or twice rather than once. Some irretrievable combination revived the projection screens, this time into a crisp, synchronized whipping up and down that snapped the pot smokers out of their reveries and even subdued the choking hilarity of most of the class. Warren, more than ever convinced he was in the hands of fools, considered getting out some paper and beginning his letter of complaint to the chairman of the Reigning Board but was stopped by a student's cry:

"I've got something," she called out and Wainwright gratefully pushed again at what he thought might be the correct key.

"What is. . .Is this. . .?" the riveted student asked. "My god! Look at this! Jesus."

The students around her leaned to take in her screen, some quickly looking away but most staring hungrily until Ringle made his way back to the wide-eyed student's computer and after a quick assessment unplugged it. The screen made a number of offended beeps, flashed a message threatening the operator with imprisonment, and went blank.

Dean Wainwright, who knew never to admit himself at fault, pushed vainly what he hoped was a more salutary key and then stubbornly but with no effect persevered in his operations until, with only fifteen minutes of class time remaining, the student computer-whiz Sean Johns, who had been hired as a technological consultant, showed up to slap in a disc, ripple his fingers across a keyboard and materialize the proper picture on the students' screens. It depicted a small central ball with other balls revolving around it at different distances. Warren stared dully at his screen; behind him, Kimee Deneen laughed quietly, and again when Warren turned to look, smiled at him and shook her head in disbelief. Wainwright exited the control booth.

"What I've 'called up' for you," he announced without acknowledging Sean John's help, "is a picture of what used to be the universe, or no, the solar system I believe it was. I'll turn it over to Dr. Ringle to explain it all to you."

Ringle, several weeks earlier, had already explained Ptolemaic cosmology, but the Medieval Literature computer material had not then arrived so now he explained it again while directing the class's attention to how the central ball representing the earth was circled by the moon, sun, other planets and so on. The pictures were jerky and unfocused, the labels of the heavenly bodies nearly illegible. As Ringle's repetitious explanation ran down, Warren, eager for the end, glanced at the computer-controlled clock on the side wall. It was seven hours and seventeen minutes slow. After it became clear that the class bells were not working either, Ringle, five minutes over time, dismissed the class. Dean Wainwright was waiting until the room cleared.

"That's it?" he said to Ringle, who was standing nervously in front of the control booth. "Five hundred dollars and a trip to Seattle, and that's it? A ball and some other balls going around it?"

"Was it that bad?" Ringle asked. "I didn't think it went too badly. They seemed interested to me. Didn't you think they liked it?"

"Of course they liked it. It kept them from having to hear a lecture on Chaucer or some other monk from back then. You think they'll stay interested in circling balls? You ever see those video games they play? They're so real they can get female characters in them pregnant. My god, balls going around another ball. Look, I don't care what you come up with as long as it has something exciting in it, something that would look good in the press release I'm going to send out about innovativeness in the humanities at Middle State. It can't be about balls going around another ball."

"If you—we—could have got things working quicker, I think they might have really liked it," Ringle said. "We didn't have time to show the epicycles and how they were used to prop up a cosmology that was failing in the face of the growing new scientific. . . ."

"Save it for your next lecture, Ringle. Epicycles sound about as interesting as balls going around another ball. Come to think of it, if we can cut classes to twenty minutes like Curtis wants, epicycles are another useless thing that can get the boot. Nobody cares about epicycles. Get something I can put in a press release, something that will get our college some visibility, something innovative. I don't have to tell you, if we can impress the higher-ups by showing them the humanities are dedicated to cutting edge excellence in all areas of performance evaluation, then we'll get the kind of recognition I deserve. Now see if you can't get something that will look good on the front page."

The kind of recognition Dean Wainwright had in mind was his salary raised to the level of the science and business deans, and perhaps an elevation of his prospect of someday becoming Vice-president of Academic Affairs. He wanted his faculty to work very hard to earn both kinds of recognition for him, and was yet to encounter any scheme humiliating or ridiculous enough that they couldn't undertake to that end, though at first even he had considered extensive computer deployment in the humanities preposterous. Then computers became popular, and Wainwright briefly changed into a cautious appraiser, then an enthusiastic booster of what he relished calling 'the electronic classroom'. But after the fiasco in Ringle's class, he had no faith that a medievalist lacking all proper ambition, or any mere faculty member for that matter, could promote his interests without serious professional help. He decided to provide some, the very best taxpayer money could buy.

"I've hired Shank Consulting to get you up to speed on your new software," he informed Ringle over the phone the next day. "Shank is flying in tomorrow."

"Dr. Ringle?" The knock had been discreet but firm.

Ringle, in spite of being prepared, nearly gasped when he looked up to see the trim, cosmopolitan figure in his doorway, at ease in a gray, light-weight suit of blended silk and mohair, supple leather briefcase with brass grommets in hand, a perfectly knotted tie slashing a deep red across his light blue shirt. Here was a visitor from another land; not even the former state-government operative Flexner who had recently been given some vague duties at Middle State could match the urbane nonchalance, the impeccable grooming, the sheer splendor of Shank,

CEO of Shank Consulting. He was a piece of work, a man you could dream of becoming.

Shank had become Shank twenty years ago. He had foreseen the incipient boom in education and grasped immediately, after a year at a real university, that the way to success was not to read books but to sell them. Acting on his insight, in the true American entreprenurial spirit, he had borrowed money, opened a used-textbook store that quickly expanded into a chain, and through dedication, hard work and charging all the traffic could bear, did well. Then an even smoother road spread before him, one without the potholes of shoplift and payoffs, the hills of inventory and tax preparation or the blind curves of competition and uncertain profits. It opened its vistas when the many regional universities his bookstores served came at last to see that their mission was to have an ever-growing enrollment, and to insure they did so by downplaying education and work and elevating entertainment and vocational training.

Predictably, this switch caused dislocations to occur and conflicts to arise, external and internal, the latter especially among the faculties of these institutions. Those teachers dedicated to the life of the mind found that other allegiances were now in vogue, allegiances that were more visible, glamorous and profitable, both to them and especially to their administrative superiors. One such allegiance was to computers, though there were many more. There was both domestic and foreign travel, there was supplemental administrative work, there was consulting with all sorts of local entities, there was grant writing, grant spending, and writing grant spending justification. As might have been expected, most of the devotees of the quiet and unglamorous life of fine distinctions, contemplation, and critical thought found to their dismay that they had absolutely no skills in recognizing a meretricious bandwagon, let alone clambering aboard one. It was to soothe these inner conflicts of principle that Shank came to the rescue, advising convincingly many an unwilling or baffled academician that what they thought was a disreputable whore cart was in truth the very bandwagon that would parade them to glory.

With his knowledge of the price of books and his sure comprehension of the soul of the modern university, Shank had become a consultant whose nearly always-heeded advice was to do what got you the most money. As a result, success now embraced him, not as a mere seller of books but as a professional, an accepted if minor satellite of the managerial elite who through many forms of hocus-pocus had always ruled the world. And if success's embrace had been a bit cool and perfunctory when he peddled books, it was now passionate and enduring, and Shank, unlike so many of the self-made who were mere boors and vulgarians, wished only to share the bounty that had come to him. Dealing with academic clients whose income level approached the insignificant, while it strengthened his sense of self-worth, allowed him at the same time to practice an egalitarian presence that won over everyone he consulted with and strengthened his reputation to the point that he was always in demand. And since he consulted on anything, the sky was the limit.

"Dr. Ringle," Shank had said, presenting Ringle his card. "I'm Shank, of Shank Education and Consulting." The card proclaimed Dr. Ross Shank, PhD, to be CEO of the firm, with offices in New York, Los Angeles, London and Nassau.

"Good to meet you, Dr. Shank," Ringle said nervously. "Please, have a seat."

Shank, eyeing dubiously the sagging, faded chair wedged in front of Ringle's scarred, decades-old desk, gingerly sat down. But he made no sign of aversion. In spite of the cramped, tacky quarters, the office, Shank knew, was Ringle's castle keep. *My office* Ringle and thousands like him would casually say, whose ancestors had no offices and who had hardly envisioned one for themselves. *My office*–claiming a place, however insignificant, in the amorphous, heartless order whose inner circles Shank orbited much closer to. Ringle, Shank could see, was a timorous, insecure man who desperately needed advice to succeed. He undid the gleaming brass clasps of his leather briefcase, removed a folder and came straight to the point.

"Dean Wainwright gave me some preliminaries on his project, and I've drawn up a few ideas that might help you implement it. I think you can see they will get you booted up in the thrust to integrate computers in all aspects of university life."

"Really? All aspects?" Ringle said, genuinely startled. "I hadn't heard of that. I thought we were just trying to get some ways to liven up classes–you know, some interesting pictures, something to appeal to our students. I didn't realize computers were going to. . . to take over."

"Maybe I overstate my case," Shanks said with a dismissive gesture, "It doesn't matter. But I think by now it's pretty clear that computers are the greatest technological innovation since the steam engine. You can't imagine the uses for them, and educationalists everywhere agree that there's nowhere they can be better used than in education. Here, take a look at this." He removed a single sheet of paper from his folder and handed it across the desk to Ringle. It was headed: Coming Soon–the Information Boulevard.

"There are quite a few computer applications listed there you could consider. But what I'd advise you to do is listen to Wainwright and whoever is above him and take your cue from them. In fact, I'm going to give you a head start. That, I believe, is what consulting is all about. In next month's issue of the *Journal of Deanship* and in this month's of *Studies in Vice presidency of Academic Affairs*, IBM and Microsoft will be placing articles announcing a new age in education brought about by computers. Wainwright and what's-his-name–Staull? is that really his name?–will of course read them and they'll fall in line faster than Marine recruits on the second day at boot camp. And here," Shank said, smiling with professional satisfaction and pulling another folder from his briefcase, "is your head start. These are pre-publication copies of the articles," and he handed them with somewhat of a flourish to Ringle. "You see where I'm coming from? Instead of just parroting what your bosses parrot about computers–which after awhile can be a little obvious, a little demeaning– now whenever the general topic of computer innovation comes up you can speculate offhandedly on particular points in the articles as though the ideas are your own. I don't know exactly what ideas–haven't read the things myself, don't know anything about computers–but when the time comes, I believe you're the kind of man who'll know how to handle the issue."

Ringle glowed under Shank's sincere assessment of his qualities. As much as he loved Chaucer and the material in all the courses he taught, he knew that when he retired, his salary, adjusted for inflation, would be little more than it was when he started. But with Shank behind him, with the two seminal IBM and Microsoft articles lighting his way like halogen headlights, Ringle suddenly saw his way down the information boulevard, and it looked like Easy Street. He could hear himself: "You know," he would say thoughtfully to Wainwright, "I've been doing some thinking about computer application. It's possible, I've discovered, for students to 'word process' their assignments on computers. I don't see why we couldn't require students to submit all their assignments typed on computers, or even submit them over the computer network. We could even have classes conducted by means of computers, maybe even directly by computers."

The last would be going too far, he realized, but then again, maybe not. Eliminating all human contact between student and teacher was insane, but that would be no impediment to doing so since it was clearly cutting edge and highly innovative and could well result in a press release by Public Relations and Public Information that no member of the public would think closely about or likely read but that would look good in any number of faculty and administrator dossiers.

Armed with Shank's articles and with the high-minded workshops and selfless free materials available from computer corporations to aid him, Ringle saw new worlds before him. Somewhere in the near future, a Director of Computer Usage would be needed in the department, maybe even one for the entire College of Humanities. And if a departmental director got a freshman comp class off from the normal teaching load to perform their directing duties, what might an astute College Director expect? At least two, maybe more, and there were tears of gratitude in his eyes as babbling with elation he escorted an understanding Shank to the elevators. Shank did understand; he had seen it many times before.

"We're going down to the computer lab today," Ringle announced a week later when new discs had arrived from the Center for Electronic Learning Enhancement.

Wainwright, now willing to let a subordinate make the test flight, was not present, but Ringle, having practiced at length with the new material, was much more adroit in the cockpit than Wainwright the previous week and eventually linked the master computer with all the individual computers in the class. After he had shown the students how they could cause to appear on their screens any of the items he wished them to see, in the time remaining most managed to view pictures of Sir Gawain, a monk, Everyman, and members of a medieval village dying of the plague. There were also the first nineteen lines of the *Canterbury Tales* in Middle English, but only a few managed to get to it. Several of the class checked their e-mail, and one was advancing on the porno web site Wainwright had inadvertently tapped into the previous week, when Ringle dismissed the class and rushed down to Wainwright's office to report the success of their project and how well plague victims and Everyman would look in the newspaper. He also planned to broach the topic of using computers to re-introduce Middle State classes in the near-by state maximum security prison, classes suspended some years before after the savage beating of a Middle State instructor over a low grade.

So computers came to the humanities at Middle State much like the Greeks came to Troy. First there was a long period of stern opposition to their gaining the citadel; then came the treacherous gift horse in the form of computer company grants that put a computer in every faculty office. Then came a TV-advertising campaign of great expense, cunning and effectiveness whose commercials showed that computers were not only fashionable but indispensable to life and that those who didn't fool with them would not be up-to-date and likely not survive. In a convincing ethical stroke, the commercials also featured former sitcom or movie actors who had played rebels on TV or in films now using computers without in any way compromising their anti-establishment principles. And it didn't take long for word to get around that computers offered hours of mind sucking diversion. Once the first faculty worms had crawled from the woodwork and had been rewarded by university administrators for computer innovativeness, the gates were thrown open and the silicon hordes marched in.

It was as though one day the mechanistic, control-oriented threat was recognized and rejected in all courses that did not deal with numbers. And the next, even the most dedicated and thoughtful opponents of the uncritical acceptance of technology were sitting before computer screens, typing away or viewing Internet pictures or playing solitaire.

In the required general science course Warren was taking, computer enhanced instruction had arrived not a moment too soon for Half-life Anderson, who now in the third year of working on his Master's degree had gone through every possible dodge to get out of the considerable work of teaching. The burdens of knowing the material well, recognizing what might be difficult for his students and devising ways to clarify it were more than he wanted to bear, as were relating the material when possible to the familiar and reviewing it carefully before each class. So in his first year of teaching, at least one and sometimes two classes each week were devoted to movies, field trips, peer discussion groups, research time or some other cover that, whatever their ostensible intent, invariably got Anderson out of work. But in fact, while most of the students avoided rigorous instructors whenever possible and were right at home with Anderson's dereliction, he felt that a few, though they never complained, held him in contempt and saw his dodges for what they were. There had been only scattered fishy looks after his showing of *Young Tom Edison* in conjunction with the course section on electricity. But then had come the disaster of bussing the class thirty miles to a grimy, stinking ice-making plant, a field trip meant to enrich a class session in thermodynamics. On that one, not even the usual toads would sit by him on the lonely ride back to Middle State. As for peer group discussions, they either degenerated into trivial chatter or caused the one or two real students in each peer group who tried to address the work to be despised by the rest. And as generally fraudulent as such discussion groups were, they still required that he often be present and even occasionally answer a question.

What Anderson really wanted was to be assigned a non-course, like those classes in French or Spanish cultures offered by the Foreign Language department. No attempt to learn the language was involved, but instead there were many movies and readings about haciendas, bullfighting and the Isle de France. Anderson thought that he could develop an excellent course in science along these lines, one perhaps stressing the many benefits to humankind that the sciences had bestowed. There could be a section on cars, one on nuclear power, on airplanes, on beauty products and aids, maybe one on sex. Students, he knew, would positively mob such a course; great teacher awards awaited him. But he wasn't sure his professors, at least the older ones, would react kindly to such a proposal. There seemed little hope but to do the work necessary to teach.

To such a state of doubt, frustration and despair, computers came to Anderson like great white capsules of some soothing drug. Now a new technology could be married to an evasion of responsibility in an entertaining union that, all else failing, could be justified as teaching computer skills. Anderson was saved, and though a mere low-paid graduate student, he soon was having as much success with computers in the classroom as any professor. Students were impressed by the rapidity with which he could find and call up any web site, and to demonstrate his mouse skills he had played a losing game of computer solitaire for the class that in its dexterity and dash was breathtaking.

"Today," he announced to Warren's class one afternoon, as he did at least once a week "we're going down to the computer lab."

Unlike the computer labs in the Humanities Hall, those in the Science Building had comfortable captain chairs for seats, much more spacious work areas, and a control booth like the command center of a nuclear submarine. Anderson, who had ordered a number of lesson supplements from the Center for Electronic Learning Enhancement, was delighted with the student response to his incorporation of computer instruction into the course. While he suspected that many were using the time in the computer lab to write messages to their roommates or to the person sitting next to them, or to work on projects from other courses or, inescapably, to view the near infinite number of pornographic web sites, at least the few who seemed to want to learn were showing almost no dissatisfaction with his new method.

"In connection with our readings on the atom for today, if you'll hit alt-F6, you'll see this material illustrated," he proclaimed from the controller's chair.

Almost everyone hit alt-F6 and watched unmoved as a ball, unfocused and circled jerkily at various distances by other balls, appeared on their screens. The central ball was labeled nucleus and the orbiting ones electrons. Warren recognized the image as the same one used to illustrate the Ptolemaic system in Ringle's Medieval Literature class, but with the labels changed.

"It was the same picture," he railed to his dorm floor mates around the dorm floor study-lounge table that night. "Only the label on the balls was changed. The same picture."

"You know, now that you mention it, I think I've seen the same thing," Plumb Bob offered. He was taking the night off to rest himself for a demanding weekend coming up. "It was a couple of years ago in a management class, when I was majoring in Management. They got computers over there way before anybody else. Any rate, in this class they showed the same picture on the computer. This one showed how the manager is the central object in an organization and all the subordinates circle him trying to get in a kiss at his ass and the sub-subordinates circle the subordinates to get in a kiss at theirs."

"I hate to say this," Shepherd said with his usual deliberation, "but the thing must be everywhere. In Agribusiness class last spring they had it to show how an agribusiness conglomerate is the central object, with marketing and retail firms circling it and farmers and everybody else circling them. Something is going on, you think?"

"Can you believe that in my country it is used showing Allah circled by the great Prophet and himself circled by various dignitaries who ran our city," Mo said. "I thought it was a load of shit."

"I've seen it, too," Jeeks said to everyone's surprise. He rarely mentioned classes other than to complain about having to work in them, and never any specifics about their content. "History. American. Fulson's class. Custer's Last Stand."

"My god," Warren exclaimed. "It's everywhere."

"That may be," Bolinger said from the end of the table, closing a book he had been reading in apparent disregard of the talk. "But is alarm the proper, the valid response? Maybe we're on to something, or maybe the unconscious union of computer people and academic people and whoever else is involved has come on to something. This balls going around balls may be sort of a philosopher's stone, a key to all mythology, a unified field theory. Think of it. It can explain everything. This book"–he pointed to the copy of *The Great Chain of Being* he had been reading–"is about the same thing, except the visual concept is more static than the balls theory. We ought to bring this convergence of design to the attention of–well, who? Ringle is interested solely in Medieval literature, Half-life Anderson in whatever it is idiot's are interested in, Plumb Bob's management profs in control, Shepherd's profs in starvation, Fulson in Genghis Kahn and Hitler. None would care about this more-than-coincidental paradigm that illustrates everything. So what do we do? I'd say we sit on this knowledge. If the one's in charge knew we'd discovered their key, they'd burn our asses down."

"Bolinger," Sola said after the appreciative silence that followed most of Bolinger's deliveries. "What are you talking about? It's just that a bunch of gougers have found out a way to use some clueless teachers to screw us and take our money, that's all."

"Friend Sola, I couldn't agree more," Bolinger said solemnly, and then laughed. "The gougers are like a central ball with the clueless teachers revolving around them and us revolving around the teachers.".

Warren knew he should be grateful for the almost unimaginable packaging of human ingenuity that made computers possible and that distributed and installed them at Middle State. The concentrating of technologies that placed the distillation of so many minds and so much calculation at the fingertips of so many was, he thought, a kind of miracle–something like a good stainless steel knife or a supply of disposable butane cigarette lighters would have been to the stone age. The analogy, he knew, wasn't quite right–Bolinger might be able to work it out for him–but he felt pretty sure that all such miracles needed careful examination before acceptance, certainly before acceptance as benign. While he suspected that in no time computers would seem as indispensable to him as a host of other gadgets and machines had come to seem to people of the past, so far the miracle of computer use at Middle State was an apparent, expensive fraud. Millions of dollars for machines that showed balls going around another ball, or something not far from it. And it was all adopted and espoused throughout Middle State as though previous to the arrival of computers, human enterprise did not exist, could not have existed. Millions of dollars for computers, and he couldn't get two classes added to this semester's course offerings. It was time to get started on his letter to the Reigning Board's chairman, and to hint in it that he was going to sue.

Warren had no idea what his instructors thought of computer usage, except for Huckston, whose university-supplied computer had displaced almost everything else on his desk. But Huckston was a special case among Warren's teachers, one whom Miss Pam had categorized with great accuracy. He was truly a Shit-head, an instinctively crafty, opportunistic one. For instance, he seldom had to be asked what he taught at Middle State, but when he was, he never replied that he taught English. His writer's sensitivity for language that might enhance his career made him alert to the fear and occasional loathing most people felt toward English teachers, and he always responded, if he had not already informed his audience, that he was in Creative Writing. This same sensitivity also restrained him from correcting students who mistakenly addressed him as Doctor Huckston, but here because of the automatic cachet accorded the title. A few times Warren had been nearby when an unknowing student addressed Huckston as Doctor and had waited for Huckston to correct the misapprehension. Huckston never did, nor did he show the least concern over Warren's witness to his deceit-by-omission, and in consequence Warren was always uncomfortable when he had to speak with him.

"Mr. Huckston," he said as he knocked on Huckston's partly open door a few days after Anderson's balls-around-a-ball class. Huckston of course preferred Doctor, but for students who thought he had that title, just the familiar, egalitarian Bill was fine. That way he could retain the prestige and add to it the admiration accorded the gifted who were humble and unpretentious. Warren and most of Huckston's other students saw through him, and invariably addressed him as Mr. Huckston just to see the near-undetectable wince.

"Yes?" Huckston said, looking up from an issue of the *Middle State Alumni Magazine*.

"I've finished my assignment for next Tuesday. Could I turn it in now?"

"I'd prefer that you waited until class—better you lose it than I," he said, shaking back a stray lock of his blond hair and hoping for an appreciative laugh from Warren.

"It's pretty long," Warren uselessly explained, "and I thought if I got it in early it would give you time to look at it."

Huckston was notorious for not returning papers for weeks.

"I should have plenty of time," Huckston said. "Besides, I like to read everyone's stories at one sitting so I can evaluate them more consistently, see where everyone stands. Just a moment." he said, as his telephone squealed out a horrible electronic noise. He sat staring at it, and Warren understood he had decided to let his answering machine handle the call. Huckston had recently become aware of the number of optional calling features available from the phone company, and, to complement his sleek, button-encrusted answering machine, he had purchased a number of the options the week before and was still enthralled with their operations.

"Let's see here," he said, leaning toward his phone to check the number and name of the caller on his answering machine's display screen. *Caller unknown,* the screen read, which usually meant either someone calling from a huge phone bank to sell him something or a student calling from a campus phone. Huckston's phone uttered the unearthly shrill three more times, Huckston looking at it intently and Warren staring at the bookshelves behind him thinking *answer it.*

With a click and a whir, the answering machine kicked in.

"Hi," Huckston's recorded voice said pleasantly, "this is Bill Huckston. I'm away from my office at this moment and unable to take your call. Please wait until after the beep and leave your number and, if you like, a message. I'll return your call when I'm able. Thank you."

"Well, shit," a voice said before the caller hung up.

Huckston snatched up his receiver, pushed a button, and waited for a moment before pushing two more. There was a short delay, and then a recorded voice came on the line and over the still open speaker on the answering machine.

"We're sorry, but the last call made to this number was from a phone system whose individual phones are not a part of Midbells's network. This call came from,"–and a truly machine-generated voice said--"Mid dul Sta tuh."

"I didn't know you could find out what number called you like that," Warren said.

"Oh yes," Huckston said, glad to turn the matter of Warren's interruption to something more interesting. "My Caller ID usually displays who's calling, but you can also dial 64 and the phone company will tell you who it is. Unless the call is from a network other than Midbell's, or if the caller has Caller ID Block installed, which keeps their number from being revealed. But I hear there's going to be a Caller ID Block Unblock soon that will override Caller ID Block."

"Will there then be a Caller ID Block Unblock Block?" Warren asked.

"I don't know. I wouldn't think they would, but I don't know."

"I'd think that if somebody wanted their number blocked in the first place, then if you unblocked it then you'd want to block it back."

"Maybe. But sooner or later it would have to stop. These options don't come cheap, you know. Eventually it would cost more than it was worth."

"Like an arms race," Warren observed, thinking it already cost much more than it was worth.

"You know, that's right," Huckston said, struck with the idea and wondering if he could turn it into another brilliant, award-winning story that he would never write.

"That's quite an answering machine," Warren said. In addition to its large number of buttons it had a screen, antenna, headset, speaker, two dials, and a joystick.

"Yes, latest model," Huckston said proudly. "I've got all the accessories I can get. Even more on my home phone. I've got an answering machine like this one, with Caller ID. Got Call Waiting where if I'm talking to someone and another call comes in, I can hang the person I'm talking to out to dry for a minute or so and check on the other call. I've got Call Forwarding where I can program in a number or several numbers so the person calling can transfer the call to those numbers."

"Gosh," Warren said, baffled.

"Of course I'm mobile, my home phone is mobile. I can carry it outside if I wanted to go outside and if I stay within fifty feet of the house and if the weather is right I can make and receive calls. Then I've got Call Selector that I can enter ten numbers and when each one calls there's a distinctive ring so I can tell who's calling without looking at the Caller ID screen. And all this is on my cell phone, too."

Warren nodded, hoping he look interested.

"Oh, yes, and I've got Call Block. Put in five numbers and none of them can even make your phone ring."

While Huckston gave his office number to his upper-division classes, he used this feature to recognize and block out the calls of the four students each semester who he thought might be prone to call him about assignments, and also, in wasted spite, to block the call of the magazine editor who would never contact him and who had most recently turned down his seven-year-old short story that he was certain could win him wide recognition if only he could find an editor of deep aesthetic discernment who could appreciate his muscular prose and recognize his powerful new voice and rush his powerful, muscular story into print. Only occasionally did Huckston doubt his talent, at present mute and inglorious, but solely because the current literary establishment preferred the minimalist school of writing. When he recalled his position as literary pioneer who had abjured the overly-refined taste of the coasts to explore the wild, abundant inner continent of the nation, he then, doubt dispelled, knew himself a writer. He also resented his cushy job that unaccountably kept him from his work of not writing stories, and he resented the woman he was living with, who he felt did not sufficiently respect his talent. He would like to get rid of her, and planned to as soon as he could turn his attention away from the task of getting an even cushier position at Middle State with less teaching involved. At every opportunity he courted any administrator he thought might help him obtain such a job, but he was never called with an offer, partly because to give himself an air of mystery and reclusion he had an unlisted phone number. Computers provided another device whereby he could receive or ignore messages, and he eagerly awaited every innovative, cutting-edge accessory their manufacturers could dream up to help him do either.

Ringle, on the other hand, seemed to Warren of a divided mind about computers, promoting them at times, muttering at the unpredictable and inevitable disasters they occasioned at others. The rest of Warren's instructors were silent on the matter. Though he did not know it, many distrusted computers and tried to see past the facile argument that they were only a tool and we choose to use that tool for good or ill. But there ultimately would be no choice whether to use them at all.

"Calona says they'll be used to form the global village," Brumley observed to Hobart and Greenman at an infrequent fast food luncheon at a franchise not far from campus. Most often they brought their own lunches and ate in their offices. "He sees his use of them as bringing about universal harmony and world peace."

"That sounds plausible," Greenman replied, first glancing back to see if an informer might be sitting in the booth behind them. "As soon as fifty percent of the world's population makes the decision to buy a computer rather than three years' worth of food and then starves to death as a consequence, population pressures will be reduced and a much nicer brand of people can then take over the global village. You effectively kill all your competitors and then live in peace."

"I don't think you've got it quite right,' Hobart disagreed. He had taken one of his paper-wrapped cheeseburgers from its small cardboard box, which at the condiment counter he had then pumped almost full of ketchup for his two orders of super-size fries. "The fifty per cent of the world's population that is starving will be *given* computers, or more likely they'll be assigned one at some multi-national corporation's electronic sweat shop. Then the jobs of about ninety per cent of the fifty percent of the world's population that is not starving will be moved to the sweat shops at ten percent of their former salary, and the astral–from the Greek, astron, star–the star-like five percent of the population–*the Real Ones,* some wag has termed them–will, I suppose, be even further above everything and everybody else. That's how it will play out." He violently plunged six fries into his homemade vat of ketchup.

"But there's something that I don't get about those things," he paused in his feeding to muse from his side of the booth. "Back here in our tawdry little arena, why are classes in composition where students are required to sit at computers called computer labs?" Chemistry labs aren't called test tube labs. Biology labs aren't called microscope labs. Why computer labs? I'm not sure even writing lab is logical."

"It's so it sounds like science," Brumley said, dabbing one end of his French fry into the small ketchup-filled paper cup on his tray. "Wainwright's—I guess you could call it an idea—-Wainwright's idea is that if he makes everything we do in the humanities sound like science, there will be more money in it. For him, needless to say."

"By god," Hobart said, enlightened but disappointed he hadn't thought of it. "That's it. Dean Marsh of Science does make considerably more than Wainwright." He began unwrapping his second cheeseburger. "Who knows? Sound scientific, get paid scientific. It might work. Wainwright is slicker than I thought."

"There's more,' Brumley said, and Greenman, sensing a truly damning revelation, looked around the franchise for eavesdroppers and motioned for Brumley to keep it down. "Some state agency–the state Economic Development Council, I think–said that teaching 'computer literacy' had to be a part of every state university's curriculum. Science and business didn't want to fool with teaching glorified typewriting, so we got it. To sweeten the deal, the state allocated thirty thousand dollars annually for computer repair and yearly replacement–Wainwright was on that like syrup on a pancake. He could actually use that money for anything, and when he announced computers would be required to teach writing, he claimed the money could buy supplies during the next budget cut–paper and stuff. And of course to supplement travel. The travelers were overjoyed."

"Did you say they replace the computers each year?" Hobart asked, unwrapping his third cheeseburger. Brumley felt sure that someday he would not bother with removing the wrap, at least on his first burger. Several years ago Hobart had suffered a mild heart attack that had changed his life. Realizing that time was running out, that he might die tomorrow, he had begun eating anything and as much as he liked, drinking whenever he felt like it, smoking again on occasion, and refusing to take a cholesterol test. "Are they that shoddy? Don't they last longer than that?"

"Maybe every year is an exaggeration. Every other year is more like it. But for god's sake, it's not just that they wear out in that time. What happens is that the computer companies will announce a breakthrough, more gigabytes or whatever they announce–sort of like horsepower in cars–that are necessary for life to go on. Then we have to buy new computers. You know the drill. But back to your first question, if Wainwright calls those classes computer labs, he gets more money to control and a higher salary. And, he gets another way to test the loyalty of his troops by seeing who will genuflect before his innovation. He also gets a sense of importance. For all of that, he'd call them Moloch."

Hobart had finished his repast and was tidying up with the double handful of thin paper napkins he had torn from the counter dispenser, mounding them on the tiny tray that had barely held his feast.

"I wish he'd use some of that thirty thousand to hurry up installing those sprinklers–that or soundproof the classrooms," Greenman said, emboldened by Brumley's frank assessment of the computer invasion. "How long is it going to take them to get them in?"

Not only was Humanities Hall being retrofitted with a sprinkler system to protect the computers, but Dean Wainwright, in order to keep the computer maintenance and replacement money flowing, was also having installed various outlets, ports and plugs in all rooms to allow every class and not just the computer labs to have access to the streets and addresses of the electronic global village.

"It's not going to take them long, from what I understand," Hobart confided loudly enough for the cooks to hear. "If he's going to get that computer maintenance money next year, it has to be installed by

March. Wainwright will ramrod the project through if he has to put on a toolbelt and strap up a few pipes himself.

"I don't see how a sprinkler system would save the computers," Brumley said. Wouldn't drenching them with water be as disastrous as a fire?"

"My god, Brumley," Greenman said. "I would think a Professor of Humidities would know the answer to that one. Aren't you keeping current in your field?"

Brumley had mistakenly told Greenman of the misunderstanding of his credentials, who had then gleefully spread the word that there was a man of real consequence in the department.

"I suppose if the computers got wet you could put them in a oven and dry them out," Brumley delivered his expert opinion. "The pottery kiln in the Art Department would hold several at a time. Stack 'em in, fire it up—I don't see why that wouldn't work"

"Maybe you could pass them through the Big Pep Rally bonfire that's coming up," Hobart speculated. "Put that miserable waste of trees to some good use."

"Look," Greenman broke in, "no computer is going to be put in harm's way in a kiln or a bonfire. And another thing, the Big Pep Rally bonfire is sacred. It's for rousing school spirit, for some ball game, I believe. It's unthinkable that it might be employed for some useful purpose."

Carrying their trays with the considerable paper and plastic each meal had generated, they reached the trash cans, concealed in cabinets with a hinged door in the upper part of one side, through which one emptied his tray's contents. After Greenman and Brumley had done their duty, Hobart, as usual, crammed tray and all through the cabinet door and walked placidly out.

Greenman was right to complain about the sprinkler system installation. Classes were being shuffled from floor to floor in a vain attempt to avoid disruption from the clang of pipes and the insolence and grumbling of the contractors doing the installation. One of Brumley's humanities classes had begun on the third floor, was transferred abruptly after a week and a half to the fifth floor, then to the first, then back to the third, the relocations generally communicated to the class and to Brumley by a handwritten note on the door of the to-be-abandoned classroom the day it was to be vacated

They stayed one step ahead of the distant drilling and smashing until the first hour exam. Ten minutes into the test a barrage of room-shaking blows from the classroom next door brought cries of protest from even the most apathetic students. Brumley, glad to be their champion, sprinted next door.

"Could you hold off until ten-thirty?" he asked the two constructions workers, one of whom was pounding with a large sledgehammer on the concrete-block wall between the two rooms. "We're having a class next door."

"Dean says we're supposed to do this," the one supervising the smashing said. The other continued to swing the sledge, powerfully.

"No," Brumley tried to command, "they're part way through a test. They can't think with this going on. Hold off till class is over. I'll square it with the dean."

He felt sure Wainwright didn't realize a class was meeting on the other side of the wall or else there had been some confusion as to where the work was to be done.

"He said we're supposed to do it," the supervisor said, a cigarette, in defiance of the no smoking regulations for the building, bouncing insultingly from his large, clasping lips. But the mighty John Henry did ground his hammer.

"I'm sure he didn't know there was a class next door or he wouldn't have had you working in here. I'll go down and tell him about the mix-up as soon as class is over."

The supervisor did not reply but looked down to see how the work had progressed. From the Vulcan-like beatings, Brumley would have thought the entire wall would have been rubble, but only a small, fist-sized hole had been opened, and that only into the concrete block's hollow interior. He walked back to his classroom door and entered, trying to be as expressionless as possible but hoping that the students would think he had at least some authority. To one appreciative glance he smiled in conspiratorial satisfaction, only to have it stunned off his face by a resumption of the great, resounding blows from next door.

"What the hell is this?" he said furiously to the narrow-eyed supervisor after rushing to the next room. "No more. Get the fuck out of here. You can finish up later. I'll straighten things out with the dean," he added, trying at least to end on a civil note.

The supervisor and his Thor, either of whom could have held Brumley out the window by his ankles, stared at him and seeing he was willing to throw himself between the hammer and the wall, sullenly filed out and down the hall.

"I'm going to see the Dean about this," the supervisor said evenly back over his shoulder as Brumley returned to his class. Thinking he had been unpleasant enough, Brumley said nothing.

"That should do it," he said to the class as he entered the room. "But they're going to tell the Dean on me," he added with mock concern, emphasizing for the class that what mattered not just to him but to all of Middle State was the uninterrupted conveyance of knowledge and the evaluation of learning.

The memo from Dean Wainwright was hand-delivered by one of his gorgeous student assistants not long after lunch.

> To: Dr. Brumley
> From: Dean Kenneth Wainwright,
>   College of Humanistic I & I
> Subject: Unacceptable Behavior
>
> I'm very disturbed over your unwarranted interference with authorized construction in Humanities Hall this morning. Two construction associates reported that you obstructed their attempts to install a computerized smoke detector and computer port prior to sprinkler retrofitting in Room 318. You also threatened them and used profanity. Such behavior cannot be tolerated.
>
> However averse you are to the integration of computers into the instructional process, such impeding of the university-sanctioned employment of high tech equipment is unacceptable.
>
> I am entering this incident on your permanent record.

The thought of telling Wainwright his side of the story Brumley found unacceptable. Explaining that the authorized construction had disrupted a test would be a waste of time. Either Wainwright didn't care, or he would be shown so in the wrong on the matter that his thirst for revenge would be boundless, and it was perfectly obvious why. Computers were his ride to glory, and Brumley knew Wainwright saw him as a possible spoiler like Old Cadoon, who had actually taken research seriously and uncovered a series of studies proving that computer enhanced writing instruction was no better than the old type, except that lots of money got passed around. More important, Brumley was aware that his irksome letter about inadequate course offerings for students to graduate on time was an impediment to administrative peace of mind, and, when he sent his next one to the state's largest newspaper, it would be clear that he didn't know when to shut up. Worst of all, Wainwright didn't like him. So speaking with Wainwright to explain–as though it needed explaining–an attempt to halt the disruption of a class examination was pointless.

Brumley decided to do worse. He sent Wainwright's superior a somewhat intemperate memo.

> To: James Staull, VP for Academic Affairs
> From: Dr. Brumley, English Dept.
> Subject: Unacceptable Memo (copy attached) from Dean Wainwright Concerning "Authorized Construction" That Disrupted a Test in My Humanities Class, and then Dean Wainwright's Twisting the Event to Make My Stopping the Disruption Appear Unacceptable Behavior
>
> Wainwright says he'll enter this unacceptable behavior on my permanent record. I'd like it also carved on my tombstone as at least one good thing I did..

He told no one what he had done, not even Greenman and Hobart. Nothing could save him now. Socrates could appear and praise his teaching and be dismissed as a fraud and extradited back to Athens. His research could be commended by a Nobel prize winner and be disregarded. He would probably be removed from the Signage Committee. It was professional suicide. He would be on the streets by next year. But what else could he do?

ten
LEO LEAR

By the time he had been escorted to University Hall and the tenth-floor offices of President Curtis, Leo Lear, CEO of Foods Unlimited and Middle State's biggest private benefactor, had once again warmed to an academic setting, one where sweet youth frolicked, supple and eager for experience and knowledge of the world. He began heating up when he stopped to banter with the two luscious student helpers at the first-floor reception desk, and neared combusting when rising up in the elevator with two more stunners who were returning to President Curtis's outer offices after delivering memos over campus. Lear's escort, Vice president Swift of Logistics and Hospitality, pressed himself into a corner of the elevator, needlessly terrified over possible sexual harassment lawsuits as the dapper, fearless Lear joked with and lightly fondled the delighted coeds.

"Maybe you could show me around after I'm through up here," Lear called to the twittering girls as he and Swift started down the hall to the president's suite. "I've got to drop by the Center for Life Form Enhancement. You know how to get to the Center of Life Form Enhancement?" he asked, easily but intensely. "Swift here doesn't and somebody's got to get me there." Looking back over his shoulder at the girls, he preceded Swift down the hall toward the president's office.

"There's the man," Lear said, striding briskly into President Curtis's plush inner suite and shaking an apprehensive Curtis's hand as Vice president Swift, his duties accomplished, quickly backed out of the office. Larson, President Curtis's Administrative Assistant for Planning, whose loathing for Lear she made no attempt to hide, lingered at her side desk in spite of her repugnance, displaying her institutional loyalty under

128

duress. Like Administrative Assistants of all stripes throughout Middle State management, Larson had originally been a faculty member but had quickly seen her mistake. Now she spent most of her time reading the *Bulletin of Administrative Assistants for Planning*, planning on how to find something to do, preferably something that would please President Curtis and cause him to recognize her potential to perform at a higher administrative level than where she was now stuck.

"Hahahaha," she laughed nervously, swishing past Lear to place a stack of folders before a slightly irritated President Curtis. "I thought you'd need these records of grants and endowments we've received over the past ten years. They're arranged chronologically by folders and by amounts within each folder. I've highlighted those donations from Mr. Cranshaw. Of Cranshaw Deodorant.

Larson assumed wrongly that Lear might feel himself in philanthropic competition with Cranshaw, one of Middle State's most wealthy and celebrated alumni, inventor of the roll-on deodorant ball.

"Thanks, Dr. Larson," President Curtis said brusquely, "But we won't need them. Take them back to filing, would you," and he waited for Larson to stiffly gather the folders and head for the door. "Just put them back where they came from."

As she went out, President Curtis impulsively grasped Lear's hand again in an awkward renewal of welcome.

"I was about to ask, old buddy," Lear said to Curtis's vigorous pumping of his hand, "is there any chance of fixing me up with one of those sweet things down on the desk, or that came up on the elevator with me? Or with a couple of them, hell, I'm a generous man. The tall redhead would do for starters. I'll bet she isn't majoring in Home Economics, right, unless it's Bedroom Management. God, what a piece."

President Curtis, who would never have spoken so crassly of having sex with Candy, the tall redhead so openly solicited by Lear, would like to have turned the lewd but highly respected little vulgarian out of his office. But alienating a multi-million dollar donor over a quibble in decorum would not sit well with the Reigning Board, half of whose male appointees had at one time or another made similar if somewhat less direct requests of him, always jokingly but with a stifled hope peering through the wet, nervous grin. And too, hadn't he reserved to himself the final approval of all student helpers who came to work in University Hall? That he picked only the most burstingly nubile females, and that the more bursting they were the closer they worked—or more often sat—to his office, signified only that he wished Middle State to project a good image. He decided that the proper tone to take—take carefully—with Lear was the one of quiet dignity he always adopted when meeting with university benefactors who might benefact it even more.

"Wouldn't be a bad idea, Leo," President Curtis responded with what he hoped was an easy laugh as Lear continued to pump his hand. "But you know I can't do that."

"Can't do it?" Lear asked, ceasing to shake hands but not letting go. "What do you mean you can't do it?" His eyes, suddenly cold, searched Curtis's face. "What the hell kind of chief are you if you can't fix up a friend? What kind of place do you run here?"

"A university," Curtis said, his enlarged smile pasted even more tightly on his face. "Just a university." Laughing it off was the only way. He tried to resume shaking Lear's hand, but the pint-sized corporate giant's arm was as stiff as angle-iron.

"Oh. A university." Lear looked at him carefully. "Sure. A university." He smiled, not quiet contemptuously, and began again shaking Curtis's hand. "Different at universities, huh? Well, let's get down to business. Maybe I can make some arrangements with one of the little rose buds on my way out."

President Curtis winced inwardly again, but felt some relief in knowing that whatever this crude buffoon, who was also an esteemed and urbane patron of cutting-edge research all over the country, might do on his own, he himself was not responsible. Let him pluck one of the rose buds on the floor behind the reception desk—Lear could buy his way out of it even if there were five witnesses and a video tape of his pluck. Meanwhile, there was business. Lear's latest proposal of a tax write-off donation to Middle State hinted at millions, which would mean hundreds of thousands coming directly to the President's account as discretionary funds—*discretionary funds*, a term that filled Curtis's mouth like some heavenly unction, since he could spread the unction as he wished with virtually no accounting to anyone. Attracting Lear's donation, or just by being at the helm when Lear made the donation, would mean a substantial raise in salary from the Reigning Board and another addition to his resume to bedazzle that larger university for which he would eventually leave this backwater school–which, he hastily added to himself, was one of the highest ranking former teacher college universities in the upper mid-south, based on Middle State's own trumped-up statistics sent to the magazine that did the rankings. And discretionary funds, in the meantime, could be used to enhance Middle State's image by remodeling extensively his present suite of offices, which in spite of their lavish appointments reminded him too much of faculty offices around campus. Teak, or Brazilian rosewood paneling, he thought, with Moroccan leather bindings for the undisturbed books on his shelves. And some interesting art, paintings of some kind, of a lake or tree, or maybe a statue of some recognizable thing, something you wouldn't have to waste time wondering what it was supposed to be. And a new stereo sound system whose sound he couldn't tell from the old one and that he would never listen to. He was tired of feeling ashamed when speaking in his shabby surroundings with Lear, whose glass and chromed offices he could only imagine, and who reportedly sat in a chair that had once belonged to a Czar.

Clearly, Leo Lear was not a man to be antagonized, though how such an unrefined little cretin could rise to near the top of the pecking order troubled President Curtis, though not enough to impede his sucking up to the man. Yes, at times Lear might appear the coarse lecher, but there was another Lear. When necessary he could become a hard-eyed, calculating exemplar of the modern corporate head, a ruthless man of consequence, a smooth rake of great wealth who could influence presidents, intimidate senators, and generally disburse wads of cash wherever it would benefit him.

"Leo," President Curtis said, moving around behind his desk and determined to get Lear's mind on the business at hand. "I'm fully aware of your interest in Drs. Critson's and Wyandotte's research and I want you to know that every agency at Middle State is ready to support any grants you may make. I believe the track records of those two researchers is ample warrant that your kind and generous support will be put to wise use."

Lear, who was slowly canvassing Curtis's office, stopped and looked at him.

"Prez, I could listen to you talk that talk all day. You university folks do it better than politicians. 'I'm fully aware'—that's good, real good. Let me try it. 'I'm fully aware'," Lear intoned, "that everybody at this place who's clawed up to the trough is already squealing to dive in and that Critson and Wyandotte are damned good at dreaming up things to spend money on. And can 'disburse' it when they get it. What I need to know is, have you got a good bookkeeper here who can do creative accounting and get me a tax write-off about twice what I deserve. I don't mean illegally. Just in ways that no honest human would dream of. You got one?"

"Well, we have an accountant—several in fact. I'm sure they'll do their best to accommodate you."

"Their best? Will that be good enough? I can't loan out any of my accounting staff to give them a hand—conflict of interest or some such shit I think it's called. Anyway, my boys are busy enough as it is. You can't loot pension funds and break unions and bribe Congress and ship good-paying jobs overseas and find off-shore banks and dummy accounts without the top graduates of our most prestigious business schools to show the way and cook the books. Quality counts. I hope, by the way, that your little business school here knows which side the bread is buttered on and are graduating people who can get the most out of their fellow man."

President Curtis, who wished Lear would sit down and keep his mind on the grant at hand, nodded uncertainly.

"I believe our graduates excel as management material. I'm confident that they can get the maximum productivity from their subordinates."

Lear paused in his examination of Curtis's hand-carved ivory chess set from India and turned to look at him.

"That's not what I mean—not 'the maximum productivity they can get from their subordinates.' I mean, how much can they get from their fellow man."

"Why, yes, I see—I think I know what you mean," Curtis said nervously. "I had a little economics years ago. We better ourselves and automatically everyone else does better. Isn't that it? The invisible hand?"

"Nick," Lear said sympathetically, sitting on the edge of Curtis's desk and turning to face him, "There is an invisible hand, and we certainly better ourselves, that part you've got right. About everybody else I don't know and don't care. The way the invisible hand works is, it grabs its fellow man by the balls and squeezes until he coughs up whatever we decide we want. That's what getting the most out of our fellow man means. It's the free market. Everybody is free to squeeze everybody else's balls. But there's a catch. Most people have a little weak invisible hand. Mine–" he held out a surprisingly large and powerful one–"mine is a real nutcracker. So if you want to get in a ball-squeezing contest with me, you're welcome to try. Want to give it a shot?" he said, rising to face Curtis and slightly spreading his legs, smiling with cruel amusement at President Curtis's discomfort. "But you've got more sense than to try, because when I got through squeezing back, you'd walk on your knees and sing soprano for the rest of your life. Just never forget, the free market and the invisible hand of the corporate person are the greatest inventions that don't exist that have ever existed."

"The way you put it," President Curtis said cautiously, "it does sound pretty appealing—to a certain type, to the right type of people. But on a more, ah, positive side, when you help your company by sending all our well-paying jobs to poor countries where they become poor-paying jobs–that's an example of your bettering yourself but also helping the starving people of the world, right?"

Lear smiled thinly and for a moment seemed to study the pattern in President Curtis's Persian carpet, which along with the hand-carved chess set had been purchased several years before to show Middle State's commitment to cultural diversity.

"Your problem," he finally said pityingly, "is that you want to take a good line on everything. The only line to take is the bottom line, which is where my money and yours and everybody's comes from. I don't mean your money comes from my bottom line, but you get the drift. The point is, I send jobs overseas to make me money. If India won't take what I offer, then it's China; if China has a problem, then it's Africa–that is, as soon as we can get taxpayer money to educate all the brutes over there. Which taxpayer money, by the way, is what we used to set up the transportation and communication and global bribing systems we needed to move jobs overseas in the first place. All those airports, satellites, subsidized shipping, bought officials–those and a lot more the public paid for, and is still paying, bless them. Democratize the costs, privatize the profits is an old and valuable saying. Hell, your place is a fine example–train our work force for us at taxpayers' expense, we'll work them until we can move their jobs to Uganda. We get the profit. And you get a cut. Just don't tell anybody. Even better, though I know you've got a start on it already, you can lure the brutes over here to train them to be our labor market over there. They don't know Middle State from Harvard, and I don't imagine you're fool enough to teach them their error. To tell the truth, Nick-o, keeping people ignorant is what it's all about. I'd be careful about really educating folks. But just don't tell anybody."

"Well, no, I wouldn't tell anyone,' President Curtis began, "but it's not all like you say. We do have a mission statement here, you know, that prescribes the broadening of the mind and the teaching of the best that has been known and thought as the central thrust of Middle State's. . . ."

"Cut the shit, Curtis," Lear said. "I know you've got to cover yourself, but you're with a friend here. Keep your customers believing they can get a cushy, high-paying job when they graduate, and they'll pile in here and keep your bottom line fat and healthy–that's your cut. So. Let's get back to this little grant thing. That's what I'm here for. I'm going over to Critson's labs this afternoon to give his balls a little squeeze and make sure he's spending my money like I want him to. He's working on a project or two for me that I'm hot to hear how they're going. The redhead is going to take me over there. Now, fix us a drink and let's get down to business. Gentleman Jack for me."

At Middle State's Center for Life Form Enhancement, where Dr. Critson of Biology presided, there were problems. Genes kept getting out. Whether they ran out or walked out or hopped out or flew out or crawled out or gnawed out or blew out nobody knew. But they kept getting out.

"We need to call Wyandotte on this one," Critson said to his lab assistant. "I don't know why chicken sperm would necessarily show up at the Poultry Complex, but it seems a logical place. Call Wyandotte."

Critson eyed sourly a long row of cramped, stacked cages that stretched down one wall of his Outer Lab and that contained various deformed chickens whose deformities were for the most part not visible and could therefore be called enhancements. 3E722 slumped near the front of one, an exhausted fowl engineered to lay three eggs a day while consuming only three-and-a-half times more high protein feed than a normal hen. Next to it, following failed attempts to produce a bare chicken to make processing its slaughtered carcass more efficient, was NF681, designed to pluck out its own feathers as they grew. It showed some promise and one of the Center's team was now attempting to incorporate muteness into the type, whose shrieks at present were loud, persistent and heart-rending.

Critson walked to the last cage in the row, one much larger than the rest.

"Good morning, Better Boy. Are you feeling your genetically enhanced oats this morning?" he said to a powerful mass of feathers at the back of the cage that fixed a black, red-rimmed eye on him. "Would you like a worm, early bird?" He poked his finger through the wire.

Like a spring-loaded projectile the mass of feathers shot forward and smashed against the door as Critson jerked his hand back and jumped away from the cage. The rooster, frenzied and determined, leapt again and again against the sturdy wire mesh, striking with two-inch-long, horn-hard and needle-pointed spurs, then stabbing and slashing with its slightly hooked beak.

"Relax, boy, relax," Critson said, vigorously prodding the bird with a scarred wooden rod he kept by the cage. "Are you the thief? Are you stealing your sperm? We'll go a long way to spread our own genes, won't we," and he gave the maddened rooster another couple of pokes before turning back to the room. Better Boy continued to slam against the quivering door.

"I don't know, Dr. Critson," his lab assistant Prosser said cautiously. "You maybe shouldn't rile him up like that. If he ever gets out we'll have to shoot him. That won't look too good."

"I may shoot him whether he gets out or not," Critson glowered, his fingers tightening on the prodding stick. "Try to make a rooster whose life is a dream and what thanks do you get? He can copulate with 120 hens an hour, and do you think he's grateful? Half those he services he kills and he'll rip the clothes and the hide right off you if you get in his way—I thought that Harpy Eagle gene was a mistake. In fact, you don't even have to get in his way: if he sees you, he'll go for you. You can't outrun him; god, the Ostrich gene was a mistake, too. Prosser, maybe I should shoot him right now. Then we can go back to theory; there's nothing wrong with our theory. I just can't figure out why it won't work. And we've got to find out why genes are missing."

Genes began getting out the first year Critson's labs began operation. Their tendency not to stay in place, in spite of all precautions, was first discovered when a crop of soybeans on the Middle State experimental farm downwind from the Center for Life Form Enhancement had produced pollen that killed every unsuspecting butterfly and bee that wandered to their blooms. Then there was the meat substitute manufactured from the same unintentionally modified soybeans. Designed to be indistinguishable from steak, it turned out to be so in every way except taste. The next year came the mouse inadvertency when mice bred for intelligence by the Center to run mazes had their genes show up five miles from the facility in seemingly ordinary mice that refused poison bait and could cleanly spring traps. Here Critson, his plans for future grants and support not yet ripe, had first considered designing cats of superior intelligence to counter the mice but sensed public relations problems if he got in a genes race whose end might not appeal to his corporate sponsors. Critson had finally hushed the inadvertency up, and for all he knew the mice were still out there, plotting. And now it was rooster sperm, specifically Better Boy's sperm, that was getting out, and from cryogenic vaults with a security system whose manufacturer swore that not even the Grim Reaper could get past.

"If you're going to shoot him, Dr. Critson, I wouldn't let Mr. Lear know about it," Prosser warned. "He's counting on super-roosters to up his chicken production. You know how he is."

Leo Lear's interest in Critson's work involved something more than super-roosters, though super-roosters and the increased profits they would bring were of immediate and considerable concern in themselves. And Critson did know how Leo Lear was. A little bantam of a man, often crude but quiet and contained if the occasion required, Lear, if balked, could become an excoriating animal. But usually he got what he wanted—as everyone knew, he had the money.

And as CEO of Food Unlimited he could make or break any

agricultural researcher in the country, supporting with huge grants those researchers who could be counted on to increase his profits and blocking funds to those whose findings–or even whose inquiries–went against Food Unlimited's central principle. That principle, in many variations, insisted on the Conquest of Nature, a precept his public relations department didn't even have to sell. If withholding funds wasn't enough to quash an upstart researcher, then he bribed university administrators with large grants to fire the troublemaker. Because Lear loved power, Critson knew that while Lear's primary, clandestine interest in genetic manipulation was not super-roosters, the great man was still drawn to the idea of a truly dominant life form like Better Boy. Come to think of it, Critson reflected, Lear's primary interest and his interest in super-roosters were not far apart.

"That boy reminds me of myself in my younger days," Lear had crowed the previous year with happy reminiscence after seeing Better Boy perform for the first time. "I never quite piled 'em up dead like he does–I'm sure you fellows can get over that hump, huh Critson–but I still did my best. Now help me out here–120 hens an hour–twenty times the normal rooster–production up, say, ten times to be conservative–ten times the production units–goddamn, Critson, you start turning out these studs and I'll feel like I'm putting my money to good use with you."

"Uh, Leo," Critson began tentatively, "We do have a little problem."

"We what?"

"We have a little problem."

"Well that's good if it's little. What's your little problem?"

"Sir, we're not sure Better Boy is passing on his breeding propensities to his offspring."

"Now what the hell does that mean?"

"You're right in calculating that Better Boy could theoretically sire twenty times the chicks an ordinary rooster could, but our theory isn't matched by reality, at least not yet. An appreciable number of the eggs from Better Boy's harem are infertile and. . . ."

"What percentage"? Lear asked.

"Around forty percent."

"Around?"

"Forty-four percent."

"What else?"

"It seems that those eggs that were fertile hatched out a wide assortment of types, and not all their characteristics were desirable or, much worse, predictable. Some were ordinary chickens. Enough of the cockerels were. . . ."

"The what?"

"The cockerels. That's a young rooster."

"Go on."

"Enough of the cockerels were like Better Boy to make entering the brooding pens dangerous, and they usually killed and ate the ordinary cockerels within the first two months. Then a good number of the super-offsprings were infertile. . . ."

"Wait," Lear halted him. "Back up. What percentage were like Better Boy?"

"Let's see, I'm not sure I've got that figure exactly at present."

"It was twenty-seven percent," Prosser eagerly offered.

"Now how many of those were infertile?" Lear asked

"Fifty percent," Critson confessed.

"Is there any more to your little problem?"

"Well, Mr. Lear, some of the fertile super-roosters died of unknown causes in the first four weeks. The ones that survived, as you can see, were public menaces and we had to build elaborate compounds to protect the workers and offer some diminished threat to the hens they serviced—and to segregate them from one another, of course."

"Of course. Expensive compounds, I'd guess," Lear said coldly.

"As for the pullets," Critson went on, ignoring Lear's implications, "we had. . . ."

"The what?"

"The pullets. Pullets are young female chickens."

Lear nodded, and Critson went on. The pullets had turned out to be a pleasant surprise that then turned out to be unpleasant. Many of them were as sexually aggressive as Better Boy, resulting in a quick die-off of Better Boy type roosters, who were forced by the rampantly libidinous hens into prodigies far beyond even the roosters' sizzling capacities. Then these red-hot pullets, as soon as they laid eggs, ate them and were on the prowl again.

So all-in-all, Better Boy actually produced viable progeny at a much lower rate than would normal, more temperate roosters. But, since such a result was only preliminary, or, given the paucity of data developed, even unreliable as a predictor of future results, further research would be needed and would likely show that Better Boy was as successful a stud as Seattle Slew.

"It sounds like a pile of shit to me, Critson," Lear said, rising to leave. "I've had it shoveled to me by the grain scoops: everyone wants just a few million more and soon the well will come in, the mine will hit the vein, the company will turn around. I'm going to keep bankrolling this farce, but I don't want you to think I'm fooled. I can cut you some slack on this rooster project, but pretty soon, there or elsewhere, I want to see some results."

While Critson had heard nothing from Lear in the time since, he had not forgotten his notice. And Lear was dropping by that very afternoon, to check on how he, Critson, was coming along with the millions he had wheedled from the little bastard. That, and as Lear had informed him over the phone, to give his balls a little squeeze.

"Yes, Prosser," he said," I know how Lear is. But I do not like a chicken. I don't even like them fried. Lear is mistaken if he thinks I'm going to stick with chicken enhancement, even if it is just a cover. I want even my covers to be successful, and chickens are too stupid to be enhanced. They don't even know what's good for them. Prosser, if I could make you capable of breeding twenty times an hour, you'd be grateful, right?"

"Well, Dr. Critson," Prosser replied blushing, "I don't know."

"You don't know? Great God, think of it—twenty times an hour!"

"There would be a problem."

"There's no problem if you can screw twenty times an hour. Your problems are over."

"But, sir, who would I, uh, mate with twenty times an hour?"

Critson looked at him.

"I mean, if I were married, could I get my wife to go along? I mean after the honeymoon? And when would I work, or even eat? And if I lived just generally a normal life—you know, eating and working and sleeping—what good would it do me to have intercourse twenty times an hour?"

"You don't understand, do you? Say you're not married—or even say you are, there's still lots of other women in the world—think of the variety, Prosser, think of it."

"But, sir, if you're not married, wouldn't there be a logistical problem? If you're mating twenty times an hour, when would you get to know enough women to have any variety? How would you arrange things, I mean getting from one place to another, without taking up so much time it wouldn't matter if you could have sex even once an hour?"

"Prosser," Critson said patiently, "if you could have big booming sex twenty times an hour, as soon as you became a celebrity you wouldn't have any problems with, as you say, logistics, other than crowd control. The problem with your thinking is that you're only considering ordinary guys. They slog along; women aren't interested in them except for marriage. Word gets on TV or in *People* magazine that you're capable of sexual congress twenty times an hour, don't fool yourself, congress will be in session."

"I don't know, Dr. Critson," Prosser said after some thought. "It sounds good, but it might get a little tiresome. And wouldn't everyone else want to be enhanced, too? Then what would happen?"

"You wouldn't get tired after I got through designing you," Critson chuckled indulgently. "I'd see to it that your ability matched your drive. Then you'd be a star. And if everyone else wanted a little enhancement or wanted to be born that way, then think of the money we'd make. But until I can get away from chicken enhancement, you're not going to be a star and neither am I. We've got to stop spending so much time looking at results and get back to possibilities. Better Boy's a failure, we might as well face it, though there's no need to let Lear know until we can figure out a way to tell him so it won't appear we've failed. I've already tried 'uncertain preliminary results'. I don't think he was fooled. Maybe we can call Better Boy an intermediate step or a promising beginning that with five year's further development could result in real progress in life form enhancement. That might do it. But we've got to be careful. Lear's been around. If we can just get back to micro-manipulation and a little recombinant action and get away from these goddamned life forms—and I mean especially chickens—we may get somewhere."

It was the lab that Critson loved. In the past twenty years since he received the Doctor of Philosophy degree in the then nascent study of genetic manipulation—and he never understood what philosophy had to do with it—he had seen laboratories in his field, and his not least among them, become expensive and complex even beyond those of the now-worried physicists and chemists at Middle State. Sensing a shift in what mattered and a corresponding tilt to the money table in the direction of microbiology, Critson's competitors in the physical sciences often dropped by the Center for Life Form Enhancement, ostensibly in a spirit of cooperation and intellectual interest, but mainly to see just what was going on that could attract so much cash.

What they saw in just one of Critson's labs was ultra-centrifuges, automated gene splicers, atmospheric scrubbers, hermetic hoods, cryogenic holding vaults, scanning tunneling electron-beam microscopes, direct access to the Center's super computer, and an array of reagents, glassware and electronic devices breathtaking in its complex design. Flashing lights and laser beams pulsed and shot through clouds of liquid nitrogen vapor that swirled about the workers in yellow protective suits who tended the temple's demands. And this was only a Second Circle lab. Similar to the Transuranic Department, the Center for Life Form Enhancement was designed to place increasingly more sensitive and hazardous work deeper into the building, with powerful but low-velocity fans pulling air from the outside toward and through these areas of sensitivity before venting it into a two-hundred-and-two foot smoke stack, out of which—also like the Transuranic's stack—no smoke ever came. Each stack, in an attempt to strengthen the image of Middle State as an institute of higher learning rather than a factory, had a complete carillon added, encircling it part way up. The carillons were played alternately each Sunday morning by the university carillonneur, a slow-witted cousin of the Chairman of Middle State's Reigning Board who was given a title he could not pronounce and whose duties were to make a Sabbath climb up the appropriate smokestack and insert a tape of carillon music in the carillon's sound system, there being no real carillon. The chemists and physicists in the Science Building were well aware that the Center for Life Form Enhancement's smoke stack had been built exactly two feet higher than theirs, with a better sound system. And the entire Center had a security system that had been proved unbreachable. Except, of course, for the missing genes.

In the Inner Lab of this grand complex Critson did his real work, the work Leo Lear had become truly interested in. His real work was immortality.

"Unenhanced life forms," Critson explained to an initially distracted Leo Lear later that afternoon, who had murmured a few words to a blushing Candy before she left after escorting him there, "lack a certain vitality after a number of cell divisions. In humans, after about fifty or so divisions, the subsequent generations of cells lose their efficiency, have metabolic wastes build more quickly and eliminated more slowly. The cell, so to speak, grows old, enfeebled and eventually can neither divide nor live."

"So?" said Lear impatiently.

"What this means," Critson went on quickly, "is that the organism made up by these cells also becomes enfeebled and cannot live. All its functions slow as each vital organ becomes less and less efficient."

"Wait. I don't divide. What's important about the cells not dividing? What's it to me?"

"Of course we don't divide," Critson said agreeably, "but when the cells that make us up don't, and they've also become invigorate, then the overall organism—us—likewise deteriorates. Or," and here he played what he knew was his trump card, "it's somewhat analogous to the decline of sexual vigor as an organism grows older. The cells can't reproduce by division, and an organism can no longer perform sexually."

"Are you saying you can keep the cells from losing their spunk?"

"Well," Critson admitted modestly, "let's just say we're working on it and hope with ample funding to achieve some real breakthroughs."

"Let me get this straight," Lear said. "You're saying that to keep me from growing old you're working on making cells that don't grow old?"

"More exactly, whose successive divisional generations retain their vigor."

Lear regarded him a moment.

"Making cells that don't grow old," Critson agreed.

"And this means that the person that has these cells won't grow old. Is that right?"

"If all goes well with our research and we can discover why one type of human cell never seems weary, so to speak, and can transfer that quality into"–he almost said normal cells but caught himself– "other cells, then I'd say you were more or less correct, Mr. Lear."

"You mean, your eyesight would stay good? Your skin wouldn't wrinkle, your belly tub? Your heart wouldn't wear out or your brain arteries start to blow? You wouldn't get stiff where you used to be limber and limber where you used to be stiff?"

To Critson's relief, he did not ask what kind of human cells never seemed to weary. Even Critson sometimes felt queasy transferring genetic material from indefatigable cancer cells to normal ones. If only those uncooperative telomeres at the end of chromosomes could be made to behave, he could program normal genes with a clear conscience, though when you were finding the key to immortality, conscience, as Critson saw it, hardly mattered. But so far, those telomeres just wouldn't go along.

"More or less. At least the statistical chances of all those things happening would be greatly diminished. Very greatly, in fact."

"What would I have to do to enhance my cells? Get a shot? Take some pills? Have a transplant of some kind, a cell transplant?"

Here was a delicate spot, Critson knew, but he was prepared.

"No," he said sorrowfully, "it doesn't work that way. So far, and I stress so far, there's no way of altering an already existing organism, one that was given an inefficient genetic makeup at the moment of fertilization. What we must do," he said, confidence easing back into his voice, "is first to test the feasibility of altering sex cells before their union with another so that the resulting initial cell will differentiate into an organism all of whose cells are, well, ageless."

"You mean it's too late for me? Or can you do something with my sex cells? That's where I'd want you to start anyway. What about that?"

"Not exactly," Critson went on smoothly, relieved at Lear's ignorance and resisting a counterproductive explanation of sex cells. "I would say that with our current level of knowledge, transforming the cells in an already existing organism into super cells is not presently possible, though that will likely be where the next generation of research is focused, as soon as we solve these first generation problems."

"But there's an intriguing possibility," he continued, seeing Lear's displeasure. "We can now clone a human, as we have done with many life forms. In this cloning, there's a real possibility of enhancing the initiatory cell, and the organism that results would be an exact copy of the one from which the initiatory cell was taken except it would, through the super cells, retain its vitality, its punch, its *lustiness*, so to speak."

"It would be immortal," Lear said.

"More or less."

"Just immortal. There is no more or less."

"I guess you're right," Critson said, still unsure if Lear was buying it.

"But if you took a cell from me and cloned it and put in these super cells or whatever you do, it might be exactly like me, but what about *me*? I'm still here, my eyesight will go, my heart start wheezing, my hair turn gray."

"The clone will *be* you. It'll almost exactly look like you, walk like you, sound like you—to your dog, smell like you. And as far as we can see, it will be immortal."

"I don't know," Lear said. "It seems like something's missing. But it also sounds like everything's in place and it looks good. This work can be patented, right? Not everybody with some pans and a cook stove can do it?"

"Of course our product can—and will—be patented," Critson happily agreed. "And no, it can't be done outside a very, very advanced laboratory, though in time we hope to get to get the cost down to around a million dollars per procedure. Though naturally, on the free market the procedure would be available to all who could meet market standards, that is, the price. We want to be fair here. I don't—and I'm sure you don't—want any scientific advancement made with your generous patronage blemished by its being labeled exclusionary or elitist."

Lear understood public relations, but he also understood the free market.

"You bet your ass I don't want it labeled elitist or exclusionary, though I'm not worried about it being either one. Now what's this little venture going to cost?"

For starters it cost a pretty five million, but all was relatively sure to come back in the forms of enhancement of his corporate image, patents on anything Critson produced, and immortality. While Lear knew nothing of the gods, he wished to be like them and was pretty sure everyone else did too and would fork over plenty to live forever. He would be glad for all who could afford it to live forever along with him, even merrier since he would be living on their money. At the same time, he wasn't sure that Critson hadn't shell-gamed him some. Knowing little of semantics, Lear could nevertheless sense the conditional, the predictive, the waffle, the hedge and the crawdad. But the possibilities in Critson's mad dream were surely greater than those offered by shaman spells and alchemist elixirs. Lear knew nothing about science either, but he was as unconsciously swayed by a lab coat as were the millions of viewers of the Food Unlimited commercials that hawked whatever industrial food product Lear was trying to manufacture and inflict on the public. Invariably, the product was tenderly displayed by a benevolent scientist, played by a handsome actor in a lab coat. Three-piece suits Lear could penetrate, but he responded to a lab coat like a churl of the Dark Ages to a priest's vestments at high mass.

And if nothing panned out, Lear's public relations department could still extract a little glitter with Lear-the-Philanthropist releases. Five million wasn't quite peanuts, but, one way or another, he'd get at least some of it back. And maybe he'd corner the whole peanut crop.

For Critson, five million was frosting on the cake, butter on his bread. Already he was rolling in grants from the U.S. Department of Agriculture, a partial one from the state, and several from pharmaceutical firms and, mystifyingly, the Department of Defense, whose interest baffled Critson though he still took their money. All together he had collected a tidy sum, constructed a stately center and installed labs that would have shamed the Manhattan Project. And how lovely they were! There, all was possibility; there were no thorny roses full blown, not even the bud or the seed. There was just the fertilized egg, the gamete, the genes at the heart of the gamete, the DNA at the heart of the gene. Everything was nearly perfect, and when Lear left, Critson was for a moment content.

But Better Boy was a failure, and genes kept getting out.

"Prosser," Critson called to the now yellow-suited assistant, who was entering data at the Inner Lab's computer prior to entering the secure area. "Did you notify Wyandotte about the sperm?"

"Yes, sir."

"Well?"

"Well what, sir?"

"What did he say? What was his reaction?"

"He seemed interested."

"And?"

"But he didn't seem to understand why I was telling him."

"Did you tell him that if that sperm gets distributed in one of those packed chicken houses he's so peacock proud of"–Wyandotte's ability to attract grants was of longer duration and better known than Critson's but was waning– "he'll know then why you were telling him."

"I did tell him it was Better Boy's sperm that was missing."

"I assume he knows who–what–Better Boy is?"

"I don't think he does."

"Did you tell him?"

"Yes. He said he didn't know anything about genetically enhanced super roosters. Confined feeding of multiple units was his specialty."

"Then we've done all we can do with Wyandotte. If his workers start disappearing, it's not our fault. But if we're ever going to get in the clear, we've got to find out how the genetic material is flying the coop. Call Electronics and see what they've got in the way of new surveillance equipment. And tell them I want a real pro on the job," he called to Prosser as the assistant unsealed the Inner Lab's door. "Tell them I want Junior White. He'll know what to do."

eleven
THE SIGNAGE COMMITTEE

Junior White, Brumley found out from Office Barnes, knew how to do many things, and would do them. Late one gray afternoon, hoping to meet Kaneesha the Voice of Delight and knowing that the first Signage Committee meeting was near, Brumley made his way to the Security offices. Fall was well along and a light rain presaged the arrival of the first really cool weather of the season that so far had been unusually mild. The rain, Brumley knew, would make it more likely that Officer Barnes would be inside and that he might learn if White was a possible ally.

"Is Officer Barnes around?" he asked through the glass partition where fines were paid and complaints turned away. A small sign at eye level read: All Conversations Are Recorded. It was an attempt, Brumley surmised, to keep the lowly and totally innocent clerks in the office from cursings and attacks by those who had so unjustly received parking tickets for the wholly blameless act of parking illegally.

"I don't know," said the student worker, whose bill cap identified him as a member of Pi fraternity, Colson's pack. "Let me check. Ms Morris," he called, "is Barnes in yet?"

When she came out of the work cubicle, Brumley's heart did not stop or race. It expanded. In one glance he saw that while not a beauty, no stopper of traffic or turner of heads, she was for him a hope of life. She was tall, slender; her thick dark-brown hair, parted on the left, was worn in the long natural style of some twenty years before. She had high cheekbones and a wide, promising mouth. Seeing that Brumley was the inquirer about Barnes, she walked to the counter, and her eyes, Brumley saw, were hazel, that mixture of green and brown that never receives its due, but in her, he decided later in a proper extravagance, were like shy galaxies formed and tinted by some stellar god of color and design.

"He isn't in yet. I'd think with this rain he should be soon. He was working Lot C the last time he called in. Are you Dr. Brumley?" she asked suddenly, her voice even more caressing in person.

"Yes, I am," Brumley heard himself say blandly as a dozen unformed and never-to-be formed replies of easy wit and impressive elaboration whirled in his mind.

"I'm Kaneesha Morris," she said, stepping to the counter. Through the half-moon hole in the glass where fines were paid and parking permits issued, smiling she reached her hand. Brumley touched it briefly.

"You said you'd drop by, but I'd about given up on you. Do you want to wait back in the snack room? I don't think he'll be out long. It's almost quitting time."

Brumley knew there would be other campus cops back there, most wearing the new, menacing black uniforms, and he wanted to get Officer Barnes' unreserved opinion of Junior White.

"He'll probably be out there until dark," he said, and Ms Morris nodded. "Did you say he was in Lot C?"

"I believe that's what he said. Do you know which one it is? Here, let me come around and I'll show you."

Showing him Lot C was not quite the equivalent of pointing out the dominating smokestack towers of the Transuranic Department and the Center of Life Form Enhancement, but very nearly was. She preceded him out the door onto the small portico, and Brumley, in spite of all the denial he could gather, began to believe that she wanted to talk to him, alone.

"You go down to that street, Rowan I think it is, and follow it," she pointed. "Lot C is the third one on the right. It's marked."

The slow rain had emptied the streets and only a few figures could be seen among the nearby buildings.

"He's a dedicated man," Brumley said. "Have you been here long? Do you know him well?"

"He is a hard worker, and so nice," she said. "I've been here for a little over a year now, and he's always been so nice–told me where to do business, who's honest, who to watch out for in the job," and she looked openly at Brumley.

"He's a good man, all right." Brumley did not feel he should speak of Officer Barnes' mission of justice for the affluent, which as far as he knew only he had divined. "I've known him almost since the day I got here too, a lot longer than you have," he said in a self-deprecating reference to an age difference between himself and Ms Morris that was likely little more than five years. "He's a good man."

"He likes you," Kaneesha said, and Brumley saw unmistakably that she admired him on Barnes' certainly modest estimation alone.

"That's good to hear," Brumley said inanely. "I like him. I'm glad to know he thinks well of me."

They stood together under the portico roof, the rain still coming slowly down, fall coming on. He was aware of his heart again, and did all he could to keep from telling this desirable, tender woman how beautiful she was to him.

"Well," he said after a few moments' silence. "I'll walk down that way and see if I can catch him."

"Do you want an umbrella?" Kaneesha asked. "We've got a dozen or more that students have left and never come back for. I'll be glad to get you one."

"No, that's okay. It's not raining very hard. Probably I'd forget to bring it back."

"You could keep it," Kaneesha said, and only with the greatest wrench of self-control could Brumley keep from taking her in his arms. At which, no doubt, he would have found in the most humiliating and punishing way how insanely he had misconstrued the feelings of Ms Morris, whom he had barely met.

"No, it's all right. I'll see if I can't hunt him down. But thanks for the offer. Thanks for the help."

As he walked bare-headed along the puddled sidewalk, he realized he hadn't even looked for a wedding ring, which meant she had one, and even if she didn't there was no possibility that such a woman wasn't living with a man. Thank god, he thought, I didn't make a fool of myself.

He met Officer Barnes trudging back to the Security Office, cheap vinyl rain slicker and covering for his hat shedding the rain, which beaded plumply on his glossy hat brim and shoes. Barnes' pleasant expression Brumely put down to what was doubtless a run of improperly permitted or parked vehicles of the latest models and highest price that Barnes had ticketed to the full extent of the law. When he recognized Brumley, his great face broke into a smile, and he raised a mighty hand in greeting.

"Ms Morris said you'd called. I'd about forgot about it. Here, you're going to get wet. Or wetter." He produced from under his coat a short-handled umbrella that he opened and handed to Brumley.

"Thanks," Brumley said. "What I need is a little information. You doing all right? Ticketing business good?"

"Slowed down a little from last month. Always does—people start to behave better. But ahead of this time last year. Gets better every year. People get worse, year to year."

Brumley nodded. No scientific study, no pronouncement from the greatest intellectuals about the decline of the West could convince him as did Officer Barnes' matter-of-fact statement. Barnes saw, and knew.

"What I need to know is about Junior White. You remember him; he used to work in Security."

"Yes, I remember him. What's he trying to do, sell you something?"

"No, nothing like that. He's on this committee that I got put on--" Brumley could not name the Signage Committee to such a man as Barnes "-- and I just wondered what he was like. Trying to sell me something? What do you mean?"

"Well, White's not a con-man, exactly. He's just out for number one. But he's up front about it. He did work here for awhile, knows a lot about police work and the other side, too. Always thinking. He went over to Electronics. I've heard he does more over there than repair radios and computers and such, but I don't know. He was in the military, in surveillance, something hush-hush. I'd say he's a fair man, wouldn't go behind your back. But like I say, he's out for number one. He won't scare, that I'll guarantee. He'll say what's on his mind."

"That's good," Brumley said. "A lot of staff people that get put on committees feel, well, uncomfortable I guess you'd say."

"Junior White won't," Officer Barnes said thoughtfully. "They had a meeting when they told us we weren't campus cops anymore. We were

'Security Associates'. White asked the fellow that told us if that meant we'd get more work or less pay or both. Didn't ask it mean; kind of like a joke, but he wasn't joking. Fellow didn't know what to say."

"I can imagine," Brumley said.

"White got what they call a 'negative performance review' not long after that," Barnes said, as though there was no connection between White's review and his asking the intemperate question. "I can imagine that, too," Brumley said. Few things frightened management more than a fearless underling.

"Not long after that he transferred to Electronics."

They stood silently for a moment, the rain now slacking off.

"I'd better get back," Officer Barnes said, looking off to the west. "It's close to quitting time and I've got to clock out. Hope I'm right about White. He's up front about things, but he's looking out for himself."

"Thanks for the info. By the way, how much longer until you retire? Didn't you tell me you had thirty-five or so years in?"

"First of next June," Barnes replied. "I can start drawing my pension then. I may stay on a while, may not. Depends on if they need me. You be careful, now. See you around."

As Officer Barnes made his way toward the Security Office, Brumley started toward his car. Where Junior White would fit on the committee Brumley wasn't sure, but at least he might be an interesting distraction. Not as interesting as Dr. Bohannon of Theater, but better than nothing.

The first meeting of the Signage Committee, itself a sub-committee of the Asteroid Preparedness Committee, was called for early the next week, and Brumley for a while had flirted with ignoring it and all subsequent ones. But like most of his flirtations he could not sustain it and found himself in his usual unsatisfied state, mildly disgusted at his cowardice. Making it all worse was Franco "Stub" Weebles of Criminal Justice and Penology as chairman, named to the post in recognition of years of faithful informing on fellow faculty to the higher-ups. Unlike the other faculty members on the committee, when yearly job evaluations rolled around the administration would have Weeble's Signage Committee service rated as invaluable with a hefty raise slipped to him for his dedication and sacrifice in chairing it. Betraying one's comrades to the higher-ups of course was not an activity listed as an item of merit to be considered in awarding raises, but there was never a problem in finding ways to grace the faithful. Weebles had learned this lesson early and had done well.

He preferred not to be known as Stub. No one addressed him directly as such, but the students, who had conferred the title on him after his first lecture over a lectern at Middle State, knew him as nothing else. He was a beak-nosed, balding, truncate of a man who was facing middle age with the same resolution he faced the sense of inadequacy his stubbiness had always caused him: he undertook violent physical exercise. Hardly a day passed that he could not be seen—bug-eyed, sweating, trying not to pant—staggering along the streets of Middleton. In fact, there were many similar figures of all ages and sizes loping day and night along sidewalks and roadways or around the several ball courts of the lavish and costly new Wellness Center or grunting and straining in a desperate vanity at ever more elaborate and expensive exercise machines. Having no useful physical work to do, and in fact adverse to the thought of such, they spent large sums of money for proper attire, equipment, memberships, nutrition supplements and occasionally drugs to do what was called staying in shape. For what, no one knew, though Brumley thought some misconception of sex was heavily involved.

"Could we get started," Weebles piped from the head of the long table where roughly eighteen of the twenty-five members of the committee sat chatting or staring gloomily at the table top. Brumley, not yet fallen into a stupor, looked up and down the table. Six women, he saw, two physically attractive enough to keep him awake if not attentive to the coming tedium. The lithe Bohannon of Theater sat across from him and down the table. Yes, as he had foreseen, she was perfect fantasy fodder, though he feared she might prove to be intensely interested in the committee's work and take seriously the heavy responsibility of being a member and make many motions about the size, material, lettering, placement, color, shape, cost and other mind numbing qualities of signs. The other distracting female, who had arrived with and now sat beside the lanky Junior White, was a staff member from the electrical shop, a robust fit for his Rosy the Riveter Comes Home Horny fantasy. White, he saw, had her full attention. On Brumley's side of the table, out of view unless he leaned forward, Warren sat uncomfortably with the other student member.

"Given the size of this committee," Stub Weebles began, "which I think that due to its importance is about right though I'd like to have seen it a little larger—but given its size I believe we should have a vice-chairman—chairman in charge of vice," he brayed at his wit, "--and a secretary. Dr. Schrimp, would you be vice-chair—a man well suited for the job"– another bray– "and Dr. Bohannon our secretary?"

Brumley could detect neither elation nor disgust from Bohannon in being chosen for a traditionally unrewarding but demanding job reserved for what he figured Stub would call the fairer sex. She pulled out a lined writing tablet and turned to a clean sheet.

"Our charge," Stub led off, " is to review signage in general throughout the university complex."

Our job, Brumley thought, is to waste our time and cover some administrator's ass while we do his job for him by making sure all signs identifying buildings look the same and are put by the buildings they signify and are spelled right. A job any moderately intelligent human could do in an afternoon.

He would have to stop this. Translating Weeble's gibberish into truth was a process both demanding and, he was afraid, endless. Why did addressing a seated group from the head of a table turn the human mind into some robotic apparatus, spouting jargon, cliches, and evasions? Maybe Junior White would pipe up as he had against the security associate label.

"But," Weebles continued, and then paused, long enough for Brumley, now fully alert, to see he was having difficulty going on. "But first, there's this problem that's been brought to President Curtis's attention. It concerns restroom signage."

From the stir that came from several points around the table, Brumley knew something was up that the insiders on the committee were already aware of.

"What we have, we've had some complaints about the signs that identify the men's and women's restrooms," Weebles went on with effort. "And we've been asked by the President's office to consider them."

"What in god's name can be wrong with the signs on bathroom doors?" Talbot of Biology asked in genuine wonder. Brumley could tell he regretted his abrupt and bewildered tone the second he spoke. "What *are* the signs on bathroom doors?"

"At present they're symbols," Stump replied. "There's a circle with a triangle beneath it and two short lines from the base of the triangle"–he turned to the blackboard behind him and drew ⅄ as he spoke. "This is on the women's restroom doors, and a circle with a rectangle beneath it like this"–and he drew ⅄ "is on the men's." He put the chalk back in the tray and turned to face the committee.

Brumley found himself in a position becoming more and more frequent with him. A non-problem of near total insignificance had been presented as an issue of real moment whose importance he failed to see. And increasingly, his failure rendered him morally suspect.

"I don't get it," Brumley said, and Talbot nodded his head vigorously in agreement. The low-level administrators present maintained solemn, nearly sorrowful aspects, while Junior White stared intently at the shiny table top. The blow was coming soon, and Brumley was afraid he would get no help. The low level administrators on the committee had already been informed on the problem and likely told what to do about it. Like Junior White, the rest of the staff members were stunned and likely amused by the proceedings but, unlike White, were cowed by the suits around the table and the unfamiliar formality of it all. Brumley wondered how Warren was taking the proceedings.

"What is it, exactly, that's the problem," Brumley asked. "Don't tell me our students–or administrators"–he looked smiling around the table and registered on the faces of several faculty members a denial of all complicity with his comment and even of his acquaintance– "are having trouble figuring them out?"

"They're having trouble, all right," a hard-edged voice came from down the table, "but it involves more than walking into the other gender's restroom." The voice was Dr. Bohannon's, and Brumley heard in it the assured self-righteous ring of a six-pound sledge hammer on a rail-road spike. He chose an expressionless, waiting look, which was the only response he had the courage to make. Evidently it revealed his ethical blindness, for Bohannon said with an edge of disgust:

"How many females do you see wearing dresses any more–as the symbol on female restroom doors depict? Do ten percent, do five percent–of our students at least? The restroom signage suggests they all do. If we're going to stereotype them at such an impressionable age into their patriarchally-determined gender roles, why don't we have figures of women on their hands and knees scrubbing a floor? Discrimination can be a subtle thing, Dr. Brumley," she said with mock-tolerance and showing Brumley she had gone to the trouble to learn and remember his name, "and we need to be alert to the forms it takes that our culture blinds us to."

"I don't get this," Brumley was surprised to see that a small woman sitting beside Conners of Chemistry dared to raise an objection. She was the assistant bursar and was wearing a dress. "I wear dresses most of the time. What's wrong with that? I don't see anything wrong with it."

"I'm not suggesting that there's the slightest thing wrong with wearing a dress *freely chosen*," said Bohannon, "or wearing pants, or wearing nothing for that matter"– Weebles, at the end of the table, smiled and nodded vigorously— "but an officially sanctioned sign implying that all women wear dresses imposes on females a traditional costume that recalls and enforces their marginalization in our culture."

The assistant bursar listened politely.

"But wouldn't a sign that had them dressed in pants–or in nothing– wouldn't that be an imposition as well? I don't get it."

"Look," Bohannon said with impatient condescension, "what's easier to violate, a woman in a dress or skirt or one in a pair of pants?"

There was an expectant silence. Weebles, a few precious memories crowding in, nodded again in fond reflection.

"Dresses and skirts are culturally enforced uniforms that permit and encourage the domination of women by men. Our organization," she said, somewhat hesitantly, "the Professional Women's Alliance, of which I am chair, brought this matter to President Curtis's attention, and we've passed a resolution calling for an end to this officially sanctioned discrimination against women."

"Now hold it here a minute. What about the men?" Junior White said solicitously from down the table, straightening slightly from a comfortable slump and barely turning his head. "I mean, don't those pants on the men's restroom signs sort of represent an official costume for men? A *culturally imposed*"–he looked innocently around— "way for men to dress? It's a lot harder to violate a man in a pair of pants than in a dress, isn't it? I mean, if a man is wearing pants, you've got to get the belt unbuckled and the button unbuttoned or the hook unhooked, and then the zipper is always going to be a problem, and then. . . ."

"What are the bathroom signs in Scotland like?" Talbot interrupted, disappointing Brumley, who suspected Junior White would have continued until the offending pants had been wrestled off over at least one work boot. He hoped Warren and the other student were enjoying this. "Maybe we could send someone to Scotland to do some research on the topic and I'll be glad to volunteer. Anybody else want to come?"

"I see," Bohannon said, smiling thinly, "that this matter is not being taken very seriously. But it will be. Dr. Weebles, could you get us started?"

Weebles had been called to President Curtis's office the previous day, the first time he had ever been so summoned, and he had been so flooded with joy and anxiety that he feared he might soil himself when he appeared and considered wearing an adult diaper. All his anxiety had been dispelled, however, when President Curtis, with the Vice president of Academic Affairs, the Vice president of Public Information, and the Vice president of Student Services in close attendance, took him completely into his confidences.

"This is the dumbest shit I've ever heard of," President Curtis declared. "It's worse than the Vietnam War stuff or those sweatshop protests. It's a goddamned farce is what it is. Bathroom door signs. Jesus Christ. That's what I'm supposed to worry about. Bathroom door signs. Maybe I'll just close the women's bathrooms, see how those dumb bitches like that. Let them piss in the shrubs. By god, that would show them a thing or two. Some people just don't know when they've got it made."

"You're absolutely right," Dodson of Public Relations agreed, "but I have to point out that not everyone will see it that way. The Professional Women's Alliance has some pretty sharp chicks in it who know which side their bread is buttered on and how to get the butter applied. Davis over there in English–she's used this gender thing to get the highest raises of anybody in the department. There are laws about sexual discrimination–federal laws," he said pointedly, "and they cover just about anything. Maybe even bathroom door signs. As much as I'd like to see their lily white asses shining in the bushes, I think we better take this one seriously. We've got an image to worry about."

"You know," President Curtis said stonily after a moment, "sometimes I'd like to abolish Public Relations. Not you, Dodson, just public information and public relations in general. Our goddamned *image*," he said with a sneer. "Everybody's shitting their pants over their goddamned *image*. You know what I'd like to do? I'd like to throw a rope on the Professional Women's Alliance and drag them behind a horse for about ten miles. There's an image I like. Believe me, they wouldn't be whining about bathroom door signs after that little gallop. But," he said with a sigh, surrendering to the times, "you're right. I suppose we will have to do something. Weebles, can you handle this?"

Weebles, within an ace of soiling himself, thought he could.

"Okay," Curtis said. "You try to handle what's-her-name—Bonnona, Banana, whatever—on the committee, the chairman of the Professional Women's Alliance, find out what they want on the goddamned doors, and bring it back here for me and Dodson to look at. Got it?"

Weebles certainly got it. A disciplined if abject player, he saw his greatest task would be to suppress his disbelief at the bathroom sign complaint and pretend to take the entire issue seriously. No principle had ever stood in the way of his advancement, and he didn't intend to let one now, not when President Curtis himself had taken notice of him.

The meeting, under Weebles maladroit direction, lasted two-and-a-half hours and was one of the most intricately absurd and therefore personally rewarding meetings Brumley had ever attended. It was not often that proof of the inefficiency, waste and sheer stupidity of the institution was so clearly revealed. Plus, there was the subject itself, a shameful trivialization of the consequential that promised along the way irony, farce, emotional outbursts, personality conflicts, and, if enough meetings were required, perhaps physical violence. Brumley could not believe that the Signage Committee was turning out so well and was mildly disappointed when it seemed at the meeting's close that a consensus had been reached and the problem virtually solved.

"Are we essentially agreed then?" Weebles asked. It was growing dark outside, and through the windows the lights lining the sidewalks were coming on. From the far end of the campus, the incessantly throbbing strobe lights of the Transuranic Department and Center for Life Form Enhancement smokestacks were becoming more evident.

"As Dr. Brumley suggested, the Greek letters ♂ and ♀–what are they again?"

"Anthro and Gyn," Brumley said, and only Conners and Talbot shot him questioning glances. Down the table, he was fairly sure he heard a stifled laugh from Warren, who with his fellow student had maintained a determined silence.

"Yes, Anthro and Gyn will be the new symbols for Middle State's bathroom doors. Like you say," Weebles nodded at Brumely with respect, "not only does their use solve the bathroom signage problem, but it acquaints our students with a couple of the less familiar letters of the Greek alphabet, and does so outside the traditional classroom format. I'd say that we've solved a thorny cultural issue and advanced education with cutting edge techniques. We should thank Dr. Brumley for such a good idea."

"It seemed like a good idea," Weebles said two weeks later when the idea had proved a total failure and he had called an emergency meeting of the Signage Committee, "but we've got complaints, lots of complaints."

The complaint he was most concerned with was President Curtis's profanity-laced rant the previous day over the failure of the bathroom signage problem to cease bothering him.

"Students," Weebles went on, "can't keep the signs straight and large numbers of them are going into the wrong gender's restroom by mistake. Don't tell me you haven't seen the red faces or heard the shrieks. Males are starting to use the general confusion to go in the wrong restroom on purpose; maybe some of the females are too. Students are starting to urinate—ah, relieve themselves–in the shrubbery. Perverts are showing up and taking advantage of the confusion to expose themselves. For god's sake, it's worse than the streaking crisis. Reporters, there are reporters starting to ask questions. This is *serious*," Weebles said, fear in his voice. "Think how this could look on our records if we don't get it solved. We've got to come up with something."

"I suppose Men and Women are still out," Brumley inquired, hoping for some action. He noticed that neither Warren nor the female student member had shown up. No doubt the first meeting, however entertainingly absurd, had been more than they could bear. This one promised worse, and Brumley was glad Warren had chosen not to come.

Weebles looked down the table at Dr. Bohannon.

"*If* we spell women wimyn," she said firmly.

"And men myn?" Brumley had to ask.

"No, not spell men myn. Men is not derived from women; women, in the cultural bias of our language, is derived from men–its very etymology shows the demonizing of women by naming them the woe of men."

"That's not the etymology of women," Brumley said as dispassionately as he could, knowing there was little use. "The word comes from wumman, Middle English, in turn derived from wifman, Old English, the wife of man." He owed his etymological knowledge, of course, to Hobart.

"Yes, you see," Bohannon pounced, "same thing, women defined only in relation to men, their wives, vassals, slaves."

Maybe the woe of man was a better etymology, Brumley thought; for Dr. Bohannon, at least, men were apparently a woe to women. Thank god she doesn't have a magic wand, it came to him, or we'd all be pigs–though Weebles with a snout and bristles might be closer to the runt's inner truth than his present form. Or maybe Bohannon was only emulating Davis of English, on the make, riding an unassailable principle and willing to sue if accused of exploiting such.

"All right, why not spell women wimyn?" one of the lesser administrators offered.

"I mentioned there were reporters sniffing around," Weebles reminded them. "They may not be able to write about perverts or pissing—urinating–in the bushes, but if we stick Wimyn up on the female restroom doors, it'll be on Paul Harvey tomorrow. Let's think about this."

"You're probably right," Dr. Bohannon finally agreed resignedly. "We don't want to be made into laughingstocks."

"Wait," Brumley said. "Wait a minute. Laughingstocks? I thought this was a matter of principle, not of careers or institutional image preservation. If we believe there's some injustice behind how women is spelled, then we should spell it in a just way, not chicken out if our personal situation is threatened. That would be ignoble."

"You know, I haven't seen you set fire to yourself over what you think is the stupidity and corruption of Middle State's administration or the general drift of society," Bohannon said, and the lack of anger or sarcasm in her voice was to Brumley a marvel. She would go far indeed. The number of scandalized eyes on him from around the table demanded a reply.

"You've got a point," he conceded with a forced smile. "To a degree we're all moral failures."

"I don't know about this moral failure stuff," Weebles interrupted, "but we've got to get this restroom thing straightened out. Our Greek symbols won't fly. Men and Women I guess are out."

"Dr. Weebles, could we have guards—or attendants—outside each restroom to give instructions?" one of the lesser administrators asked.

"Too expensive."

"How about a recording played over a speaker by the appropriate door that said Men. Men. Men. And Women. Women. Women?"

"That's probably too expensive, too. And anyway, it would drive you crazy. Think about it: you go in, you get settled, and it's Men. Men. Men. Or," he quickly added, "Women. Women. Women."

"Hey, what about pictures, you know, of private parts?" Junior White offered, elbowing lightly the absolutely bewildered electrical shop technician who again sat beside him. Brumley caught the glint in his eyes.

"You know," Brumley said with encouragement, after a moment of shocked silence had passed. "You know, that might be an idea. It would show the students that Middle State is not a prudish institution but one on the cutting edge, so to speak, of educational innovation."

"I don't know," Weebles said uneasily. He had heard *cutting edge* and *educational innovation* and that had to be good; but not all was right. "Private parts on the doors? Put those up and believe me, those reporters would have a film crew here before the paint was dry."

"You've got a point, I guess." Brumley pretended to give up reluctantly on a possibly brilliant solution. "Would there be other objections?"

He hoped to keep the ball rolling, and Junior White gave it a mighty kick.

"Yeah," he said. "How big would we make the cocks? And, uh, what state would they be in, if you get what I mean? We wouldn't want to intimidate any genders."

"Look," Weebles burst almost in tears, "we can't keep waffling around. We've got to. . .."

And then his one great idea came to him.

"Listen," he said excitedly, "Wait. What about this. Oh, yes. Let's take the Greek alphabet symbols again and liven them up a little, make them unmistakable, more life-like, more *cutting edge*."

"Let's hear it," Dr. Bohannon said encouragingly, and Weebles described his solution. Brumley, catching the unbelieving looks of Talbot and Conners, pronounced the idea one of the most innovative he could imagine, and Weebles' brainstorm, at once conciliatory and clarifying, was passed unanimously. By the end of the week the graphics department had drawn up trial versions of Weebles inspiration for him to submit to President Curtis, and the Signage Committee, its labors successfully complete, was disbanded. The signs were to be as follows.

For the males, ♂

For the females, ♀

twelve
OLD CADOON

Warren had been named to serve on the Signage Committee by President Curtis, who skimmed Warren's lucid, compelling letter about not graduating on time with alarm and also a sense of deja vu. He distinctly recalled seeing this letter, or one like it, not long ago and unwillingly summoned Administrative Assistant Larson to clear up the matter and assign the uppity brat to some punishing task disguised as an honor.

"Oh, yes, Dr. Brumley in the Humanities College wrote you about this last year, last spring, remember?" She had rushed down from her office when President Curtis had buzzed her. "You didn't want to read his letter at first, but I told you it might be important."

"Did I answer it?"

"No, sir, you didn't."

"Why didn't I?"

"I believe you were busy. It was just before your recruiting trip to Cannes."

"Did you answer it?"

"No, sir."

"Do you think I should answer this one?"

"Yes, sir."

"Why, Larson? Expand a little without me having to pry it out of you."

"Well, sir, Warren–that's the student's name, Christopher Warren–says he took all the courses his first three years as spelled out in the catalog. Now that he's a senior, not enough of the remaining courses he needs to graduate are offered this year, so he'll have to stay an extra semester or year. He points out it will cost him several thousand dollars—he itemizes it pretty thoroughly—and neither he nor his parents can afford it. And, he adds, he doesn't want to go another year; he wants to graduate in the four years he planned on."

"He can't afford it, huh," President Curtis said with a satisfied smile, settling back on the thick, supple leather of his chair. "That means his parents can't be too important. I don't think we have a problem. Send him Number Four."

Number Four was a standard letter that expressed great concern at the correspondent's problem but sincerely regretted that a deadline or a violation of university policy or a lack of funds or some combination of these were involved and that nothing, therefore, could be done.

"Yes, sir. Number Four."

"And bring it by before you stamp my signature on it. I want to add a personal note of sympathy. I'll even sign it myself. Has that teardrop machine come in yet? I think Dodson said he would get us one."

Vice president Dodson of Public Relations had learned that institutions could now purchase a device that produced saline drops of exactly the average size of human tears and with a chemical composition indistinguishable by gas chromatography from the real article. In whatever amounts might be called for, randomly or in a pattern, the device would sprinkle the drops on an envelope, a letter, or even a legal document.

"I don't believe it's arrived yet, sir."

"I suppose we'll have to do without it, then. Now, somebody named Brumley wrote a letter similar to this one of what's-his-name, Warren. Does Brumley not have the courses to graduate either? I thought you said Brumley was on the faculty."

"He is, sir. His letter was about Warren, about Warren's not graduating on time. Warren is a student of Brumley."

"Well I'll be damned. So this Brunley's a do-gooder. That means he may be a real troublemaker, though he's so far down on the totem pole he can't be too much of a problem. Come to think of it, I believe he's the one Staull said wrote a memo that made Dean Whatever-his-name is over in Humanities look bad. A wise-ass memo."

"Sir, Brumley is one of those who doesn't know which side his bread is buttered on," Larson said. She had never liked Brumley, who she knew was not impressed by her quick and successful rise from teaching in his department to being an Assistant to the President.

"In that case, keep an eye on him. And if tries to help this Warren brat out, let me know."

"Yes, sir, I will, sir. But did you read all of Warren's letter?" She knew he hadn't.

"I read enough to know I didn't want to read any more. So," he unwillingly picked up Warren's letter, "he can't graduate, let's see. . . ." He began to read it.

"What the hell! Who does this little bastard think he is, anyway? 'If I can get no satisfaction from you, I will take my case to the Reigning Board'. What is this, a threat? And where'd he learn to write like that—'no satisfaction from you, I will take my case'? And how does he know anything about the Board? He's just an ordinary student, isn't he; he's not in Student Government or a fraternity? Maybe this Brumley is clueing him in, maybe this is a conspiracy of some kind."

He looked at Larson for confirmation or at least sympathy. She assumed her most solemn expression of pained commiseration.

"Just because we screwed up," President Curtis fumed, "doesn't mean he has any right to complain, not if he knows what's good for him. Now we've probably got to do something."

"If you don't mind my saying so, sir, I'd just go ahead and send him Number Four and see how it comes out. If nothing else, it'll be a delay, and time is on our side, as the song says. Needless to say, we don't admit any fault, but he's young—maybe a show of sympathy and understanding will satisfy him. And if not, there are still Numbers Five and Eight to give us even more time."

Number Five announced that the problem was real and that President Curtis was looking into it. Number Eight announced the formation of a committee, or, if the problem might result in a lawsuit, a Task Force to examine the issue.

"You, know, sir, we're starting to hear lots of complaints like Warren's. So far most students just go to their department chair and swallow whatever excuse they're given and then go the extra semester or year without much more fuss. But if there's any publicity of Warren's situation, there might be an organized movement, with real publicity."

"Organized?" President Curtis said with alarm. "Publicity? Goddamnit, why wasn't I told about this problem?"

"Oh, you were, sir. In this memo I wrote you over a year ago. I outlined the situation, as you can see, as being due to your budgeting money to non-instructional areas with a corresponding shrinkage of available instructors and hence of courses offered."

She handed a copy of the memo to him with some trepidation. President Curtis looked at it. In the margin, in his handwriting, was scrawled: Don't bother me with this.

"Yes. As I recall, I had other executive decisions to deal with at the time. Listen, why can't we give him a full scholarship, a free ride for the extra semester or year?"

"It might work, yes. But he says he doesn't want. . . ."

"All right, I remember, he doesn't want to go an extra semester or year; he wants out. What's the matter with him, anyway? Doesn't he know these are the happiest years of his life? He ought to be grateful for the opportunity for an extra happiest year of his life, or even two or three. Especially if he doesn't have to foot the bill. I don't think he knows which side his bread is buttered on. Maybe if I talk to him I can get him to see the light. Meantime, put him on that idiot Signage Committee."

The call from Curtis's office requesting him to meet with the President left Warren both hopeful and frightened. Brumley as well was unsure which response was appropriate.

"Maybe your letter impressed him," Brumley said. "Maybe you made your point. He's got to be a reasonable man. Anybody can see how wrong it is to require students to have certain courses to graduate and then not offer them. Especially as conscientious as you've been in following the prescribed schedules."

He was far from sure Curtis was a reasonable man, or one whose reason operated to a decent degree unfettered from self-interest.

"Dr. Brumley, do you think I ought to dress up when I go over—wear a tie?"

"No. Be who you are. He's got your story from your letter; he wants to see what you're like."

"What do you mean? I mean, why?"

"You know, just to judge you. Be yourself, you'll be all right."

President Curtis, Brumley was sure, prided himself on sizing up those who appeared before him, gauging their weaknesses.

When Warren walked into President Curtis's opulent office, Carl Colson was sitting at ease to the side of the enormous presidential desk, the brim of his cap with its Pi symbol pulled low, shading his eyes. Warren, thinking the receptionist who directed him in was unaware of a meeting in progress, started apologetically to back out.

"No, no, come on in," President Curtis boomed. "Carl and I–do you know Carl? Carl Colson, Chris Warren–Chris, Carl."

Colson let the faint smirk he'd been wearing morph into a hearty, innocent greeting. Warren nodded.

"Yes, Chris and me are in Dr. Brummey's class together."

"Brumley," Warren corrected him.

"Oh," Colson said, his features tightening slightly in resentment. "Brumley, right. It's one of those humanities classes. It's required," he said to President Curtis, to explain why he would even be in such a class with Warren and taught by Brumley.

"Yes," President Curtis said in a clipped voice, the name Brumley reminding him that troublemakers were everywhere.

"But have a chair, Chris. I got your letter and I want to tell you that I thought, if our students can write this well, if they have such a way with words, well, I'm proud to be president of this university. Are you a natural at this writing stuff or did somebody teach you how?"

"Dr. Brumley did."

President Curtis glanced quickly at Warren to find an apparently guileless face.

"Well. Is that right. So, let me get. . . ."

"Dr. Curtis," Warren said without looking at Colson, "do you mind if we talk alone?"

Colson stiffened in his chair. President Curtis for a moment said nothing but easily regained his composure.

"No, why no. Carl, could you excuse us?" As Colson slowly rose and walked to the door, Curtis gave him a thumbs-up. "You're doing great work with Student Government, Carl my man. Keep it up."

"You know Carl, you say?" he said to Warren after Colson had gone out. "One of our better students. He was just saying his fraternity was looking for some new upperclassmen pledges. Pi Iota. They're a great bunch, those Pi's. And you know, Chris," he said, growing serious, "I might can fix you up in that area. I read your letter, as I said. Now I don't want to point any fingers or play the blame game, but it's pretty clear to me that someone, somewhere dropped the ball. I don't know why the courses you need aren't offered. . . ."

"It's because there aren't enough instructors who can legitimately teach them," Warren said, more assertively than he knew he should. "Even if a professor gave up another course they were scheduled to teach so that I could get the ones I need, some other student would then have their required courses taken away. The problem is too few instructors."

"That is a possible perception, and that's unfortunate," President Curtis said smoothly, "and maybe I can make up for the mistake. I'm prepared to offer you free tuition for the entire next school year so you can return to Middle State and get your diploma."

Warren, to seem considering the offer and to show gratitude, said nothing for a few moments.

"President Curtis, that's nice, but I'd still have a lot of expenses—books and dorm fees and food. . . ."

"You know, Chris," President Curtis said with affected expansiveness, "you know what I'm going to do? How about I throw in dorm fees as well? How about that?"

"Sir, I appreciate it, but I want to graduate on time, with my class. There are others in the same boat with me, two, maybe three guys on my dorm floor who can't get the courses they need to graduate on time. I'd like to have my courses offered; I imagine they would theirs too."

"Chris, you drive a hard bargain. Much of this is up to the scheduling rotation of your department and the full-time equivalent demands in that budgetary area. And you know that the percentage of monies allocated by the state to higher education as compared to state per capita income has declined over the past decade. But let me look into it. Just remember my offer if nothing turns up. Heck, we might even be able to work out something on your incidental expenses, on books and such, food even, even walking around money. And remember," he said confidentially, "Carl's fraternity is looking for upperclass pledges next year. Meanwhile, I'll find out what I can about your situation and get back to you."

"Larson," President Curtis called over his intercom after Warren had gone, "Get a Number 4 ready to send, one appropriate to this matter. If he won't jump on the free-ride train in two days, then send it. It'll at least buy some time, maybe shut him up altogether, I don't know. He's hard to read."

Two hours later, Warren was in Brumley's office, telling Brumley and Hobart what had transpired.

"A free ride, huh?" Hobart marveled. "There's something behind all this. They want you to go away, or your complaint to." He took a great pull from his quart-sized coffee mug.

"You might consider taking him up on it," Brumley suggested.

"I don't know," Warren said.

"How much would it cost our cherished institution," Hobart mused, "to hire adjuncts to teach the freshman comp courses to free up, say, you and me Brumley, to offer Mr. Warren here the necessary upper-division courses? Probably not as much as his free ride would. Why not do that for now, then hire enough instructors to make sure the problem doesn't keep recurring?"

"They'd rather buy off or threaten or buffalo the students. They don't count on you"–he turned to Warren–"pushing the issue. So they try to handle the students individually. That way they don't have to admit publicly being wrong. And they can save monies for other budgetary areas. . . ."

"Oh god," Hobart winced, "you're talking like them: 'saving monies for budgetary areas'. Or is it *arias*, conflation from Old French and Latin, lower atmosphere, meaning hot air about hiding and wasting money. 'Let us sing a budgetary aria'."

"That was irony, you know that," Brumley said. "I'll never talk like them. But you get the point. What Curtis doesn't want is for his spending priorities–you like that?–to be made public, especially if they show all the blather about concern for students to be. . .well, blather."

Warren knew little about budgetary areas and monies and spending priorities and didn't want to. He wanted the required courses he needed to graduate to be offered. But the free ride was tempting.

"I'm going to think about the free ride," he said. "But maybe if I don't say anything for a while he'll can get those courses offered."

"I'm going to write the Board," Warren told Brumley later that week as he handed him the Number Four Larson had finally forwarded to him. Brumley read through the bureaucratic clot of insincerity. Due to an unfortunate coincidence of scheduling complexities and budgetary constraints, it was possible to finally decipher that nothing could be done. Thank god, Brumley thought, Warren knew a dodge when he read one.

"Did you tell him in your letter you'd write them?"

"Yes."

"Then do it. Write the Board, everyone on it. Can you get their addresses? I can help you if you'd like. Just say the word. In fact, I think I'll do a little writing myself, to a wider audience."

"Would you mind checking over mine when I'm through?" Warren asked. "I'd rather write it on my own, but I don't want to make any mistakes—I don't mean spelling or anything like that. I don't want to be too humble. Or angry. But I'd rather write it myself." He was beginning to sense that involving anyone else, anyone that Curtis or the Board could get back at, was not the thing to do.

"Be glad to check over it," Brumley said, fairly certain Warren would get the tone about right. "You can type it on my computer if you'd like. I've got classes tomorrow morning; if you're free, drop by and help yourself."

"Thanks. I probably will. By the way, how did the Signage Committee turn out? Anthro and Gyn still going up on the doors?" He laughed at Brumley's mock-innocent face.

"I think they're out," Brumley replied with exaggerated sadness. "Stub—Dr. Weebles—took the committee decision to President Curtis who called in Vice president Dodson of Public Relations who literally passed out when Stub showed them an 8x10 blowup of the markers that Weebles had the Graphic Arts division draw up. Curtis chewed Weebles out so bad that—at least according to Conners of Chemistry—he shrunk another two inches and shit himself. Then, the story is, he bolted from Curtis's office and ran the roads all night in his suit and tie and was found three miles out of town the next morning by Junior White, unconscious in a ditch. Poor guy. He'll pull through, but he'll never be the same."

"What's going to happen? What's going on the doors?"

"Who knows? According to Talbot, the Professional Women's Association has about been convinced by President Curtis that Men and Women would be fine if all faculty women at Middle State are given a five percent raise next year in addition to the usual one. If they're not convinced, Vice president Dodson came up with a urinal for the Men's doors and a commode for the Women's. There could still be confusion, I'd think, but I believe Dr. Bohannon and her group will see the light."

"So nothing will change?"

"Not quite. Someone—in this case the female faculty—will get a bigger cut of the pie, though probably still not their fair share and for the wrong reason. And someone else a smaller one, someone with no power whatever. We'll find out who soon enough."

A week after Warren had sent a copy of his letter to each member of the Reigning Board, Sola overtook him on his way back to the dorm late one afternoon.

"Want to hit the smokestack after the Asteroid Program tonight? I've got some good stuff." Climbing one or the other of the smokestacks to the phony carillon to get stoned had become a recent tradition among the type of student who saw a rightness and nearly a duty in smoking pot on a smokestack that never smoked. Over the weekend Warren had written two papers for his classes and was caught up on his readings for tomorrow. He deserved a break, and besides, Sola, through careful research and experimentation, always managed to find the best marijuana on campus and at the best price.

"Why not," he said to Sola. "What time does that asteroid thing begin?"

"Six. Got any idea what it's supposed to be?"

"Asteroid preparedness. Didn't you know? This is Asteroid Preparedness Week. There's a meeting on it at every dorm this week."

"Can you believe it?"

"I can believe anything about this place. I used to be prepared to graduate in four years. Now I've got to be prepared for an asteroid. Are you going?"

"Might as well. See what it's about. It'll be right after dinner; no sense going back to the room."

Asteroid Preparedness Night at Wilder Dorm, the first of the dorm programs, was to be presided over by Cutter of Emergency Preparedness with assistance from Half-life Anderson, specially hired for the occasion to handle any thorny technical questions that might arise. Vice president Hays was saving himself for presentations to the faculty and hopefully to administrators if President Curtis reversed his decision that managers were exempt from such wastes of time. But with Cutter's blundering help Hays had grudgingly lowered himself to produce a program sure to be both entertaining and educational for the students. It opened with a computer-projected image on a large screen at the end of the cafeteria. It showed a ball with other balls going around it, which elicited to Cutter's surprise a chorus of groans and catcalls from the audience. Half-life Anderson rose to the occasion.

"No, no, this isn't what you think, it's not a model of the atom. This is the solar system and . . . ."

"Where's the asteroid?" a voice asked.

"We're just about to get to it. I'll have to use this laser pointer to show you where the asteroid might come from. Okay, it would be somewhere out here in the far reaches of outer space. . . ."

"Between the orbits of Mars and Jupiter, mainly," Bolinger called out with dismay, trying to disguise his voice and direct Half-life to some accuracy.

"Yes, but not always," Half-life said triumphantly, "because it could--" he slashed the ruby dot of the laser down to the third ball from the central ball–"because it could at any moment hit the earth."

"Wait," Warren said. "Not at any moment, right? I mean, the asteroid's not conscious; it's not waiting to spring on us."

"It might be," Bolinger piped up, seeing he could drop his disguise and keep the ball rolling while seeming to be on Half-life's side. "There might be intelligent life on it. Maybe aliens are guiding it and will blast off of it in space ships before it hits and then land and take things over after most of us have been wiped out."

"Well, that's not very likely," Half-life said uneasily, turning to a baffled Cutter for support that was not forthcoming. "I mean, there's no evidence that there's life on the asteroid."

"No, but there's a chance there is," Shepherd threw in from the audience. "You can't rule it out completely."

"No, I guess not, not completely."

"What's the chance of the asteroid hitting us? Is it as good a chance as there being life on it?" Warren asked. "I read somebody had calculated there was a very good chance of intelligent life somewhere other than earth. Isn't that right? Maybe it's on the asteroid."

"Gee, I don't know," Half-life admitted, his laser pointer, its mission forgotten, flashing blindingly around the cafeteria. "But if it is, we ought to worry about the asteroid hitting us first. That's the first thing that would happen."

"Yes," Bolinger agreed, glad again to be backing his instructor. "But we shouldn't forget the possibility of alien invasion. I think we should have an Alien Invasion Week sometimes soon, just in case."

Cutter made a note to raise the possibility for such an observance to Vice president Hays the next day, while Half-life Anderson, unsure if his leg was being pulled, went on with his presentation as most of the students, singly at first and then en masse, left for their rooms or wherever else they were going.

"I think Half-life is an alien," Bolinger proclaimed before he left Warren and Sola to go back to his room, "but not an intelligent one, not unless he has a plan to lull us into a stupor and then take over our minds. He's working on taking over our minds now—the stupor part he's got down pat."

Angling across the Quadrangle toward the library, Warren and Sola picked up the pace. It was already near eight o'clock.

"Do you think the truck will be there?" Warren asked.

"Should be. It has been every night for the last two weeks."

A university maintenance truck, an extension ladder on its rack, was being parked regularly behind the library and only a short distance from the base of the Center for Life Form Enhancement's smokestack. Since the steps around and up the stack began ten feet off the ground, they had used the convenient ladder twice before to reach them.

Once they climbed to the steps, Sola pulled up the ladder behind them and leaned it lengthwise on the winding stairs up to the carillon, then followed Warren up to the carillon enclosure. They stopped before entering to take in the view from a hundred feet up.

"Evening, gentlemen," said a voice from the dark beyond the carillon control panel. "Have you left me a way down?"

"Hey," Warren said after the shock had subsided.

"Hope I didn't startle you. I thought if I kept quiet you might go away. But I remembered my hoist and thought you might have found it. I couldn't get down if you pitched it down."

"We didn't see anything. What are you doing up here?"

The owner of the voice moved toward the door into the moonlight. He was an old man, or at least older than anyone who climbed one of the smokestacks without authorization ought to be. "Looking around. Thinking. I try to get up here at least once a month, until winter comes. My name's Cadoon. Matt Cadoon. I used to teach here. I'm better known as Old Cadoon."

"How are you," Warren said, shaking his hand. The old man, now that Warren could take him in, looked wiry and fit.

"Mr. Cadoon," Sola said, doing likewise.

"I notice you boys didn't give me your names–no, no," he said waving off their attempt to do so. "Better that you don't. If I get caught and you get away, then I won't have to lie, not that I'd mind lying in such circumstances. How'd you get to the steps?"

"We used a ladder."

"One you took–borrowed–off that maintenance truck parked by the library?"

"Yes, sir."

"Did you pull it up behind you?"

"Yes, sir."

"Good. If you hadn't, you wouldn't be worth talking to."

"How did you get up?" Sola asked.

"I've got a portable block-and-tackle with a harness. I hook it with a pole about three steps up, on the outside of the steps. Then I hide the pole, get in the harness and pull myself up. Getting on the steps is the hard part, but I can still manage pretty well. Then I carry the whole apparatus up a little way and hang it so it's under the steps. It's invisible from the ground and evidently, since you missed it, pretty much so from the steps."

"You just climb up here and sit?"

"No, I climb up here and sit and think. Or stand and think. Did either of you bring a bottle or a joint with you? Don't worry, I won't hit you up for a share of either, or inform the authorities. It's hard enough for me to get up and down here unimpaired. Age is impairment enough. But don't let me stop you. Have at it,"

"No, we didn't bring anything," Warren lied. "We just wanted to climb up here."

Old Cadoon regarded them for a moment and moved back to a pile of cushions beyond the carillonneur's seat.

"Sit down," he said. "Though there's only one chair. Let's keep the doors open and have a view. You can't tell they're open from below. I've checked."

"So," Sola said after a long silence, "why do you come up here to think?"

"Good view," Old Cadoon said. "A good view made better because it's off-limits. Besides, I get a little exercise climbing up."

"What," Warren finally ventured, "do you think about up here?"

"Usually it's the same things I think about when I'm down there."

There was another silence. From below an occasional voice could be heard, along with the sound of cars whose headlights moved in vague patterns about the streets. From their vantage point far above the lights that illuminated the sidewalks and drives about campus the stars stood out even in competition with the moon. Only the frantic strobe lights atop the stacks defiled the sky, and from where they sat they could see none of them.

"What did you teach?" Doug asked.

"I was in the English Department."

"That's my major," Warren blurted out, but Old Cadoon said nothing.

"Are you retired?" Warren tried again.

"Yes," Old Cadoon replied. "Forcibly retired, more or less."

Warren and Sola, both embarrassed, said nothing.

"What forcibly retired means," Old Cadoon said easily, "is that they gave me a choice of retiring right away or teaching four sections of freshman composition each semester until I retired voluntarily. I hung on for a year and got in a few good licks. But I couldn't take it. Besides, I had my time in, a little pension coming."

"Sorry, boys," he said after a moment. "I didn't mean to get started.

Crank up that joint or crack that bottle. I'm sure you brought one. Most everybody who comes up here does."

"What did you do that made them retire you?" Warren asked. He wanted Sola to produce the joint, but was still cautious.

"I let them know that I knew they were self-serving, dishonorable hypocrites. Who weren't smart."

"Who? You mean the administrators?" Warren still wasn't too sure who fell under the heading of administrator or why they had control of teachers, who to him ought to be in charge.

People like President Curtis were pretty surely administrators; Eigleman had to be; the Vice presidents were. But what about Dr. Cole, or even Dr. Brumley. They both taught, though Cole didn't teach much. What determined an administrator and what did they do? Were administration and management the same? And how was it they could forcibly retire someone?

"Yes," Old Cadoon said, "and those who hoped someday to be administrators, the faculty who hoped to. But listen, you can't be interested in this. Surely to god you've got better things to do"

"I've got Dr. Cole mad at me," Warren offered. "He is an administrator, isn't he?"

"Oh yes. He is indeed an administrator."

"And even President Curtis– he may be on my case, too. I was supposed to graduate this spring but they didn't offer the courses that I had to take and I've got to come back another year. I told them I didn't have the money, but it doesn't seem to matter."

"You haven't told them they were self-serving, dishonorable hypocrites, have you?" Old Cadoon chuckled.

"No, sir."

"That's good. Doing so would be neither polite nor wise. Tell me something," he said after they had watched a few random headlights move about below. "You say you're an English major. What book is big on campus these days?"

"I don't know," Warren said. "What do you mean?"

"Is there a book," Old Cadoon said from the dark, "probably a contemporary novel, that's assigned in freshman composition courses by a number of instructors or that students are reading on their own?"

"I don't think so," Warren said. "I don't think they read novels in freshman comp. I didn't have to."

"Me either," Sola said. "We had a book with stories–essays–in them."

"Do you remember who wrote them?" Old Cadoon asked. "Montaigne? Hazlitt? Orwell?"

"I don't think it was any of them. They were about multiculture."

"But no novel?"

"No."

"Were the essays any good?"

"No."

"Do you say that as an expert in prose style, as an analyst of argument? Or were they just no good?"

"They were all alike, except one would be about how bad it was to be discriminated against because the person writing it was a woman. Or black, or gay or an Indian–a Native American."

"Sounds insightful. They weren't as interesting as *The Catcher in the Rye*, I'd be willing to bet. Ever hear of that one?"

"I've read it," Warren said, with more pride than he meant.

"Well I'll be damned," Old Cadoon said, leaning forward for a better view of Warren. "Read it on your own? I mean, was it a class assignment?"

"No, sir. Well, Dr. Brumley mentioned it in class so I got it."

"Brumley, eh?" Old Cadoon nodded. "I read his letter to the editor about the student who–say, I guess you're the student. Am I right?"

"Yes, sir. Chris Warren."

"Chris Warren. Now I remember. That was a courageous letter Brumley wrote, a dangerous one. Curtis had to answer it, or one of his lackeys did, which means Brumley's in serious trouble even if he does have tenure. Wonder how they'll get him." He stared out beyond the railings.

"But back to Salinger. Did you like the book?"

"Yes, okay. It was depressing. But I couldn't put it down."

"I picked it up almost forty years ago," Old Cadoon said. "That was the big book back when I first started teaching. Not many college students escaped reading it, or wanted to. After it came *Lord of the Flies*, then *One Flew Over the Cuckoo's Nest, Catch-22, The Lord of the*

Rings. Around 1980 that all stopped. Something happened, I'm not sure what. They stopped having freshman read novels. I complained, but I complained too much and was ignored. Actually, though, I didn't complain enough."

In the southeastern sky, one bright star cut easily through the moon's obscuring glow. From below there were fewer indistinct noises, and only an occasional pair of headlights traced along the streets.

"Nice night," Sola finally said.

"Yes, it is," Old Cadoon agreed. "Now and early spring are good times to come up here. I like early spring better–better sky. Orion's still out–the Pleiades, Sirius."

"That's Jupiter, I think," Warren said, indicating the bright star in the southeast.

"You sure it isn't Saturn?" Sola suggested.

"I don't think so. Saturn isn't that bright."

"If we had binoculars, we could tell."

"Gentlemen," Old Cadoon announced from the dark, "I'm impressed. Not many students know the night skies, or even that there are night skies. Television declares the glory of God, and the Internet showeth forth his handiwork."

"That's pretty good," Warren said, smiling.

"Not many would have recognized the allusion," Old Cadoon said, "or the commentary. I'm afraid, boys, that things are bad."

"I don't know," Sola protested. "Students aren't that sorry, are they? Things can't be that bad."

"Maybe I do judge the students too harshly. But your friend here isn't going to graduate this spring, and I imagine his grades are pretty good, right?"

"They're ok," Warren said.

"GPA?" Old Cadoon asked, unfazed by Warren's reticence.

"Three point eight."

Old Cadoon whistled.

"And yet you're not going to graduate. It'll cost you, what–several thousand more? And everybody–Cole and Curtis did you say?–is just weeping sympathy but there's nothing they can do except find some way to get rid of whoever exposes the truth–Brumley, I'm afraid. Yes,

I'd call that bad. Maybe if you had lower grades, they might pull some strings and correct their mistake. Maybe."

"Come on," Warren heard himself say with more disbelief than he should have. "You can't mean they don't want good students to graduate."

"Not if you mean by good students those that make high grades so they can become corporate lawyers or public relation experts or organization men in general. Or, god help us, organization women. Women can now much more easily join the ranks of the plunderers and call it liberation. No, they want that kind of student to graduate. But real students? Best that they disappear. They could cause real trouble down the road. Just look at Middle State—and it's like every other third-rate university. Even the second- and first-rate ones are starting to resemble it. If they have a higher purpose any more—and god knows I'm not talking about their 'mission statements' or any such crap—it's to train the young to hold jobs in corporate America. As though the only dream of the young is to have money to buy things."

He stood up and stretched.

"Maybe that is their dream. Maybe it always has been. I had another one, but it doesn't matter now. In fact," he said laughing, "any more I'm not even sure what it was. Who knows? Maybe Brumley does, maybe he has the same dream—you should ask him. I'd love to meet him and ask him myself, but I'm not exactly welcome on campus. Anyway, it is a beautiful night. If you get situated right up here, like we are now, you can't see those strobe lights. And the stars—and planets—are still up there. And I'm still able," he said, moving past Warren and Sola toward the stairs, "to get up and down these steps and spend a peaceful—and tonight a heartening—hour or two up here. But I must be going. Hope it's not too late for you to enjoy that joint. Goodnight, gentlemen. It's been a pleasure."

They heard the occasional muffled clang of Old Cadoon's descent until he wound to the other side of the stack and, as he neared the bottom, stepped more softly.

"That must be some kind of contraption he's got for pulling himself up," Warren said.

"And letting himself down."

"That's something. Him and all."

"It is."

"I wonder if he comes up here any particular day?"

"We could try next Wednesday," Sola said, producing the joint from an undetectable slit in his belt. "You don't think he'll take our ladder, do you?"

"No," Warren said. "Fire that thing up."

Sola, who through long practice had perfected the talent, was soon blowing amazingly dense and near-perfect smoke rings out over the railing.

"Could you get smoke rings out of a smokestack?" he mused as Warren took a mighty hit.

"Notlikely," Warren squeaked, then exhaled and gasped for air. "Anyway, there's never any smoke, here or from Transuranic's stack. I saw a fire in one of the Transuranic hood lines when I was here for summer orientation. Three years ago. But I don't remember any smoke coming out of their stack even then. Why do they even have them if no smoke ever comes out?"

The answer was simple, but was kept very quiet. The smokestacks with their towering heights were covert safety devices that functioned, should some truly massive leak of plutonium or escape of genetically altered organism occur, to spread the contamination over a large, distant area far downwind from Middle State. This expedient would mean more people or a larger ecosystem would sicken and perish much more slowly and less noticeably than if the poisons should settle in a small area just around the two research facilities and cause a sudden, spectacular die-off. Critson of the Center for Life Form Enhancement had yet to inform anyone higher up of the missing Better Boy sperm; Jenkins of Transuranics had written off the disappearing plutonium as an inescapable by-product of his research. Both were hoping no one would notice their problem, or care if they did.

thirteen
JUNIOR WHITE

Rumors of plutonium getting out from the Transuranic Department had not even registered with President Curtis, who almost daily faced career-threatening problems that were much more immediate. Constantly crouching in wait outside the range of his total control were the never-ending investigations, some criminal, of the Athletic Department; the shocking costs of faculty and administrative travel to increasingly exotic and expensive foreign venues; the rumors of rigged bids and kickbacks on the contract to build Middle State's multi-million dollar Wellness Center; and the gush of so-called scholarships pouring out to just about anybody or anything that applied for admission to Middle State. In the blink of an eye, any of these beasts could drag down his dream of moving up.

And now another one: Too Few Courses. The kid Warren's letter to the members of the Reigning Board President Curtis could easily handle. But that bastard Brumley, splashing Middle State's malfeasance across the letters-to-the-editor section of the *Journal* in a letter Curtis imagined was read by everyone in the state and to which he had to have Dodson of Public Relations write a long, inadequate bureaucratic gobble in reply—that was real trouble, that was airing our dirty linen *in public* as Dodson had written. The secret, President Curtis knew, was to keep Middle State's dirty linen in his own Laundromat, where he controlled the washers, the detergent concession and the change machines. This publicity, this whole mess, clearly endangered his career prospects, and President Curtis knew he would have to stifle Brumley, who might persevere and keep the heat on until the muddled injustice of Middle State's policies were too evident to weasel out of. Then, in an act that would be tantamount to admit being wrong, he might actually have to re-allocate money to academics that would be much more productively spent elsewhere to increase his chances for a better-paying, more prestigious presidency. Defusing the Too Few Courses crisis was clearly a top priority, even though the best strategy, President Curtis realized, might be simply to keep quiet and get rid of Brumley.

So plutonium was far down the list of his concerns, since a scant amount of plutonium, however chemically corrosive and radioactively lethal, was journalistically inert and provided no stimulating visuals for TV reportage. Besides, if there really was a threat, it was remote and too difficult for the local media or their audiences to understand. All of this meant that President Curtis, who had been briefed some time before by Administrative Assistant Larson on the plutonium rumors and long since forgotten them, was unprepared for the alarming developments she brought in with his morning coffee and Danish.

"There's a story here you might want to see, sir," Larson said as she placed the breakfast tray along with a newspaper on his desk littered with blueprints for another remodeling of Guildview, the presidential home. "It may have some bearing on the problem at Transuranics. Maybe at the Center for Life Form Enhancement, too."

"Oh, god," Curtis sighed, looking over the front page. "Which one–this one on the Uranium Enrichment Plant?"

"Yes, sir," Larson said with her tinkly, inappropriate laugh. She had recently learned from the *Bulletin of Administrative Assistants for Planning* that administrative assistants for planning should plan to keep their positions by being cheerful when delivering bad news to their superior.

"Let's see," President Curtis skimmed, "workers had been assured all was well; no dangerous substances; no hazard pay; foreman ate a tablespoon of uranium salt to show it safe; plutonium was present–isn't plutonium what Jenkins is so jumpy about over in Transuranic?–management hid information; incidence of cancer twenty times normal, blah, blah; management destroyed documents; government investigation; possible criminal charges. Criminal charges! What paper is this?–my god, the *Journal*. As if I didn't have enough problems. Quick, get Jenkins on the phone, now."

"We've got to keep the news of our plutonium getting out from getting out," he told a disheveled, panting Jenkins, who arrived still wearing a white bonnet and white cloth galoshes. Larson had dug out her earlier memo on the plutonium rumors and gone over it again with a now fully-alarmed Curtis. "You see what's in the paper on this Enrichment Plant crisis. Their plutonium is the same as our plutonium, right?"

"Not exactly, sir," Jenkins replied, his breath almost recovered. "Theirs was mostly the 239 isotope, which is fissionable; ours is nearly all 238, which isn't, or virtually isn't, but ours is more highly emissive of alpha. . . ."

"Jenkins, I'm not interested in a science lesson. How's it going to look on TV, in the newspapers? Plutonium is plutonium, right? It's bad stuff. That's all that's important–Joe Six-pack thinks it's bad stuff. Maybe it is bad stuff, I don't know. All I know is that we've got a potential problem on our hands that once it gets out of our hands will be a real problem. Look at this--" he shoved the *Journal* at Jenkins— "criminal charges, possible criminal charges. You know what that means? It means I might not be moving up the ladder, maybe not even president of this place. It means you won't be director of anything except maybe a shovel brigade. We won't look good in orange jump suits, Jenkins. Get your ass to work and find out what's happening to that plutonium. And do everything you can think of; money is no limit. In fact, it's just as important that we be seen trying to solve the problem as actually solving it, if you get my drift. You do get my drift, don't you?"

"I think I do, yes sir. And I've already had some ideas. It involves extensive, clandestine surveillance of our labs and the personal lives of our workers that will show we're willing to subvert the Constitution to find out where we're screwing up. I'm going to get Junior White in Electronics on it immediately. But it would be all right if we did solve the problem, too, wouldn't it? If we did find out what's happening to the plutonium?"

"Probably. I think so. But if what you find out makes us look bad, keep a lid on it, understand? I'm sure there won't be any embarrassing reports you have to write."

It was clear President Curtis expected no reports, and Jenkins understood that if necessary the missing plutonium was to be swept, perhaps even literally, under the rug.

"Jenkins," President Curtis called to him as he was leaving the office, "wait a minute. What the hell are those white things you've got on?"

When Junior White got the work order for a furtive installation of miniature cameras and microphones in all the hot side labs of the Transuranic Department, he was delighted. Not only would he receive the fillip of donning a spiffy pair of white overalls and cloth galoshes while doing the job, but also, whether he needed it or not, he could drape a respirator around his neck and appear truly a specialist and ready for any emergency, such as the pickled egg and whiskey fart Blubbo Hunt released one day deep in the Transuranic Processing Lab, an emission of such fetid toxicity that it tripped the building evacuation alarm, shutting down work for part of the morning and earning Blubbo the gratitude and respect of every hourly worker in the department. Even without the premium of exotic, eye-catching clothing, the hot side was a much sought after work site by all maintenance workers since one was not likely to be disturbed there by supervisors and there were many opportunities for relaxation and entertainment..

"All right, you shit-heads," White announced to the lounging technicians comparing their fantasy football teams in the change room. "Gab time is over. Horseplay is over. Old Junior is here to put in cameras and bugs and they'll be watching and listening to every scratch of your ass from now on—got a monitor in every big-wig's office up to the head of the FBI."

"Go to hell, White," one of the workers offered. He watched White eagerly climb into a pair of white coveralls, proudly fasten the hideous respirator around his neck, and slip the white cloth galoshes over his shoes.

"Carry this for you?" the technician asked, reaching for White's large work kit.

"No, my man, oh no," White quickly took it. "This stuff is highly confidential. If it fell into the wrong hands, there's no telling what laws could be broken with what's in there. Better let an expert handle it."

They went through the change room door into the hot side corridor.

"White's here," his escort said to the several lab technicians sitting or napping on upturned fifty-five-gallon drums containing low-level radioactive trash. "I think he's got some girlie magazines for sale."

"Not for you pricks, Brown. Nope, the party here at outlaw roost is over," White announced as they entered the lab. "From now on you've got to keep your minds on your work. Higher ups are afraid you're fucking up the world. What I've got in the old case here are mini-cameras and bugs that you're not supposed to know about that I'm putting in so you can be spied on."

"We're already spied on," the technician Brown retorted, pointing toward a surveillance camera in an upper corner of the lab.

"That thing? You call that thing a spy camera?" White said with disdain. "This is the only one in the room, right? Don't tell me you haven't figured out how to beat it—here, just look at this," and he pointed to a long, low cabinet along the wall just under the camera. "Let's take a look and. . . ." He opened the door and there on the bottom shelf among a comfortable bed of cotton glove liners and white shoe galoshes the technician Crumb was fast asleep.

"Plutonium's in the meadow!" White shouted at him. "It's in the cows!"

Crumb opened one eye and seeing it was White, languidly gave him the finger and rolled back to his nap.

"Well, not too hard to see how that's done," White nodded to Brown after he had closed Crumb back in. "Just duck out of the field of view, like you're looking for something you've dropped, and then snake into that cabinet and you're set. Nobody at the monitor is keeping up with every move in here—in fact, half the time nobody is at the monitor, and when they are, half that time they're asleep or reading one of the magazines I sold them. If they don't see you duck down, you're out of mind as soon as you're out of sight. You losers aren't being surveillanced and you know it. All this camera does is make the chicken shits who work hard anyway work even harder."

In the next lab, the blinds over the window of the emergency exit doorway to the corridor were tightly shut, and an elaborate frame that held an optical device and a photo of the empty lab taken from the same location as the camera sat in place over the lens of the lab's surveillance camera. A poker game was going on in the center of the room, complete with popcorn, beer, and cigars.

"All right, get your hands up, boys; game's over," White proclaimed as he breezed in behind Brown. "Here, give me a cut of that pot—watch it now, watch it. Better behave, you're all going to be TV stars now."

He walked over to the duped camera and inspected the apparatus while the poker game resumed.

"Not bad, not bad. But when I get through putting these babies in,"—he held out a handful of the mini-cameras— "the game is over. You won't be able to flip a coin without a reprimand. And I've got mikes, too."

"White," the current dealer said, shuffling with vigor, "what good does it do to tell us they're putting them in? We'll figure out how to beat them too."

"Yeah," said Faulks, the sullen organizer of the game, who came in shortly behind White. "You're wasting your time."

"Uh-uh. I don't think so. I've got some in here—let's see," and White rummaged in a small case he carried. "All right, here's one so small it looks like a speck of dirt; you couldn't find it in a month and for all you know there may be twenty more in every lab. And they don't need cables any more—all of them have their own transmitter that can be picked up a mile away if you've got the technology. And we've got the technology. I'd say your poker game has been shut down— permanent."

"Then what do we do?" asked the morose Faulks, who at some risk not only organized the poker game but also supplied the beer, snacks and cigars. Strangely, while a small cut of each pot was set aside for him to cover the cost of refreshments and provide a small profit, once the game began he went back to his work and never played.

"No problem," White said expansively. "First of all, since they don't trust me and have some shit-head coming over tonight to put in cameras I don't know about, you're going to have to have some way to interfere with mine and his both. What I can do for you is, I can put together a little interference device that will distort every picture sent out from a lab so that it looks like there's some screw-up in the receiving end or in the monitors, or there's some unknown buzz from electric lines or something. They'll go crazy trying to find it. But you'll have to be careful using it. Turn it on, deal the cards for about an hour, then stop the game and clear everything out and start acting like you're working and turn it off so the picture comes clear and they can see what busy beavers you are. In a little while–don't set a pattern–turn it back on and start dealing. If you won't set a pattern, maybe some days don't even use it, they'll spend years trying to find out what's wrong. They're $399.95 each. You've got forty people working back here. That comes to less than ten dollars a man, though I'm sure you'll want at least four of old Junior's distorters. You'll probably be using two at all times with a couple in reserve. So for less than forty dollars a man–a mere two hours' pay–you can catch up on your sleep, deal the cards, play chair soccer, shoot the shit, or, when the women are allowed to work back here, get in some grab-ass. What do you say?"

"Wait a minute, White," Faulks said. "That's the cameras. What about the bugs, the mikes?"

"The bugs? The bugs are no problem." He held out a handful. They were near-perfect replications of small insects. "I make them, and I'm the only one putting them in. I've got to tell the shit-heads where I put each one, but I can put together another little device that can be set up in a room that can distort the signal in a way that they'll never figure out what's wrong. And," he added, "with every purchase of White's Non-patented Picture Distorter, I'll throw in not one, but two–yes, two–White's Non-patented Sound Distorters. You can't beat that with a stick."

Within two days after the Plutonium Containment Task Force began with great care and an enormously expanded surveillance team to monitor the operation of each hot side lab, both picture and sound quality of the surveillance equipment began fluctuating between high resolution pictures of a busy, purposeful lab to long periods of fuzz and distortion and once to a wrestling video, a confusion which necessitated the hiring of four new electronic technicians to track down the problem. Eight months and two supervisors of electronic technicians later the problem had not been located, and all the technicians and many of the original surveillance team had been assigned to the labs as laboratory technicians. Once initiated into to the benefits of the hot side, none ever reported anything amiss. But in spite of added change room procedures, heightened radiation monitoring, and revised accounting techniques, the plutonium kept getting out.

The brooding technician Faulks knew how the plutonium was

getting out. He was stealing it, and it was a breeze. Even before he had hit on the distraction of the poker game, he had found little trouble in pilfering miniscule amounts at a time. With a small but excellent metal lathe at his home he easily turned out inch-long tantalum cans of a slightly greater than 1/4-inch inner-diameter. Plutonium would not eat through tantalum as it would steel, and since the plutonium came to the Transuranic Department fabricated into rods of exactly one quarter of an inch diameter, all Faulks had to do—a lunch hour gave him more than enough time—was hack-saw off in the hoods a small pellet of plutonium from a rod, fit it into one of the tantalum capsules, place on a cap of tantalum and weld the can shut in the micro-welder installed in the hood line. He then placed the tiny can in the litter on the floor of the hood and later slipped it inside a slightly larger capsule of a tough tungsten alloy and welded a top on it. Finally, he would pass the capsule, whose surface was highly contaminated with microscopic amounts of plutonium merely from being in the hood line, out with the usual trash into a decontamination box where he washed it until, wrapped in lead foil, it could pass in his pocket through the radiation monitoring devices without detection. Once he had started the popular poker game, the entire procedure accelerated, and over a period of seven years, with great circumspection, he had collected almost a pound of plutonium in nearly a hundred capsules. He kept them in a flat metal box under the rug beneath his recliner, the considerable heat they gave off wafting up through the chair's framework and providing a soothing relaxant after a stressful day stealing them.

Faulks knew he didn't have enough plutonium to make a nuclear bomb; he was pretty sure he didn't even have the right kind of plutonium for doing so. But it hardly mattered. All one needed to make a good-sized city uninhabitable for months and poison and kill a fair number of its unsuspecting citizens was to distribute a pound of plutonium through its streets.

How to do this he'd had only a few vague ideas, aware that he would likely kill himself in pulling off any of them. He could cut open each capsule on his lathe, but on contact with air the plutonium pellet inside would immediately begin to smolder and fill his home and his neighborhood with the smoke form of plutonium oxide. How long he would last, even wearing the full face respirator he had stolen from the lab, he wasn't sure, but well before he could cut open the hundredth capsule most of the others would have already burned and the unimaginable contamination be centered in his basement workshop. What he needed to really do a job was a portable, even automated lathe, a sort of tiny but extremely heavy-duty automatic can opener mounted in the bed of his pickup truck, along with an as yet ill-defined ejection mechanism that he could drive through some gray, hostile city on a damp or rainy night, opening and then propelling each capsule at precisely predetermined points to smolder insignificantly in the middle of busy streets until the entire metropolis was permeated with invisible dust of the most deadly substance known to exist. Faulks found dark satisfaction in knowing that, in essence, plutonium was not found in nature. It was strictly man made and, like all scientific discoveries and technological innovations, had certain side-effects that hadn't quite been foreseen. He wanted everyone—not just the scientists—to know and understand humanity's blind handiwork. No political or ethnic or religious or class cause motivated him. It was personal. Humankind, by its own standards, was a mistake whose instinctual powers and evolutionary cunning far outstripped its wisdom, nowhere more evident than in its suffocating, destructive overpopulation and its creation of such substances as plutonium. Brought together, plutonium could cancel the overpopulation and that would eventually extinguish the plutonium and a cosmic imbalance be rectified. Whether he would ever carry out his cleansing act, Faulks wasn't sure. Just giving his idea potential by having the plutonium was comforting. As was knowing he was secretly one of the most powerful men on earth.

Huckston was not one of the most powerful men on earth but would liked to have been—not necessarily to lord it over others, but because being such would mean he could do anything he wanted. One thing he wanted was never to teach freshman composition again, and he had a plan to get out of it, one that would disrupt only a few other classes that met near his.

The noise from Huckston's eleven a.m. class had several times almost drowned out Brumley's next-door attempts to impress upon his freshmen the importance of coherence in their writing. For two weeks, eruptions of gaiety and celebration, successively increasing in volume and duration, had burst from Huckston's room and flowed down the fourth floor corridors of Humanities Hall. And each time the festive sounds swept into his room, Brumley to his annoyance felt in himself and saw in his students an initial flash of cheer, quickly fading with the realization that the joy and festivity were elsewhere and that for them, for now, Duty kept the books.

On the way up the stairs after the class, Brumley overtook Greenman.

"What's going on in Huckston's class?" he asked him.

"Is that where it was coming from? What are you, next door to it? My god, it was loud enough at my end of the hall."

There had been music, great outbursts of laughter, a rhythmic stamping of feet.

"Is today the first time you've heard it?" Brumley asked as they stopped on the fifth-floor landing. "It started a week-and-a-half ago. He showed a movie that Tuesday, then on Thursday there was a big cheer about five minutes into class and from the noise in the hall he must have dismissed them just afterwards. When I went by his class at the end of the period, the room was already empty. Then this Tuesday the really good times started. Lots of laughs; he must have been telling jokes. . . ."

"They were somebody else's jokes," Greenman interrupted. "Huckston can't tell one, you ever hear him try? Forgets details, or gets the sequence screwed up or bollixes the punch line. Same thing with his stories. You ever notice that he's Director of Creative Writing but never writes anything?"

"Well, no, I don't keep up with him any more than I have to," Brumley was pleased to admit. "Isn't he coming up for tenure this year. Rumor says from now on you'll have to publish to get tenure. How does he expect to get tenure if he doesn't publish anything?"

Greenman looked at him closely.

"All right," Brumley said. "As I was saying, today there were lots of laughs again, and then an appreciative murmur, then quiet for a while with occasional outbursts after that. And then the real party began. The room was empty again when I went by and the waste-can beside the door had empty pizza boxes stacked by it. I believe he had pizzas delivered."

"He must have furnished beer as well, going by the noise. No band?"

"No, just a tape player, I think," Brumely said as they started again up toward their offices. "At first, fool that I am, I thought it might be something legitimate–maybe some Renaissance music or Delta blues–but I think it was contemporary rock. That went on for awhile until, like I say, he let them out early."

"What class is it, you know?"

"I think it's comp," Brumley said. "He was bitching when the semester began about having to teach a section of it two semesters in a row. I think this is the period when he has it."

Greenman, who like Brumley and Norens and Hobart taught two sections of freshman composition every semester, stopped, gripping the stair rail tightly and swaying for a moment.

"Two semesters in a row, huh? One class each semester. What does the shit-head do to get out of it? Whose ass does he kiss?"

It was Brumley's turn to regard Greenman with disbelief.

"You know the answer to that, or at least part of it. He was Cole's major supporter for the chairmanship; that doesn't hurt him any. But you may not know, and it's probably more crucial than his support of Cole, that he's also a great smoocher of Wainwright's fundament. Huckston takes him fishing and plays raquetball with him. Probably cleans his fish and loses the games, I'm not sure."

"My god," Greenman said. "I didn't know that. That's amazing. But what I really mean is, what are the details? Does Huckston just say from his end of the boat 'I don't want to teach freshman comp; I'll clean the fish'? And Wainwright says back 'You will! Why, I don't think you should have to teach freshman comp'. It can't be like that. They've got to have some finesse, some–shall we say–delicacy."

"Greenman," Brumley said as they reached the eighth floor landing, "do you think we're the only ones who know what kind of work and despair that freshman comp is, or has become? I mean those of us who have to teach it? Everybody knows, or can pretty well imagine, Wainwright included. When someone pleases him, especially when they're obviously trying to please him–as Huckston does, or Calona or Davis–Wainwright knows how to truly reward them. Suddenly he finds some make-work administrative job for them or some non-duties.

Maybe puts them on the Studies Abroad shuttle. Or he'll let them–and only them–know he's thinking about giving selected faculty members some released time from teaching to do research, and they'll come bounding down to his office the next day with some project and what they get released from is freshman comp. It's all winks and nudges, without the courage to actually wink or nudge."

"You're right," Greenman said, lowering his voice as they went through the landing door into the Humanities Department corridor. "I guess my question now is, do they know what they're doing, do they say 'I'm going to delicately kiss some ass to get out of work or to get tenure or more money' or whatever, or do they just do it without a pang of conscience, as though it's not odious and dishonorable?"

"Probably both," Brumley said.

Greenman thought a moment.

"I'd still like to know what Huckston is up to."

Huckston was up to the mark. The fall semester was nearing its end, and with student evaluation of instructors looming Huckston liked to have at least a two-week run at requiring little work and giving high grades in his classes and in general turning them into disports of jubilation before students filled out the standardized form evaluating how well they liked him. Supposedly the accumulative score he gained on these forms, as for all instructors, was used along with service and, not far in the future, research, to determine his yearly raise, and Huckston was taking no chances that his superior knowledge of how to manipulate the evaluations would go unrewarded. If rated highly enough as a teacher, his reward, in addition to a bigger raise, would be to get out of teaching, especially freshman comp.

"It will break my heart, I mean break it," Huckston exclaimed to the woman he was currently living with, "if I'm buying pizza for those little illiterates and letting them out of class and they don't rate me on up there, around a 2 or so. I think I really am at least a 2 as a teacher, maybe a 1.5.

Huckston's woman was distracted from his worried mutterings by a new TV program about an ordinary group of attractive, affluent and hilariously entertaining friends who lived in a large city and were endlessly joking and having fun and sex and never working.

"Wouldn't you think I 'm a 2 at least?" he begged, throwing back his gleaming blond hair impatiently. "I mean, I work hard to be a good teacher and get those scores up there. Every class period I review to see what works and what doesn't. I'm pretty sure pizza works well, and I know high grades just before evaluation do."

Huckston's woman didn't know what he was talking about. She did know he was a conniving blowhard who pretended to know stuff he didn't. He never shut up, and her early hope that his motor mouth was evidence of his command of the language and the intelligence he pretended to had long ago vanished. Since he was fairly generous and undemanding, more so than most of the bums she had lived with, she overlooked the frantic self-justification behind which he hid his insecurity. But she knew sooner or later he would connive against her. Huckston had a reputation to uphold as a volatile, uncurbed genius who any day would publish something and stagger the world with his transforming power of language and get out of teaching forever. One way he tried to uphold that reputation was by living with a different woman every two or three years. She had figured him out without much trouble and planned to drop him first.

"Why don't you just teach like you always do, like everybody does? Isn't it kind of unfair or something to make things fun and easy just before they evaluate you just so they'll rate you high? That's not a real way of telling whether you're a 2 or 1 or whatever."

For a moment Huckston was silent, but he was processing at supercomputer speed.

"There's a difference," he began to sputter, now running his fingers rapidly through his mane.

"I'm a 2 or maybe a 1—I know I am. You've got to treat them right if you expect them to treat you right. It's like the Golden Rule, without the religious overtones, of course—the Golden Rule as just good ethical sense. If I'm not careful, the little bastards will rate me low and I won't get the raise I deserve as a 1 or 1.5. It's a matter of ethics, don't you see?"

"I guess," she said, hoping he would get off his irrational justifications that were beginning to embarrass even him.

But she did see. By now she saw Huckston with great clarity. Meanwhile, on the television, several of the untroubled, handsome males of the program had fallen into a large water fountain, and the beautiful but momentarily disdainful females were predictably destined to follow them shortly. She had lived in a large city, several of them. The more lonely and unfriendly they became, the more rabidly television proclaimed them the locus of comity and love.

"Everybody tries to please the students," Huckston went on unchecked. "They all do it or otherwise no one would get a high rating. Our students hate those composition classes; they hate all their classes. I'm just honest about it. There are plenty of instructors who don't make them work and cover it up. Not me, I'm up front about it. It's just for those one or two weeks. . . ."

Two of the gorgeous females of the show, one of whom by dint of her horn-rimmed glasses and her hair worn in a bun was supposedly plain, had been pulled shrieking into the fountain and were now vigorously splashing water on two passing cops, who were smiling benevolently on the fun.

Huckston's woman, who had had dealings with cops, decided what she was watching was bullshit, like Huckston. It was everywhere.

When he came to Middle State, President Curtis was determined not to preside but to rule, and to do so over every aspect of academic life. He began by discarding the old method of judging a faculty member's worth by the estimate of those who worked with them and replacing it with a wholly objective system that gave administrators the final determination. Middle State's student evaluations were a part of his plan and were thoroughly scientific. They presented the students with twenty-five statements about an instructor and his class with five possible responses for each statement that ranged from highly agree, a 1, to agree, to neutral, to disagree, to highly disagree, a 5. The ratings of each of the twenty-five statements were added together and then divided by twenty-five to produce a two-digit number between one and five–2.1, say, or 3.8–which was an objective and unassailable measure of the effectiveness of a teacher. This number was a central component in the larger, completely objective and highly scientific overall assessment of a faculty member's performance, which also included two more two-digit numbers from one to five, one derived from the service component, and the other, eventually, from the research component. Various weightings would be given to each of the three categories' numbers, and when all were summed and divided by three, a final number resulted that allowed administrators to reward those faculty members who agreed with their lunatic projects and penalize those who didn't. This method was much superior to the old way in that it covered prejudice and favoritism with several coats of bogus impartiality.

Though proclaimed to be nearly infallible, the system was constantly being adjusted by Vice president Yount's ever-growing Office of Assessment and Evaluation, which last year had discarded the previous, three-year-old student evaluation form for a more up-to-date one that the company selling it insisted was much more reliable, though the earlier one had been touted as unimprovable. The day that samples of the new one were distributed to the faculty, Brumley, Norens and Hobart took copies to their weekly lunch meeting at El Bullo to discover their fates.

"Here's one I like," Hobart pointed out during a lull in his attack on a plate of refried beans. "'Instructor's knowledge of the material was adequate' If one very much agrees, is that a plus or a minus? Do you see? Was it only *adequate*? Or if you very much disagree, was his knowledge much more or much less than adequate?"

"Try this one," Norens said mildly. Brumley admired her careful reserve and often felt its superiority to his own ever-simmering sense of outrage. "'Instructor's knowledge of material was without depth.' Wouldn't you think that calls for a judgment of character? And isn't there some question as to whether students would know whether the knowledge was without depth?"

"Give high grades and they'll think you have lots of depth," Brumley observed gloomily.

"Oh, 'tis a mighty instrument," Hobart chanted. Cole and Wainwright invariably referred to the questionnaire as an instrument, for the scientific connotations.

"Is it true," Norens asked innocently, "that when your number based on these instruments is determined they're going to engrave it on a plaque to be hung in your office?"

"Or two plaques," Brumley speculated. "One for your office and one to wear around your neck."

"Whether a plaque or not, we're stuck with this big, stinking albatross," Hobart proclaimed, tackling his Super Enchilada now that the beans were disposed of. "If Old Cadoon's exposé of the utter hollowness of these 'instruments' didn't discredit them, nothing will, ever."

"Old Cadoon?" Brumley asked. It was Old Cadoon again. "What didn't he stand up against?"

Brumley sometimes wondered if the Old Cadoon of Hobart's tales existed. He was fairly sure he had met Cadoon before Cadoon's retirement and recalled no signs in him of the fearless warrior against stupid power that Hobart graced him with.

"Oh, many things, many things he didn't stand up against," Hobart said. "No one could take arms against all that goes on. No, Old Cadoon seemed to choose only those issues whose implementation was closest to the hearts of Middle State's management, the issues whose exposure and thwarting would be most likely to infuriate them. But I think his little research into the validity of Student Evaluations was the capstone of a legendary life, his magnus opum, as I heard Wainwright say last week about his yearly Five Year Plan."

Norens had finished her tamales and ordered another beer; Brumley, who wanted several more but who had a batch of freshman themes awaiting his attention, decided to nurse the one he had and hear Hobart out.

"Someone on the departmental Evaluation Committee—may they ever be anonymous and their name be blessed—it was me, by the way—slipped Old Cadoon the grade point averages for every class and the corresponding student evaluation number for each one. No names, just two numbers—grade average and student evaluation number. Cadoon got Fairmont of Statistics to run a statistical analysis on the data. It showed an overwhelming correlation between grades and evaluation scores—the higher the grades, the higher the scores, and vice versa. Big goddamned surprise, huh? A disinterested baboon would have known that was the case. Cadoon meticulously arranged the data, analyzed and interpreted it with Fairmont's help, wrote it up clearly and succinctly and gave the results to our good Dean Wainwright, who read it with great care and determined to get rid of Old Cadoon as quickly as possible. Especially after the next day, when Old Cadoon accosted him just before a meeting of the college Evaluation Committee and asked if the study didn't show that high student evaluation numbers at best meant nothing and likely meant that the supposedly best teachers were instead just the easiest teachers who betrayed their discipline to get more money. Wainwright muttered something about an insufficient sample, and Old Cadoon immediately volunteered to mount a much more extensive study—statewide, nationwide, he told Wainwright, and he wouldn't even ask for released time from teaching freshman comp.

"Few administrators have ever been in the bind Wainwright found himself in. President Curtis, who despised Old Cadoon too, had decreed these instruments. They were used throughout the university except in the Business College, which didn't do anything it didn't want to. The pretense was that the forms were wholly accurate and a fair judge of what was good teaching. But here in Old Cadoon's report was near unshakable proof of the obvious—that they were not only fallacious but indicated just the opposite of what they claimed to indicate. Now of course Curtis and Wainwright and everybody else knew the truth, but for administrators, easy teachers *were* the best teachers, who didn't flunk anyone and kept the enrollment figures up. Since the students saw easy as best also, Old Cadoon's study was declared at odds with 'the literature'—that is, with the false information the instrument-selling companies peddle their instruments by—and therefore invalid.

"Also, to emphasize management's resolve to muzzle the truth, Wainwright told Old Cadoon that unless he retracted his findings, he would fire Dr. Johnson as chair, since he suspected Johnson of giving out the data on class grades and rankings and felt, too, that Johnson liked and respected Old Cadoon. Old Cadoon immediately gave up his quest and surrendered all his data and copies of his report."

"Wainwright actually threatened him with that?" Norens asked.

"He did."

"And Old Cadoon dropped it all?"

"Every bit of it."

"He was even better a man than I thought," Brumley admitted. "He wouldn't reveal you as the source and protected Johnson."

"Sort of protected him," Hobart said with restrained glee. "Wainwright fired Johnson the next week. Told Old Cadoon that he didn't say he wouldn't fire him if Old Cadoon turned over the material, only that he would if Old Cadoon didn't turn it over."

They sat silently, Hobart spooning in his Viva Zapata ice cream sundae.

"You know," Norens finally observed, "it's not just that they don't care about teaching, other than claiming they do. They don't care about research, either, not if it produces results they don't like."

"Truth is a terrible thing," Hobart agreed. "It ought never to be a concern of a university."

fourteen
BOOKS

The mild, colorless fall had brought only an occasional cool spell but many slow rains that left the trees largely bare and Middle State's campus looking even more desolate than usual. Trudging towards the library and picking his way through the rotted and fermenting fruits along Gingko Walk, Brumley for a change felt at one with the campus. Chairman Cole, either because of Brumley's smart-ass memo to Wainwright or the letters supporting Warren, knew a pariah when he smelled one and was clearly avoiding him. Even more ominous to Brumley, he was almost sure that Huckston and Calona and Davis had begun falling silent and averting their gazes when he walked into the coffee room. And while no student could have known or likely cared about his growing isolation, he imagined those he was meeting as they hop-scotched through the smashed gingko fruit were careful not to catch his eye.

Down the way, far past the library and near the athletic complex, he could see the snowy cupola of the just-constructed Wellness Center. *The Wellness Center*. A place to heal those sick of thought and study but repelled by the idea of useful physical work. It was a Taj Mahal of restoration containing one heated outdoor and two indoor swimming pools, racket and volley ball courts, two gymnasiums, spacious areas stocked with exercise machines resembling medieval engines of torture or siege, rooms filled with ping pong and pool tables, and corridors lined with banks of video-game machines to rejuvenate 20-year-olds exhausted from becoming well. What had it all cost? Some staggering figure had been announced at the project's joyfully heralded inception, a figure undoubtedly exceeded as the construction went on. But who cared what it cost? If no one cared about the overseas travel shuttle, the enormous pool of university vehicles, the athletic racket, the unexamined avalanche of computer and gadget purchases, the inevitable, staggering administrative featherbedding. . . .

Brumley couldn't go on. He tried to attend to avoiding the gingko fruits, several of which he had skidded on in his bleak reverie, but it was no use. The scholarship program! The near-innumerable scholarships, thrown out like confetti to almost any student who applied for one, regardless of need or, Brumley suspected, even aptitude. When an undergraduate himself, he recalled, he had known only one fellow student, poor but brilliant, who held a scholarship. Where did the money for Middle State's largesse come from? And why was there such abundance? The official rationale he could hear swelling and puffing—*to provide educational opportunities to as broad a spectrum, etc., etc.* But there had to be something else at work. He tried again not to think about it. The whole system was as rotten as the gingko fruits that splattered the sidewalk, and the answer to who cared how much anything cost was obvious.

Aside from nobody else, or nobody else who mattered, he cared. That was his problem. His intemperate memo and letters—these and just his skepticism about Middle State's direction that he did not try to hide all counted against him. Brumley knew he didn't have a chance. Retribution was gathering. Before such transgressions as his, tenure was gauze to the whirlwind.

Even the machines had been alerted. At the library, where Brumley spent more time than he felt was good for him, the computerized check-out system had begun persistently to identify him as a special user, not as faculty, and in spite of repeated assurances by the circulation desk that like all faculty he could keep books for three months, the stamp in the books stubbornly continued to proclaim them due back in two weeks. Not even a phone call to the office of Dean Gobel of the Library, who lavishly promised to correct the problem himself, had satisfied Brumley that anything would be done, and he felt confirmed in his growing sense of having already lost his job.

"Are you going to the pep rally Friday night?" Ms. Varner at the library check-out desk asked, once Brumley had found one of the two books he wanted. She had a tray of cards from the card catalog on her desk and was feeding them into a copier of some sort attached to a computer. Her long dark hair had recommended her to him since she began working there several years earlier, but as usual he had been unable to get beyond pleasantries.

"I don't think I can make it this year," Brumley said. He prided himself on never having attended any university sports event in the years he'd been at Middle State, seeing no sense in giving aid to the enemy. Nor had he ever attended the Big Pep Rally, held yearly before the Big Game between Middle State and Southern State—or maybe it was Eastern State, Brumley could not remember. These schools were fiercest of rivals, along with Northern State and Western State, for the Higher Education Fund allocated each year by the state legislature. Administrators at all these former teacher-college universities were insistent that winning athletic teams were of immense importance in determining whether a school got a fair space at the state-budget trough, though they knew virtually no one cared one way or another about the teams—not the students, the alumni, the legislators or anyone else other than a few local, middle-aged lawyers, businessmen and politicians who, unable to interest themselves in anything worthy or useful, became sports boosters. Through the Reigning Boards, comprised largely of those like themselves, they controlled the schools.

"Do you think many people will be there?" Brumley asked, shamefully entertaining the thought that showing an interest in what the administration considered important might save his job. "What goes on?"

"Oh, there's lots of cheering and the band plays—you know, lots of school spirit. And President Curtis speaks and then the coach. If there are any players who have anything to say, they do. Then they light the big bonfire. A lot of people come—more than come to the games most times."

Attendance at the games was, Brumley reflected, low. When by oversight he had found himself driving by the stadium while a game was in progress, he had often noticed—had strangely enough been almost embarrassed to see—that rarely was the great bank of stadium seats over a third full, those in attendance huddled almost self-consciously around the fifty yard line and close to the field. Mercifully, some twenty years ago when the needless new stadium was being built, no one had demanded a completely encircled playing field. Had there been such, the miserable attendance would truly have been apparent, though likely it would have made little difference in the funding of the football program, which had a life of its own, separate from the student body, academic programs, or any other part of the university. Many of the players had never read a book. Some had never seen anyone read a book. A large number stayed in school by majoring in Physical Exercise and Leisure, where they were given A's regardless of their class performance or attendance; others, with what Brumley thought unusual foresight, chose to master Criminal Justice, preparing for an eventual place in the penal system. Occasionally the administration coerced faculty members to raise a star athlete's grade, or, simply raised it on the athlete's transcript with no one's knowledge. The head coach was paid more than the university president, who was paid three times more than any faculty member. No one had ever been able to find out how much the football program was budgeted each year, let alone how much it spent.

"You know," Brumley said weakly, feeling years of resolve collapsing, "maybe I'll go. It might do me good to get out. Are you going ?"

"I doubt I'll make it this year," Ms. Varner said. "We're trying to get this all entered by the end of the week"–she indicated the card catalog tray on her desk— "It's part of President Curtis's paperless campus initiative. We're changing from the card catalog and putting everything on the computer."

"Everything on the computer?"

"Yes, we've been doing it for over a month, ever since we got a grant from the computer company to get it started. Everybody's doing it, all libraries."

"You mean there won't be card catalogs any more?"

"No card catalog, but there will be a catalog. It's all going on the computer."

Brumley felt a pang. The search down the drawer fronts for the proper tray, the sweet slide of oak on oak, the touch search through the cards, copying the call number, or else, if there were several needed books, carrying the tray to a tall desk with high stools to copy the numbers there. Even at Middle State there were usually other faculty or students using the catalog, walking around one another, waiting until the user of a drawer near theirs had finished. The process was tactile, communal. The new way would be as isolated and TV-like as it could be made. The beautiful cabinets, finely crafted and built to last, their odor that Brumley could only call of the promise of knowledge, would now at best be relegated to some obscure corner, replaced by a bank of plastic-enshrouded, soulless screens, designed for quick obsolescence.

Now I'm the champion of the old card catalog, he thought and inwardly shook his head.

"We're going to have a number of terminals all through the library where you can access the electronic catalog," Ms. Varner continued. "Here, this is roughly what it will look like."

She shoved a disc into her computer, pushed some buttons and, after a few flickers and a false start or two, a colorful picture appeared on the screen welcoming the viewer to beautiful Middle State University, which was rated sixth by a prominent news magazine as a bargain school among all upper-mid-South and lower-mid-West former teacher-college universities. She then caused another picture to appear specifically welcoming the viewer to Middle State's library and asking if the viewer wished to continue. The screen didn't say how one was to continue, but she smoothly directed an arrow to the question and clicked. The screen then changed to a picture of a computer screen with various choices presented the viewer.

"Wait," Brumley said. "How would you know where to click—or even to click—if you didn't already know?"

The librarian looked at him.

"That's just how it's done," she said. "Everybody, or at least the kids, knows that's how you do it."

"But how?" Brumley continued doggedly. "I mean, even if they knew, how did they know? Were there instructions by the computers they first used that told them where to click if they wanted to continue? Is it the same for all computers at all libraries?"

"I don't know. I doubt it, but I'm not sure."

Brumley knew the hopelessness of pushing the issue, but among the unreflective there seemed to be an assumption that children were now born with an ability to use computers that was instinctive, like suckling.

"Will there be instructions by the terminals here that will tell me where to click and such?" he asked, trying to be practical.

"I don't think so," Ms. Varner laughed with amused tolerance, "but it may be necessary for the Luddites."

"I'm not a Luddite," Brumley said, as dispassionately as he could. "I just don't think the library should assume people know how to do things they've never done before. Just because you spend your life fiddling with those things doesn't mean everyone has."

"You may have a point. But most people are already familiar with computer usage. They have to be."

"I know," Brumley agreed, "but that's only because the advertising campaigns the computer companies ran ten years ago convinced everybody that if they didn't get the things they would lose their jobs or their children would flunk out of school or they would look out-of-date. All computers have really done is increased control."

"What do you mean?" the librarian asked, more apprehensive at Brumley than at his message.

"Control of the powerful over the weak."

"Over the weak?"

"Us," Brumley said, trying to stop. Nothing was worse than having an opinion in such matters. To most people it was like having an opinion on breathing.

"We don't have any say in how, let alone if, these things are used. I like the card catalog," he said, wildly shifting ground. "It's *real*, substantial, I can touch it. But that doesn't count. In fact, it's almost suspect to bring up such an objection. That's how powerful this gadgetry has become. It's like cars."

"Cars?" the librarian asked, now truly worried. Fortunately, Brumley thought, there's no alarm system at the desk.

"All this monstrous pile of information computers store up, or whatever they do," he plunged on, "it's too much, it's just overwhelming. What's worthy is lumped in with what's insane and the insane wins. And when things go haywire–when the computer is *down*–then whatever you're trying to do just ends. It's become the biggest dodge in the history of human bungling: 'the computer is down.' Don't tell me you haven't heard that yourself."

"You know, you're right there. But they still do a lot of things."

"I'll admit that with computer games and the web and the Internet they've done a lot to divert and stupefy the weak. Like television does, but now you get to take an active part in it. Interactive stupefaction, it ought to be called."

"Maybe so," she agreed laughing, beginning to see that Brumley was harmless. "But they're here to stay."

She handed Brumley the book she had been checking out for him. It was due back in two weeks.

"Ms. Varner, I know this is probably futile since I've already been through it twice, but I'm supposed to be able to keep books for three months. I never keep them that long, but all the books I've checked out recently are stamped due back in two weeks. Is there any way you could check up for me on why the computer is doing this?"

"I can surely try," she said, and began typing on her computer keyboard.

"What?" She jerked back suddenly, typed some more, looked puzzled, typed further, pushed some buttons. She looked up at Brumley.

"I'm afraid our network is down," she said without a sign. "If you can't wait around, I can try later today and give you a call if I find out what's wrong."

Since he never got the call, Brumley assumed she never discovered what was wrong, or else discovered nothing was wrong after all. Nor did he see her when he arrived Friday night, as he vaguely hoped to, at the Big Pep Rally, where he slunk after a long inner debate in which all that was cowardly and small in him won.

A fairly large crowd of exuberant, mostly male students, roused from another long, empty night in their dorms and drawn by the sounds of the marching band, faced the enormous, wasteful stack of bonfire logs, before which a sizeable speaker's stand had been erected. President Curtis and Coach Seighel crowned the stand, along with the most ambrosial and cavortive of the female cheerleaders, who exhorted the crowd to beat Southern while male students mobbed to the front for the best view of what pumped and pulsed under the cheerleaders' butt-twitcher skirts. Brumley, mesmerized by their peppy bounces, their shakes, their oiled and flashing kicks, was mortified to find he too was surging forward for a better view and let himself be pushed back into the crowd. Such as they, he reminded himself once more, had not been made for him.

President Curtis, trying to appear informal and uncalculating, finally stood and strode to the front of the speakers stand, perfunctorily thanking the cheerleaders, who moved like momentarily serviced fowls to the back of the platform, the smoothed feathers of their pom-poms falling still.

"I can see Middle State's spirit is ascendant tonight," he proclaimed with rehearsed spontaneity. "And much of it is due to our fine cheerleading squad. Let's give them a hand."

A great shout, with undertones of moaning, went up.

"If I were Southern and were here tonight to see all this support, I'd be worried," President Curtis continued and was drowned out by enthusiastic shouts of what he took to be agreement that bounced the cheerleaders to their feet, squirming and kicking.

"Yes sir," he went on, dropping into the colloquial and for a moment actually appearing at ease, "they may have a —seven?" he turned questioningly to Coach Seighel.

"Eight," Seighel said uncomfortably.

". . .eight game win streak over us, but I can see from how aroused we are here tonight that tomorrow may be another story. Yes, they've come a long way just to be defeated. . . ."

Another, somewhat contrived salvo of approving shouts again goosed the cheerleaders into a sensual frolic that President Curtis smilingly waited through.

". . .to be defeated by. . . ." he attempted, but the outcry, now clearly unrelated to anything he was saying, spread and rose appreciatively, exciting another galvanized frisk, this time ending in the cheerleading squad's competition winning Folies Berges Ass Flash, which brought forth a roar so primal and sustained that President Curtis, now alert, had to speak pointedly to the flushed and panting cheerleaders, who somewhat primly took their seats.

"As I was saying," he continued, "they've come a long way. . . ." An anticipative chorus of cries died weakly when the cheerleaders sat immobile and President Curtis glared at the more unrepressed of the enthusiasts.

". . .a long way just to be defeated by our team."

He had meant to turn a phrase here, feeling that his Ph.D. in Communications should occasionally be flaunted by a little Churchillian eloquence to show he was a communications expert who could use language other than to obfuscate and mislead. "By our stalwart gridironists" had not quite rung true, even to his gummed ear. Neither did "our valiant student athletes." He could not abide using what he considered the insipid nickname Middle State's first president had bestowed on the school's athletic squads when a track team from those bygone days had won the conference high-hurdle relay, the high and long jumps, and the pole vault: the Kangaroos, or Roos, as it was often endearingly shortened. "To be defeated by our roused and ready Roos" had actually crossed his mind, only to be savagely dismissed. *Roos!* How much respect was drained from his position when the university he ruled had as its mascot a goddamned kangaroo, a grotesque, hopping, idiotic butt of a thousand jokes. Surely his great vision of himself as a more highly paid, free-spending president at a larger university was forever out of reach when the hiring committee of that richly endowed institution saw that his otherwise impeccable resume was sullied with the presidency of Kangaroo U. He was afraid that even now, in his own fiefdom, a small number of students and many faculty ridiculed him as, what else, the head of the kangaroos, Captain Kangaroo himself.

"Coach Seighel, what about it?" he said, covering his bleak reflections with heartiness and gladly surrendering the microphone to the neanderthal Seighel, who grasped it like a club and stared vacantly at the crowd.

"President Curtis," he grunted, "cheerleaders. . . ."

A roar from the pent-up crowd unleashed the quiveringly eager cheerleaders, as renewed as Aphrodite, whose nympholeptic shimmies not even President Curtis's icy stare could still.

"I thank you all for your support," Seighel said, once the orgiastic rooting had subsided, "and all the boys on the squad do, too. I want to tell you we're ready for tomorrow. There was a lot of hard hitting in practice this week, and I believe last week's game is behind us. We got our heads up and if we can just play some hard-nosed fuhball tomorrow and give it a hundred-and-ten percent. . . ."

Why, Brumley thought as Seighel droned on, was it always a hundred-and-ten percent? Clearly any effort over one hundred percent was impossible. Did this suggest that Coach Seighel and all other football coaches at every level actually knew what hyperbole was, and every week, at pep rallies, pre-game, post-game and half-time shows, consciously used a poetic device to stress dedication, or the need for it, in their players? But why not a hundred-and-one percent? Or a hundred-and-thirty-two percent? Two hundred might be an exaggeration too large to be swallowed even by sports fans, but why always a hundred-and-ten percent? Modesty? The comfort of cliche? The tyranny of the decimal system? And in football, how does one add ten percent more? Gouge more savagely? Butt with even more fury? Fall down harder? The cheerleaders, Brumley thought, his mind turning to a higher, sweeter realm, they were giving a hundred-and-ten percent on that last bump-and-grind routine, but they were closer to the crowd and more individually distinct than the football team. They could be joyously certain that a large number of hungry eyes were deliriously appreciative of every bit of ass they showed or shook, so even a hundred-and-twenty or maybe a hundred-and-fifty percent effort could be called forth in those circumstances.

". . .tackle, hit hard and keep their quarterback contained," Seighel fumbled on. "I told the boys if we play team ball and don't make any turnovers and give it a hundred-and-ten percent, we're gonna win this fuhball game. They're a good team and we're looking for a dog fight. But if we play smashmouth fuhball and keep the turnovers down, I believe they'll think they've been kicked by a kangaroo!"

The bursting students, sensing another opportunity, exploded with applause, and the cheerleaders shot to their feet and gave it a hundred-and-ten percent.

"And now," President Curtis intoned, taking the microphone, "the moment we've all been waiting for—the Middle State Bonfire, and let's get it burning, like the school spirit I sense before me. And this year we've got an added touch. Dean Gobel, come on up here."

Brumley saw Dean Gobel of the library move through the crowd and climb up to the speakers stand.

"Thank you, President Curtis. . . ."

This time the cheerleader-instigating shouts were so disorganized and inopportune that they were barely noticed, even by the cheerleaders.

"...tonight even the library wants to get in the old Middle State spirit and do our part to see that Southern knows what a marsupial mauling is."

He waited above the puzzled silence, then went on.

"So tonight, in keeping with the drive for academic excellence that is the hallmark of Middle State," and he turned fawning toward the impassive President Curtis for approval, "and in a joining of athletics and academics based on cutting edge technology, we at the library want to show that we can do our part for school spirit."

An uncertain cheer went up from the crowd, and as the band struck up a militarized version of "Light My Fire," Brumley saw a number of students and library workers, Ms. Varner elatedly among them, filing from a university truck that had been parked at the fringe of the rally. Most were sacrificially bearing aloft what at first he thought were small, elongated coffins, perhaps each one representing a member of the Southern football team. Then he realized they were nothing other than the library's card catalog drawers, still containing the cards. The workers and students, some carrying the drawers, others signs proclaiming the arrival of the paperless university, snake-danced through the cheering crowd to the great stack of logs behind the speakers stand where flames were already starting up from carefully laid, kerosene-soaked rags and kindling. As the bearers of the trays reached the periphery of the stack and flung the card-filled drawers into the interior, the flames grew higher, climbing up through the logs and whirling the spilled cards upwards, some of them ablaze. The band blared, the cheering grew louder, and Brumley saw President Curtis from the speakers stand reach down to a passing tray and pluck out a handful of cards.

"Here we go," he said excitedly, now wholly given to the moment. "We've got"–he picked out one of the cards and from the light of the flames read– "Fitzgerald, Edward, *The Rubiyat of Omar Khayyam* to get things going. And here's–hey, I've heard of this one–Fitzgerald, F. Scott, *The Great Gatsby*," he said beaming to a chorus of groans from the students, who recognized a book required in the humanities course. He flung the handful of cards like confetti into the air and the cheerleaders, sensing from his tone and act that anything could go, began a sustained routine of such erotic frenzy that the band, in spite of the director's admonishments, gradually doubled its tempo. The fire, as if fed in part by the maddened music, grew roaring to a great height, cheered by the jubilant crowd, and the final cards of the card catalog, along with the drawers of seasoned oak, were hurled into the flames, the burning cards now rising madly on the updraft and burning out to cold ash, far above the celebration.

It can't be, Brumley thought, it just can't be. Not far in the future, he felt certain, it would be books.

Books often caused problems at Middle State, especially for the bookstore. Only a few days after the Big Pep Rally, Brumley found in his mail box his book order form for the coming spring semester, which had been carefully typed by Miss Pam and submitted some weeks before, well ahead of the deadline. His form had attached to it a bookstore form headed REJECTED, and underneath the heading, in a list of reasons purportedly explaining the rejection, was checked the enigmatic phrase: Too Big. There was nothing else.

"Miss Pam, excuse me," Brumley said to the secretary, more harried than usual now that the semester was coming to a close. "Do you know what this means?"

Miss Pam inspected the form.

"No," she said, considering, "this is a new one. At least I've never seen it checked. It's Ratliff, he's in charge over there. Do you want me to call him?"

"No, thanks, I can do it," Brumley said. He didn't want to add to the already overworked Miss Pam's duties, and besides, he would like to see if Ratliff's rejection was as insolent as it appeared.

Not that he could do much about it if it were, but the further out on the limb he went at Middle State and in spite of his fear, the more he also relished the exuberant sense of danger. What, he wondered, would it be like to venture out so far that the limb broke, or he slipped off? He knew that was a possibility he needed to consider before any further rash letters or memos tossed him out of the academic tree once and for all. Timidity and fear were his usual round, but his few sips from the cup of assertion and courage had been bracing.

Going back to his office, the way nearly unimpeded now that the elaborate sprinkler system and computer wiring work was almost complete, Brumley considered the offending form and the list of criteria on it that Ratliff had for rejection. There was Too Expensive, Too Early, Too Late and Too Dirty, this last unclear and disturbing. There was his own defect, Too Big, then Too Many, and Too Different, also puzzling and as troubling as Too Dirty. And then a final one, Too Bad, which had the same baffling ambiguity as Too Big and which might overlap Too Dirty but also, rather than being a category, could be just a malicious dismissal of the order, no explanation forthcoming.

"Hobart," he said to the nodding giant, apparently lulled asleep by the swirling screen-saver pattern on his computer, "wake up and tell me if you understand this."

Hobart looked sourly at the form, collected himself, looked again and laid it on his desk.

"Your order is Too Big," he said with great satisfaction.

"I know that. Jesus. What does Too Big mean? Don't screw with me here; I've got enough trouble as it is. What does Ratliff mean by Too Big?"

"All I can do is speculate, and you've got to promise me that you will not, based on my speculations, write any letters to editors or memos of any kind whatever to administrators, even fawning or congratulatory memos. Okay? Now, first, it may mean that you have ordered more tomes for your classes than some unwritten rule of the bookstore says you're allowed to. Your order is therefore Too Big in the sense that there are more books than permitted, though likely Too Many would be checked if such were the case. Or, with more subtlety than we should grant Ratliff, the *contents* of the books are Too Big, that is, the themes, issues, ideas therein are overly ponderous, weighty beyond what Ratliff feels is the ability of our young scholars to mentally lift and carry. Or perhaps the order was not Too Big in the sense of too many books but in the more specialized sense of Too Heavy to meet another unwritten rule governing the maximum shipping charge allowed any one instructor. Then, maybe the *print* is Too Big; other editions might have smaller print, hence smaller weight, but that possibility overlaps Too Big in the sense of Too Heavy. All of these, except for Too Big in the sense of too intellectually burdensome, are easily defensible by Manager Ratliff, and even in that sense his rejection would be justifiable to some."

"Oh god," Brumley moaned, "what does that idiot over there think I can do if his instructions don't make sense. I don't understand what's wrong and I wouldn't know how to change it if I did. Here, let me have it," and he snatched the offending form from Hobart. "Who is this Ratliff? I'm going over there and get this straightened out."

"Brumley, wait, slow down a minute. Call him; don't go over there to his territory. You're in no position to make a scene, as much as the uncivil little prick needs his ass kicked. You don't know the score. Listen," Hobart said firmly, "that bookstore was a large part of the end of Old Cadoon, did you know that? Have you heard of Old Cadoon and the Bookstore Exposé."

"No, I haven't," Brumley groaned, unwilling to calm down. "And not another Old Cadoon story. Old Cadoon is gone. What good is he? Or his stories?"

"Brumley," Hobart said severely, "what are you saying? Old Cadoon's stories are invaluable. He had the courage to lift the mask and show what he saw. He could lift the mask. You need to hear this one, to know what you're up against. Sit down."

Grudgingly, Brumley took a seat. Hobart was generally more reckless than Brumely had ever been, but Hobart also knew when prudence and restraint were called for. Besides, Brumley in spite of his impatience knew all the Old Cadoon stories were good ones, and this one he had never heard.

"It was long ago," Hobart began, settling in his chair as though they were seated before a comfortable fire, "before you got here I think, and it was Old Cadoon's first counter-culture research project. His infamous 'Report on the Bookstore' came out of it, written to document the vacuity, inefficiency and perhaps corruption of the store's operation. He was just Cadoon then, but he was beginning to realize who he really was," Hobart recalled, staring off into the mythical past. "He originally entitled his report 'Report on the Baub and Trinket Store', but Greenman and I talked him out of it.

"What set him off was three consecutive semesters of having his class schedules disrupted by the failure of one or more of the books required in the classes to arrive at the bookstore on time. He went to Moore, who was chairman then, with his complaint and Moore, who didn't recognize what Cadoon was becoming, listened to his complaint and when Cadoon said he was thinking about writing a report on the situation, Moore encouraged him, thinking that like most faculty Cadoon was long on bellyaching and short on action.

"That was Moore's mistake. Cadoon–it's about now that I think of him as the inchoate Old Cadoon, the a-borning Old Cadoon, so to speak–decided that if they wanted research, they'd get it. I tried to talk him out of the project, but he had heard the trumpet and said Ha Ha to all my entreaties."

Hobart, pleased with himself, stopped to see if Brumley caught the allusion, and when he saw he did, continued.

"So Old Cadoon designed and sent out a survey to every member of the old College of Arts and Sciences. Over fifty percent, it turned out, had experienced some kind of screw-up with the bookstore in the past year–books not ordered, wrong books ordered, or, the most common, too few books ordered. All of these caused considerable modification in careful sequences of reading in a variety of courses, which old Cadoon had to admit didn't seem to bother anyone but the instructors.

"He gathered and analyzed his survey, wrote a concise introduction to his data, presented it in a careful, easily understood tabular form, then in a painstaking analysis showed the magnitude of the problem and mercilessly exposed the implications of a bookstore's determining the conduct and often the content of university courses. His case, as I saw it and every other faculty member who read it, including the toads, was airtight and incontrovertible.

"It was controverted and deflated by being ignored. He had determined to follow channels, unlike," Hobart said pointedly, "some hotheads who send reports or memos directly to the president or to state newspapers. So he took his data and report first to Chairman Moore, who you'll remember had encouraged him to write it.

'Here's the Bookstore Report you encouraged me to write,' he said, and saw the blood drain from Moore's face.

"'Well,' said Chairman Moore, 'well. I got a copy of your survey, but. . . .'

"'Did you fill it out?' Old Cadoon asked.

"'No. I hadn't had any bookstore problems so I didn't think there was any reason to respond.'

"'Actually there was,' Old Cadoon pointed out. 'I'm trying to get the facts to determine if the bookstore is doing its job, and I needed–wanted–information in their favor as well as against it. But I've noted in my introduction to the report how many surveys were returned–it was eighty-six percent, by the way–and that those that weren't returned were likely those of instructors who had had no problems. Or, those who had problems but weren't bothered by them.'

"'I'll get this to the Dean,' Chairman Moore said, setting the report in his out tray, and Old Cadoon said he saw then that I was right in my estimation of his undertaking. He had wasted his time.

"Two weeks later, he found Chairman Moore in his office.

"'What's the word on my bookstore report?' he asked Moore.

"'I took that down to Dean Ogg'—he was dean then. 'He's looked into it and the bookstore is taking the report under advisement and working to correct the problems your research highlights.'

"Old Cadoon heard no more about it, except that until the day he retired and beyond, the wrong books or not enough books or no books continued to arrive or not arrive and not a damned thing changed. They still haven't. The bookstore, Brumley, is impregnable–from the Latin, suggesting it can't be screwed. But it can screw you, just like it did Old Cadoon. After all that work to benefit the true university, he saw that real research was not wanted, that whatever constituted the smooth running of the bookstore was more important than the careful imparting of knowledge, and that management was a bunch of self-serving, dishonorable hypocrites. Nothing changed, except that from there on out Old Cadoon was a marked man. So you'd better tread carefully here. Don't go to the bookstore; call Ratliff and make whatever changes to your order form he wants. Smaller, evidently. Make everything smaller."

Middle State's bookstore was aglow, as orderly and antiseptic as a music store in a mall. In fact, Brumely noted when he got there after ignoring Hobart's advice, a good deal of the bookstore was given over to music recordings, though not nearly so much as to T-shirts, sweatshirts, shorts, logo caps, rainwear, umbrellas, backpacks, stickers, huggies, decals, pennants, banners, cosmetics, soaps, medicines, and two aisles of greeting cards for every conceivable event in order to free students from having to write a message of their own. There were picture frames, beer mugs, coffee cups, water bottles, all with official Middle State logos on them; there were videos, wallets, key chains, sunglasses, license plates, stuffed animals, and much more. There were even yo-yos, and some dusty Rubick's cubes.

Books occupied less than half the floor space, and the great majority of those were textbooks. Hobart was right; he should not have come to this wholly insensible shrine of consumerism. But he had decided to come humbly—at least the spirit of Hobart's advice he would take—and ask Ratliff what baffling flaw had invalidated his book order. And here he was, a smile of affable compliance in place, ready to scuff and shuffle an apology when his mistake was explained to him. If he had a hat, he imagined, he would be twisting it in his hands.

Two idle employees at the check-out register directed him to Ratliff, who was half-way down an aisle, polishing a mug.

"Hello," Brumley called out with the little heartiness he could muster. "How's it going?"

Ratliff paused, looked at him carefully, and resumed polishing the mug.

"Okay," he said.

"Keeping them clean, huh?" Brumley heard himself ask.

Ratliff put the mug back on its shelf and turned to Brumley, waiting.

"I got this form from you," Brumley said, holding it out, "and wanted to clear up what it means."

Ratliff paused before accepting it, then took it, glanced at it, and set it down by the mugs.

"Your order was Too Big," he said.

"I saw that," Brumley managed to reply civilly, with an effort that he felt separated viscera deep inside him. "I don't know what Too Big means—too many, too heavy—what?"

Ratliff regarded him with a faint smile, whether of amusement or contempt Brumley was unsure.

"Too Big," he said. "The books are too big to fit over here on our textbook shelves. You've got to order smaller books so we can put them out on the shelves."

"You've got to be shitting me," Brumley blurted in disbelief.

Ratliff's smile disappeared and he looked coldly at Brumley.

"No, I'm not. We've got to have the textbooks in order on the shelves—it's a rule. And if the books are too big, then they won't fit and we can't put them out."

"Yes," Brumley said, "yes, I see. But is there any reason why you couldn't keep the books that are Too Big back in the storage area and have a sign on the shelves where they would be located telling students to ask for someone to get from the back any of these books they're required to read that you think are oversized?"

"Yes," Ratliff said and looked at Brumley.

"What is it?"

"There's a rule that says we've got to display the books on the shelves, and if a book is Too Big to fit on the shelves, then it can't be displayed."

"Could you make the shelves bigger?" Brumley asked, determined to go down every obvious path, as long as he could control his anger.

"No."

"Why? Would they take up some mug space?"

Ratliff, who was reaching for another mug on which he had detected a smudge, halted and turned to Brumley.

"What's your name?"

"It's on the form you sent me."

Ratliff grabbed the form from the shelf and found Brumley's name.

"Well, Mr. Brumley, let me tell you we're short-handed around here. We can't be running to wait on students and building new shelves and doing whatever faculty members want done. This store is a business, and it's got to show a profit. And you know why? Do you know what our revenue is used for?"

"To stock mugs?"

"No, not stock mugs. It's used to pay off the bonds for developing the university's Robert O. Masher Golf Course. What about that, huh? That farm may have been donated to us, and it may have been donated for a tax write-off, but it didn't come with greens and a club house on it. A golf course costs money, and this bookstore makes our golf course possible, though I doubt, " he said with a sneer, "that you ever play."

"No, I don't play. I've got work to do. You know what Mark Twain said about golf."

"Who?"

Brumley was so stunned he could not even feel superior.

"Look," Ratliff said. "If you want books, get the right size. Hell," he continued, relenting somewhat, "there are all kinds of books in the back. Go back there and take your pick. You're bound to find something; more goddamned books than you could shake a stick at. Books about everything. You'll find something. And none of them are Too Big."

Brumley declined and left Ratliff reaching for another mug. He would have to choose other texts—but which ones in his first order were Too Big! He had neglected to find out. Facing death he would not turn back to ask Ratliff.

The two idle bookstore employees chatting with student workers at the checkout slots didn't even look up as he went by.

"Better keep an eye out," Brumley called to them. "I might be stealing a book. Or a mug."

Out on the sidewalk, he tried to think through the encounter but knew already what he would conclude. Ratliff could not be moved; a tightening garrote would not move him. Chairman Cole, should he appeal to him, would be fearful of troubling a higher administrator to resolve the situation, so he would be no help. There was only one thing to do: he would have to alter his courses, choose new readings, rewrite his syllabi. He would have to make sure his books were not Too Big.

The intense, thin and sour Stevens of English never ordered books that were Too Big, or excessive in any way that would upset Ratliff. Stevens had come to Middle State three years before from a job at a great research university, where after a trial period of six years with small classes of brilliant students he had distinguished himself by publishing nothing and doing nothing. Subsequently cut loose to make his way upon the then slack waters of academic employment, he had wound up at Middle State as a result of an adroitly written, wholly misleading resume he had slaved over for weeks in hopes it would give him at least six more years of comparative leisure until he was exposed and once again had to move on. His effort had worked beyond his wildest imaginings. What he found at Middle State was a majority of students so ill-prepared and indifferent that he felt utterly justified in despising them, as well as the university that enrolled them and the region that gave them birth—and feeling this way, why then put forth effort to educate such carpenters, cosmetologists and clods that his students were so obviously destined to become? Looking more broadly around him at Middle State, he realized that as long as he knew which side his bread was buttered on, played his cards right, and kissed the proper ass, no one cared whether he worked or not. Clearly it was only right that he expend the little energy he could summon in working to get out of work. He occupied his considerable intelligence by immersion in trivia, mainly sports statistics and the numbing minutiae of movies and early television programs. But he still feared, in spite of his eagerly displayed willingness to be a team player, that his dedication to taking it easy might not be recognized for the wholly logical and justifiable position it was and that the production of some kind of tangible evidence of his academic worth would be necessary for him to remain in this utopia he so completely loathed. But producing almost anything would take some effort, even of conception. Brumley had the misfortune to pass his office as Stevens was pondering his dilemma.

"Brumley," he called, "you got a minute? Come here, would you; I've got an idea to try out on you."

Brumley, loaded with a new book order form to fill out for Ratliff's approval and a batch of freshman composition papers to grade that evening, reluctantly complied. Not only did he have work to do, but he had begun to feel uneasy about Stevens, who, despite his brilliance and occasional guarded friendliness, was beginning to smell like a rat and more and more to betray an unfamiliarity increasingly common to most of the newer members of the department with what they contemptuously called the traditional literary canon.

"What is an 'idea'?" Brumley asked.

"Actually, I don't have an idea, I've had an insight. My insight tells me I need an idea that I can expand on and get published so I can get tenure at this disgrace of an institute of lower learning, and then a raise and promotion. Do you have any idea what that idea could be?"

"Nothing that would be publishable," Brumley replied. His ideas were mostly of how a number of the works of literature that he taught kept him going, but he knew only too well that absolutely no one was interested in that. At present, a present he prayed would be short, the trend in his discipline was to show that poems, novels, stories and plays either meant nothing or revealed some great moral blindness in the author or in the period in which they were written. The scholar or critic writing about these works was wholly free of such blind spots of any kind and therefore he or she was superior to every author and in fact superior to just about everybody.

"Come on," Stevens said impatiently, "surely you've got something. Shakespeare, you like Shakespeare, don't you? Everybody likes Shakespeare even if they don't read him. Got any ideas on Shakespeare?" It struck Stevens that if Brumley came up with something, he, Stevens might have to read some of the Glorious Swan.

"Greenman says that Shakespeare despises sycophancy more than any behavior," Brumley said impulsively, not intending offense but aware of the applicability to Stevens, who, however, would never see it.

"Greenman." Stevens snorted dismissively, shaking his head. "He actually believes, you know, that everyone in management here is a sell-out."

"Oh, they are," Brumley agreed. "At least that's what they're becoming."

"Come on, Brumley, you know that's not so. Anyway, for an organization to run smoothly there's got to be cooperation, consensus. Otherwise nothing would ever get done."

With effort, Brumley remained silent, but was now assured that Stevens was a player who likely was guided by two moral principles: I want to do it, and everyone else is doing it.

"You'll never get anywhere with an attitude like Greenman's," Stevens cautioned him. "But whatever it is with him, I need an idea. I believe I could do something on Shakespeare's attitude toward women, how he didn't respect women or like women or something like that. Or how he liked them, but not in the right way and therefore didn't like them at all but just thought he liked them and was trying to fool people. There's enough in Shakespeare that I ought to be able to find something like that."

"It's been done," Brumley said. "It's been done for Shakespeare, for Chaucer, for Milton, Dickens, Joyce—it's been done for every male writer. Twice for every male writer; several female writers too."

Brumley had gamely tried to plow through a few such studies, believing they had a worthy premise, but found them predictable and written so shabbily, so indecipherably, that it was hard to believe that anyone who taught writing or who read great writing could have produced such murk, or at least not have recognized their throwing of darkness over what was basically so clear.

"Okay, okay," Stevens withdrew his proposal. "Women as victims of a repressive society–I mean culture–are out. Now, what about homosexuals. Or gays. Or I believe it's now okay to say queers. How about queers in Shakespeare?"

"Shakespeare *was* a queer."

"Shakespeare was a *queer*?" Come on." He looked at Brumley as though it was one of Greenman's transgressive beliefs that would never get him ahead. "You're kidding."

"The sonnets," Brumley said. "They're pretty unequivocal."

"Oh, yes. But there is some question about that." Stevens had read at best three of Shakespeare's sonnets but knew there were questions about everything, that all was relative, and he hoped to suggest that Brumley was an inflexible, unconscious ideologue in his not seeing the many sides of the issue of whether or not Shakespeare was a queer.

"Yes," Brumley said flatly.

"So maybe I should steer clear of queers," Stevens conceded, 'not that I've got anything against them. In fact, some of my best friends are queers. It's just that I wouldn't want my sister to marry one. Hey, what about Blacks, or Afro-Americans–I mean African-Americans? Are there any of them in Shakespeare?"

Brumley waited a moment.

"Othello."

"What? Othello? You're shitting me; Othello wasn't an African-American."

"No, but he was black, or black enough. A swarthy Moor, I believe he is called."

"Well I'll be damned–are you sure?"

"Yes."

"How is he treated? Is there racism in the play he's in? Maybe I could show Shakespeare is a racist."

"Maybe," Brumley said slowly. "And then there's Caliban, who's kind of a monster but because he's on an island taken over by Europeans, he's seen him as a victim of the brutality of colonialism and imperialism."

Stevens looked closely at Brumley. "That's a hell of an idea. Can I have it?" he asked. "What play is what's-his-name–Calabash?–in? Has this been done or is it original, your idea?"

"It has been done," Brumley said. "Over and over. For everybody."

"All right, I'll take your word for it. How about Hispanics? I'd love to find a wetback or two and show how Shakespeare was against Latinos and Chicanos and muchachos and those kinds."

"No Hispanics."

"Then what am I going to do?" Stevens wailed. "If women have been done and queers have been done and African-Americans, and if there aren't any Spics, I can't think of another category of to write about and.... Wait a minute. Wait. What about animals? What about Shakespeare's attitude toward animals? He wasn't a vegetarian, was he, though I could work around that, maybe write about his attitude on vegetarians, or vegetables even. But if he was against animals, I could write about that, about how he disempowered them. Do you know where he stood on animals?

"No, but I think he had the usual attitudes toward them of his times."

"What was that," Stevens asked, reaching for a pen.

"I imagine he thought humans were superior to them and were to use them for food and clothing and labor, but...."

"Great god, that's it," Stevens exclaimed, relief flooding his narrow face. "He privileges humankind above animals, marginalizes animals, adds to their exploitation. Probably was an abuser, too. This is unbelievable, this is a gold mine. But wait. Has anybody done this?"

"....but," Brumley cut back in, "I was about to say, he probably liked dogs and maybe cats, cows, horses, chickens. He knew they were important, had to. But I imagine he got upset at them every now and then. Whether some imbecile has manufactured a flaw Shakespeare had in his presentation of animals, I don't know."

"What about the lesser known animals?"

"God, I don't know," Brumley replied tiredly. "Who gives a damn. Couldn't you find something good to say about Shakespeare instead of what a blind, unsympathetic man he was? He actually is a great writer, I think. He knew everybody laughs and suffers in pretty much the same way."

"A great writer?" Stevens repeated in alarm. "You can't get anything published along that line. And what people share in common—come on, Brumley, you've lived in this hole too long. You can't write about how well a poem works or how well a novel hangs together or how art touches us all. You write about how writers privilege this or that, or about victims. About how great writers aren't great at all. Or how bad writers are as good as great writers."

"I know," Brumley agreed, too dispirited to argue. 'The rats are sinking the ship. The Harpies of the shore are plucking. . . ."

"What's that?" Stevens interrupted. "Is that from Shakespeare? Does he have rats, does he marginalize rats in his plays, or sonnets? Doesn't he say there's a rat in Denmark or something like that? That's a slight on rats, because he's using—is it a simile?—to say something is wrong in Denmark, which is a subtle way of disempowering rats. That settles it; I'm going to write on rats in Shakespeare. Maybe,"—his eyes lost focus—"maybe there's a major article on this—rats in the Renaissance. Or maybe a book, a book on rats in literature in English. Brumley, thank you, bless you. I've found my subject. I think I'll start writing a grant proposal tomorrow to fund my research on it. Let's see, can you think of any examples of rats in literature?"

Brumley, who could think of a few without much effort, was pleased to lie and say he couldn't. He left Stevens chortling to himself, and, making his way to his office to re-order his books and begin grading the forty-four soul-eating freshman composition themes, he decided that Stevens had found a topic that fit him perfectly.

fifteen
BOLINGER

Bolinger's particular threat to the world was manifest early, virtually from the cradle. At a family gathering, when he was a plump four months old and in the midst of a diaper change, his dreadful Aunt Delores had rushed extravagantly to his crib and bent to gush and goo at him. When her cold eye and false smile were rightly positioned, the infant Bolinger had pissed powerfully into both. His discernment was second only to his intelligence, and in kindergarten, preferring a pencil to finger paints, quiet assessment to the snatch-and-run, and a window to the educational TV screen, he broadened his reputation as an eccentric and therefore a disruptive. Most of his well-meaning but limited grade-school teachers treated him as an intelligent dancing bear whose graceful if weighty mental flights were amusing but so discordant with good common sense that they could be ignored. This made him an immediate outcast among his fellows. The loneliness he felt from their indifference and the scars from their ridicule he bore as best he could.

In middle school, the portly Bolinger refused to take interest in any organized activity involving a ball and did not try to hide his wonder that others did. He compounded this heresy by knowing more than he should and asking questions in class that too often exposed hypocrisy, ignorance and stupidity in his teachers. Predictably, his life became even more of an affliction, one that all the intelligence in the world could not understand or justify.

"Why in foreign movies on TV do the actors' mouths not seem to be saying what we hear?" Mr. Folik, his ninth-grade science teacher asked. "It doesn't look like the two are together. Ever seen it? Know what I mean?"

Bolinger sat alertly at his desk, wondering if no one was responding because the answer was so obvious or because of Folik's murkiness. He could not imagine that they did not know.

"Nobody?" Folik happily asked.

"The sound—their speech— is dubbed in in English." Bolinger said levelly. "Whatever language the film is in doesn't have their sounds--" he almost said their phonemes— "coinciding with the English translation."

Some of the class turned in surprised enlightenment toward him; Folik as well looked startled at the revelation.

"Yes, that may be part of it," he said, "but that's not the main reason. The main reason is that foreign movies come from overseas, and since light travels faster than sound, the pictures and the voices don't get here at the same time. That's why the actors' mouths and what they say aren't together."

Bolinger's mild but unyielding response, pitilessly exposing Folik's ignorance of acoustics, electromagnetic radiation, movie production and distribution, television transmission and finally film history, resulted in the usual resentment of the class and the unforgiving enmity of Folik. Several weeks later, in the class section devoted to astronomy, Folik had another stumper.

"You know when you're going around on a merry-go-round, it tends to throw you off, centrifugal motion. Now, why don't we all fly off the earth? It's rotating. Why doesn't it sling us off?"

"Gravity," Bolinger said. He did not elaborate.

"Gravity may help," Folik nodded tolerantly, feigning generosity before crushing the know-it-all, "but the real reason is that the earth is going around the sun and that helps hold us down to the ground." He sketched a crude diagram on the board of the earth going around the sun, with some arrows pointing this way and that, establishing his theorem.

"What about at night?" Bolinger asked.

"What do you mean?"

"At night we face away from the sun. That ought to add to the forces that would throw us into space. Your vectors would show that if you put them on the dark side of the earth. Although maybe," he added desperately when he saw the look on Folik's face, "maybe we do fly up off the earth when we're asleep and don't know it and then come back in the morning with the sun. But I guess not. Not everybody sleeps at night."

The idea struck him as worthy of being true. It struck Folik and most of the class as insolence and lunacy, more proof of Bolinger's oddness that would have to be tormented out of him.

The torment had its culmination during his first year in high school, shortly after Coach McGraw's gym-class talk on tolerance and self-esteem, subjects recently required by the State Educationalist Board to be somehow incorporated into all subjects. Like physical education courses everywhere, Coach McGraw's stressed triumph and humiliation, and he resented encouraging tolerance in those who could intimidate and cause pain and resented even more granting self-esteem to those who couldn't.

"Everybody's unique," he read in a monotone from the approved instructional sheet. "Everybody's valuable. We should tolerate differences"—he shot a quick, ironic glance at his more favored bullies of the athletic teams—"and those who do not have your advantages have other valuable qualities."

The lesson took. The more intuitive of those with physical advantages sensed the rush of self-esteem they would gain by intolerantly persecuting and humiliating the meek and defenseless and were primed to apply their lesson a few days later when Bolinger's English teacher widely broadcast her dismay over Bolinger's well-argued homework essay on the tyranny and corruption of sports in schools. The word of his grotesque misconception spread quickly. Walking home after band practice in the early fall afternoon, Bolinger had turned down a narrow street flanked largely by vacant lots when a car that had been tailing him sped by and then pulled over, disgorging five of the more sadistic and brutal members of the football team. They were on him quickly, muttering threats and shoving his soft, unresisting body. Two pinned his arms, while the others produced several rolls of surgical tape stolen from the sports medicine room in the school's athletic complex. With a speed and dexterity befitting their athletic training, they quickly, tightly and completely wrapped Bolinger.

"Piece of shit," they panted. "Think you're pretty smart."

"No," Bolinger said evenly, but that was all.

Unaccountably, they left him a small breathing hole and laughing derisively piled back in the car and sped away. Bolinger lay like a large grub, the slow tears of helpless despair running along his nose and down the white tape that covered his face.

The street was uninhabited except for two houses at one end and was seldom traveled. Bolinger lay quietly, his lower legs and arms gradually losing feeling, until he heard a car approach, brake, and then a door open and footsteps coming toward him. He knew with a sudden agony much worse than his physical pain what he would have to do.

The good Samaritan, who saw from Bolinger's scattered books that likely a boy was mummified within the wrappings, began unwinding the tape from his head as gently as he could.

"You okay ?" he asked, once Bolinger's mouth, set in a forced, horrid smile, appeared.

"Yes, sir. Just a little tied up"

The man shot him a quick look and continued pulling away the tape, finally freeing Bolinger's arms, which like his legs had gone to sleep to the extent that he couldn't help free himself or stand for several minutes after the last tape was removed.

"Who did this ?" his liberator asked gently. "Do you want me to call anybody ?"

"No," Bolinger said with a laugh so artificial and forced that for a moment he thought his whole pretense might dissolve and he collapse to the sidewalk, weeping with humiliation and loneliness.

"Just some guys," he managed. "They got me good," and he continued with a story that turned his torture into a harmless and amusing prank some high spirited acquaintances—having none, he could not bring himself to say buddies—had pulled on him.

"Do you need a ride?" his undeceived benefactor asked, hoping to spare the boy any more pain.

"No, it's okay," Bolinger said, unsteadily gathering his books. "I just live two streets over."

By the next day he could see word of his chastisement had spread throughout the school, and from then on his alienation was nearly complete. Through it all, Bolinger's one desire was that his parents never know what happened. They never did.

But they sensed his isolation and persecution and suffered at his lot.

They were awed by his intelligence, entertained by his wit and proud of his courage and good nature. His mother often wished his tormentors would find an additional victim who would come armed to school and extract a rightful vengeance whose details she could not bring herself to elaborate, other than it caused the parents of the departed bullies intense and prolonged grief. Aware of how inconsistent and wrong her thinking was, she still could never dismiss it. His father felt his son's inner strength and depth of spirit and knew he would survive. But he also wished to kill certain of Bolinger's classmates and then their fathers, ideally the former in front of the latter as in a howling mass they were chasing his son home on his bike. *Hurts, doesn't it?* he would say as the police placed him in the back of a patrol car to begin a journey that would end with the gurney, the lethal drip, and his unrepentant, triumphant smile at the mothers of the victims behind the one-way viewing mirror. A Catholic, he could never bring himself to confess these violent, disturbing fantasies, mainly because doing so would betray his son's loneliness and sorrow, not to say his own helplessness, to one as ineffectual in the matter as himself. And he knew he could never repent. After all, the true wrong was elsewhere and would never be admitted or even recognized by its perpetrators, who would prosper or fail regardless of their incidental cruelties. Bolinger's father came gradually to believe there was no justice, anywhere.

By far the most intelligent student in his high school class, Bolinger continued exposing sufficient intellectual shortcomings among his teachers that his grades often suffered. He was not granted admission to the Honor Society, whose members were chosen by these same teachers, and his less-than-perfect grades were not enough to gain him a scholarship at a real university. Nearby Middle State's offer of free room and board was a godsend to his parents, and Bolinger, whose failure of discernment here was easily excused by his age, enrolled there gladly, unaware that Folik and most of his teachers had attended Middle State or schools like it, schools that in the not-too-distant past had promoted themselves from Teacher Colleges to Universities. He had a dream.

Though it never regressed to the nightmare of his earlier days, his dream of finding at college likeminded students who demanded to know was short-lived, and even before the beginning of classes, he knew something was terribly wrong. And yet there were kindred spirits at Middle State, even friends who were not kindred spirits. A month into his freshman year, Bolinger found himself discussing with Warren and Sola the purpose of life. Jeeks, drunk again, was lost in a dream of fulfillment, his cheek on the study-lounge table by a half-eaten slice of extravagantly topped pizza.

"The obvious purpose of life," Bolinger declared, "is to destroy life."

"You mean, like the food chain, that kind of thing?" Sola asked.

"In part, the scrimmage of appetites, yes, but I'm just talking about humans. And not solely our appetites for square hamburgers."

"Wars," Warren observed. "Wars and persecution and all that. We live just for that."

Jeeks, stirred by the unfamiliar profundity of the discussion, partly lifted his head.

"Pussy," he announced, his head easing back toward the pizza slice, "only answer."

"Jeeks notwithstanding," Bolinger grinned, "I have something else in mind. Unbridled sex, while enticing, is not the answer, not with our brainless overpopulation at the root of it all. Bridled sex may hold some promise, but probably not."

Jeeks made an incoherent but vaguely dissenting noise.

"Maybe there is no satisfying answer," Bolinger went on, "not in the sense that the purpose of life accords with our deepest wishes. But I think we can establish from the evidence what the true purpose is, however unpleasant. It's to end life."

"When we slaughter a cow," Sola said—he was awed by Bolinger but always tried to contradict him— "we're not trying to end life, not all life. We're killing the cow to eat so our lives can go on. Just like the cow kills grass—do they kill grass?—so its life can go on. We don't want to kill all the cows. They probably don't want to kill all the grass."

"We're the highest form of life," Warren said. "What's our purpose? Just keep on eating and breeding until we evolve to something else? Then what does the something else do—go on eating and breeding? Maybe in wars and all our purpose of life is to end life, though the winners just want to end the lives of the losers, it seems to me. What about it, Bolinger?"

"Wars, pogroms, persecutions, genocide. They're all to my point in a way. But I mean something else. . . ."

"Pussy," Jeeks insisted thickly from his pizza.

They waited.

"Only. Answer."

"What I mean," Bolinger went on unperturbed, "is that we're not ending life conscious of what we're doing. It's not like a war or persecution or such. Just the way we're living is ending life. We're overpopulating everywhere; we're warming the globe, holing the ozone, acidifying the rain, eroding the fields, poisoning the ground water. We're cutting the forests, polluting the rivers, expanding the deserts, wasting the soils, extincting the animals."

"Extincting?" Sola challenged. "Is there such a word?"

"Ask the Passenger Pigeon," Bolinger said. "We're not just killing life, we're killing the possibility of life. We're killing the goddamned *ground*. And the water. And the air. Maybe we'll find some way to kill the sun. Come to think of it, now that we're destroying the ozone layer, we've found a way to make the sun kill us."

"I don't get it," Warren said, slipping a half-full beer from Jeek's nerveless right hand and passing it around. "Doing all that stuff isn't on purpose. Nobody sets out to destroy life."

"It's the purposes we don't recognize that are the real purposes," Bolinger said, taking a pull from Jeek's beer. "Of course nobody intends to end life. But at the same time, everybody knows what's up. Take Jeek's pizza slice, or, same thing, this beer," he said, holding up the can like Yorick's skull. "Think what had to happen to get it here. First the aluminum ore had to be strip-mined and shipped and processed. How much coal or oil had to be burned to do it, with more strip mining and air pollution and acid rain and global warming as a consequence? Then the metal had to be formed, the barley for the beer grown in agribusiness fields with oil supplying most of the energy and poisons everywhere. The grain had to be dieseled to a brewery, the beer gas-guzzled to a brightly lit, energy consuming store. And to get us–except" he nodded toward Jeeks–"to drink it, it has to be advertised on TV's that are manufactured and run on energy from coal. Mostly from coal. Maybe a little nuclear thrown in to round out the picture. It's the same for everything, every little seemingly innocent thing we do or buy or use. We're killing life and we know it. But somehow we refuse to know it, and go right on. So I'd say the purpose of life, based on the available evidence, is to end life."

"Okay," Sola said, "Suppose you're right. What do you do? If it was a can of beans instead of beer and we were starving, you can't just say I won't eat the beans because I'm ending life– I don't mean the bean's life; I mean, like you say, all that's done to get the beans to you is ending life. What do you do?"

"We could grow our own beans," Warren observed. "I don't know how but I know it can be done. My grandparents raised a garden every year."

"We could even make our own beer, even grow our own ingredients, except maybe the sugar," Bolinger reflected. "Actually, I don't know how to grow the other stuff either. But people could learn; I could learn."

"Nobody would do it," Sola said. "I don't think. Maybe if you had some kind of law people might, though I doubt it. I can't see me doing anything for myself that I could pay somebody else to do for me."

"Then Bolinger is right," Warren said. "The ending of life is so far gone that there's no changing it."

"But we're having a big time," Bolinger added. "In fact, I believe Jeeks still has a full beer under his chair, and we might as well drink it. Let's drink to having a good time in America. It'll last maybe fifty years, and then what will happen will happen. I see no solution."

They turned to Jeeks, struggling to lift his head, but he nestled closer to his comforting, lavish pizza and resumed his untroubled dream.

Bolinger was a marvel to many of his college instructors at Middle State, who very rarely saw his like. And they were miracles, some of them, to him. Talbot of Biology, Mulholland of Psychology, Hobart, Norens, Greenman–were delights to him, for they let him challenge them and seemed to admire and enjoy his speculations, though the truth was they were more taken by the fact that he *would* speculate. To others he was a threat. His suffering throughout grade and high school years had taught him to recognize quickly those who would not have their knowledge–or lack of it–questioned, and so at Middle State he no longer suffered unintentionally. Harmless lame-brains like Half-life Anderson he tried to ignore or to entertain himself with their inexcusable ignorance. For mental martinets like Fulson of History, he simply dropped their classes. Extraordinarily high grades were a breeze for him in courses he liked, but he still made high grades in those he didn't. His fellow students, no longer quite the ravenous pack of fearful conformists of his high school days, mostly accepted or at least tolerated him, but it was in Brumley's humanities class, one of his favorites, that he found that he would never be safe.

"Let's try to apply this next reading to the present, to our own time and lives," Brumley had said the previous meeting of his humanities course. "Instead of *The Prince*, think of the title as *The Leader*, or *The Boss*, and substitute that word for prince throughout. And don't think only of a country as what this leader is head of–think of anything, a corporation or a church or even a university. Remember, everything we read in here is a waste of time if you don't try to apply it to your own life."

Or are incapable of, he wanted to say, or won't. But as usual he kept silent, tact—or kindness– winning out over sincerity, though he thought cowardice might also be involved. He felt that most of his students who found Machiavelli repellant did so not because of the calculating courtier's bleak assessment of mankind, but because his name was hard to spell. Still, at the next meeting Brumley came to the discussion of *The Prince* as he did to most of his classes, assuming that everyone in the class had tried to do as he suggested and had thought as they read–if they had read–of their own world in terms of Machiavelli's assumptions.

"First of all, we need to recognize that Machiavelli calls for the kind of leader he does in order to unite Italy and drive out its several conquerors. Do you remember the situation in Europe during the 1500's from your second semester World Civilization course you took as freshmen?"

World Civilization, once proudly called World History, was required of all freshmen; the two humanities courses like those Brumley taught were required during or after the sophomore year. Brumley saw no lights go on in anyone's eyes, and a flash of guilt told him he wasn't altogether sure what the situation had been himself. Colson and his wretched brothers of Pi fraternity furtively looked at one another: *Oh, sure–how well we remember World Civ and whatever.*

"In other words," he went on, "Machiavelli wants his advice to a leader—his discussion of how a leader ought to act and be—to be followed in order to free his country from foreign oppression, something that most of us ought to appreciate."

Then he made a mistake.

"Why is that so?" he asked.

He felt an immediate tenseness grip the class and realized most had been just drifting along to the hum of his voice.

"Why do I say that most of us should appreciate the fact that Machiavelli wants to free his country from foreign oppression?"

"Because it's bad?" asked Gordon, an ever-hopeful student near the back.

"The basic reason, I agree," Brumley replied. "But why should *we* feel sympathy with Machiavelli's goal?"

"Is it because we know that foreign oppression is bad?" a diminutive and usual silent girl offered.

"That's right," Brumley agreed encouragingly, as though a real advance had been made in answering the question. "But why is it that we especially would think it was bad?"

Bolinger's hand shot up.

" Eric?"

"It's because of all the stuff we had to read in freshman comp about how bad it was to be oppressed—to be an Indian or a black or a woman and to be oppressed. Evidently the assumption was that we didn't know it already."

With Bolinger, Brumley knew, it was best to practice the old courtroom precaution of never asking a question to which the answer wasn't already carefully circumscribed, but he was curious enough at Bolinger's answer to risk letting his own question slide for the moment.

"How did you know it already?" he asked, hoping Bolinger might eventually produce what he was fishing for.

"You have to read all that stuff in high school, or at least we did in mine. Every year. How racism was bad, how sexism was bad. It made the teachers feel like they were courageous or something."

He ceased speaking, but Brumley stood waiting and finally nodded for him to go on.

"I figured that to speak up against the powers today and be really brave was too dangerous. Racism, sexism–nobody's going to shoot you or laugh at you now for being against them. A long time ago you could get in trouble for doing it, but not now. So you make students read about how bad those things are and you can feel noble. And probably help your career."

"Eric, I'll get a little ahead of ourselves and say I think you may agree with the spirit of a lot of what Machiavelli has to say."

"I agree he's generally accurate; I don't agree with him, though."

"Good enough," Brumley said, relieved that this time Bolinger had given his considered opinion without offending anyone or showing Brumley not to be thinking very well. "But I still want to know why *we*, as citizens of the United States–formerly the Thirteen Colonies–might feel sympathetic toward Machiavelli's ends."

Bolinger looked down, but Brumley sensed he felt the answer was perfectly obvious; Warren was surreptitiously reading *All the King's Men*. Colson and his pack were snickering again at the pointlessness of it all.

"It's because the British ruled us and weren't fair," Kimmie Deneen asserted. "It's part of our past to resent it."

"Thank you," Brumley said, stunned at Kimmie Denee and noting the rush of enlightenment on many faces. He was reassured by their comprehension, but why hadn't they seen the connection themselves? Was it simply that doing so required the conjoining of two separate pieces of information that most knew but were incapable of bringing together? Or as likely, when he had stressed *we* as a key concept in answering his query, the *we* to them could only encompass a present-day age group or zip code or income level–something demographic that could have no extension whatever into the past. After all, so many of them lived sealed in a world where the privileged wanted no past, only an artificial present and a fantasized future. The colonists, British oppression, the War of Independence–all of it, in that dismissive twist so many of them gave the now-discredited word, was just *history*.

"Let's get back to *The Prince* itself," Brumley said. "Machiavelli has an *end* for his advice, a goal, something he wants to see accomplished by putting his advice into practice."

He wrote *Ends* on the board and underlined it. A general scuffling of notebooks being opened and pens searched for followed. He felt sure that for some in the class, their only note for the day would be the word *Ends*, underlined.

"I mention this now but want to look in some detail at his advice, which contains his *means*"–he wrote *Means* on the board, and it was dutifully recorded by most of the class— "his means of realizing what he wants, namely, the freeing of his country. Freeing his country is the *end*–or it constitutes the *ends*–of what he wants. Now, when we've looked at his means, then we can consider a larger issue that underlies Machiavelli's writings: can one's ends justify one's means of reaching them? Do you understand that, ever heard the phrase 'the ends justify the means'?'

Neither Kimmie Deneen nor Warren nor the pre-med majors nor the other two or three dependable students appeared to have–surprisingly, even Bolinger appeared blank.

"We'll come back to it after we've looked at *The Prince* in detail. Or all the detail twenty minutes allows."

The committee that had designed the course required that the students read only the opening chapter of *The Prince* and then the central ones that contained the heart of the work. Brumley had always been both exhilarated and depressed by them. There one found Machiavelli's advice on how a prince should conduct himself to keep power, both the qualities he should have and the ones he should pretend to have but on no account ever practice. Brumley dove in.

"Machiavelli has a fairly consistent way of presenting his advice or argument. He'll start off by saying something like, in a certain area, a leader ought to have such and such a quality–for example, in the area of giving out government construction projects or grants or tax breaks, it would be wonderful if he could be open-handed, generous, spend and grant favors left and right. *But*, Machiavelli will quickly add, doing such is in the long run, or sometimes in the short run, not a good idea and it's better to be just the opposite. How would you classify, in all the areas he discusses, the first choice and then the second?"

Brumley knew the question was far too involved and vague. He tried again.

"Put it this way: he says that between a leader's being generous and tight, tightness is better; later, between being loved or feared, feared is better. Now, how would you compare generosity and love to stinginess and fear?"

No one wanted to try, until finally Bolinger spoke up.

"The first of each pair, the ones he advises against, are ones we think of as good, as qualities people ought to have. But the second of each pair, the qualities a prince really should have, are bad."

"Exactly," Brumley said, delighted that Bolinger had answered for a second time without bringing in wholly relevant and important side issues that disturbed the rest of the class, often including Brumley. "So Machiavelli says, and notice that he gives plenty of examples that support his point—remember how you were told to support your general assertions in freshman comp"—Brumley wasn't sure that many were being taught anything in freshman comp other than the easy piety Bolinger earlier had referred to— "Machiavelli says that in spite of what we say and maybe even feel is good conduct by a leader, history shows us that just the opposite kind of conduct is the effective one. Let's take whether it's better to be loved or feared. As he says, *everybody* knows it's by far better to be loved, surely on a personal level. But for a leader, if he's loved, if he's been kind to everyone—commuted prison sentences, handed out money everywhere, respected his opponents—what does Machiavelli say that does to his ability to rule, to be a boss and keep his country or whatever he's leader of united to some common purpose—in other words, what does it do to his ability to command people's loyalty?"

Most of the class looked studiously at their book.

"Anyone want to make a try here?"

"Doesn't he feel like nobody will follow him if things get bad," a pre-med major offered.

"Right," Brumley said, "good. Now, why does he say this is so—what reason or argument does he give to support his assertion, his thesis?" He hoped the concept of a thesis was still being taught in composition, but likely it had been abandoned as being too limiting to the free expression of the students.

"He says," Brumley was again gratified to hear Kimmy Deneen say, "that people can't be trusted. They like you as long as they can get something from you, but when they may get in trouble for being your friend, they'll drop you. Though they'll act like there's another reason."

"Kimmy Deneen," Brumley said, moved, "that's very well put. You may even go Machiavelli one better," and seeing her face fall from what she evidently thought was censure, he tried to correct himself.

"I don't mean you're like Machiavelli," he went on, knowing the smile he offered could not ameliorate his misconstrued remark. "You just broaden his field from politics to all human interaction. And you may well be right. Look, let's get to the heart of the matter."

Most of the class re-opened their notebooks or poised their pens anew.

"Machiavelli says that a prince or leader can keep his position—and thereby keep an orderly, united, strong state that can among other things resist outside conquest—not by being loved or by being generous or by being truly religious, that is, by following Christian ethics. Instead, he can have loyal subjects only by scarring them to death, through fear of his power. And this is because, to Machiavelli, humans are fickle, false, quick to cheer you in good times and stab you in the back and leave you bleeding if you can no longer do anything for them."

"Now, the real question is, are humans, is human nature, like that?"

No one wanted to speak after his blunder with Kimmie Deneen, and Brumley felt once more how difficult it was in a class to get everything right—impossible, in fact, though there was no choice but to keep trying. To prove how often one could go wrong, he tried to outwait them. Saying nothing, striving to keep an alert, friendly face, he simply looked from one bowed head to an occasional puzzled face to another bowed head.

"I don't think it is," said Colson, who occasionally felt it to his advantage to pretend some engagement with the class. Brumley often wondered how the Pi Iota fraternity had come by his tests, which was all that could explain the four arrogant twerps in his class. Unlike Colona, who to advance himself in the administration's favor had become faculty advisor to one of the lesser fraternities, Brumley did not court their presence or give them unearned high grades.

"Go on," Brumley said.

"I just don't think it is," Colson carefully clarified his point, barely keeping a straight face when one of his brothers hidden behind him snickered at their leader's successful hoodwinking of an instructor.

Of all in the class, Brumley thought, it would be Colson who sooner or later, in an extravagant and cruel way, would prove Machiavelli's assessment of human nature correct. "What do you base your position on?"

"I don't think most people stab you in the back. I mean, I don't see it."

"So, like Machiavelli, you're basing your position on experience, in your case your own experience. Machiavelli, as you read, generally uses historical examples rather than personal ones to support his argument, but in both cases neither of you is idealizing human nature. In other words, you're both saying, here's what human nature is, as shown by what humans do—right?"

"Uh huh," Colson said, vaguely comprehending.

"Can you give us some specific examples?" Brumley asked.

"You mean mine?"

"Sure." Brumley decided to press him as far as it took.

Colson thought.

"When we have rush and guys come and we see if we want them to join, we. . . ."

"Rush?" Brumley asked in feigned innocence. Let the little shit think at least somebody doesn't have any idea or interest in what fraternities are or do.

"Our fraternity. We're in a fraternity."

"And you judge who you want to join?" Brumley couldn't help himself.

"Yeah."

"Okay."

"Well," Colson continued, and Brumley was gratified to see him disturbed to realize that someone he mistakenly believed had standing and power knew nothing about fraternities. "Well, when we have guys visit and they want to join but aren't Pi material and aren't picked, then we don't stab them in the back or anything."

The class for the most part sat dully, but Brumley saw Bolinger stir in his seat. Even Colson appeared puzzled at his example. He had ventured into treacherous waters.

"Let's see. . . ." Brumley began, but Colson, trying to flounder to redemption, elaborated.

"I mean, you know, they've come over to the house and feel lucky to be invited and then when we don't pick them and they feel bad, we don't stab them in the back. We still speak to them and all. I speak to guys who aren't Pi's all the time."

He turned for confirmation to his fellows, some of whom were still trying to contain their choking incredulity that Colson was actually taking part in a class.

"Do you speak to just any guys who aren't Pi's or only to those who wanted to be Pi's but weren't good enough?" Bolinger calmly asked from the back.

"I'll talk to anybody. Almost anybody," Colson shot back.

"Would you talk to me?" Bolinger asked matter-of-factly.

"Why would I want to talk to *you*?" Colson sneered, and his brothers looked back contemptuously at the audacious worm.

"Because, like you said, or implied for Dr. Brumley, human nature is basically friendly and kind. And since you're human, you'd talk to me because you're friendly and kind and not snobbish and cruel. You can prove Machiavelli—the guy we're reading—wrong by talking to me."

"Huh!" Colson grunted, turning back around and glowering at his desk top.

"I think we need to get back to the details," Brumley announced as though no harpoon had been set and Colson impaled in uncomprehending fury at his desk. "We've seen that Machiavelli wants a strong leader and wants one in order to unite Italy and free it. But he thinks that can happen only if that leader is more or less ruthless, rules by fear—but of course doesn't take any of his subject's property, which would be a mistake based on another rather low view of mankind that he holds. Anybody remember what he says there?"

"'Men sooner forget the death of their fathers than their loss of patrimony,'" Warren read and looked up. Colson's stupidity and Bolinger's exposing it had called him from his novel.

"Exactly, good," Brumley said. "In other words, as a leader you can have their fathers executed and they'll get over it before they will your taking their property—their patrimony. Pretty harsh, huh?"

Warren had read Machiavelli's comment from their translated text, and most of the students began thumbing fruitlessly through their books to find and mark the passage.

237

"It's on page 423, about half-way down," Brumley informed them. "Now, there's another point to Machiavelli that we should consider as it relates to our time. While he says we should avoid being merciful and generous and actually avoid nearly all the virtues if we're going to be an effective leader, we've got to do what as concerns those virtues?"

"We've got to pretend to have them, to put up a front," Bolinger said, with a delighted smile that made Brumley smile back at him and nod in agreement.

"Fine, Eric. Do you—or does anyone—remember what it was he claims is most important to pretend to have?"

"Religion," Bolinger quickly replied. You've got to pretend to be religious above all else."

Machiavelli was explicit on this point, but Brumley could clearly see that several of the class, including Jenny McDaniels and others who liked praying on the corners of the street were either shocked or confused by Bolinger's answer.

"Why do you think he feels that to stay in power you've got to pretend to all the generally accepted virtues, especially religion, but have none of them?"

He pointedly looked away from Bolinger and around the room. Colson, somewhat recovered from his urge to rip and tear Bolinger into the pieces of offal he was, tried to establish himself again as actually caring about this Mack-whatever guy.

"If you're not good to people, they won't like you and you'll be voted out."

Brumley considered for a moment.

"You mean really good to them?"

"Yes."

"Not just pretending to be?"

"No. I don't think." Colson began to feel his platitudes were getting him nowhere. Behind him, his brothers were beginning to twitter again.

"What about being religious?" Brumley asked, and hoped someone would cut in and un-skewer the oaf. No one did, and Colson thrashed on.

"He'd need to be religious or god would punish him by having him not be reelected."

"Dr. Brumley," Bolinger signaled from his far corner.

"Yes?"

"A good example of religious hypocrisy in our time," he began, as though Colson had never spoken, "would be the TV evangelists who have gone to prison for stealing from their audience. Those and politicians who love to go to a prayer breakfast with Billy Graham the anti-Semite and get their pictures taken praying over their pancakes."

There was an angry mutter from several points in the class and a shaking of heads here and there. Colson, who not only had been lanced by a creature insignificant beyond contempt but had now been cast away, sat adrift, incapable of retaliation, in white-faced silence.

"How does that relate to Machiavelli?" Brumley asked.

"It's complicated," Bolinger said carefully, frowning. "The Prince needs to keep people guessing, off-balance, so he can push them any way he wants. So he rules ruthlessly but pretends by his show of being religious that he's good. But also, he goes along with the general hypocrisy of Christians, to keep up a front and give lip service to being Christian but generally go on being self-centered and covetous and thoughtless about others. So everybody feels the prince is like them. I mean, in his going to church and praying in public and all he's obviously like them, but in the way he actually is, he's secretly like them. So they feel he's a regular guy. He's sort of like the King and Duke in *Huckleberry Finn*. And like TV evangelists. People aren't smart. If you announce you're a preacher or put up a show of being a devout believer, you can take their money a lot easier."

After that, no comment from the class was likely, so Brumley went on. There were only a few minutes until the bell.

"What about keeping up a front in general? Is that a commonplace, really an industry, in our time?"

"I don't think we keep up a front," Colson dove in for a last, desperate attempt to rescue his unexamined life. "We're not like that. That's just a bunch of bull, what he said," and he gestured with angry repugnance at Bolinger.

"I don't know," Bolinger rowed back in as though punting down some gentle stream. "Every corporation in America has a public relations division to 'put a spin,' as they call it, on whatever atrocity the corporation is responsible for. Our government does it best of all—they lie about almost everything. We even teach public relations here, at Middle State—you can actually major in it, study to become an expert in lying and covering up. You can get a degree in it. And television is nothing but a lie. That's all it is. But I think pretending to virtues we don't have is pretty human, pretending to be what we wish we were. Or much worse, what we want people to think we are. I mean, there are some people who every now and then make it a point to try to answer a question in class and pretend to be interested when in fact they never read an assignment and cheat whenever they can and consider the whole subject of the class to be useless garbage. They're trying to fool their instructor that they're serious and real interested."

Colson, Brumley saw, sat positively paralyzed, too shocked for the moment to feel the murderous rage that would surely come later. As for now, any lashing out would verify Bolinger's fatal thrust, but to sit silently after such a smooth lancing was nearly ripping him apart. He turned quick to glare with pure hatred at Bolinger.

"Yes, there are students like that," Brumley said reflectively, as though he recalled from many years back witnessing such dishonorable fakery. "I've seen it. Every instructor has. And you know something," he went on innocently, the malicious way before him perfectly clear, "there's nothing more obvious to a teacher than that kind of student."

He looked with mock sorrow at the floor, and in a tone that of course excluded all in the class from such a category, said in a final machiavellian twist, for which he felt no shame whatever:

"The worst thing is that they're so conceited and stupid they never see what transparent weasels they are," and the bell dismissing class rang almost approvingly but, for a change, too soon.

II

sixteen
THE PARTY

"C all! Me Ishmael," Bolinger commanded, striking his fringed
buckskin-clad chest with a clenched fist. Costumed as a Sioux
chieftain complete with war-bonnet, he was handing out small cards
with his name and phone number to every girl who stepped out of the
elevator into the dorm study-lounge area where the dorm floor costume-
or-not party was underway.

"Also called Big Sperm Whale," he would add hopefully to each
of the mainly uncomprehending but surprisingly large number of girls
who had been attracted by the mysterious classified ad in the previous
week's student newspaper. The ad was for the dorm floor's second annual
Hellcome Back party celebrating the beginning of spring semester,
and the floor's occupants, having optimistically decided that the poor
attendance at last year's inaugural party was due to insufficient publicity,
had elected a willing Sola to be its organizer and promoter.

"Everyone write me up an ad," he had requested at the informal
gathering in the study-lounge, "typed, please, and on standard paper.
Try to make it as brief as possible, but attention-getting. Maybe we need
a committee to evaluate them."

No committee was forthcoming and only Bolinger submitted an
ad. To Warren's amazement, Bolinger was taking an Introduction to
Advertising class in this, his last semester at Middle State. He had told
no one but Warren.

"Why?" Warren asked. "Why would you take such a course? You'll
hate it. You already hate it."

"Know thine enemy," Bolinger replied. "I know they *are* mine enemy; I want to know their methods. Besides, already I've learned to write a counter-ad, a non-ad, based on only two weeks' of class."

Bolinger's ad read:

> Lonely, lost, good-hearted males, longing for similar females or any females, are having a party. Almost everyone welcome. Wilder Hall, 8th floor, January 30, 8 pm.

"It's honest," he protested with suppressed laughter to Sola's disbelief on scanning the effort. "Wouldn't you want an honest description of a party you might go to? Women like honesty, don't they? Is Plumb Bob in his copularium? Hey, Plumb Bob," he called down the hall, "do women like honesty?"

Bolinger and Sola waited.

"Depends," Plumb Bob called back.

Sola took the writing of the ad on himself, and the eye-catching result had been a great success, standing out blaringly from the twittering idiocy of such usual *Middle State News* classifieds as: "Patti-cake, Thanks for an mega-good time last weekend. Sigma Delta love, Pumpkin"; or "Rho Zetas, Massive kegger last Friday. Yours in Alpha Delt Pride."

Sola's ad read:

> Christian Orgy
> Serious-minded abandon with godly revelers. Costume, street clothes, or no clothes required. Free drugs and alcoholic drinks prohibited by unjust laws. A new tradition. Wilder Hall, 8th floor, Fri., Jan 30, 8pm. Free. For all.

The ad's success, Warren insisted, was its broad appeal through clearly expressed paradox, and he readily conceded that his early insistence on godly *bacchants* was needlessly allusive and literary. *Revelers* had been a compromise between it and Jeek's more straightforward *motherfuckers*, which lost its considerable support when Sola pointed out that the student newspaper would never print it and that the promise of wild, irresponsible and possibly dangerous males was clear enough without obscenity. He was right, and the women poured in.

Warren was ready for some revelry. Over the holidays he had talked at length with his parents about having to return to Middle State an extra year to complete the course work for his degree. His father, unfamiliar with academic procedures and too good hearted to believe in institutional indifference and incompetence, did not understand the situation and offered to borrow money on their house to finance the extra year, an offer Warren refused. Either he would borrow the money on his own or would work during the year. Or maybe he would just drop out. After all, he had made a good start on his education and thought he knew enough to continue it on his own for as long as he could foresee. An education was everything, a diploma nothing. Or, as evidently everyone else in the world thought, the other way around.

But for now, the decision could wait. Hoh, from a slightly raised platform of loading-dock pallets at the far end of the study lounge, had cued the music and cranked the volume up a notch, while Jeeks as Mahatma Gandhi came prancing with gong and loin cloth down the hall and into the shrieking crowd in the study lounge, a pint of tequila stuck in his waistband.

"Not bad," Shepherd said to Warren as Jeeks dropped to his knees for a moment of transcendent meditation before a quivering, full-bodied girl in a gymnast's suit. "Not bad at all."

They surveyed the action while Hoh jacked the volume up even more and the elevator bell clanged its door opening to disgorge some dozen more newcomers, half of them in costume.

"Look," Warren exclaimed. "My God—Kimee Deneen."

She was the last passenger off and was wearing easily the most splendid costume of the night. It was an old fashioned prom dress, black satin, tight over her hips and upper thighs and then flared, with glitter in her hair and on her face. She smiled appreciatively at Bolinger's routine, took his card and spoke with him for a moment. Catching sight of Warren, to his astonishment she waved in his direction, and had he and Shepherd not been standing against the wall, he would have assumed her greeting was for someone behind them. She made her way through the increasingly animated dancers and up to Warren.

"Hi," she said, though he could hardly hear her for the music and the roaring in his ears.

"Hey," he managed. "Nice outfit." He did not dare look her up and down.

"I thought it would go along with the theme."

The theme, Warren thought. *What theme?*

"Theme?" he said.

"Of this." She indicated the crowd. "You know. The party, the ad. It was irony, wasn't it? I thought wearing a prom dress to an orgy would go along."

Warren was speechless; he could tell that Shepherd, too, was stunned.

"And in case nobody caught it"–she looked playfully at him–"I wore these," and she glanced down at her feet.

Warren, looking down slowly, saw she was wearing holed, worn and dirty sneakers.

"All right!" he said appreciatively, and, gathering confidence, "That's great. A prom dress to an orgy. I don't think there'll be much of an orgy, but it looks like things are picking up."

Hoh's warm-up tape was doing its job. Already the party was spreading down the hall, and the few occupants of the floor below who had not gone home or elsewhere for the weekend were expectantly coming up by the stairs, drawn to the pulsating beat. Plumb Bob, surrounded on the dance floor by four writhing coeds, was pleasantly assessing them for a nightly partner. Warren was prepared for him. To make sure he eventually had a place to sleep he had volunteered to be in charge of refreshments and had put the beer keg in his and Plumb Bob's room, knowing that Plumb Bob would need at least some privacy well before the party ended and would have to go elsewhere. Plumb Bob rarely granted his aspirants more than an hour's time, but Warren was taking no chances. He had a story due in Huckston's class on Monday and would need at least a little sleep to finish it up over the weekend.

Farther down the hall, Sola and Mohamed's room had been designated the smoking area and was furnished with black-light posters, lava lamps and an exhaust fan rigged by Hoh and Shepherd. It was getting heavy use.

"Like a beer?" Warren asked Kimee Deneen, who appeared content to stand by him. Shepherd had retreated to the smoking room with a bag of his harsh but passable homegrown for free distribution.

"Sure," Kimee Deneen said, the glitter on her eyelids flashing like tiny promises from a land of dreams. "Anything to eat?"

"Yes, but I don't know what. Want me to bring you a plate?"

"I'll be right here," she said.

The refreshment room, as Sola had christened it, was strategically located in Linton and Well's room directly across the hall from the smoking room and was stocked with open bags of potato, corn, wheat and rice chips and seven kinds of dip in their plastic supermarket cups. Bolinger, deputized by Warren to provide the food, had been thorough within the bounds of chips and dip, but had evidently decided to forego elegance in their presentation. At the last moment Warren had realized there were no paper plates or plastic spoons and had managed just to get them in place just before the crowd began to arrive. Now, ripping open the untouched rice chips, he started to prepare two plates, then, inspired, put four dollops of dip on one and heaped a mixture of the four chips on the other. If she wanted chips and dip both, she would have to stick with him. In his room, after a brief wait in line for the keg, he sat the two plates down on Plumb Bob's bed, filled two plastic cups, hugged them gently to his chest with one arm and picked up the two plates with his right hand and threaded his way with care down the hall, where he found Kimee Deneen talking with Plumb Bob.

"My man," Plumb Bob said. "You brought us food." But he laughed easily and looked around the room as Kimee Deneen relieved Warren of a plate and cup.

"This is good," she said, seeing the two plates. "We can share."

She took a healthy pull on the beer—ahh—and licked the foam off her upper lip with a tongue that needed no glitter.

"You know Dr. Brumley is supposed to chaperone?" Warren told them. "He said he couldn't get here until nine but to start without him—he didn't want to put a damper on things."

"Do you like him?" Kimee Deneen asked, turning away from Plumb Bob, who, unaccustomed to disregard, stood for a moment and then moved charitably and unoffended back into the crowd of dancers where he quickly had two partners. Across the lounge, Bolinger whooped with delight as a startled girl in a cowgirl outfit stepped from the elevator and found herself the center of his improvised Chickasaw corn fertility dance, Bolinger whirling, bending and straightening, beseeching the great spirit.

"Yes," Warren said, only slightly distracted from Kimee Deneen by the general turmoil. "A lot. He tried to get some courses added so I could graduate this spring, not that it did much good. He got some other instructors to do what they could, too. I like his classes. Do you?"

"Yes. He's helped me out a lot. I think I'm doing better. He really likes what he teaches, doesn't he?"

Hoh had dropped the volume slightly; a slow dance was coming on, calming the crowd somewhat before he cued some classic Stones.

"More than most of them. He wants us to like it, too. And to think about it. I wish he wouldn't get so irritated when nobody answers questions and he thinks we haven't read the stuff. I mean those of us who do read the stuff. He tries not to show it, but you can tell he's pissed."

"I sure read the next day's stuff when he does. That's one thing I get out of him, to really read. I used not to read much, and when I did, not think much about it–I mean apply it to me."

"He's interesting. At least he's interested in what he teaches."

They had moved down the study lounge wall to a table and sat their plates there. Kimee Deneen ate with relish and, after seeing Warren's expression when she again licked the foam off her upper lip, dropped her eyes and thereafter unselfconsciously used her fingertips.

"Are you graduating this year?" Warren asked.

"No. I didn't do very good my freshman year. Then I switched majors. It'll take an extra year. What about you?"

"Me, too–an extra year. But like I said, I should have this spring but they didn't offer the courses that I had to have to graduate."

"I don't get it. Can they do that? Or not do that?"

"They can do about anything they want, I think. I wrote President Curtis about it and the people on the Reigning Board. Brumley wrote Curtis for me, too–did you know about that? He's in some kind of trouble about it, I think, or that letter or article he wrote to the state newspaper–did you hear about that?"

"No. Just lately?"

"A few weeks ago. Actually, he didn't say he was in trouble. But he did say he'd made Curtis look bad, and I felt from the way he said it there was something wrong. Outside of class I've only seen him once since break, to ask him to chaperone tonight."

"He's okay," Kimee Deneen said, and then with a twinkle in her starry eyes: "Why didn't you ask Dr. Huckston to chaperone?"

"Good God," Warren said derisively, and both of them laughed.

"I never did get my final story back from him last semester," Kimee Deneen said. "He never gets things back until after you've forgotten what you weren't sure about in your answers or what you felt good about."

"I don't mind it that much, but he doesn't show up a lot of the time. And he's always trying to entertain."

"Do you think he really lays it on just before teacher evaluation?"

Warren was struck by the idea.

"I never thought about that. You're right. Pizzas and goofing off–and it was all just before evaluation. What a jerk."

"He thinks he's god's gift to the females. You notice that?"

"Yes. Embarrassing. That gold chain."

"Shaved chest. You notice?"

Their voices were about drowned out by the music.

Ooh, the storm is raging, higher and higher it burns; gimme, gimme shelter, the lyrics went, the sweet guitar filling in.

"Shaved? No, I didn't. How do you know?" he asked before he realized its possible implications.

"One day he unbuttoned his shirt one button too many and you could see the line where he stopped shaving."

Warren wondered why anyone would shave his chest, but didn't want to seem naïve and didn't ask.

"He thinks he's an *artist*," he said.

"But I don't think he writes anything," Kimee Deneen said. "His story he read last week I thought was bad. 'The Life of John Williams'."

"It didn't seem right. I thought so, too. I didn't know what to say.

"Look," Kimee Deneen said suddenly, her attention drawn to the elevator. "Dr. Brumley."

Brumley, arm-in-arm with Norens, was just getting off, both reacting with great delight to Bolinger's greeting–by now slurred, from firewater, he explained with slow dignity. Looking around, they spotted Warren and Kimee Deneen across the lounge and, bumped and jostled, began to make their way toward them through the dancers.

"I see you started without me," Brumley said. "Good. Chris, Kimee Deneen, you know Dr. Norens, I believe."

Warren had been in her American Literature class his sophomore year; Kimee Deneen the next year. Both said hello, awkwardly holding their beer cups by their sides.

"Where's the keg?" Brumley asked, looking around. "I might as well break the law, make things official. You want one?" he asked an already inquiring Norens.

"Down the hall, third door on the left," Warren told him, pointing toward the hall's entrance. He hoped the fan in the smoking room was doing its job. He was relieved at Brumley's unconcern over the beer, but was unsure what his reaction to pot might be.

"Just remember," Norens said, laughing at the pair as Brumley headed toward the beer, "I wasn't here; I saw no alcoholic beverages being illegally served—or anything else we could be hauled in on. Such as aiding and abetting revelry, maybe."

"Are you teaching American Lit this semester?" Warren asked uncomfortably, having spent a good part of his life hiding his doings and feelings from most adults.

"Yes. What are you taking—or what were you able to take?" Warren saw she was aware of his situation.

"I've got Dr. Brumley's British Lit class and Ringle in Medieval Lit. A science requirement and a couple of electives. Humanities. And Dr. Huckston's creative writing course."

"That's around twenty hours," Norens said, almost in disbelief.

His two-hour electives were a course in stonemasonry and in basic building construction, taken in the event that if he dropped out he would at least have something to fall back on.

"I'm in the British Lit class and humanities," Kimmee Deneen volunteered. "And creative writing with Dr. Huckston."

"It's Mister Huckston," Norens corrected her, as Brumley, returned with four beers on a tray.

"Huckston's here?" Brumley asked, trying to keep the irritation out of his voice and looking toward the elevator, where to his surprise he saw the disdainful faces of Colson and one of his pack surveying the crowd. Colson sneered at Bolinger, then with a start recognized Brumley but managed to recover his superior air before letting the door close and evidently descending to find more appropriate company. Brumley made no sign and turned back to the group.

"No, he's not here," Norens smiled, as did Warren and Kimee Deneen, whose glitter Brumely was doing all he could to ignore. "I was saying, he's Mister Huckston, not Doctor Huckston."

Brumley said nothing. While taking almost no account of his own earned doctorate, he could not bear the title's false appropriation by such a fatuous poseur as Huckston, who, though careful not to claim the title outright, would never, he knew, correct the many students who so addressed him. And yet Brumley felt that setting the record straight made him appear a puller of rank, or else a man proud of what he knew was too often an empty honor. How many PhD's did he know at Middle State who, once awarded the doctorate, had seen it only as a ticket to the Big Rock Candy Mountain and appeared never again to take thought of or even to show any interest in the subject matter of their discipline. Or of anything else, other than creature comfort. He recalled once trying to engage Nutter, Chairman of Psychology, in a discussion of social categories as psychological projections—of all human constructs as emanations of the mind's structure and processes. Probably the idea was absurd. Nutter had appeared to listen, but Brumley had the sense of addressing a surprised and somewhat amused rock, a sense confirmed when Nutter, to show that he too was a thinker, countered with his secret, unique theory that all atoms were little suns and the electrons were planets and that the solar system was a little atom in a bigger universe. Brumley had stood dumbstruck, vaguely realizing that he had been involved in a contest that he had no idea was a contest, and that Nutter was not only deeply stupid but dangerous. So was Huckston, but there wasn't much Brumely could do about it.

"Did the Signage thing turn out like you thought?" Warren asked.

"Yes, It's going to be Men and Women. The old symbols will be on the doors, too. For foreign students who don't yet know the words."

"Gyn and Anthro never had a chance."

"None. Not a chance. Not a chance," he repeated more loudly, leaning toward Warren as Hoh granted the Talking Heads a few more decibels.

Letting the days go by, water running underground.

Greenman and Hobart had been right—his memos and letters were poison. They were, yes, *in writing*, one even *public*, and constituted a record that couldn't be ignored, especially the foolhardy letter to the editor questioning President Curtis's policy and causing him to defend it. Brumley knew what it all really meant, what his efforts for justice had done—he had at least lifted a corner of the mask of pious concern for students and the life of the mind that management at Middle State was careful always to keep in place. To fully expose all the rat-holes into which a great deal of the money allotted Middle State flowed would take—a task force, he decided wryly. The wasted money could easily have hired sufficient instructors to allow Warren to graduate on time. But lifting the mask—in other words, telling the truth—was as Hobart knew the most dangerous of all transgressions. Soon, Brumley knew, a day of reckoning would come for him, and his transgressions would not be forgiven.

Brumley looked at the stacks of examination booklets. He was a fool. Only too well he knew how long it took many of his colleagues to return papers—Huckston, when he was first hired, often did not hand back a graded exercise of any kind until just after student evaluations, with only three weeks of the semester left. No one seemed to have cared. Other professors graded so perfunctorily that for all the good it did students they might as well have not returned their papers at all, which, he suspected, some did not. And there were many, even in the humanities, even in English, who gave tests that could be graded by a computer and thereby avoided ever reading a student's work or requiring them to write.

Without looking at the name on the outside, Brumley opened the top humanities test booklet, hoping it would not be one of the few lucid, insightful efforts that would then mean one less nugget to later gleam from the pail of mud and offer him some relief. Nor did he want one from the bottom of the mud bucket itself, one that would so demoralize him that he couldn't go on without a drink. A somewhat above-average paper was the way to begin, one that showed some actual acquaintance with the material, some real attempt at comprehension, however incomplete, one that he could make suggestions about that might stand some chance of being taken. This was not to be his night. The first booklet's author had turned his skills to the question What does Tolstoy think of Ivan Ilyich's life before he falls ill? Brumley began to read.

> In the Death of Ivan Ilych Ivan Ilyich lived in Russia but he managed to do well in life. Tolstoy the writer thought Ivan was a man who sat goals in his career field and then achieved them. He started out as a lawyer but worked his way up the ladder and was a judge. One time when he didn't think he was making enough money he quit his job and got a better one for more money. He believed he could be anything he wanted to. He also had a house with all the latest furniture. He enjoyed his job alot. . . .

Brumley looked out the window at the snow. Thirty-two more to go, provided he could re-read and grade this one. Somewhere in the stack the brilliant eccentricities of Bolinger or the clear common sense and clear prose of Warren or some unexpected student's real attempt to know the work would shine out of the great darkness. He would welcome their work at the same time they served to set off—what? The deficiencies, Brumley euphemistically decided on, the deficiencies of most of their classmates.

He put the paper back on the stack and, unable to risk another defilement of Tolstoy's great story, picked up the top one from the British Romanticism stack. Turning to the essay answer, he stumbled amazed to the third paragraph, which read

> Wadsworth himself was once a conservative and later became a liberal. Society finally got the best of him and he changed. This upset some of the other poets who were diehard conservatives like Shelly, who wrote a poem about it.

Hopelessness swirled around him like some final blizzard. Why go on? he thought. There was nothing he could say to help this student, whose agony at having to sit in the class, at having to read material so foreign to him or her that it might as well have been in Sanskrit or semaphore, Brumley could not imagine. Or was it agony; was it

anything? Had the divide become so great that nothing from the past, nothing that required disciplined thought, could any longer have meaning or worth to so many Middle State students? If another rumor was true, that President Curtis wanted to reduce all one-hour classes to thirty minutes and all longer ones accordingly, while at the same time increasing the supposedly standard teaching load to five classes per semester, maybe he was right to do so. Students didn't care how many classes instructors had to teach, and many would welcome shorter classes, some no classes. So wouldn't everyone be served, even gratified, for such a debacle? Everyone, he thought, except the students who wanted to know. And the faculty, the ones who had not yet lost all idealism, given up on their discipline and found a way out of the demands of teaching.

He went back to the humanities stack and, bracing himself, began reading a second booklet's attack on a question he had labored over: "Socrates in the *Apology* held there was a certain kind of life that was not worth living. What kind of life was it (use the phrase he does) and, briefly, how does the *Apology* demonstrate that he follows his own advice?

He had gone over the term 'unexamined life' three times in their discussion of the work, and, without stressing the connection, had tried to impress on the class the Old Stonemason's faithfulness to his principles. He turned to the paper to see how well he had done.

> Socrates believes that you should live a life to its fullests. Your life style should be to try to obtain as much wisdom as possible. Socrates was told that he was a wise man. To prove this he wondered around the land gaining knowledge and becoming a well rounded individual. He realized that for example a blacksmith was an expert in that field but not in the field of farming so he would ask a blacksmith questions about that profession. This gave him the best possible information on that subject. He felt that everyone should try to learn as much as they could.

Brumley put the paper back on its stack, pushed his creaky, worn chair back and stood up. The snow, he noticed, had let up some. He walked to the door and took his coat off the hook. He looked back at his desk. Refused tonight, the stacks would still be there tomorrow; they weren't going away. He stood there for a moment longer, then hung the coat back up, returned to his chair and sat back down. Picking up the first humanities test with its affirmation of what it saw as Ivan Ilyich's enviable life, Brumley opened it and began to write his pointless suggestions in the margin. At the end of the week, forty- three freshman composition themes would replace these stacks, and they would be worse.

"Huckston?" Brumley, bleary-eyed, whispered the next morning to a chuckling Hobart as the curtains at Blair Auditorium drew majestically back to reveal Huckston sitting on stage with studied unconcern in a row with Wyandotte of Agribusiness, Jenkins of Transuranics, Critson of Biology and Mills of Economics. To the right of the lone lectern were President Curtis and Vice president Staull.

"Quiet," Hobart said loudly over the slowly hushing crowd of faculty members. He apparently had time to comb only one side of his head that morning, the side away from Brumley. "I want to see how this is done, recognizing Huckston for research. How has he found time to do any research? All he does is apply for administrative positions. I've got an idea what he's done, though."

"Maybe he published an application," Greenman whispered from the other side of Hobart. "Or a series of lessons. You know, on hearty commraderie, eager cooperation, team playing."

"Kissing ass, " Hobart agreed.

"Whatever he's done, it's worked," Brumley pointed out. "He's going to be recognized and rewarded for research. Maybe they'll tell us for what."

As the nervously expectant faculty grew quiet, Brumley braced himself for what he knew would be the crackpot research requirements devised to help President Curtis advance in higher education management, requirements whose promised benefits would never be kept. A formal gathering where they would be proclaimed had seemed to Curtis the best venue in which to set them in stone, but initially he had other ideas on how to coerce the faculty into inflating Middle

State's reputation as an institution dedicated to excellence in research and thereby help him get the hell out of there.

"It's for damned sure we can't require them to do research and not show them we mean business," he had fumed to Vice president Staull a month earlier after reading in the *Regional University Presidents Quarterly* that all upwardly mobile regional university presidents should have on their resumes an impressive list of publications they had intimidated their overworked faculties to churn out. Prior to this enlightenment, President Curtis was largely unaware of research, having ceased doing any on the completion of his dissertation for his Doctorate of Communications degree, which to his annoyance had required the reading of several books and the summarizing of their contents. But once alerted by his trade journal to the heretofore unrecognized importance of research in such schools as Middle State, he had moved decisively and called a planning session to form a strategy that would get the lazy, irresponsible dolts who taught at Middle State off their worthless asses and hacking out some publications he could enter on his resume as proof that he was a man who thirsted for knowledge that could get him ahead.

"Maybe if I fired a few who haven't done any research it would get their attention. Fire some with tenure to show them nobody's safe."

Administrative Assistant Larson, who in the background had been dusting the various plaques, sports items and military figurines that cluttered the walls and shelves of President Curtis's office, lay down her feather duster.

"Not without first having made research a requirement for raises—or promotion or tenure. Retroactive, of course," she said with her compulsive, tinkling laugh. "And even then you couldn't get rid of the tenured faculty without a great deal of legal trouble."

President Curtis turned his heavy face toward her and stared.

"On the other hand," Larson quickly added, "it might not be all that much trouble. We'd just have to respond to each lawsuit brought by the tenured faculty members we'd fire—brought at their own considerable expense by the way. The university attorney, of course, would handle our side of it, and since the university attorney is paid for by the taxpayer, there's no problem for us. No real problem."

She trailed off under President Curtis's silent regard.

"What she means," Vice president Staull interposed, "is that there must be a better way than firing those who don't publish—or who don't do research, we should say, though we've got to equate doing research with publishing research. Don't want to give anyone the idea that mental application means much without publicity. But as I say, there's got to be a better way than firing all those who don't publish to make those who already publish publish even more. If we could be sure that the ones we hire to replace those we fire would do research, then I'd say green light, throw the shiftless bastards out on their faces. Probably the new ones these days will do anything we tell them to, but we can't be sure. So we've got to find some way to make those who don't publish publish so you can get their work on your resume to show how you've whipped this cow college into shape."

"But don't call it a cow college," Larson admonished cheerfully from across the room where she was dusting the ivory chess set. "We wouldn't want anyone to know that's how we really thought of this place, would we."

After a quick glance in her direction, President Curtis and Vice president Staull went on with their planning, and Larson, who had run out of things to pretend to dust, finally slipped out and closed the great mahogany door behind her. President Curtis was silent a moment.

"You think you're doing someone a favor," he said, jerking his head toward the just closed door, "getting them out of teaching. And what happens. They think they're king shit. Or queen shit. She sits around reading one of those damned administrative assistants' journals to get ideas from. I tell you, Staull, good help is hard to find." He looked morosely at the figures in his plush Persian carpet and then turned decisively to Staull. "What we've got to do is to *make* the help good—you don't just find it. And we'll start by making those useless drones we've got in teaching who aren't doing any research do a little something for us for a change."

"I agree," Staull agreed smoothly, "and how about this for openers. First, we want to keep the salary gap between the haves and the have-nots on the faculty as great as possible—not as great as that between the faculty and management," he laughed confidentially, "but still pretty large. Our present system, the old 'performance-driven merit system'— you remember coming up with that one?"

President Curtis nodded modestly. The phrase had come to him in a dream one night early in his taking over at Middle State while planning daily with his henchmen on how to sow terror in the faculty, who over the years had come to believe that teaching was more important to a university than running it. And, since their salaries were small, believed for the sake of accord and cooperation that raises over the years should balance out. With one semantic stroke–the 'performance-driven merit system'–Curtis had made money king at Middle State, had placed competition far above community, and had assured by setting college against college, department against department and instructor against instructor that, thus diverted, he could manipulate them all. His assumption was that no one would be responsible or would work unless he forced them to, and that they should do only the work he thought valuable.

But exactly what constituted meritorious performance under such system was never quite made clear, and while Brumley and a large number of other faculty saw the scam for what it was, no one spoke up. One year, when an old college friend of President Curtis had been selling the then-new portable tape recorders, faculty members who made extensive use of them in class, or, as one perceptive instructor in Social Work had done, required all his students to purchase one, were seen to perform with stunning merit and to be on the cutting edge of pedagogical techniques and were given raises that were the bitter envy of most of their colleagues. The next year, however, tape recorders had fallen from grace, and the dozens of instructors who emulated their more prescient fellows of the previous term found that tape recorders were without innovation and therefore lacking merit altogether. Merit, it seemed, in all the areas of faculty assessment, was an amorphous, indefinable thing, changing swiftly and unaccountably with the times, and President Curtis liked it so. It meant that knowing and teaching the material of one's discipline became inconsequential, and that theatrics and gadgetry, in ever shifting forms, were in the saddle. It also meant no one could ever do enough.

"Like I've always thought," Vice president Staull went on, "the old performance-driven merit system is made for research to fit right in."

Their final plan was to pick four or five cooperative faculty who had published something and reward them inordinately from the usual skimpy raise pool, which would never be expanded, and to do so in a solemn ceremony that hallowed the whole concept.

"After all," Vice president Staull, chuckling, reminded President Curtis, "the biggest part of the faculty have just one goal–to get more money than their colleagues. Throw out a little loose change for them to fight over and they'll be at one another's throats for the duration."

Being at one another's throats would keep them off his ass, and President Curtis felt he had again made an executive decision that would soon result in a resume to stun the search committee of that bountiful university that awaited him just down his career path by showing he could make underlings swallow a dose of anything he could concoct. Very much to very few, very little to very many–that was a motto to live by, assuming, needless to say, that he was one of the very few who got very much. And since not only he but Vice president Staull and all deans and chairs throughout Middle State had a much better chance of rising there, or of vaulting to a similar but better paying position elsewhere, by launching themselves from the backs of the faculty, the new requirement for research was sure to be hailed with fulsome enthusiasm by all administrators. Unless there was a catch.

"There's one other thing," Vice president Staull hesitated before leaving. "Will we–that is, will management–have to do any of this research? This is an initiative only for the faculty, isn't it? I mean, we're listed as faculty, but this is for, well, classroom faculty, right?"

President Curtis said nothing for a moment, watching the alarm grow on Vice president Staull's smooth face.

"No, Staull, for god's sake no," he said, laughing suddenly and shaking his head. "We won't have to do any of it. We have enough to do finding work for others to do for us. And then finding a cover so it seems there's some urgent, noble reason for making them do it. No, don't worry. This is strictly a 'faculty initiative'. But I've got a bonus."

"What's that?" Vice president Staull asked, relieved and beaming.

"We won't have to read any of it either."

If President Curtis's ambition explained Research Recognition and Reward Day, it did not explain Huckston's presence among those to be recognized and rewarded, and Brumley, like Job, was impatient to know why.

"You're right," Greenman persisted, his voice lowered, "Huckston has never done anything. He's Director of Creative Writing, but he never writes."

On the stage President Curtis nodded to Vice president Staull, who rose and approached the lectern.

"He never writes much, no, at least nothing of merit," Hobart rumbled. "But he directs! Perhaps he's done research on directing—that's from the Latin *regare*, to rule."

"Quiet," someone hissed from behind them, and on stage Vice president Staull cleared his throat with professional modulation and looked solemnly at the audience.

"We're here today to celebrate the launching of a new and, I think we'll all agree, an exciting innovation here at Middle State." He paused to let the excitement build.

"Many of the faculty have come to me with the complaint that research takes a back seat here, that Harvard and Yale and the like aren't the only places that can do top notch research."

"Now where," Hobart wondered aloud, "is the top notch located? I think I know where the bottom notch is."

"Quiet," someone else hissed, apparently eager to hear all of Vice president Staull's exciting message.

"It's pretty close to the back seat," Hobart raised his voice defiantly, looking around. Brumley saw now that both sides of his head were uncombed.

"Some have asked," Vice president Staull was going on, "how a teaching load of four to five classes a semester could possibly leave time for any research, let alone meaningful research? The answer lies in our conception of ourselves, our own sense of self-worth. We are a university. But there are many institutions of higher learning. How do we distinguish ourselves from them? How do we market ourselves as something different from, say, a junior college? The solution is clear: we—and by we I mean the faculty—we support, even demand research from ourselves. I think a new motto for us might be Excellence in Research, to be added to Excellence in Teaching and Excellence in Service."

"What is Excellence in Service?" Brumley wondered aloud, and Hobart glanced at him knowingly but said nothing.

"So the answer," Staull went on, "to the complaint of how can a teaching load such as we have here leave time for research is, quite simply, find time. Now in the future—you've probably heard the rumors—we may have a substantial reduction in classroom contact hours per class meeting—counterpoised by a slight incremental augmentation in classes per semester—but for now we must find time to dedicate ourselves to a new excellence that can go proudly on our resumes and be properly rewarded and that can make Middle State an even finer university than it already is. Those faculty members here on the stage are proof that time can be found," and he turned to nod with manly confidence at the expressionless honorees.

"Let me introduce them, or rather, since they are well known to most of you, let me introduce their work to you—and let's hold our applause until the end."

President Curtis, in the interest of cutting this crap as short as possible, had instructed Vice president Staull to limit his introduction to two minutes or less and dispense with needless ceremony.

"First, Professor Jenkins of Physics. Professor Jenkins," Staull said, referring to his notes, "has secured more than $6 million in Department of Defense grants over the past ten years, as well as grants from Middle State's own College of Business, to fund ongoing research in his Transuranic Laboratories, specifically in—plutonium usage enhancement, is that right? His department's labs employ over forty scientists and technicians and supports a considerable graduate student population. His latest of several publications is "Where Has All the Plutonium Gone?", a rebuttal that appeared in the *Bulletin of Plutonium Enhancement Scientists.*"

Hobart stirred and leaned toward Brumley.

"Poisons the world. Teaches one or two upper division physics courses per semester. About five students per class. Grad student grades all tests and exercises and teaches the classes when he's traveling. He's usually traveling."

"Next," Vice president Staull went on after Jenkins had nodded modestly to the crowd, "Professor Mills of Economics. Professor Mills has just published in the *Laissez_Faire Journal* an article entitled, let's see, "Supply and Demand, Thank God" in which—I hope I've got this right; some of this stuff is pretty high-powered—in which he shows that a basic law of economics can be simply stated that when the rich and powerful *demand* an even greater portion of the common wealth, the poor and powerless must *supply* it. I know that sounds obvious, but Professor Mills has some formulas and graphs to prove it, am I right," he said, turning to an impassive Mills, who nodded abstractly, apparently already thinking of a corollary to his rule, or perhaps a refutation. "His research was supported by a grant from the Departments of Commerce, Defense, and Justice."

"Teaches only every other semester. Travels to give pep talks to corporate executives," Hobart explained, this time well above a whisper. "Tells them greed and theft are good."

"How do these guys get out of teaching full time?" Greenman whispered cautiously, who like most of his colleagues in Humanities taught around a hundred students per semester in four classes. Mulholland of Psychology, on the other side of Brumley, also leaned forward to hear the answer.

"The College of Business is big business," Hobart informed them, and several rows to the front and rear. "Many students major in business. America's youth dreams of becoming investment bankers. Starving grad students and adjuncts teach the big introductory courses. Mills gets small classes and few of them. Supply and Demand, didn't you just hear? College of Business is rich and powerful and demands more money and less work."

Hobart's voice was rising. Heads turned in their direction, and Brumley hoped President Curtis wouldn't hear the disruption from the stage and fix on him as part of it.

"Now we leap from Economics to Agribusiness to honor our next faculty member. Professor Wyandotte here has recently received a very large grant—the amount is still secret—to fund construction out at our agribusiness holdings of the Leo Lear Addition to the Chickens Unlimited Poultry Complex, which will be dedicated later this term. This grant follows a series of grants from the Departments of Labor, Commerce, Agriculture and Defense as well as ones from the Leo Lear Food Unlimited Foundation, other agribusiness corporations, and our own College of Business, to construct, staff and administer the Poultry Complex itself. His most recent of many publications to come from his work appeared in the book *Chickens en Masse* and is entitled 'Minimum Feed and Floor Units per Poultry Food Unit for Maximum Profit Units.' Efficient mass production of mega-unit foodstuffs is the cutting edge in agribusiness, and I think we can all admire Professor Wyandotte's long standing contributions to this field. It's finger lickin' good, I'd say," and Staull winced theatrically at a scattering of good natured groans from a few breathlessly enthusiastic faculty members eager to show their full support of whatever was being promoted.

"Makes dumb animals suffer," Hobart said matter-of-factly. "Kills farming. Makes rich assholes richer. Poisons the world."

This time his voice was hardly lowered and was heard all over the audience, even over Vice president Staull's continued enthusings from the stage. Through his alarm, Brumley noted that of the faculty who heard Hobart, about as many frowned as nodded in agreement.

"We can indeed be proud," Vice president Staull went on, mistaking Hobart's censure for an involuntary whimper of admiration from some awe-struck junior instructor. "Certainly Professor Wyandotte's cutting edge research is justly commendable. Now, next to be recognized. . . ."

"And rewarded," the just-seated Wyandotte briskly reminded Vice president Staull, who thinking at least some sycophant would join in, laughed wildly but alone.

"I wouldn't want to leave out rewarded, no, and the next to be recognized and rewarded is Professor Critson of Biology."

"Microbiology," a voice from the audience said flatly. It was Talbot.

"Microbiology?" Vice president Staull said, distracted and unsure if there was antagonism in the voice. "Do we have such a department?"

"Just Biology," Critson said with disdain. "Not everyone's on the bandwagon yet. Just a little departmental factionalism."

To the side, President Curtis stiffened with displeasure, annoyed as usual when a matter of real import that would not affect his chances for advancement was forced to his attention.

"Whatever the case," Vice president Staull said lightly, "Professor Critson has just been given a multi-million dollar series of grants from--" he referred to his card labeled Critson, Prof.– "the Department of Agriculture, the Department of Commerce, the Department of –Defense? is that right again, Defense?" To Critson's affirmative he looked momentarily perplexed but went on– "from the Pharmaceutical Cartel Research Foundation, from the Leo Lear Food Unlimited

Foundation, and, of course, from our College of Business, all going to Professor Critson's Center for Life Form Enhancement. His latest paper, appearing in the prestigious journal *Life Form Enhancement Studies* is "Containment of Genetic Delivery Substance of the Order Gallinaceous." I think we can all agree, and I mean this seriously, that there is nothing this world needs more than a little life enhancement."

"Frankenstein," Hobart said, this time loudly enough that even Critson and the others on the stage almost heard him correctly. "Faust. Monsters. Goddamned concepts from the black lagoon of nightmares. The end of humanity, of nature."

"And now, last but not least," Vice president Staull went on, distracted only slightly by the disturbance of Hobart's comments.

"Yes, least," Hobart spoke loudly but affably, and President Curtis, who had now spotted the noisy, unkempt troublemaker, suspiciously regarded from the stage Hobart's relaxed demeanor and cordial tone. He was accustomed to troublemakers choked with suppressed rage and inarticulate over some flagrantly unjust decision he had made, and he enjoyed watching them sputter impotently their sense of justice violated as he waited for them to flounder to a stop before dismissing them. But this fat, uncombed insurgent was all relaxed amiability, exuding the air of one who assumed the floor was open, that it was not only perfectly right that he speak up whenever he wished but that he was expected to. Meetings such as this, President Curtis intended, were to be regimented, with those at the front in charge and those in the audience subservient and respectfully silent while they were told how it was going to be. Ceremony, he knew, had as its major if not sole purpose the imposing of the hierarchy.

But next to the corpulent slob of a troublemaker sat what President Curtis recognized with a shock as yet another troublemaker, this one slumping down in his seat, trying to disassociate himself from the agitator beside him, which was reassuring, but still, maybe there was a conspiracy, maybe the whole scurvy faculty was about to mutiny, to rise and hoot him and his research initiative from the stage, thumb their noses at his plan for them to take on another load that would show how hard he could make them work. They could do it, and he knew they could, and, if they stuck together, there was nothing he could do about it. Fortunately, they were cowards. He glared again at the corpulent troublemaker's accomplice. It was *Brumley*, he believed, that was his name, the one who pretended to give a damn whether students graduated in time. Brumley, who not only had the effrontery to go outside the chain of command and write him, the President, a letter about the matter, a careful, respectful letter infuriating in its reasonableness, but who had then *gone public* and forced him to order Vice president Dodson of Public Information to draft a public reply derived from Number Four that dismissed most of Brumley's complaint as alarmist, expressed sincere concern over that brat Warren's plight, and, to all who were ignorant about what could be done, explained that nothing could be done. Yes, he knew that this whole issue of having insufficient faculty to offer the courses students needed to graduate in four years could mean trouble for him. But then, he could be pretty certain no one who mattered would care about students graduating in four years–in fact, keeping them around an extra year meant wringing another year's money out of them. Besides, didn't he have an Office of Student Affairs or some such shit to look out for them? He was covered. Brumley might write letters, but Brumley was afraid–that fact President Curtis could see by Brumley's pretended unawareness that the lout beside him was not playing the game by the unspoken rules. But neither was he outright recoiling from the noisy agitator as was the nervous instructor to the lout's right. Brumley was not denying his evident friend. That was bad. But keep them at one another's throats, he remembered and was reassured. He knew how to keep that dog fight going.

"No, no, not at all least," Vice President Staull laughed nervously, feeling in spite of the heckler's serene bearing that all was not under control. "Not at all least is Professor Huckston of Humanities. Professor Huckston, while not in a field where big killings can be made in the grant department, nevertheless, while serving as Director of Creative Writing, has had an article published recently in"– he glanced at his Huckston, Prof. card–"*MSAM,* a periodical that has published over the years many articles by a variety of authors."

To Brumley's horror, Hobart rose to his feet, applauding noisily.

"I hope everyone will join me," he said widely to the audience, "in acknowledging that even a Humanities instructor can do the old top-notch research–and do it in spite of having served not only as Director of Creative Writing, but also, if I remember correctly, as Assistant to the Dean, and as Coordinator of Overseas Travel to Bulgaria for Creative Writing Students—all, of course, with reduced teaching load."

A few utter impercipients in the audience began applauding, but quickly ceased.

"And the journal where the article was published," Hobart quickly went on, not giving Staull a chance to recover, "what was its name again, Dr. Staull—the *MSAM*? Few of you outside the community of creative artists are familiar with that publication, and I think we should all be fully informed of Professor Huckston's achievement."

On stage, Huckston sat rigid, his face reddening, while neither Vice president Staull nor President Curtis could collect themselves sufficiently to intervene.

"The acronymic-like appellation of that periodical somewhat obscures its stature," Hobart boomed on. "Do you have the full title of the *MSAM* in your notes there, Dr.Staull, so we may honor its contributor of the research? No? Professor Huckston, would you please inform us?"

Huckston rose from his chair, crossed the side of the stage and charged down the steps that led to the auditorium floor. Never taking his maddened eyes from where Hobart sat, he passed up the aisle to just before Hobart's row, down which Hobart waited pleasantly, as though Huckston's actions were no more than a placing of himself to be better heard by the assembly, who by now were either stricken or gleefully anticipating what might develop.

"What are you trying to do?" Huckston managed. "What are you doing?"

"Why, to have you tell us what *MSAM* stands for. So we can all appreciate you and this grand research innovation that somebody who won't have to do any of it—who couldn't do any of it—has dreamed up to promote themselves," Hobart observed with a smile and affectionate nod toward the stage and President Curtis.

Almost weeping with anger, Huckston spun away and sped up the aisle to the exit. Behind him was silence, except for President Curtis scrambling up to command the microphone.

Before he could get there, Hobart, as collected and amiable as ever, surveyed the shocked but expectant crowd and held up a magazine with a bright but indistinguishable cover.

"*MSAM*," he announced loudly. "*Middle State Alumni Magazine*."

He flipped it open and before President Curtis could blast out a dismissal, Hobart announced: "Here's Professor Huckston's research article, which we need to recognize and reward," and on the stage Presidnt Curtis, who had approved the article and read it several times, could not help but pause to hear.

" 'Look out! There's a new world coming! Or so says Middle State's forward-looking President Dr. Nick Curtis, whose leadership in the encouragement of cutting-edge research at Middle State had resulted in our institution being ranked by a national magazine as fifth in research among all non-doctoral, former teacher-college, upper-mid-south universities. Under President Curtis, research at Middle State in biotechnology, nuclear applications and free-market economics are helping us toward a perfect world where there will be no hunger, no disease, and no conflicts.'"

Hobart looked up from the magazine. "And," he declared sadly, "no humanity, no humans, and no world." He turned to the audience. "You've heard the opening of Huckston's cutting-edge article. Now let's give a big hand for all these researchers—The Four Horsemen accompanied by Fraud."

eighteen
COLUMBO

Hobart's dauntless critique of Middle State's research initiative made him a marked man whose calm courage so intimidated President Curtis and the rest of management that they decided not to confront the obese screwball but also not give him more than a ten dollar raise each year for the next five years. Administrative Assistant Larson was assigned to research other modes of revenge that could be surreptitiously taken without anyone having to face Hobart directly. Brumley, on the other hand, and even Greenman for sitting beside Hobart, were also marked men, but who seemed easy to beat down. But all-in-all, Hobart's disruption and the suspected existence of co-conspirators hardly checked President Curtis's desire for advancement through the labor of others, and overall, Research Recognition and Reward Day was a splendid victory for management at Middle State. Among the faculty determined to charge from the gate, Davis of English already had a leg up on the publication racket and was hot to trot away.

"Brumley," Norens hissed, beckoning frantically at him through his office door, "she's posted another one," and he rose and followed her down to Greenman's office where Hobart was urging Greenman to move the damned screen down or up, whichever way you're supposed to so they could read Davis's second installment of her study of "Columbo."

"Where did she get to last time?" Greenman asked, scrolling away.

"The Queen's whorehouse in Chicago, I think," Brumley tried to recall.

"That was it," Norens said modestly. "Do any of you dirty old men know what comes next?"

"I know some of the verses, but not their order. Maybe there is no order, though I think it follows a loose chronology. Of the voyage."

"Here it is," Greenman said. "I've got it."

They all leaned forward as the lead-in to Davis's study appeared on the screen in full color with a photo of a vastly glamorized Davis in the upper right-hand corner, Middle State's logo in the left, and an accurate but massively incomplete biography of Davis preceding the text.

"Scholarship goes Madison Avenue," Brumley observed.

"Everything goes Madison Avenue," Hobart added, and they began to read.

"As explained in my prefatorial remarks in the opening version of the work treating 'The Ballad of Christopher Columbo,' or, as I choose to abbreviate for the sake of brevity, simply 'The Ballad of Columbo,' or, 'Columbo,' the following examination or provocations are strictly preliminary and I invite suggestions of all sorts on their content and style. As you recall, the study tends toward an unmasking of the poem's sub-text, revealing that by ironic reversal the imperialist, racist, sexist Columbo of real life is actually, in the poem, a trickster whose uninhibited libido and frolicsome abandon undercuts the entire dismal record of European male dominance while ostensibly lauding it, and points to a decided non-male hand behind the strategy. I will say no more but begin for now with verse three and end with verse four. Please keep in mind that the chorus (see my first installment) comes between the two verses, as it does all others in the poem. Verse three:

> The rain did pour, the wind did howl,
> But that didn't bother Columbo;
> For he was down below the deck,
> A-pounding on his Jumbo.

Verse two, one remembers, has Columbo soliciting ship and cargo from the Queen, who is promised by the wily conquistador a whorehouse in Chicago in return for her sponsorage. The leap here in verse three to the perils of the voyage (and Columbo's jaunty disdain of them) subtly suggests that the Queen has perceptively fathomed the windfall a Chicago whorehouse would bring—not only to herself, one intuits, but to her land and people—and has funded posthaste Columbo's expedition. Skipped over completely are the mundane awarding of the grant, the purchasing of supplies, the solicitation of applications and the interviewing and hiring of the crew, loading, making sail, etc., which by their very absence are significant since ignoring them allows full play to the intrepid voyage unblemished by inconsequential details.

And how savagely pours the rain and mightily howls the winds! Yet true to his devil-may-care nature, ceaselessly insisted upon from his alley-beshitting days of verse one and thereafter, Columbo is untroubled by those elements that deities from Posiedon to Aeolius have hurled at his nautical forebears. No cowering, patriarch-fearing he; no, Columbo, true to his choric manifestation as masturbator, is below the decks, out of the inclement weather, not from awe, not from fear, but only for comfort, a-pounding on his Jumbo.

This action is not, I think, to be seen as masochistic disdain, a thumbing, so to speak, of his Jumbo at the gods, but a serene acceptance of fate that has much more of the feminine than is usually associated with the imperialistic tendencies of the true Columbo. Keep this in mind. Note, too, that realistic consistency is maintained in that the author has Columbo pound not a penis or member, certainly not a winkie or pee-wee, but a Jumbo. The genitalic prodigality (balls hanging to the ground-o) granted Columbo in the chorus renders anything other than a jumbo lopsidedly—or, more precisely, lopfrontedly—inappropriate. The auto-erotic element illustrated here in verse three will now gradually give way to other forms of sexual gratification, as will be immediately apparent in verse four.

> Columbo had a stout first mate,
> He loved him like a brother.
> And every night upon the deck,
> They cornholed one another.

The abrupt switch (even allowing for the intervening chorus, which, recall, occurs boisterously between each verse) from one mode of sexual release to another begins a progression which I shall explore at greater depth later in the study but which here I merely call to the reader's attention for his/her own consideration. Other elements of this verse demand more immediate treatment.

First there is the artistry. Columbo's relationship with the crew member is not with just any crew member, but with his first mate, his chosen one ("mate") above all others ("first"). He is furthermore a *stout* first mate of endurance and strength, with suggestions of steadiness and tenacity of character subtly attendant in the diction. Though Columbo's love for him goes beyond the quiet respect of familial affection, beyond the mere brotherly (as stated in line two), the non-egalitarian and unashamed nature of their commitment (commitment because they rollick "every night") is emphasized by the location of their nightly spooning. Here is no bilge buggery, no hammock hunching, no "here is the key to my cabin" surreptitiousness. Far from it! The display of affection is performed upon the deck itself, in full view of the crew, openly, without shame. The very etymology of their act is in keeping with the high poetic achievement of this verse (and, some would argue, of the entire poem). *Cornhole* is a compound formed from *corn* and *hole*, and its coinage is traceable to a native American myth in which Flutter Dove, sharply rebuking an exploiting white usurper of her culture who wishes to purchase genital sex from her with a bag of corn, points first to her genitalia, declaring

"This hole money hole."

Then her anus—

"And this hole *cornhole*."

So in keeping with the feminine, highly affectionate regard Columbo is shown to express for his first mate, a somewhat anachronistic but clearly ironic allusion to the consequence of his voyage of subjugation is inserted into said regard in a historistical sense. That is to say, mythic echoes from a non-privileged culture appear retrospectively in a privileged culture's canon in such a way as to undercut the ascendant culture's claim to intellectual hegemony, a clear counter text to Eurocentric primacy that is the poem's putative sub-text. (For his generous attestation of the etymology of *cornhole*, I wish to thank our own legendary Dr. Hobart, who so often sheds new light on the origin of words.)"

At this point the screen was blank, Davis apparently having progressed no further.

"Hobart," Norens managed, "how could you? She actually believed your etymology for—that word? She didn't even check?"

"Perhaps I shouldn't have been so extravagant," Hobart admitted. "I was joking. She doesn't joke."

"You know who she'll claim the author is," Brumley said.

"It won't be Henry VIII," Greenman chuckled. "But royalty, right?"

"My god," Norens finally managed, "she's mad."

'You think so?" Hobart said, rising massively from his chair. "Wait until raises come out for next year. Then you'll see who's crazy."

Norens herself was not crazy but sometimes felt it a considerable task not to be. Unlike Brumley or Hobart she did not think all was lost at Middle State and refused to believe that what she taught was often irrelevant or opaque to most of her students. She tried to let the few good students she had be representative of them all, even taking a few moments each evening to recall from her day a student's insightful question or comment or one of their well-written papers or exams. Or, more often, when nothing offered itself, remembering a particularly well-made point of her own that she hoped had clarified for a class, or for at least one or two members of it, some difficult portion of their reading.

Just yesterday, for instance, in her American literature class, she felt she had turned a near-disaster into at least some insight. They were discussing Frost's "Stopping by Woods on a Snowy Evening," and she had asked someone to characterize the speaker of the poem.

"That's very interesting," she had managed after Jack Timmon's tentative response. "Why do you believe it's Santa Claus?"

Following Jack's justification, she had gently explained that in New England and other northern states there was a time, before automobiles, when people in winter traveled in sleighs pulled by horses, they really had, so it was not just Santa that might be found behind Donner and Blitzen and Dobbin.

Dobbin, and she laughed now in her pillow. If only she had said that, though the irony would have been wasted. Dobbin would just be another reindeer to them, provided they recognized Donner and Blitzen as such. She wrenched herself back to a more positive train of thought.

"In fact," she had said to the class, "how do we know the speaker is riding in a sleigh? The poem never says so."

Most had thought there was a sleigh, and she hoped she had made them see that behind their conclusion lay cultural assumptions they didn't know they knew–New England snow, a time before automobiles among many–that made them see a sleigh as the vehicle of choice. She then essayed some general comments on shared knowledge as necessary to understanding not only poetry but any literature. Could they think of any examples?

That they could not–in fact, that for the moment she could not–simply proved, she told them, how unrecognized these assumptions are. After class in her office, hoping some of the class might stop by to discuss the topic further, she had finally decided "Because I Could Not Stop for Death," which they had read earlier, would be a good illustration of the matter for tomorrow's class meeting.

She smiled drowsily at the prospect, and, pleased that she had salvaged something from that day, tried for sleep. But down the road from her house, which stood some two miles outside Middleton, one of Junior White's superannuated drug dogs kept in a well-maintained pen behind his trailer was persistently howling. Was the moon out, she wondered. Was it a mournful howl? Maybe, she thought, before dropping off to sleep, it was actually an indefatigable, businesslike alert that a large cargo of illicit drugs was passing by, slowly.

Junior White's dogs were the only problem with living where she did, in a small house in a still rural area not yet developed into one of the near-incredible subdivisions that for over ten years had been mushrooming all around Middleton and several miles out from it. They had names like Maple Elm Fields and Gatedborough and Castlereigh and Oak Creek Heights. Such places, built largely in former corn and soybean fields, did not allow barking dogs. Nor did they allow dog houses, gardens, clothes lines, non-regulation outbuildings, or bird feeders. Some, it appeared, did not allow trees. As far as she could tell, the two she drove past going to and from Middle State each day did not allow children, for she had never seen any at play, and certainly not at work, on the large, perfectly groomed lawns or anywhere else in the developments. In fact, except for the proliferating landscape workers who mowed the lawns and tended the permitted shrubs, she never saw anyone at all in these subdivisions. But of course people lived there, and Norens was certain they all saw their enormous houses as dream homes. Dream homes, that expressed the personalities of their owners. Since all were of the same phony chateau style, Norens had concluded that the owners, by remarkable coincidence, all had the personalities of bogus French counts from the Loire valley.

On coming to Middle State, she had barely avoided such a house.

"This one," said Sally Utley, the realtor she had contacted months before, "should have a great resale value."

The house in question was a rambling ranch-style with five bedrooms and two-and-a-half baths, a rather modest dwelling compared to the four French provincial mansions Utley had led her to earlier that day. Norens, not quite sure what a half-bath was, allowed herself again to be led through a labyrinthine interior, enduring the praise of the walls done in Moonglow (with the Hot Pink exception of the rumpus room), the plush, light gray wall-to-wall carpet, the gaudy light fixtures and the considerable remainder of knobs, closets, pantries, cabinets and appliances.

"It was eighty thousand when it was built, five years ago. It sold for eighty-six two years later and ninety-one two years after that," Utley said reverently.

It was presently listed for ninety-five thousand.

"Sally," Norens said, "I need to make it clear that I can't afford half that. These palaces we've been to are three times the size I need. There's just me; I won't need a three-car garage or three bedrooms. Or two-and-a half baths."

"So you really are looking for a starter home," Sally said, barely avoiding an inflection equating starter home with sty. "Most new faculty members at Middle State look more for the second tier level. Dr. Wyandotte last year bought a home in Maize Field Estates that's already gone up ten thousand in listed value. Have you met him yet? He's in the paper a lot, the chicken guy."

Norens recalled that in their initial phone conversation before she arrived, Utley had seemed completely understanding of her desire for a very modest but well-built house in the country or a quiet part of town that would last, as far as she could see, for the rest of her life.

"I'm not into big houses and such," Norens recalled saying, and was now amazed that she had taken Utley's lack of comment as the realtor's tacit accord with Noren's belief that acquisition and display was to their present world what bread and circus was to Rome.

After renting an apartment for a year, she found what she wanted, a small farm house and five acres whose owner, an elderly widow, was moving into Middleton to be near relatives. An old but still sound barn, once a shelter for animals but now reduced to storing machinery, came with the purchase, as did a small tractor and implements with which Norens kept some of the open part of the acreage mowed. She had even learned, with the help of the widow's son, to plow, disc and cultivate a garden plot, even considered raising some animals though she knew nothing about doing so nor anyone who did. The rest of the farm's eighty acres was rented for row crops to an agribusinessman who lived several miles away. Except for the occasional howling session from Junior White's dogs, the place was quiet, and she felt secure there, even purposeful, though unsure what that purpose was. But she did not feel crazy, at least when she was there. Lonely, yes, but not crazy.

nineteen
SCHOLARSHIPS

Vice president Flexner of Recruitment and Retainment had come to Middle State from a series of consulting jobs with several state governments that were establishing lotteries to help shift the burden of taxes from the rich to the poor. His specialty was the design of compressed-air ping-pong ball machines used to select numbers for the lotteries in a clearly random way so as to give the appearance of strict probity within the larger fraud. He was also a facilitator who facilitated public acceptance of state-run lotteries through TV commercials implying that fifty million-to-one odds gave everyone an excellent chance at becoming a multimillionaire for an investment of a mere five dollars or so. He also made certain that each commercial suggested the state skim-off from the lottery would be used for educational purposes.

"Someone Is Going to Win!" his most successful advertising campaign trumpeted. "Why Not You!" and the joys of attaining great wealth were depicted by a fictitious winner quitting his unspecified but demeaning job, driving in a newly purchased sports car to Las Vegas, and taking the patsies there for even more money by winning at their slot machines.

As for the educational purposes the lottery money was earmarked for, two predominated. The first was to educate road builders that because of increased state revenue from the lottery even more lucrative than normal payoff contracts awaited those who contributed plentifully to whatever political party was running state government. The other, and lesser, purpose was to educate state university officials that Flexner and his cohorts were valuable men who deserved high paying jobs where they could keep their bamboozling skills sharp until some state or even the national government needed their services once more. The governor himself had hinted to President Curtis that Flexner would be an excellent addition to Middle State's management team, and Curtis, by hastily moving sections from the Office of Student Services, the Office of Public Relations and the Office of Outreach and then combining them, had quickly created a new Office of Recruitment and Retainment. Flexner was its vice president and, unlike all the vice presidents except those of football and basketball, could see President Curtis whenever he wanted.

"Here's what I think we should try," Flexner said, leaning forward to hand President Curtis a slim folder. "I'll go over it, but it's all in there."

"First, I spend a lot of time—too much, in my opinion—in supervising my staff's evaluation of scholarship applications and applications from those who want to be Leo Lear Scholars and other applications in general. My purpose is recruitment—and retainment, of course, but for the moment let me concentrate on recruitment. I believe I can join recruitment with our scholarship program, which are already bed buddies in a way, and enhance recruiting without tying me down with a lot of unnecessary paperwork."

Curtis understood perfectly, but was always suspicious of Flexner, even more than he was of that dandy Shank of Shank Consulting, whose sartorial chic Flexner almost equaled. Anyone who wore thousand dollar suits, imported neckties of the most fashionable patterns and widths, a silk handkerchief in his coat pocket and hand-made Italian shoes must know something important. That Flexner had the governor's imprimatur was another indication he should be watched, as was his close friendship with the immensely wealthy Heft, a much-courted Middle State alumnus who had invented the plastic bag. But exactly what to do about Flexner, President Curtis wasn't sure. He glanced at the first of three pages in Flexner's folder. It contained in large letters the word LOTTERY.

"We want more students, right?" Flexner asked, breezing on before Curtis could react. "And we want everyone to get a college education, since every student can learn and at a high level. That being so, and since the legislature, when they determine our budget, doesn't know and doesn't give a damn what our students' entrance test scores are or what their high school grades were–they just want enrollment numbers–we could save my office a lot of time and effort evaluating applicants if we just distributed our scholarship money by lottery."

He paused to let Curtis's alarm develop.

"By lottery?"

"By lottery."

"You mean, we don't give scholarships based on outstanding secondary education records or on high college entrance test scores? Or on the student's need? My god, Flexner, this lottery scam may work at the highest levels, but you can't think it will go over here."

"But I do think it will. Let's consider the situation." Flexner leaned back and began enumerating with his right hand. "First, we continue giving scholarships to all who have supposedly earned them and begin the lottery system only with next year's freshman class. We both know–even if not many others do–that we offer some pittance of a scholarship to almost anyone who applies for admission and is capable of filling out a scholarship application. Am I right?"

"Well, not *everyone*," Curtis began, but Flexner was prepared.

"According to figures I got from Vice president McGowan in Admission and Registration, $500 scholarships were awarded last year to eight students who misspelled Middle State on their scholarship applications. We have one student, though this is a special case, on a full athletic scholarship who scored a 4 on his college entrance test. Random guessing should result in a 6, so he's not only dumb, he's unlucky. Also, our requirements that a student must have a C+ or better average for all their high school classes means at present that 68% of high school grads are eligible."

He handed Curtis another sheet on which those and other supporting data were arranged.

"Sixty-eight percent. We're getting smarter by the year, and those figures prove it," Flexner said, laughing heartily and shaking his head. "Sixty-eight percent. But you'll notice that for various reasons–having poor parents or no parents being one, and having rich and influential parents being another–we have over 250 students on scholarships that had high school grades below a C+ average."

"We've got to help the poor. And the rich," Curtis protested. "You've been up with the big boys, you know that."

"Of course," Flexner said, surprised that Curtis thought he was criticizing the situation, "but what we can't stand is word getting out that we give scholarships, sometimes quite large ones, to bonehead offsprings of generous donors to the University Foundation. Or to the children of local politicians or influence peddlers."

The University Foundation was a separate financial entity established by Middle State that was privately administered and not open to public scrutiny, though its funds were open to Middle State's managers. Its establishment had been suggested by local moneyed interests and legitimized by local politicians. It functioned roughly as Middle State's off-shore bank. "That can't happen, no," Curtis agreed, alarmed. "But I still can't see what advantages we have by substituting a lottery for our current system of evaluation."

Flexner looked at him coolly for a moment and began to enumerate again.

"First, since we give scholarships to just about everyone anyway, we might as well inject a little fun into the process and do it by draw. Second, as is clear, the reason we give scholarships so lavishly and indiscriminately is to get ever-growing enrollment figures, though of course you've got to piety-mouth a little about an educated citizenry and falling behind China and all that. But that crap aside, what the state gives us per student is far more than we pay out for all but the biggest scholarships, so it hardly matters how capable a student is who gets one. A body's a body; the legislature counts a blockhead the same as an Einstein. Plus for blockheads we can justify a whole office of Blockhead Advocates and get funding for that. So Middle State doesn't gain anything worth discussing by giving scholarships to the deserving. Third, if my office didn't have to go over these meaningless high school transcripts and test scores they all send in with their applications, we could give more time to making the scholarship lottery a real, an exciting, recruitment tool. And don't forget retainment—we could work on that, too."

Curtis was speechless. Flexner was right, but he was too right, and what was worse he lacked the cowardly circumlocution Curtis expected throughout Middle State's administration and faculty. How anyone could soften the truth of Middle State's recruiting practices he wasn't sure, but faced with Flexner's unabashed analysis, open lying about them was clearly preferable. Sometimes he found himself thinking that the absurd suggestion raised by the faculty fool they had finally forced into retirement might be worthy: namely, that the state legislature should prohibit all publicity and recruiting attempts for public universities. Cadoon, the fool's name was, a troublemaker who didn't know which side his bread was buttered on, who had the temerity to suggest the outlawing of established university practices directly to him in front of many others at the reception for new faculty some years ago. Curtis had laughed rudely in Cadoon's unintimidated and calmly assessing face, and when Cadoon asked him why shouldn't it be outlawed, found himself humiliatingly unable to reply. Two years later he covertly orchestrated Cadoon's forced retirement.

But Cadoon–Old Cadoon, he'd heard him called–in spite of persistent and troubling rumors to the contrary, was gone, and now Curtis had to deal with the likes of Flexner, whose principles and practices were much closer to Curtis's than to Old Cadoon's, which caused Curtis real concern. He wasn't sure he could use Flexner, or get rid of him if he couldn't. On the other hand, he sometimes thought Flexner was using him.

"I hear what you're saying," Curtis said, "and in theory this lottery initiative sounds good. But I think we ought to have others assess it. I think what we need is an ad hoc committee or, better, a task force to evaluate this thing and get the mechanics ironed out. Give me a couple of days to appoint the task force members and I'll––."

"I've already got the mechanics ironed out," Flexner said, a slight edge in his voice, "not a wrinkle in them. I didn't make lotteries a cash cow in eight states by not knowing how to iron the mechanics. The mechanics are on page three in the folder. I believe I just evaluated the proposal to you and, like you say, you heard what I was saying and found the theory sound. So you've got a sound theory and the mechanics ironed out by yours truly, the generator of over a billion dollars revenue per year for eight states. I don't much think a task force is necessary here, though I generally like the idea of task forces when there's not much else doing and like to serve on them, especially when doing so involves travel at taxpayer expense."

Curtis shifted uncomfortably in his high-backed swivel chair, fear stirring deep within him. It was one thing to deal with some hesitant, principled leader of the Faculty Senate or an idealistic student. They were honorable and rational. Crushing them was easy. But Flexner, with his tailored suits, shoes undoubtedly made from the hide of an endangered species, and a brazen presumption—to his very face—that he, Curtis, was as calculating an opportunist as Flexner himself—well, that was another matter. Likely whatever happened with Flexner's lottery proposal, even if scandalous, would soon blow over, forgotten in a month by a public that didn't care anyway. But Flexner, with poise and determination, was turning Curtis's own arguments against him, was twisting his favorite corporate cliches and ploys to his own advantage.

"Then let me revisit these mechanics," Curtis went on, so flustered that he overlooked not having visited them in the first place. He withdrew page three from the folder.

"Okay," he said, skimming its opening paragraph, "when a graduating high school senior requests information from us, you want to send in our response, at the bottom of the letter, a series of five numbers between one and thirty printed in black."

"The color doesn't matter. We might need a task force after all to decide on the color, and some other minor details," Flexner said, whether mockingly or not, Curtis was unsure.

"These numbers you want to identify as 'Money Codes' and inform the student. . ." Curtis read rapidly ahead, ". . .inform the student —this isn't half bad—that when they come for Summer O there will be drawings held throughout the two-day period in the form of numbered ping-pong balls chosen at random by a revolving, compressed-air ping-pong ball machine and, depending on how many of their Money Code numbers match the ping-pong ball numbers, they will get various sized scholarships."

"There are two problems here," Curtis announced, then leaned back confidently in his throne-like chair. "The students who don't match a number are going to be very disappointed, very disappointed indeed, in our not giving them something positive, something that shows the world is on their side. If you turn down their application for a scholarship on a lack of academic merit, most kids can accept that, even if they don't like it. They know what they can and can't do. But turn them down because fate appears against them, they'll find another fate. They'll go to a different school."

In spite of himself, he looked at Flexner triumphantly, who looked imperturbably back.

"Go on," Flexner said after a moment.

"Go on where?"

"To the second problem. You said there were two problems."

"Oh, yes, "Curtis recalled, shocked that Flexner could breeze by what he felt was a crushing objection. "The second problem is that you mention only high school seniors. You overlook the large number of non-traditional students—older students— now coming to college and who must make up an increasingly large percentage of our enrollment if we're going to continue to grow and get ever more funds from the state. How will they get chances at a scholarship? Remember, they're more mature than our average freshman. They may believe this entire lottery plan is a hollow fraud."

"Let's take problem numero uno first, just to be consistent," Flexner said jauntily. "Each prospective student has five numbers, from one through thirty. We draw five numbers at each drawing during Summer O. If we have six drawings—say one after each meal while they're here —we can let the task force decide that—chances are very good that everyone will have at least one of their numbers drawn. The more of their numbers that match, the higher their scholarship. And don't worry, we can arrange the numbers so we always have a little discretionary money for use by the president's office left over each year. At the same time, we cover the possibility of a few not having any of their numbers match by offering them a booby prize, which we'll call the Luck's Favorite award—a scholarship bigger than ones given to those matching the most numbers. This heightens suspense. Even the born losers feel they have a shot. So there's no problem here. Everyone is happy."

"As for the problem of the non-traditional students who won't come to Summer O and may feel the whole lottery idea is disgraceful—well," he said with a gracious smile, "screw them. Chances are very good they've lost their jobs to Mexico or Bangladesh, or will soon, and have households and family fairly close to Middle State and not enough money to go to school anywhere else. They don't need the inducements of scholarships. They're stuck, they've got no choice. Plus, if the taxpayer money you're spending on getting the foreign students to come here and pretend to get an education is effective—that is, if we're getting lots of them—then we need local non-traditional students even less—the Chinks and Chili Peppers and Rag-heads can more than make up for the loss. They pay five to ten times more tuition than a local non-traditional, don't they? Let Chong and Pablo and Farouk make up the difference. We can forget the non-traditionals, though it would be best to have a big program to recruit then and a support office for them and whatever else it takes to cover our asses. We could let the task force make the big decisions on all that. That about takes care of your two problems, right?"

"More or less," Curtis said weakly, and then involuntarily burst out. "Flex, letting those who presently have scholarships based on merit—or who may have them based on such," he corrected himself after Flexner's quick bark of disdain— "letting them keep theirs and starting the lottery with a freshman class, that may help, but even in that freshman enrollment pool the high school seniors who have good grades and superior test scores will want scholarships that give them what they deserve. They've worked hard; they've got brains, or at least the kind of brains that let them do well in school. They may not want any part of a university that gives out scholarships by lottery. We could lose intelligent students who see through–I hate to use such a term—through such an embarrassing hoax.

"An embarrassing hoax, huh?" Flexner's smile was dangerous but still amused. "We're already running an embarrassing hoax, as down deep you know, but we can overlook for the moment how well my plan fits in with the reality of Middle State. If the intelligent student who won't come here when they see we conduct ourselves like some snake-oil enterprise—if they feel we disregard their hard work and academic talent, screw them, too. Everybody works hard, all high school students do. Ask them. Ask the education experts. And as for brains, brains cause trouble. Look at the Vietnam War. Students started thinking, criticizing, and things weren't the same until the draft ended and they all decided to become stock brokers and investment bankers. I don't think we'll ever have a problem like that again, but encouraging brains won't help guarantee it. But look, none of this matters. What matters I've already pointed out: brains or boneheads, who cares? For either one we get the same amount of funding, the same amount of money to play with."

Curtis was overwhelmed and had no choice but to approve the plan, though he would never have done so without the halo of the governor's approbation floating above Flexner's well-coiffured head. Two weeks later, a fuller version of Scholarship Lotto from Flexner's office appeared on his desk. In the packet was a sample letter for the prospective student drawn up by Dr. Calona, a former instructor in the English department who had recently made a vertical transfer to become Assistant to the Vice president under Flexner. The letter was complete with a lottery number and was couched in the appropriate rhetorical style.

Dear JOE/JESSICA STUDENT

How would you, JOE/JESSICA, like to win an all-expense paid, four-year trip to Middle State University? That's right, an all-expense paid, four-year College Education for JOE/JESSICA STUDENT could be yours if the numbers below are matched during one of our exciting drawings at MSU's fun-filled Summer Orientation this summer. Just check out our enclosed catalog and the other information, chose one of the Summer Orientation sessions, mail the enclosed statement of intent and bring your numbers with you! JOE/JESSICA, we hope you'll chose the warm, friendly campus of Middle State to be your home for your college career. Middle State, as you undoubtedly know, was recently rated highly as a bargain university among all upper mid-South and lower mid-West former teacher colleges by a national magazine. And you, JOE/JESSICA STUDENT, could be attending, free of charge. So get that statement of intent in today and get ready for fun! And for money!

See you soon JOE/JESSICA!

Sincerely,
Dr. Jude Calona, Asst. VP
Recruitment and Retainment

(Entrant does not have to be present to win. Lesser scholarships are offered based on the number of numbers matched during the two-day Summer orientation period. Entrant may attend only one Summer Orientation session. Scholarships are contingent on entrant's attending Middle State University. Entrant must be eighteen years of age or older or an applicant to MSU to qualify. Certain restrictions may apply. For full details, write Middle State University Foundation, 243 Dorsey St. Middle State Station.)

twenty
SMOKESTACKS

The maintenance truck, with Junior White's name now neatly stenciled above the university seal on the doors, was parked in its usual slot by the library, the ladder hung on the left-hand side. Warren quietly lifted it off its rack and walking well off the sidewalks angled toward the Center for Life Form Enhancement's smokestack. The area underneath the bottom of the steps was in shadows and no one was around. He could see no block and tackle hanging from the steps, but Old Cadoon had said he placed them undetectable from below so he likely carried his device some distance up the steps before stowing it. He might be up there; Warren couldn't tell.

At the top of the ladder he crossed to the steps, pulled up the ladder and wedged it against the railing that followed the outside of the stairs. Half-way up to the carillon booth he stopped to rest, listening and surveying both the view and the area at the smokestack's base for indications that he had been seen. He saw nothing and continued to wind his way upwards.

"Anybody here?" he called uncertainly before he stuck his head above the floor of the carillon's platform.

"In fact there is," Old Cadoon's voice came from part way around the stack. "Are you friend or foe?"

"It's me," Warren said, pretty sure he was a friend but not wanting to presume. "Chris Warren."

'Ah, yes," Old Cadoon said, as Warren came into view and sat down in the one chair. "The gentleman who knows the stars but isn't graduating on time. Taking the air tonight?"

"Yes, that and I like the view from up here."

"You'll get no stars tonight, not that this spring sky has the vivid constellations of the fall." Old Cadoon glanced upwards. "And certainly not with these clouds. They're hardly moving that I can tell. But at least they're not low enough to catch the strobe light glare—ever see that? Makes the strobes ten times as obtrusive. A glory about the smokestacks."

"There's something about that in the *Ancient Mariner*," isn't there? A glory?"

"By god, son, you do amaze me. One recollection I believe to be accurate from my twilight days at Middle State was its students' inability to remember anything for more than a day or two. Which may be another way of saying they couldn't learn, or maybe didn't want to." He resumed gazing out over the campus. "But I'm not altogether sure which, if either. I think I asked you before: do you think my assessment of the modern- day student a little harsh?"

In spite of being fascinated with Old Cadoon, Warren naturally wished to side with his own, but he thought a moment before replying.

"They're not dumb, most of them. I was just thinking, my freshman year there were twelve of us in my dorm section, and really only one— well, two if you count me—was very serious about school—no, that took school seriously—and he was a music major. Five of them flunked out, and a couple more made pretty good grades, they just didn't seem—well, interested."

"Would you say," Old Cadoon interrupted, "they didn't seem *moved*?"

"Yes. That's right. Either they just got through or liked to show off getting good grades, but they never got excited about anything, never talked about the courses they were taking—weren't moved, you're right."

"'Education must ultimately be limited to those who demand to know; the rest is just sheep-herding' a great man once said, or something near to it. In a way," he said thoughtfully, "the students you describe waste their time coming to college. There should be trade schools—honorable, respectable, demanding trade schools—or corporate financed apprentice programs for them, since it appears we're stuck with corporations. In colleges, by sheer numbers and attitude the—shall we say, uninterested students–poison the students who should be there. Universities"–Old Cadoon straightened up on his stool and looked out angrily over the campus– "operate under the same illogical and ultimately ruinous notion that our economy embraces–they've got to grow, forever–the faster and bigger the better."

"I kind of feel like that sometimes–that it's more a company than a school."

"I have an analogy, a theory, for what modern public–and many private–universities are. In fact, I have several. Would you like to hear one?" Old Cadoon's irritation had passed and he fell back into his ironic pose. "I'm sure a twenty-year-old would like nothing better than to hear an old man's maunderings."

"What is it?" Warren had his own theory of what the university was: Hell.

"The modern university is like an artesian fountain. Do you know what an artesian fountain is, Mr. Warren?"

"Yes, sir. It's a fountain that comes from an aquifer whose source is higher than where the fountain is."

"I see you've had a good geology course."

"No, but I want to take one. Now that I'll have to go an extra year, I'll be able to get one in. One benefit of being screwed, I guess."

"Again I'm astounded. By being screwed, I take it you mean that you've got no satisfaction on your complaint, or on Brumley's complaint on inadequate course offerings."

"No, sir."

"Is Dr. Brumley still working on it?"

"I don't think so. He's done all he can."

"And probably more than he should have, at least for his own good. He sounds like what we need more of these days but won't get."

"Did you know him. Before you retired?"

"I may have met him. Don't remember. But I'd like to."

Warren said nothing. Maybe he could get Dr. Brumley to come up with him to meet Old Cadoon. Why not?

Old Cadoon stood up and stretched painfully.

"I'm feeling the chill in my bones tonight, Mr. Warren. Let me put my Artesian Well Theory on hold until we meet again, if it should so be in the stars."

"Sure. You want to go ahead of me? You can use my ladder; I've got it pulled up and can put it in place. We can both use it and you won't have to put on the harness."

"Son, you're indeed a thoughtful young man."

When Warren hung the ladder back on the university pickup behind the library, a head leaned out from the driver's side window.

"You mind me asking what you do with that thing?" Junior White asked.

Warren, whose first impulse was to run, heard nothing but curiosity in the question and lowered the ladder onto the brackets and walked up to the cab.

"Girls dorm?" White asked.

"No, sir. We—I—climb up to the smokestack steps and go on up. I pull it up after me. We're careful with it."

"It's not my ladder," White said indifferently, "though I've got to keep up with it. I'd watch climbing those steps. Not many bolts holding them to the stack."

"It's usually just two of us. Hey," he said, recognizing White, "you were on that committee, the one about signs. I was on it till I quit going. And weren't you in the newspaper last week, about taking in those dogs?"

"Yeah, that's me, both times," White said resignedly. "Yeah, got my picture in the paper."

"I thought it was a good story. Not everyone would take them in."

The student newspaper article praised White for giving a home to the elderly campus police dog Toker, which while still active and in good health had reached a certain age that disqualified it for further constabulary service. An accompanying photo showed White at his trailer in the country taking the dog out of its clean and well-constructed pen for a walk. Other dogs, also retired from their city and state trooper jobs of sniffing out drugs could be seen in their pens in the background. The university dog had an electronic device with an antenna on its collar that the story identified as a shock collar that could be activated by White if the dog began to bark and disturbed his neighbors.

"Middle State staff worker gives home to unwanted dogs," the headline read. "Thinks of neighbors too." A few regional newspapers had also picked up on the story.

"Yeah, good story all right—I even got a call from Curtis, gave me a raise for"—he snorted in amusement—"'increasing institutional visibility.' I didn't think taking in old dope dogs was increasing institutional visibility. I should have asked for a grant to buy feed for them."

"They were all dope dogs?"

"Yep. Mostly Labs or some kind of hound. I don't want anything that bites. Just steady dogs with a good nose and voice. And needing a home. You ever have any dealings with Toker?"

"No, sir. I don't think I ever even saw him."

"Probably didn't. They usually took him to the dorms—you stay in the dorms?—over holidays. If he smelled any pot, the cops and student informers would keep an eye on that room after the kids got back until they got something definite and then bust whoever stayed there."

"How do they know when he smelled some?" Warren asked, intrigued and sensing he might find out something very helpful here. Sola stored his primo and Shepherd his grocery bag of homegrown by raising one of the dry, fibrous ceiling panels in the dorm floor study lounge and placing their stashes on the panel next to it.

"Oh, he'd light some incense and put on some music," Junior White replied straight-faced and then laughed with Warren. "No, he barked. Or bayed. Toker was half coon hound. Most of the dogs sit down or turn around three times or something like that. But Toker with the hound in him would just open a big, full bay, or if there was lots of sign he'd hit a steady chop like he'd treed. That's why they took him through the dorms only on holidays, when no one was around. A little hard to keep what you're doing quiet when old Toker opened up. That's okay for traffic stops on campus and such, but he was a little noisy for undercover stuff. Those people in security never gave a thought to that little feature when they got him." He shook his head in fond remembrance. "I used to work over there. Biggest bunch of strong-arm crooks in the country. Except for Barnes. But that don't matter. Just doing their jobs. Anyway, that's how old Toker let them know he smelled pot."

"That was good, you taking him in."

"Um," White grunted. "But I wish they'd never done that story in the paper. I'm not much for publicity."

"It got you a raise, though."

"Just peanuts, though it was the biggest I ever got."

"Do you work in the library? Your truck is usually parked here."

"Whenever they need me," White said. "I mean, I put in the security system and service it, the one that sets off that alarm if you try to get out with a book that hasn't had its magnetic strip demagnetized when you checked it out.'

"So that's how it works," Warren said.

"Usually. You ever have it go off on you when you'd checked one out right?"

"No, but I've seen it go off on somebody who had."

White snickered with delight.

"Got everybody's attention, I bet? My doing," he admitted. "I slipped a little counting chip in the circuit that trips the alarm every two thousandth person that goes through the gate, whether they've got a book or not. That place always seemed pretty dead to me; I thought a little action every few days would liven it up some, get the old joint jumping. I just wish I had some way to make it go off when a shit-head or two I know tried to breeze through. I'm working on that one, though the only thing I've come up with so far is to plant a magnetic strip on them."

"Are you doing–have you been doing–security work just now?"

"Well, not exactly. I had to beat the after-hours security system to get in and get back out, but no problem there–I installed it, too. Just doing a little research."

"What on?"

"Oh, dog training, and where good hunting areas might be. I get books and government documents and things and copy what I need."

Warren didn't ask, but he was sure White had installed the coin-operated copy machines, which likely meant his copying was free.

"What do you hunt?" Warren asked.

"Oh, whatever's in season. Listen," White said, "about climbing those towers. Very many want to climb them? Is it a fad like panty raids used to be, or protesting war or pollution? If they do, I can leave this truck here every night. Of course, it's a little inconvenient if I'm not doing research, which I'm about done with, but for, say, five dollars per person per night I'd be glad to rent the ladder out. You think there's much demand?"

"No, not much," Warren said, wanting to protect his method and fearful he was now priced out of it.

"Didn't think so. It's not my ladder in the first place, like I said—belongs to the taxpayer. But come to think of it, I'm a taxpayer. And I'm responsible for it. So I may as well make as much off it as I can. That's what it's all about. You don't need a utility truck for anything, do you?" he asked, indicating the pick-up. "This one is yours for twenty-five a night."

"Is that right," Warren said with no enthusiasm.

"I know she's not the type you take a woman somewhere fancy in—though it's been done. But I can cover the university logo on the door. If you need to move anything or just get out of town for a while, look me up. Junior White. Electronics," he said as he started the truck. "And help yourself to the ladder anytime you want—it's free to you."

He put the truck in gear and backed out of the space and pulled away.

President Curtis was delighted that Leo Lear had seen the story of Junior White's big-hearted adoption of over the hill drug dogs and that he wanted to meet this lover of man's best friend, even if these best friends were not at present the kind Lear could raise in suffocating, filthy conditions and sell for food.

"Larson," President Curtis said over the private intercom Larson had had installed between her office and his so he would not have to communicate with her through his two secretaries, "get down here. If you would."

Larson arrived quickly with two large steaming mugs of amaretto-laced coffee and closed the great mahogany door of President Curtis's office with a switch of her broad but flat ass.

"Just like you like it," she cooed as she handed the mug toward President Curtis, who indicated she should set it on his desk. Larson had begun a month ago to draw her fingers lightly along his as the mug was exchanged, and President Curtis, who was learning to spot a potential sexual harassment suit when he saw it, wanted to thwart this one and at the same time avoid a scorned Larson's fury. She was, in fact, a great help in keeping his life free of the many important concerns that he deemed beneath his notice, but she also knew too much about how things were really done at Middle State ever to offend too deeply.

"Mr. Lear will be here this afternoon,' he said, inhaling the fragrant odor from his mug and awaiting Larson's displeasure. Lear, as usual, would arrive in a lubricious daze from passing among and bantering with the voluptuous student workers in the president's outer offices and, again as usual, pay Larson no attention at all, for which she despised him.

She said nothing.

"He wants to meet with Junior White," President Curtis explained.

Larson nodded and waited.

"Look, goddamnit, I know Lear can be a hard pill to swallow. But nobody—*nobody*—is more important to Middle State than he is. With the poultry complex and new artificial turf on the football field and the Center for Life Form Enhancement he's already staking us close to ten million. If we're going to get the rodeo complex and the Supply and Demand Center built or that ethics lectures stuff funded, we've got to let him know we appreciate him. So suck it up"—he regretted the phrase the moment he said it—"and remember which side our bread is buttered on. He'll be here around two. Get hold of White. Get him off his death bed if you have to—hell, out of his coffin. Just see he's here. And if he drinks, see that he's sober. One o'clock sharp."

"Yes, sir," Larson said, softening before such take-charge assertiveness and remembering the importance of being a team player to eventually being a team owner. "I have his number on my computer. Would you like to serve him the invitation yourself, or would you rather I extended it?"

"You. Just tell him Lear wants to meet him, that should do it. He came with no problem to get his raise. Even if he is just staff, he's no fool; he's heard of Lear. Meantime, two other things. Tell Stub Weebles from now on he's Director of Signage; we've got to get the poor bastard off the roads Give him released time from two classes each semester and five thousand more a year. And figure out something for him to do if he asks."

"He could inspect the signage. Every two weeks or months?"

"Something, I don't care. He's been hit twice by cars since that bathroom sign mess, running along like an idiot. That's all he does. He's a laughingstock; he's making us a laughingstock. He's even trying to get time off to run in some Iron Man stunt. Or Dumb Man stunt, I don't know. Yes, have him inspect the signage–but no reports, understand. He's definitely forbidden to write any reports. Just inspect. In fact, he can inspect my door plaque, he can polish it. Yes, make sure that's part of his job description."

President Curtis had mounted on the door to his suite a great, bronze nameplate with engravings deeper and more ornate than those on the tomb of an Argentine general.

"Yes, sir. And the next item?"

"Let Hays know his ride on the asteroid is over. No more surveys, no more reports, no more press releases, no more kit distribution, no anything. Asteroids are out. In fact, emergencies in general are out. If we have a disaster, it's cheaper to have Public Relations take care of it than be bothered with his preparedness bull shit. You know something? I should put Emergency Preparedness in with Public Relations," he reflected, "but then I'd have one less vice president. So that's out. Tell Hays to back off. Give him a raise for a job well done and let him figure out something to do."

Larson, scribbling in her notebook, nodded as she finished recording the orders and rushed to her office to call Junior White. She left behind her coffee cup to retrieve just before noon in hopes of getting an invitation to join President Curtis in his daily catered lunch from the Alumni Club, a ploy that had never worked and did not work this time, since Junior White had sauntered in a half-hour early and was already sitting at the side of President Curtis's desk, a plate heaped with grilled pork tenderloin and a three-layered salad on a reed place mat beside him. President Curtis, waiting for his sopa de lima to cool and nibbling on crisp tortilla chips dipped alternately in freshly made guacamole and a rich, pungent salsa, was delivering the punch line of a joke as Larson entered. He had chosen his joke to match what he considered Junior White's level.

" '_____ well put them in, too,' she said. 'You wouldn't cheat a blind girl, would you?'"

White, his back to the door, laughed appreciatively until he saw President Curtis's goatish smirk wrench to propriety and looked back to see Larson. He normally would have liked repeating President Curtis's waggery for Larson's benefit, but in such surroundings he knew to follow the lead of whoever was in charge and ostentatiously assumed an air of innocent solemnity.

"I believe I left my coffee cup this morning," Larson fluted, all merriment and camaraderie. She peered around awkwardly to overlook the cup that sat in plain sight where she left it.

"It's over there," Curtis said testily and turned back to White. "Did you try these chips? They're hand made by some of our Mexican cooks every morning–patted out and baked on a stone slab over an open mesquite fire. They're very good with this home-made salsa–everything in it grown at the university farm, and none of that genetically modified stuff either. Tomatoes, onions, cilantro, four kinds of peppers. Made from an old Mexican senora's recipe. Even better; it's made by an old Mexican senora. Actually she and her family grew the garden. Had to import them. Nobody in the Ag. Department knew how to grow a garden, can you believe it? Have to smuggle in Mexicans, though they do work cheap."

Larson, who could no longer sustain her mock search for the coffee mug, picked it up.

"Any orders for me?" she asked coldly.

"No, not right now," Curtis said, his attention still on White and the lunch. "Maybe later. Oh, yes, could you see we have some ice and water for Lear. Just have Edna bring it in."

He tested his soup, found it sufficiently cooled, and began spooning it in as Larson, defeated for the moment, whirled and swept out of the door.

"That's Dr. Larson," Curtis said apologetically. "My assistant."

They sat silently gazing at the empty doorway.

"Ass is too flat," White observed, and Curtis nodded resignedly. The buzz of one of Curtis's intercoms interrupted their reflections.

"Dr. Curtis," one of his secretaries said, "Dr. Swift just called and he's twenty minutes out with Mr. Lear."

"Thanks, Edna," Curtis said and turned to White. "That means they should be here in about forty-five minutes. Swift will either take a short cut and get lost or be pulled over again for leaving his turn signal on for twenty miles, or he'll run out of gas. I wish Lear would fly in on his corporate jet to our airport rather than Swift having to pick him up at Nashville. He took me up in it once. His own jet. Own pilot, got a TV in it, a bar. We were in Las Vegas before you knew it."

Only a few state universities of Middle State's rank at present kept a private jet for their top management and Reigning Board members. Still, President Curtis hoped someday to rise above the clouds as a member of that godlike group of flyboys—and flygirls, he would add now, knowing that gender-slighting had become yet another pitfall he had to avoid if he were ever to get anywhere. Lear's flying him like Hermes from Middle State to Las Vegas, while elating, had at the same time almost crushed him with a sense of his limitations and the distance between his aspirations and his present state. He had immediately applied for four open positions at real universities, each of which ignored his credentials and chose candidates who he felt were vastly inferior to him in intellect, managerial ability and people skills. President Curtis could see that to make it big, to strike it rich, he'd have to write some memos that would make those beneath him on the ladder put their shoulders to the wheel, their noses to the grindstones, their hands on the plow, buckle down and earn even less bread with even more sweat of their brows to bloat his reputation and fatten his resume. And looking up the ladder, he'd have to kiss some ass. And Lear, whose recommendation for a more lucrative job even Henry Ford would have cherished, was about to make his ass available.

Lear arrived only fifteen minutes late, five of which had been spent in lewd banter with the gorgeous student workers in Curtis's far outer offices. The other ten minutes were due to an emergency stop for gas a mile from campus and Vice president Swift's inability to find the fuel-door release.

"Nick-o, my boy," Lear said, shaking his head in mock disbelief, "you still know how to staff your office. Hand pick them yourself, I'd guess. Where's that red-head that was here last time?"

"Candy took an emergency medical leave before the term was over last year. Hasn't come back."

"Too bad," Lear said. "Hope she's okay," and he turned to Junior White.

"So. I take it you're Mr. White," Lear said, extending his hand. "The man who gives shelter to poor unwanted mutts. And an expert in security, I understand. Leo Lear. Good to meet you."

""Mr. Lear," White nodded, shaking his hand, his face blank.

"Old dope dogs," Lear mused. "There's lots of people who'd like to slip a little strychnine in their feed bowl. But those people aren't too smart. are they?"

"No, sir," White said.

Lear looked at him closely and then, satisfied, turned back to Curtis.

"Nick, how's the hammer hanging? You getting any? Any of that stuff behind those desks out there? That short blonde? Put me up in the room next to hers tonight—and none of that 'it's a university' crap this time. She's ready. Even that helper that drives me up here was getting overheated just hearing me talk to her."

"That was Vice president Swift," President Curtis said, hoping to get Lear off of Cookie, the blonde who had caught his fancy.

"Vice president? You've got a vice president driving the limo? God, Curtis, you live in a beautiful world. I guess when you don't have to show a profit, you can do anything. By the way, your vice president can't drive worth a damn, though I don't guess that matters either."

"Leo, would you like a drink," President Curtis asked to change the subject, indicating the antique walnut sideboard with the bottles of special reserve bourbon arranged carefully by the ice bucket.

"Turned one down once," Lear said briskly, taking a chair, "been sorry ever since."

He took the glass Curtis poured for him and turned again to White, who sat quietly watching the two.

"Get Mr. White one," Lear said amiably, and Curtis hesitated only a second before rattling three ice cubes into a second heavy glass etched with a gold-filled Middle State logo and splashing in the bourbon.

"Mr. White," Lear said, pulling his chair toward him. "Like I said, I understand you not only love man's best friend, but that you're a good man with security. Am I right?"

"I know a little about it," White answered. "Been at it, on and off, for ten years."

"Surveillance? Investigations?"

"Little bit of everything. Worked as a clerk in Army Intelligence and picked up a few things there. . . ."

"I've got Junior's resume and records right here, if you'd like to run through them later," President Curtis began, indicating the file folder that Larson had brought to him that morning, complete with a page of her own comments on what she considered pertinent features of White's employment history.

Lear waved his offer aside.

"The more impressive the resume, the more I smell bull shit. Anyway, I've already looked into Mr. White's record," Lear said. "Go on, Mr. White."

"Well, after the Army I hired on here as campus cop. . . ."

"Hear that," Lear said to Curtis. "Campus cop. I like that. Not a 'security associate' or a 'public safety officer.' A campus cop. Good." And he nodded for White to continue.

"Campus cop for four years. Then I went to trade school at night and then they put me in Electronics."

"After you asked some asshole boss if being re-designated 'security associate' meant more work or less money or both–right?"

"More or less."

"What do you do in Electronics?"

"Different stuff. Put in security systems. Other things."

"What other things?"

White looked at President Curtis.

"You can tell Mr. Lear," President Curtis said. "He knows about these things."

"No," Lear said quickly, "I don't know about 'these things.' I've heard of them, I imagine, but I don't know that they go on. If they go on, they go on; I just don't want it known I know about it. Don't forget that."

"I won't," Curtis said meekly. Junior White smiled with admiration.

"All right, Mr. White, what other things are you familiar with?"

"Bugs. Microcameras. Phone taps. And computer surveillance. That's a whole new field, computers, the best one yet for keeping tabs on what goes on."

"Yes," Lear said encouragingly.

"There's people's e-mail. You can get in and read it pretty easy. If you know what you're doing, you can get anything they've got on their computers–bank records, appointment calendars, anything they've written. And where they've gone on the Internet–airline tickets, motel stays, books they've ordered, phone numbers they've looked up, causes they've donated to, stuff they're interested in."

"Stuff like pornography?"

"Yes."

"Good. What else?"

"I'm just talking about home computers. Workers' computers can be hooked into a firm's central computer—that's legal, by the way—and certain things looked for and marked, like how fast a secretary—I mean," he said blandly with a look at Lear, "an administrative associate—types or what Internet sites they go to or how often or what e-mail they get or send, or how much solitaire they play."

"You appear to know the laws about surveillance, Mr. White."

"Pretty well."

"Good. Anything else about security and computers?"

"There's how security can use their own computers."

"You mean. . . .?"

"To keep up with people. You can get all kinds of data on everybody from everywhere. Medical, vital statistics, legal, deed offices, membership rolls, credit card use like where they buy stuff and what for and when and how much. Telephone records, school records." He looked apologetically at the slightly bewildered President Curtis. "Anything. You can store them all and cross-reference them in lots of ways, to subjects, other people—anything. And get the info fast, if you got the right equipment."

"Can you get that information without, as they say, running afoul of the law?"

"A lot of it is public records. A lot isn't. But you can get what isn't without too much trouble, and almost without anybody knowing it. The biggest problem is running into the FBI or CIA trying to get at it the same time you are."

"In other words," Lear said as if to himself, "you can keep tabs on everybody. Everywhere. All the time."

"Pretty well. Except for ones that don't have computers or aren't on the Internet."

"They don't count," Lear observed absently. "So, you can keep tabs. . . . You know, I'm bankrolling Critson for a little project and if everything there works out, knowing everything that's going on everywhere would fit right in."

He took a long, appreciative pull on his drink.

"Good stuff, Nick my boy; my regards to the taxpayer. Mr. White, are you recording this conversation?"

White was silent for a moment. He reached to his university-shirt pocket and removed a cheap appearing mechanical pencil and his pack of cigarettes. He placed them on President Curtis's desk, and Lear and Curtis both stood and bent over them.

"The eraser is a microphone. The pencil rests against this little metal strip on the pack."

"Tape recorder in the pack?" Lear asked.

'No. Small transmitter. I left the receiver and microrecorder in the big potted plant in the office out there. Pick them up on the way out. Or come in and get them tonight."

"Break in?"

"Security check."

"I see. What if someone watered the plant with your receiver and recorder in the pot?"

"The plant's plastic. Anyway, my stuff's waterproof. They look like the artificial rocks around the stalk. I've got different cases to match different backgrounds."

Lear sat back down, smiling, and looked at Curtis.

"Get us another drink, all around, would you Nick. And give Mr. White the rest of the day off. We'll talk tomorrow about these projects you want me to buy into. What are they, by the way?"

"Oh, there're several," Curtis said eagerly but somewhat disappointed that the carefully crafted begging speech he'd prepared to soften and persuade the great corporate prick was for naught. "There's the Rodeo Arena, the new turf for the football field, the Ethics Lecture Series, the. . . ."

"The Ethics Lecture Series, huh? Now, by god, there's a winner. White, I want you to go to those. You, too, Nicky-boy. Hell, maybe I'll go. We can pick up on the definite weaknesses of the ethical, not that they've got a chance anyway. Put me down for a big write-off for that one. And Mr. White—you mind if I call you Junior?—Junior, what do you feel about being put on my payroll? Not give up your job here right away—Curtis here may need you—but just be on my payroll for a little consultant duties to start off. Expense account if there's any travel. Per diem, too. I imagine you'll want to find homes for your dogs if your extra duties take you away from home too often. But I won't ask much from you until hunting season is over–about September or October, right?"

"I didn't think hunting season opened until November, most things," President Curtis volunteered.

"Tell you what," Lear went on, ignoring him. "I'll pay for boarding the dogs if you'll give me just a little bit of whatever game they might find out in the wilds. The later in the season the better. Female of the species only. Everything sound all right so far?"

"Consulting, huh?" White nodded. "Sounds pretty good."

"Best job in the world, though in your case it won't last too long. If I decide to hire you full time, which I'm almost sure I will, you'll have some actual duties to perform. But I'll start you off as consultant at twice what you're making here, and when I hire you full time, five times as much."

"Five times!" President Curtis gasped before he could stop himself. White would be making as much as his average vice president.

Lear laughed easily. "We're talking about another world here, President Curtis," he said with a dash of scorn to the title. "I believe if he agrees to my offer, Mr. White will do well in it. He seems to know which side his bread is buttered on. How about it, Junior?"

"Deal," White said.

"Now," Lear said to White, placing his empty glass on the near-mirror surface of Curtis's desk, "if you'll come over to my suite in the Alumni House, we can work out some details. Provided, of course, that Nicky here is going to give you the day off."

"Consider it done," President Curtis said with forced heartiness. "And Mr. Lear–Leo –tonight Julie and I expect you for dinner. Can you make it?"

"I think so. Unless me and Junior can get that sweet little blonde and some of her friends to attend a party we'll hold for them this evening. I may want to award a few scholarships. But I can drop by your place first. And by the way, until he's on my payroll, Junior is on yours–use him as you need him."

"Great, I will–but tonight we can discuss the Rodeo--" Curtis began, but Lear, Junior White following in his footsteps, had already cleared the door.

twenty-one
ROUTINE FACTS

"How can you say that? How can you still teach here when you say Middle State students don't know anything and can't learn anything?" Calona said as he passed through the small coffee room where Greenman, his usual caution abandoned, had just made the rash claim about Middle State students. Davis, getting coffee and ignoring Brumley, Hobart and Greenman seated around the table, paused to see if anything might develop that could be used to her advantage.

"You didn't hear the whole story, my man," Hobart said, ignoring Calona's disdainful look. "It might do you good to hear the results of Greenman here's little experiment from which he concludes that there are certain shortcomings in today's college student. It's based on research, and research, as surely you must have seared upon your brain at Research Day festivities, is going to become very important here at Middle State. As long as it's done by the right people and doesn't make any waves."

He reached deep into the grease-spotted paper sack on the coffee-room table and extracted the last of a dozen donuts, its sugar glaze now almost liquified. Calona, trapped, watched with distaste as Hobart took almost half the donut in one bite.

"You do want to hear the story, don't you?" Hobart asked, chewing. "I knew you would. Professor Greenman, run it by us again, would you?"

Brumley didn't want to hear the sad tale again, but Calona's reaction would be worth the distress. What he especially did not want to see was Greenman's consternation in having to make a negative if true statement in the presence of a truckling informer like Calona, who would have pretended to teach a class of scraggly coconuts without blinking if it would have helped him toward his career goal, which he was closing in on now that he was Vice president Flexner's assistant and no longer teaching freshman composition. But for Greenman, the closer his children came to college age, the more cautious he became in speaking the truth, especially a truth that conflicted with official truth. One very important official truth proclaimed by Middle State's management was that each year, according to college entrance test scores, Middle State was attracting ever-more accomplished and intelligent high school graduates. Management was also beginning to advertise Middle State as the Harvard of the Heartland and would resent evidence to the contrary. Always mindful that he had a family to support, Greenman was fearful of what form management's resentment would take. He was too old and too undistinguished in any way other than his commitment to his material and to teaching it well to get a job elsewhere. Like so many others at Middle State, he mostly kept its reality to himself, aware that knowing the truth—or letting it be known that he knew it—would indeed set him free, but only from his job, which basically he loved. President Curtis, he felt sure, had marked him sitting next to Hobart at Research Recognition and Reward Day, and Greenman was afraid.

"There's no need to go over it again. It's too depressing," Brumley said, trying to relieve Greenman, who surprisingly shook his head.

"It's depressing, all right," he agreed, and looked straight at Calona. "I was going to assign my comp classes Catton's essay 'Grant and Lee'– you probably know it, a classic comparison-contrast approach, and a damned good one, I have to say. Going to assign it Monday for today. I mentioned it to Hobart that morning and made the mistake--" Hobart smiled as he finished the donut "--of wondering if anyone in the classes would know who Grant and Lee were. He pulled out this quiz–I've got a copy if you want to see it–with ten questions about the Civil War: What was the capitol of the North, of the South, what century did the war begin in, who were the main generals, who won. That kind of thing. I told the class I usually didn't give a quiz on material before they had read it, but this time was an exception. For all they knew, it was for real–counted on their grades."

He stood up and walked past Davis, who was still alert for advantage, and got half a cup of coffee and threw a quarter in the payment mug.

"I just went over the quizzes. Want to know the average score?" he asked a now unsure Calona, who nodded slightly in feigned indifference.

"Three point eight. That's thirty-eight percent, average. One student got nine right, one seven, the rest—well, the rest resulted in an average of three point eight."

"But you can't expect them to know everything," Calona exploded indignantly to cover his ignorance of the answers to two of the sample questions. "They're not here because they know everything already. After all, we're supposed to teach them."

"Two didn't know who won the Civil War," Brumley supplied, seeing Greenman was too burdened to go on. "How many were in the class?"

"Twenty-two."

"That's about ten percent." Hobart said, wiping his sticky fingers on his pants. "College freshman and ten percent don't know who won the Civil War."

"But that's just rote memorization," Calona objected loftily. "Surely you don't see such boring efforts as a way for students to learn?"

"Do you think knowing which side won the Civil War is important, here, in the country where it was fought? And for the reasons it was fought?" Greenman asked calmly.

"Well, yes and no," Calona waffled with stout conviction.

"Merciful god," Hobart said, hoisting himself up. "Friend Calona, you'll say anything. 'Yes and no.' What that response means, if I may borrow a page from your rhetorician's manual, is *yes* in agreement with reason, common sense and I imagine even your own best instincts—but *no* so you can pretend to salvage some withered way of being in the right in this matter. But tell me, how will anyone know who won the Civil War other than memorizing the fact? Or what the quadratic equation is, or who wrote *Paradise Lost*? You act like these memorizations are presented to students as a list without context by robotic teachers who give no explanation or significance. That's not the way it is. It is absolutely—from the Latin ab-solvere, meaning to release from, and I'll let you figure out the implications—it is absolutely necessary to memorize, retain, remember. Somewhere, someone taught you that rote memorization—by which you mean memorization in general—is bad. *And you remembered it*, and believe, no doubt, that you're empowered by that knowledge that you came by from rote memorization. So why do you sneer at the process and effort it requires when that sneer is informed by–owes its existence to–the same rote memorization it so smugly dismisses?"

"It's not the same thing," Calona said hotly, "not at all." But he did not elaborate.

"I can't see why we should expect them to know just facts," Davis finally weighed in.

"I don't expect them to know just facts," Greenman said, "but I expect them to know some. Actually, I expect them to know a lot."

He turned part-way in his chair to gaze through the grime of the large coffee-room window that overlooked the roof of the new College of Business building. Down the way, the strobe lights of the two great smokestacks pulsed out their unwearied message of danger.

"Anyway, there's more to this than just an ignorance of 'facts'. It's not just that two students didn't know who won the Civil War; they couldn't even figure out who won it. Don't you think they've heard the saying 'the South Will Rise Again'? What South did they think was referred to? Rise from what, why need to rise? Didn't they have the curiosity to wonder what the phrase meant? Or think about this: you know the license plate, the one with a Confederate battle flag filling the background and a caricatured figure of an irate, musket-carrying Confederate soldier glaring out, with a caption that says 'Forget, Hell!' You see them attached to the front bumpers of pickup trucks everywhere–I'll bet at least one of the students who didn't know who won the Civil War has one on his truck. Didn't he–or she–stop to ask, Forget What? No, it's not that they don't know who won the Civil War, it's that we're sending to college those who *don't care* who won the Civil War or any war or anything else that isn't immediately personal and offers instantaneous gratification, usually physical. And they can't be taught to care, hardly any of them. By the time they get college age, it's too late."

"I'm not at all sure about that," Davis said, Calona temporarily silenced. "I'm having some real success in my Gender, Race, Class and Colonialism in Literature course. I haven't required any rote memorization since I concentrate on injustice by the privileged culture against the marginalized. . . ."

305

"Really!" Hobart exclaimed. "Injustice by the privileged culture. That's fascinating. I had no idea there was injustice done by the privileged culture. Are you requiring your students to remember that fact and any examples supporting it? If you're going back over to your office, I need to check my mail; you can tell me more on the way," and he escorted an animated Davis out of the coffee room, donut crumbs and flakes of sugar falling from his shirt front.

"There's much more injustice than you would think," she was saying. "Have you been keeping up with my examination of 'Columbo'? I've been sending it by computer to the department. I think it establishes conclusively and sheds new light on. . . ."

"Yes, yes," Hobart's rumble tailed off down the hall, "tell me more about Columbo. I've greatly enjoyed your study."

Calona got his coffee and sullenly went back to his office. Brumley and Greenman sat silently for a moment.

"Why don't they care?" Brumley asked. He meant the students, and he was sincere. His life-long assumption that to know was to be human–could it be wrong? Or had he simply chosen the wrong things to know? Brand names, loopholes, where the fun was–had those become what counted, all that counted?

"Haven't you heard why they don't care?" Greenman asked. "I can't recall the figures exactly–never accuse me of rote memorization–but a huge percentage of what are virtually infants, kids from two to five or one to six or something, watch maybe three to six hours of television daily. The figure goes up as they age. When they're that young, the passive– and it can only be passive–soaking in of those nervous, attractive images and their sound tracks fundamentally changes the neural networks that are forming in kids' brains. Their brains are physically different from what they would be if confronted by the real world. This is a fact; they've used MRI's and such to show it. TV is now an evolutionary force of the first order, more powerful than the weather or the stars. These kids are not the same as pre-tv kids, not even as kids from thirty years or so ago. And they don't grow up to be the same kind of adults. Now I'd guess those damned video games and computer crap are starting to work on them too."

Greenman was not even glancing fearfully around for eavesdroppers.

"You think it's a conspiracy?" Brumley asked smiling.

"Not a conscious one," Greenman replied after a moment., but he did not smile in return. "The really dangerous conspiracies never are conscious. There aren't any meetings of plutocrats in board rooms or thought police in back rooms to determine the future. But you can bet that if a passive, unthinking, uncaring, utterly self-centered average citizen is what will keep the powerful in power and make them more powerful, then, yes, there's a conspiracy and we're in—dare I say–a brave new world."

That afternoon at El Bullo's, the phony Mexican restaurant where many of Middle State's faculty went to avoid the undergraduates who flocked to the bars closer to campus, Hobart arrived with a tidbit from one of his many secret sources, a retainment proposal from Vice president Flexner's office to President Curtis that solved decisively the loss of student enrollment at Middle State due to students flunking out. His plan was simple and brilliant. It required instructors to give only A's and B's as course grades. In one stroke his plan would abolish the need for counseling services and for remedial courses in arithmetic and in basic reading and writing to prepare students who couldn't add or read or write for the remedial courses preparatory to the pre-math and pre-composition courses in which a passing grade was required to enter Math 101 and Freshman Composition and receive college credit. It also did away with the irksome tasks of determining which students had flunked out and which one's were on the Dean's list, since no one could flunk out if they never made below a B and everybody was on the Dean's list.

"I've heard nay-sayers cynically suggest we should just give a Bachelor's degree to anyone who sent us $50,000," Flexner's cover memo read. It had been approved and signed by him but written by Colona. "This is a cockamamie idea that would mean a greatly reduced physical plant, a much, much smaller faculty and staff, and perhaps even reductions in management personnel. This is not permissible.

"Alternatively, limiting grades to A's and B's will result in the following benefits:

1) Assurance that neither the physical plant, faculty and staff, nor management will be downsized by reason of this innovation.

2) A guarantee that no students will be lost due to 'flunking out,' since an average below a C is required for that to occur.

3) The likelihood that, since high grades will raise a student's self-esteem, students will be happier and feel they owe their sense of well-being to attending Middle State. They will therefore stay here and neither transfer to another school nor simply drop out of academia altogether

4) National recognition will accrue to Middle State when our excellence in grade point averages is publicized. Such publicity should result in more students, a larger budget allocated to us by the legislature, and a corresponding growth in all managerial areas.

There could, however, be a problem. Resistance could be encountered from those on the faculty who persist in having standards in what they call their 'discipline.' Such can be overcome as follows:

1) Make faculty raises, promotion and tenure contingent on giving high grades.

2) Fire untenured faculty who refuse to give only A's and B's.

3) Harass tenured faculty who refuse to give only A's and B's through discriminatory scheduling, selective enforcement of enrollment guidelines, appointment to inane and spurious committees, and cancellation of various seniority benefits.

Likely the carrot of 1) above will achieve the desired result, but the sticks of 2) and 3) may be necessary for those faculty members who do not yet understand the need for higher education to be pro-active toward societal demands.

Get back to me on this. And if it doesn't fly, what do you think of assigning grades in each class by lottery? I've got several ideas here."

"Our problem is," Hobart announced, "we've been marginalized

"Marginalized it is," Brumley agreed, thumping down his empty beer mug on the table. "Do you remember when people got screwed instead of marginalized? 'African Americans are screwed? Lower income groups are screwed'. . . ."

"'Colored folks are screwed' is how it went," Conners of Chemistry corrected him. "'Poor folks are screwed'. There was truth at one time. Back in the good old time."

"It was changed to marginalization by those who think marginalization is a great wrong if done to them or to someone far away, usually in the past," Hobart observed, pouring salsa on his basket of tortilla chips. "Margin, by the way, is from the Latin, *margo*, border. Hence, we've been exiled. Or, yes, screwed."

Brumley felt he was already over the margin and that Greenman's fears of losing his job for criticizing the slightest aspect of management policy at Middle State were justified–not for Greenman so much as for himself. He had received no response to his memo to Vice president Staull about Dean Wainwright and authorized construction, and other than President Curtis's offended, ghost-written editorial reply to his letter to the editor, all was ominously quiet on that front. But Brumley was sure much was happening. Wainwright had extravagantly ignored him as they passed in a crowded hallway between classes the previous week, and Cole's replies to his greetings were clearly becoming more and more distant. Brumley was indeed a marked man and he knew it, and to avoid marking himself further he told no one except Hobart and Conners the news that broke in his British Literature class that week about the Continental Divide.

"Wordsworth and his friend," Brumley explained to the class, "were something like college students today on a road trip, or on spring break."

He reconsidered.

"That's trivializing the event," he said to the class containing not only Warren and Bolinger but several other genuine students, as well as Kimee Deneen, who since her early days at Middle State was becoming more and more–alert, informed?–Brumley wasn't sure how to characterize her. She was still as beautiful as ever, maybe more so.

"It's better to say they were like two curious, intelligent students who entirely on their own–no institutional coddling–went off to see Europe. It was called the Grand Tour in those days. We've already talked about their arriving in France a year after the fall of the Bastille, before the revolution was betrayed. Remember Wordsworth's response– his remembered response we should say because he wrote *The Prelude* around ten years after he was there. Anyone remember the lines?"

"Bliss was it in that dawn to be alive;
But to be young was very heaven,"
Warren quoted accurately from his seat off to the side, and hearing

that young voice recite feelingly Wordsworth's mighty tribute to youthful belief in the better world moved Brumley almost to silence.

"Yes," he said, deciding to postpone his remarks on memory and apostasy for a more advanced class that he would never teach. For now, let them sense their own possibilities, and for a moment he could almost remember a very heaven himself.

"But back to the road trip," he continued. "The passage I asked you to read for today is called 'Crossing the Alps', and there's an issue we need to clarify before we go any further. Did you see that Wordsworth and his friend were anticipating crossing the Alps but took a wrong turn and 'crossed' them without knowing it. Did you understand what 'crossing the Alps' meant?"

No one hazarded a guess.

"It obviously doesn't mean traversing the whole mountain range, since they're expecting to accomplish it in a very short time that morning, and then do so unknowingly in just a few minutes. That any help?"

It wasn't. Not even Bolinger or Warren or the ever-improving Kimee Deneen seemed to know.

"It was clearly something very important to Wordsworth, this 'crossing the Alps', whatever it means specifically–and by the way, I'm not looking for any deep hidden meanings in the act, not at the moment anyway. But it was important, and when he finds out he's 'crossed' them and didn't know it, it unleashes–dare I say it–a torrent of emotions, a powerful reaction. To understand that reaction, though, we've got to know what 'crossing the Alps' means. Let me ask you this," he said, turning to the board and drawing a crude shape of the United States. It was a device he had used for some time to clarify Wordsworth's passage.

"About right here, running along the crest of the Rockies, is what?"

"The Continental Divide," Bolinger said, and then, "Ah, yes," the whole point becoming clear to him.

"Right. And those of you who have traveled out west and crossed it, didn't you–doesn't everyone–pile out of the car at the point where you cross and take a picture of the family with the big wooden sign in the background naming the pass and its elevation and announcing that at this point you are indeed crossing the Continental Divide?"

He saw a few nods and smiles of agreement and felt well on the way to once again clarifying Wordsworth's reaction.

"But without the sign, say someone had stolen it for firewood, and you were looking forward to crossing the divide and at the next gas station found out that you'd already crossed it, how would you feel and, much more important for the passage from *The Prelude*, why would you feel it?"

And then he made a great blunder, out of what perversity he wasn't sure.

"By the way," he said, "what *is* the Continental Divide—what does it divide?"

No answer, though Bolinger and Warren glanced around as though they knew but, in Bolinger's case at least, were incredulous that no one else did.

"My god," Brumley blurted and immediately regretted it. "No one knows? Now think a minute—you've heard of the it from the cradle. The Continental Divide, the Great Divide, Across the Great Divide, adventure, exploration."

"Is it the North and South, the Civil War?" a misplaced pre-law major asked.

"North and South?" Brumley managed to keep the disbelief out of his voice. "No. Actually, the divide itself runs north and south, so if anything it divides the East and West. But any north-south line we draw would do that. What determines the Continental Divide? It will be the same criterion that determines the crossing of the Alps."

Kimee Deneen finally answered the question, and Brumley forged on, now wondering how mystifying his clarification-by-analogy of a central passage in Wordsworth's poem—actually, a central passage in human understanding of itself—had been over the years when eighty percent of his students did not comprehend what he had assumed was the familiar, illuminating side of the comparison.

"And had never asked," Hobart solemnly observed after taking a long pull at his El Bullo Grande beer. "Think how often they had heard that term, the Continental Divide. And you say quite a few had been photographed crossing it? They didn't even care enough to ask what it divided, maybe didn't think it was worth asking."

"I know, I know," Brumley intoned. "It's terrifying. A sign indicates it's important. You—or your parents—have heard it's somehow significant. So you take a photo. And that's it. I can't stand it. They don't even have the knowledge of adventure."

"Maybe that's the problem," Talbot of Biology mused, who along with Conners of Chemistry had joined them that afternoon. "There isn't any adventure anymore. We've filled up the world, can get anywhere, see anything, at least on TV. And those phony video adventures, those monstrous games without consequence. And outer space, that's a joke; forget that."

"It's not just heroic adventure that's gone, though it's gone," Brumley pointed out. "The Colorado River is just an amusement park ride now with a screaming raft of tourists shooting the chute every ten minutes. Dentists climb Mount Everest between patients. And you can't just strike out into the unknown on foot anymore. There are posted rules even in the wilderness and satellites to look out for you. But there isn't any real adventure anywhere. Worst of all, there's no imagination left for adventure in ordinary life. There's just *fun*."

"Fun that you have to buy," Hobart said. "I'm sorry, Brumley, Conners, I'm sorry," and they were astounded at his tone. "We're teaching people. We're trying to, I think. And most don't want to know anything and see no use in knowing anything. Except how to get a certificate that will allow them to do something that's too often boring and unfit for a human to do so they can get money to buy things that they hope will make their lives fun. I'm afraid that's how it is."

And Hobart, disheveled, ill-dressed, the tolerated curmudgeon to departmental careerists, out-of-date and eccentric, turned his head from them.

"I've got to stop drinking beer on Friday afternoons," he said.

Early the next week Brumley heard a familiar voice speaking with Hobart in his office, and a few minutes later Hobart appeared at his door.

"Another one gone, I hope to a better fortune," he said. "That was Flytrap Jackson."

Hobart's attempts the previous semester to help Flytrap, and Flytrap's determination to do his best, had finally resulted in four papers at the end of the course that were sufficiently readable at the fifth-grade level to allow Hobart, against his every principle except generosity and compassion, to pass Flytrap with a low D.

"I should have known what would happen," he told Brumley at the beginning of the present term after meeting his eight o'clock second-semester freshman comp class for the first time to see with dismay among his new students the eager, beaming countenance of Flytrap Jackson, ready for another go at it.

"His first theme," he said, handing the two pages to Brumley.

Flytrap had suffered a relapse. In the three-week break between semesters, whatever he had learned apparently was lost.

"He'll get a little better—maybe back to where he was at the end of last semester," Hobart had said. "I'll have to pass him this time, since I've already sold out. And over next summer he'll forget the alphabet. As they say, no good deed will go unpunished. Poor bastard."

Since then, Hobart had been silent about Flytrap. There was nothing left to say.

"Gone? He's gone?" Brumley asked. "Dropped your class?"

"Dropped out of school," Hobart said. "He was working thirty-eight hours a week and would have worked more but Global has to pay benefits for more than forty. Just the twelve hours of classes he was taking were too much. And there's a rumor that Global is going to move all or part of the plant to China. He looked like he hadn't slept for days; looked terrible. Nearly cried. He thanked me for my help. I tried to tell him it would be okay, that he was okay."

"Did he say what he was going to do?"

"No, and I didn't ask. He's a good kid," Hobart insisted. "He'll be a good neighbor someday, if there are neighborhoods anymore."

It was the next day when they found out that Flytrap wasn't going to do anything any more. On his way back to his home, some sixty miles east of Middle State, Flytrap's car, travelling at excessive speed, had struck head-on the massive concrete pillar supporting an overpass. Either his fifteen-year-old car's steering had failed, the Middle State student newspaper speculated, or Flytrap–Jackson, they called him of course–had fallen asleep at the wheel. Likely the latter, since there were no skid marks. He was dead at the scene.

"Asleep at the wheel?" Brumley inquired carefully of a shaken Hobart the next day.

"And dead at the scene," Hobart replied.

Looking carefully away, he indicated two stacks of papers on his desk.

"His last paper is in there. I did what I could."

"I know," was all Brumley could offer.

twenty-two
PLUMB BOB

At Middle State, students kept dropping out. In spite of the abundant scholarships and loans for all, regardless of the endless parade of entertainment and diversions, and notwithstanding management's considerable pressure on the faculty to give high grades, students kept dropping out. Many—some from seeking only pleasure and some from utter bafflement by their course material, or, overlapping these two, from being completely and irremediably averse to sustained or even sporadic study—many, it was clear, did no work whatever and, no matter how many easy courses or indifferent instructors they enrolled for, finally flunked out and were declared ineligible to attend Middle State for a year. After that year, many never returned. For others, the scholarships, so numerous and casually given, were often inadequate to cover a large part of the ever-growing costs of attending college, and they, too, disappeared from the rolls. And the university-sponsored diversions and recreations, while for many providing yet another welcome and fatal distraction from their studies, were for others inadequate to quell their loneliness or homesickness or alienation, and they as well left Middle State, never to return.

But many who were lonely stayed, as did many who partied incessantly and many who cared nothing for what they studied. Plumb Bob cared for his many chosen and then abandoned major fields of study, largely because their profusion allowed him to switch from one to another as long as his money, accumulated from six years of Air Force service, held out. As handsome as Apollo, and in sexual matters with as little conscience, he was at the same time as unselectively friendly as some god of pure compassion and love. He neither gravitated toward nor sought out those who through arrogance or physical attractiveness or money or self-confidence topped the social pyramid. At the same time, no one was beneath Plumb Bob's notice or regard. The most timid, lonely freshman would be alarmed, then suspicious, then elated, his world brightened when the smooth, handsome Plumb Bob, behind him in the cafeteria line, asked him about the weather or the cafeteria menu or the freshman's courses and then asked him where he wanted to sit. And then a week later, call him by name with a friendly wave from across the quadrangle. Only with non-glamorous women did Plumb Bob have to take care, having seen the pain his affability could cause when his attractiveness and the shock of such uncommon attention were so readily taken for something else. The hot, good-looking ones were likely not to get overly expectant or possessive, but even with them he had to be heedful. Promiscuous but not indiscriminate, Plumb Bob was irresistible, without conceit or pride, and he did well.

He was doing all right when he arrived with his tray and a lissome girl with black lipstick and a ring in her eyebrow at the cafeteria table where Warren and Bolinger were eating their lunch of square hamburgers and fries. The table shortly filled with the usual collection of disparate types that Plumb Bob had attracted or shown his goodness to: a shy black student from Chicago, a small-engine repairman from the motor pool, two striking, predatory female transfers from a near-by junior college who, having partied through that institution, transferred to Middle State in hopes of finding wilder parties, more drugs, and better looking males. And, incongruously, Colson, who thinking the two hot transfers were with Warren and Bolinger had determined to elbow out those two losers, especially the fat smart-guy, who by alphabetical fate had been paired for the semester with Colson's latest girlfriend in their Introduction to Advertising and Marketing class and who frequently confounded Hokes the instructor with some of the dumbest questions Colson had ever heard asked. The questions weren't even about the television commercial each pair of students had to produce as their sole class work for the semester, but had to do with deep things, philosophical things, that Colson hated and that Hokes the instructor seemed to as well.

Ignoring everyone else, he took a seat and introduced himself to the transfers as the next Vice president of Student Government and began explaining to them the importance and intricacies of the democratic electing of the officers of that wholly ornamental and useless institution.

"First," he intoned loftily, "you've got to realize that most students don't vote, which doesn't matter because those who don't aren't usually in fraternities or sororities. So it's a contest among the greeks. . . ."

"You mean the Turks don't have a chance?" Warren asked, to the bafflement of the two transfers.

"What do you mean?" Colson asked suspiciously. "Who are the Turks?"

"Long-time foes of the Greeks," Bolinger threw in.

"Oh," Colson glowered, "right. A wise-ass again." He had not forgotten Bolinger's rout of him the previous semester over something in a class, which made him think of Bolinger's present close collaboration with Aimee Brooder, his girl and one of the sweetest pieces of ass on campus, poisoning her untroubled mind with ideas and questions best never conceived. Nearly unbearable was the thought of this pudgy worm writhing around her, *talking* with her, engaging her attention that only he should command, with thoughts and ideas that he could never command.

"No, not at all," Bolinger said matter-of-factly, and Colson turned smoldering back to his two neophytes, who unable to engage Plumb Bob were shifting attention to Colson.

"So," he geared back up, trying to subdue his anger, "you've got just a small part of students voting, and it's the ones who ought to control things because they're the only ones who care. But usually it comes down to the Pi faction—that's my fraternity, Pi Iota—and the Alpha sorority against the Sigs and Delts. They're the two biggest fraternities and sororities so each pair tries to get the smaller greek organizations to vote for their candidates. We switch back and forth which bunch wins every year so it's democratic. Whoever is elected can put it on their resumes—see how it works? Being vice president should look good on my grad-school application."

The two transfers neither knew nor cared what he was talking about. They still had hopes that Plumb Bob might invite one or both of them to his room that evening, or that Colson might ask them to a fraternity party where Plumb Bob might incredibly show up and invite them to his room, or any room for that matter. It was testimony to Plumb Bob's power, Warren thought, that these svelte, pampered darlings were even in the proximity of a shy black boy, a silent and watchful small-engine repairman and a girl with black lipstick and a ring in her eyebrow. Or, he had to admit, Bolinger. And himself.

"You say to make it democratic," Bolinger remarked, "but you mean make it look democratic."

"No, I mean make it democratic, like America."

"I don't get it," Warren observed. "How is it democratic if only a small part of students vote and those who do rig the election?"

"I just said," Colson replied, the heat rising, "that those who vote are the only ones who care, so those who don't vote don't count."

"Why don't they vote?"

"How should I know?"

"Maybe it's because they think the whole thing is a put-on popularity contest among the self-appointed elite," Bolinger said.

"What's the 'self-appointed elite'?" Carlson sneered. "I'm not a 'self-appointed elite'. I can just get elected because people like me better. Especially than those who don't vote."

"Sounds like Machiavelli," Warren interjected, knowing it was a mistake.

"Who?" Colson asked suspiciously, the name troublingly familiar.

"Machiavelli. He wrote *The Prince*. We read it in Humanities last fall. He believed that to be a good ruler you had to be calculating and ruthless and keep up a false front."

"Whatever," Colson said, sensing the traits were meant to apply to him and his views on the Student Government election but the connection not quite coming. He turned back to the two transfers, both of whom were shooting seemingly blank but deeply envious looks at Plumb Bob's interest in the black lipstick they wouldn't be caught wearing under threat of torture.

"But your views are like his," Bolinger refused the contemptuous dismissal. "He believes that most people can't be counted on and in general are pretty sorry—remember? And that a real leader is perfectly justified in misrepresenting himself or downright lying about an issue, or whatever"–he lightly emphasized the word–"to get to the top. Isn't that what you're saying?"

"No," Colson said with heated conviction, and then lost his way. "I said that since most people don't vote then they don't deserve to get elected. I mean, the guy running who knows what he wants and what side his bread is buttered on deserves to be elected. It doesn't matter what 'the issues' are."

"Well," Bolinger said, embarrassed for the cock-sure, fatuous defective. "But shouldn't a candidate"—something told him not to say *honorable candidate*—"shouldn't a candidate tell people where he stands on the issues and encourage them to vote? That's what keeps democracy going. Look at the Greeks, at Athens. When the big shots started counting on and playing up to people's ignorance and stupidity and apathy, that brought the whole bunch down, the whole city."

Bolinger spoke as though Colson not only remembered the *Apology* but knew enough Athenian history to see the work's application to Athen's fall from greatness. Colson did not recall those things. But he did remember that he was looking at an egg-headed underling who wasn't even in a fraternity and who by means of the unfair advantages of retained knowledge and reason was humiliating a Pi and a candidate for the Vice presidency of the Student Government who had the complete attention of two hot pieces that wouldn't give the egg-head the time of day. He leaned forward belligerently and pointed a clean, well-manicured finger at Bolinger.

"Fuck the Greeks," he said. "You've got to get the right people into Student Government who'll do the right thing or they won't even let us have a Student Government. Like back in the Vietnam War—Vice president Timmons told me when he interviewed me—they suspended the Student Government."

Bolinger's and Warren's smiles infuriated him, and even Plumb Bob and the black student seemed amused.

"What is the right thing?" Warren asked.

"And who is they?" Bolinger added.

"The right thing," Colson asserted, "is what the people in charge want—that shouldn't be too hard to understand. What President Curtis or Vice president Timmons want. If you don't go along, they might cancel Student Government. What would you do then, huh?"

"I don't know—I don't vote," Bolinger said levelly.

"Take 'them' out and shoot them?" Warren speculated helpfully.

"Burn the school to the ground and start over? Maybe then I could get the courses I need to graduate."

"Jesus," Colson said, rising to leave. "You're crazy."

The small-engine repairman looked on with interest while the two transfers, seeing all was lost with the now totally absorbed Plumb Bob and recognizing Warren and Bolinger as definitely unsound to be seen with if they were ever going to get in with the in-crowd, serenely left their trays for some harassed bus boy to deal with and followed Colson toward the door. Warren watched them go.

"You through?" Bolinger asked, standing up and carefully placing the empty mustard and ketchup packages on his tray. "I'm going back to the dorm and work on my TV commercial. My partner wants to star in ours–she's Colson's piece, by the way, did you know that?–and sizing her up, it looks like I'm going to have to write, direct, film, edit and screen it. To be around her I'd pay to do it, but luck was with me for a change. You ready to go?"

"Yes, but I may as well go over to the library," Warren answered, indicating Plumb Bob and his consort. "I won't be able to get in my room for an hour."

A week later, Plumb Bob had just finished lunch with Shalanda Jackson and Kwanona Young, two massive and voluble girls who were dumbstruck only for a moment when Plumb Bob asked if he could join them, introduced himself and began to tell them, when he had finally asked their names, about a guy he knew in the Air Force named Young and was Kwanona maybe kin to him? From St. Louis? The girls would exclaim about the event for days.

He noticed the two men in dark suits regarding him as he took his tray to the conveyor belt, and as he began walking back to the dorm, they fell in on either side of him.

"Mr. Pope?"

"That's me," Plumb Bob said affably, but he did not slow down and the two suits, expecting him to stop immediately, slowed in anticipation and then had to speed up to overtake him as he walked unconcernedly along.

"We'd like to talk with you a minute," the stockier of the two said.

His suit was dark blue and he wore a white shirt with a blue collar and a bright red tie.

"Sure." Plumb Bob moved considerably off the sidewalk to allow the file of students to pass unimpeded and turned to the two men.

They glanced at one another.

"Would you mind coming with us?" the thin, sunken-cheeked one said, but neither started off.

"It depends," Plumb Bob said. "What's on your mind?"

"I'm Vice president Timmons of Student Affairs. This is Dr. Shelburne of Counseling and Testing. We need to talk to you."

Plumb Bob stood smiling easily, waiting.

"Could you come with us."

"Let's try again—what's on your mind?" Plumb Bob repeated, and Vice president Timmons readjusted his entire over-bearing bearing.

"There's a matter that has come to our attention," he said deferentially, "one concerning some of your fellow students—female fellow students— that we need some information on."

Plumb Bob looked puzzled.

"That doesn't tell me much. What matter?"

"Mr. Pope," Dr. Shelburne said impatiently, "it would be better for you if you just came quietly. We have information. . . ."

Plumb Bob laughed and then quickly apologized.

"I'm sorry. You sound like a character in a bad movie: 'better if you came quietly.' Tell you what—just tell me what's on your mind and I'll come as quietly as one of these folks walking along here would." And he looked amusedly up and down at the men's suits.

"Tell him, Shelburne."

Shelburne quickly surveyed the students filing past and lowered his voice.

"Mr. Pope, we have reason to believe that you are having sexual relations with a large number of women students."

Plumb Bob, expressionless, waited.

"Is our information correct?"

"Well, I'm not sure what you mean by a large number. But maybe."

"We'd like to talk with you about the matter if you don't mind."

"Talk away," Plumb Bob said. "But I'm not giving out any names."

"Any names? We've got the names, at least some of them."

"What do you want, then?"

"We need to discuss your—behavior."

"My behavior?"

"Yes."

"You mean—the women?"

"Yes."

"Well," Plumb Bob considered, "okay. But no names. Lead the way."

The way was to Vice president Timmon's lavish Office of Student Affairs in one of the older, former classroom building that had been extensively and sumptuously remodeled for various administrative offices. Along with the usual complement of desks, chairs, computer consoles and sublimely stacked coeds, the commodious suite contained a reading room well-stocked with comfortable sofas and chairs and set about with shelves containing pamphlets and booklets on every conceivable aspect of Student Affairs. There were fully illustrated booklets on meeting partners, propositioning or courting, foreplay, sexual positions, condom donning, sexually transmitted diseases, stain removal, what to tell Mom and Dad, legal rights of cohabiting partners, impotence and priapism, nymphomania and frigidity, and multiple orgasms, all with cautionary notes on the dangers of such a powerful drive as sex and the need for great deliberation and restraint concerning it and its irresistible ecstasy. There were religious tracts by prominent preachers, strutting and thundering in print against fornication except in holy wedlock with procreation as the sole purpose of the act, which when so performed you couldn't believe how good it was. There were pamphlets offering pregnancy counseling from Our Little Sisters of Infant Mercy and others from the Council Against Overpopulation and Female Oppression. Some admonished against multiple partners, whether in rapid succession or all at once, while managing to make both possibilities sound highly interesting.

Through a side door was a viewing room with several large-screen TV's and racks of video tapes on virtually all of the topics treated in the reading room. There were also display cases of vibrators; of passive and active dildoes of an astonishing range of girths, lengths, colors and textures; of condoms, condom dispensers, lubricants, diaphragms, IUD's; of garter belts, erotic lingerie, whips, ropes, Arab rings, knotted silk scarves, seatless chairs, and on the ceiling there were mirrors.

On all the booklets, tracts, fliers and pamphlets, as well as at the beginning of each video, appeared: Middle State University Office of Student Affairs. Excellence in Student Affairs. Except for the student workers and a few administrative associates, the office was empty and had the air of an elaborate movie set.

Vice president Timmons led the way, Plumb Bob behind him and Dr. Shelburne bringing up the rear. The secretaries and student workers fell silent as they went by and began whispering to one another after they passed.

"Have a seat, Mr. Pope," Vice president Timmons indicated after he had closed the door to his office. Instead of moving to the high-backed swivel chair behind his desk, he half-sat against the top edge, facing Plumb Bob. Dr. Shelburne stood expectantly to the other side.

"Carol," Vice president Timmons said over his office intercom, "bring me the printout sheet we were going over this morning."

Almost immediately the door to Timmon's office opened and the secretary entered, carrying a folder with the printout sheet. She handed it to Vice president Timmons and as she turned to go, looked lingeringly at Plumb Bob, who smiled and nodded to her.

"Now," Plumb Bob said as she closed the door behind her. "What's up?"

"Well, Mr. Plumb Bob," Dr. Shelburne quickly said, "from what the printout tells us, I'd say you are, or usually are," and he guffawed, nodding vigorously, looking to Vice president Timmons for approval that was not forthcoming. Timmons instead looked somberly at Plumb Bob.

"You know what this is, Mr. Pope?" he asked.

Plumb Bob looked carefully at the printout sheet Vice president Timmons held.

"A printout?"

"Oh, yes, you may say that," Dr. Shelburne leapt in. "But this is a telling document. You know what it tells? It says. . . .well, let me ask you a little something."

Plumb Bob, slightly slouched in his chair and studying Dr. Shelburne, looked up slowly.

"Do you know"—Dr. Shelburne walked to Timmon's side and consulted the printout—"Charlene Foley?"

Plumb Bob thought.

"Name's familiar. What does she look like?"

Dr. Shelburne laughed derisively and adjusted his tie.

"You know," Plumb Bob said, sitting up in the chair, "there wasn't anything funny in what I asked. I asked an honest question. What's so funny about it?"

'Oh, nothing, nothing at all," Dr. Shelburne said with mock levity, and Plumb Bob continued to stare at him until he dropped his eyes.

"Our printout doesn't tell us what she looks like," Vice president Timmons said. "But you say the name is familiar. Is that of Whitney Bushart? No? Megan Green? Ginny Collins? Amber Scott? Dawn Skipworth? Eve Skipworth, Dawn's sister?"

"Sure, the Skipworth sisters. Sundown to sunup, couldn't forget them," Plumb Bob said fondly. "Hard to tell apart, but I remember them."

"What about those other names? Do they bring anything up, so to speak?" Dr. Shelburne interposed, looking to Vice president Timmons for approval.

"I don't believe Mr. Pope finds anything amusing here, Shelburne. I don't believe he's laughing."

"No, sir, he isn't."

"Neither am I," said Timmons, turning back to the printout. "Let's try—Stacey Kline? Leah Tapp? Kiki Cunningham?"

"Kiki, yes, Kiki, I do remember her. Real black hair, brown eyes. Wildlife Management major. I was one too for a while. We had Turkey Management together."

"Turkey Management?"

"You learned how to figure out how many wild turkeys to have killed each year."

"What do you remember about Kiki?" Vice president Timmons asked.

"Like I said, black hair. Brown eyes. Wildlife Management major."

"Did you know she dropped out of school for a semester?"

"No."

"Do you remember anything else about her, other than what she looks like?

"Yes."

"What?"

"Quite a bit. But I don't give details."

"Mr. Pope, why do you think we're asking you about these things?" Vice president Timmons asked.

"You're trying to get some info on these women."

"Info on these women? You mean—Mr. Pope, let me assure you we have no interest in these women other than safeguarding them."

"Yes," Shelburne added emphatically, "safeguarding them. Excellence in student affairs is our motto."

"Shelburne, let me handle this. I don't imagine Mr. Pope is interested in our mission, are you Mr. Pope?"

"Probably not."

"Kiki Cunningham," Vice president Timmons said, returning to the printout. "So you didn't know she dropped out of school for a semester?"

"No."

"Do you know why?"

"No."

"She had an abortion, Mr. Pope."

Plumb Bob waited genially.

"Do you know how she got pregnant, Mr. Pope?"

"Fucking?"

"See here, Mr. Pope," Dr. Shelburne gasped, pointing an admonitory finger at Plumb Bob. "You can't talk to us like that, you can't just say. . . ."

"Easy, Shelburne," Vice president Timmons held up his thin hand. "You know," he said to Plumb Bob, "you might be a little more proper."

"You asked me how she got pregnant. I ruled out artificial insemination and immaculate conception. Only fucking was left. What did you want me to say—sexual intercourse or something like that?

You've got enough sex toys in those display cases out there to stock a Wal-Mart whore house, and you want me to say 'sexual intercourse'?"

"All right, all right. Fucking it is," Shelburne conceded. "You're right, that's how she got pregnant. Fucking. We're agreed on that. Now"—he walked to his chair, sat down, then leaned toward Plumb Bob—"do you know who the guilty party is, Mr. Pope?"

"You count Kiki?"

Shelburne uttered a cry and walked to the far end of the room.

"All right," Timmons said, "we'll count Kiki. Do you know who else might have been involved?"

"No."

"Were you?"

"I don't know."

"Is it possible that you were?"

"It's possible."

"To be frank, Mr. Pope, all the women whose names I've read had abortions, and all of them named you as the impregnator."

Plumb Bob waited, unalarmed.

"When we consider that only a small percentage of our women students who have abortions list anyone as the father, your name cropping up ten times is dismaying, truly dismaying. Could you have been involved in all these cases?"

"I don't know," Plumb Bob said, standing up and walking to Dr. Shelburne, who was now holding the printout sheet. "Let me see that sheet a minute."

"Oh no you don't," Dr. Shelburne said, jerking the sheet away. "There'll be no revenge on your victims."

"Revenge on my victims? What are you talking about? I just wanted to check those names again. Besides, you've already read them out to me, right?"

Still guarding the printout sheet, Dr.Shelburne moved around the desk.

"We did read them out," Vice president Timmons said.

"Timmons, goddamnit—yes, yes, we read them out to you. Here, look at them. Do what ever you want."

"Another thing," Plumb Bob said, ignoring the printout Shelburne shoved at him. "They weren't victims. They were willing volunteers. None of this victims stuff. Did any of them complain about me?"

Timmons looked at Shelburne.

"None of them did, sir, but if we leaned on them a little we could probably. . . ."

"Shelburne, shut the hell up. Mr. Pope," Vice president Timmons said, "pay no attention to Dr. Shelburne's comment. He's so dedicated to the welfare of our students that . . . ."

"And to Excellence in Student Affairs?" Plumb Bob suggested, returning to his seat.

"Yes, to excellence in–yes–so dedicated that he sometimes gets carried away in looking for ways to insure their welfare. They're so well taken care of that we often have a hard time over here finding something to do. Right, Shelburne?"

"Yes, sir. Carried away."

"So we're not going to 'lean on' anybody, right Shelburne? I think you can see, Mr. Pope, that such a thing will not stand."

Plumb Bob was silent and looked flatly at the two men. Dr. Shelburne took a ball- point pen from his pocket and clicked it several times before a glance from Vice president Timmons stopped him.

"How did you get that printout?" Plumb Bob asked suddenly.

"We got it from the clinic. I said that."

"That's illegal," Plumb Bob observed. "Privileged medical information. Private. You can get in a lot of trouble–you and the clinic–in getting that information. Do Kiki and the others know you have it?"

"No, they don't know," Shelburne volunteered belligerently, not seeing Vice president Timmon's furious gesture to keep quiet. "But it's not necessary for them to know. You might be interested to learn that our having this list is not illegal. Before any student can get an abortion at the clinic, they have to fill out a voluntary form in the Pre-screening Office, which is in the same building as the clinic–in fact you have to go through it to get to the clinic–and Counseling and Testing along with Student Affairs runs that office. Women who come to see about an abortion and fill out the form we give them–fill it out on a strictly voluntary basis, of course–thereby make it a part of Middle State's records. We're required to keep it confidential but can use it for official university business. What we're engaged in now, in case you don't know, is official university business."

Vice president Timmons had turned his chair to look out the window.

"I suppose the girls know that the—what did you call it?—the Pre-screening Office is not a part of the clinic?"

"We have a sign posted indicating as much," Shelburne said loftily.

"How big is the sign?"

Smiling wryly, Vice president Timmons turned back in his chair.

"Shelburne, I don't think we're dealing with a twenty-year old here, someone who hasn't been around. Mr. Pope appears to know how things are done. As for your last question, Mr. Pope, the sign is not large, and most of it is taken up with our motto, Excellence in Student Affairs. It's located, as I'm sure you'll ask next, above the entrance door. On the inside. The fine print states that the Pre-screening Office is not a part of the clinic and that filling out the forms is strictly voluntary. And to anticipate your line of questions even further, we tested a similar sign in one of Dr. Shelburne's general psychology classes and found only one student in two hundred mock visits ever bothered to read it and she found it of no significance. Didn't seem to understand its implications. Of course, we don't explain the implications at all, though as concerns the real sign, no one has yet asked about it or apparently even noticed it. When you're thinking about an abortion, you generally don't have the fine print on your mind. So in response to your suspicions, no, what we're doing is not illegal. We're simply trying to help certain students. In a difficult time for them."

"Sounds like you're doing a good job," Plumb Bob said blandly.

"Oh, yes, we're trying," Vice president Timmons said. "We don't want to lose enrollment through drop-outs caused by unwanted pregnancies. Or wanted ones, either. Flexner over in Recruiting and Retainment wants us to give the pregnant woman all the aid necessary to keep her in school and then enroll the child when it's born. That's an idea, but I think it's illegal. So we work on keeping women from getting pregnant. And that's why you're here, Mr. Pope. Now, Dr. Shelburne, you have the floor. It's your baby from here on."

"Yes. Thank you," and Dr. Shelburne walked to gaze out the window behind Vice president Timmon's desk, who turned in amazed irritation to look at him.

"What are you doing?"

"Just looking out the window here," Shelburne said abstractly. "Just casually looking out the window."

"Shelburne, Mr Pope is over here. He's the issue, not the parking lot."

"I just wanted Mr. Pope to relax, sir."

"And looking out the window will help him?"

"Yes, sir," Shelburne said, glancing sideways at Plumb Bob and lowering his voice, which Plumb Bob could still hear perfectly well. "I try to put the subject at ease before springing the hard questions on him. It's a technique you learn in psychology to get what you want from your patient."

"Shelburne, ask him the questions, for god's sake. I told you we weren't dealing with the ordinary shit-scared student here. Go on. Ask him."

"Yes, sir. All right. Mr. Pope, have you ever heard the term 'sex addict'?"

"No."

"Do you know what a sex addict is?"

"I'd imagine it's somebody who's getting more sex than you wish you were but aren't."

"No. Definitely no. It means a person who is driven to have sex, who does not observe the restraint and denial such a dangerous force as sex deserves, who has sex as often as conditions or their conscience will let them. Who is often compulsive about sex. That's what a sex addict is, and they're a destructive force; they should be locked away. Do you recognize anyone who fits that description, Mr. Pope?"

"Do sex addicts like sex?"

"Well of course they do."

"Then it's everybody."

"Everybody!"

"That's right."

"How can you say such a thing? Sex addiction has been added to the list of psychological deviations. It's an official mental disorder now. How can it be a disorder if everybody has it? Answer me that."

"Who put it on the list?" Plumb Bob asked. "What do they get out of putting it on? Sounds like a scam to me."

"Shelburne," Vice president Timmons said quietly. "Let's drop this. We won't get anywhere with Mr. Pope. Write him down as an unreformable recidivist–surely that's an official disorder in your book. The truth is, I'm afraid, that he likes to–as he says–'fuck'. Women like him to 'fuck' them. And he won't quit 'fucking' them for forty years or so. Am I right, Mr. Pope?"

"I don't know," Plumb Bob said.

"Anyway," Vice president Timmons went on, "we've done our job. We've set up a service in the Pre-screening Office, we've collected the data, we've analyzed and acted on it. Mr. Pope has been counseled, so you're covered, and he was counseled about his many affairs with female students, so I'm covered. Our job is done. Mr. Pope, you're free to go."

"I was always free to go," Plumb Bob said with an agreeable nod. "I just wanted to hear what you two had to say. Good to meet you."

There was no stopping Plumb Bob, but there was no need to stop him. He was without social or pecuniary ambitions, was untroubled by any political or governmental outrage, and took no thought for tomorrow, certainly none for posterity. Protecting the moment, staying free from annoy, and doing what came naturally were his unexamined and even unconscious guides to living, and with his looks and his easy congeniality life had been a sweet ride. If he stayed away from married women and the girlfriends of mobsters, it always would be. In Plumb Bob, who could always be handled by being left alone, the existing order saw no apparent threat, and the few broken hearts and guilt-haunted lives that were his inevitable legacy were largely cancelled by the roses of Dionysian ecstasy he scattered about. Life was good for Plumb Bob, and if he didn't rock the galley that he could so easily have sunk, he would always be free to go.

twenty-three
THE GREAT CHICKEN BREAKOUT

"Never perform an act, issue an order, or hold a ceremony that doesn't benefit you in multiple ways," President Curtis read grandly from a laminated card to Vice presidents Staull and Swift, who stood attentively before his desk. "One of the twelve rules of Management Theory," he said with brisk respect. "If you want to get anywhere, you'd better follow it. The other eleven, too. As long as we're having this Chicken Addition dedication tomorrow, I intend it to benefit me to the maximum extent feasible. You might take a lesson here"

He leaned back contentedly in his new swivel recliner. It was custom made, framed in oak and titanium, padded with the latest space-age foam, and covered in soft leather with area heating and ultra-quiet vibrating units from scalp to ankles. He had ordered it after Leo Lear's last visit, and it had arrived, a soothing reassurance of his station and infallibility, just after Research Recognition and Reward Day whose mixed results President Curtis still hadn't sorted out. He was pretty sure the faculty—or enough of them—would knuckle under and start churning out some research, but there had been the small and momentary insurrection exposing that flunkey's research published in the alumni magazine that may have made a mockery of the whole show. But, he thought, what the hell—as long as that bunch of do-nothings got busy publishing some nugatory rubbish that could go on his vita, who cared what they thought about his initiative or the ceremony to launch it, though he would like to have fired and maybe had arrested those who didn't think his initiative and ceremony were on the cutting edge of several things. As for the other flap, the Too Few Courses thing, as soon as that troublemaker Brumley got his, which wouldn't be too long, and that whining student shut up, the whole bothersome mess would be over and swept under the rug once and for all. Meantime, the new, be-gadgeted chair would ease the crushing duties of the administrator, which, unknown to President Curtis, Hobart had once observed were one with the White Man's Burden and the Awful Responsibilities of the Rich.

"Swift," President Curtis ordered, "you pick up Lear at the Alumni Club—provided he hasn't slipped into one of the girls dorms—and do it by nine-thirty. Be at the Poultry Complex at ten. I'm giving you a free twenty minutes to get back on track after you get lost, or to walk to a gas station when you run out of gas—neither of which will happen, right?"

"No, sir," Swift reassured him. "Limo's all tanked up and I do know the way—it's only a mile or so."

"Sure," President Curtis said. "Sure. Now, Staull, run over the goals of this ball-buster and give me the schedule again."

"Would you like the schedule first, then fit the goals in? I think it would give a clearer picture."

"Staull, I don't care."

"All right. At ten o'clock Lear arrives from the Alumni Club. All the others will already be assembled. . . ."

"Who've we got? Besides Lear?"

"There's Lear, like you say, there's the Chairman of the Reigning Board and four other members, six of our vice presidents and three directors, six agribusiness executives, the contractor, the mayor. Two dirt farmers for show, and you and I. Assembly is at the parking lot of the Poultry Complex. When Lear arrives the shovels will be distributed and the ground broken—and remember, it's for the Leo Lear Addition to the Chickens Unlimited Poultry Complex, not the 'Chicken Addition'. Then Lear cuts the ribbon to dedicate the overall complex. Your two-for-the-price-of-one ploy—it's brilliant."

"So you're still with me on putting the groundbreaking and the dedication together?"

"Yes, sir—like I say, it's brilliant," Staull reaffirmed.

"Perfectly okay, sir, great idea," Swift agreed.

"I didn't want to waste two mornings, even if I would get to make a speech both times. Lear wouldn't come but once anyway, so if I couldn't get a little butter on my bread twice, then I say put the two together."

He surreptitiously turned on the lower-back heating unit of his chair, satisfied with his decision.

"Now, what else."

"After the ribbon cutting. . . ."

"My speech. When does it come?"

"Just before the ribbon cutting, to build suspense and tension up to that big moment. After Lear cuts, we tour the Complex, see the chicken-raising process. The protective gear is in place; Professor Wyandotte knows the drill and we can let him take charge and lead us inside after the ribbon is cut. We should be in and out in fifteen minutes, maximum. That's the schedule. As for the goals, you get to cozy up to Lear, cement the grant, impress the Reigning Board members with your leadership abilities, get the attention of those other corporate executives, and get your picture in the paper–the press is alerted and will be there."

"Any TV coverage? What about TV? That's what really matters. All those shovels, action."

"The local stations were notified. We haven't heard back from them."

"So no TV."

"It looks doubtful."

President Curtis stared resignedly at his Persian carpet.

"You know," he said, "with all the good jobs for little people going down the tubes and everyone flipping burgers or mowing yards or driving taxis–no offense, Swift–you'd think TV would like some interesting footage that showed something good happening to the economy for a change. Like this dedication. Lear is getting a hell of a tax break here. I've got some sweet discretionary monies coming to my account. Even a dumb-cluck like Wyandotte is getting more money than a professor deserves. But no, TV is too busy out finding some sex-with-a-minor to lead the five o'clock local with. What a world. But to hell with them. I think I can realize my goals regardless of TV. Now, let's make sure all this goes as planned. I've got a one-thirty tee-time tomorrow, and I intend to be there. You hear that, Swift? Get Lear there by ten."

Only his ability to flatter and fawn saved Vice president Swift of Transportation and Hospitality from his chronic and acute ineptitude. Kissing ass was his sole competence, and even there he embraced whatever sacred loins were before him with such shameless ardor that a visiting corporate head, accustomed to subordinates writhing from his ass like lampreys, would first feel disgust at the vice president's truckling, only to pass finally, under Swift's relentless sycophancy, to tender forbearance toward the cheery, obsequious, pitiable stumblebum. No matter how much luggage Swift left sitting at the curb as he sped away with a visiting dignitary pounding on the limo's glass divide; no matter how many wrong meetings or classrooms had to turn him and the guest lecturer he was guiding away; no matter how often he forgot the essentials—once food and drink– for a reception; no matter, even, that once he had slammed the lid of the limo's capacious trunk on the treble fingers of a celebrated visiting pianist whose concert that night, though played with great fire, was clearly unbalanced—even then, Swift's gushing apologies and later praise had so mollified the testy performer that he never mentioned the mutilating act to President Curtis. So long as Swift could grin and bear, scrape and bow, smile and pucker, he would survive.

When he arrived at the Poultry Complex a few minutes early with Leo Lear, even President Curtis took note, but when ten o'clock came and a general milling around in front of the Chickens Unlimited Poultry Complex still went on, he edged up to Swift:

"Where are the shovels?" he hissed.

"The shovels? They're in the trunk, I think," Swift said feebly, starting toward the limo.

"You think?"

"Yes, they are, I think."

"Well," President Curtis forced himself to smile indulgently and lower his voice, "get over there and get them. We're not supposed to stand around here like a bunch of chickens. And what about the hard hats?"

"Hard hats?"

"Yes, goddamnit, hard hats. You've got to have hard hats for this stuff—good image, safety-conscious, that kind of thing."

"Hard hats," Swift said.

"You didn't get them, did you," President Curtis said through his rigid smile. "You are the dumbest piece of shit I ever had stuck to my shoe. Get over there and get the shovels."

The shovels were not in the limo's trunk but in the passenger compartment where Swift had stowed them the previous night, being unable to find the limo's trunk release or the hidden keyhole. Forgetting he had put them there, he unwittingly handed Lear in among the blades and handles twenty minutes before at the Alumni Club. In the drive to the Poultry Complex he had wondered at the strange noises and curses sputtering from the intercom, but put them down to Lear's irascibility at having to attend any function he didn't want to.

Trembling at President Curtis's displeasure, Swift found at last the trunk release and, seeing the trunk empty, suddenly recalled where he had placed his cargo, plunged through the rear door of the limo, and began extricating the shovels–twenty-six chrome-plated ones for the body of officials and the gold-plated one for Leo Lear. Simply unsnarling them was problem enough, but he tried to embrace, grip, balance and wedge all of them in this arms and elsewhere so he could back out and carry them complete to the dignitaries as one grand presentation, almost trapping and injuring himself in the limo before falling out backwards with three shovels onto the parking lot. Once his dilemma was recognized, President Curtis rushed to divert the attention of the reporters and photographers present while the rest of the officials turned away and began discussing the sheet metal building they had been standing before, Leo Lear among them but aloof and resigned. The two farmers came to Vice president Swift's aid, each twice stacking and carrying a manageable five shovels while Swift, gratefully noting the efficiency of the stacking method, removed and attempted to do likewise with the remaining seven but gave up after a third try. Finally, holding and tucking them at awkward and impeding angles from his hands and from beneath both arms, with the handles of two jutting and scissoring obscenely from between his legs, he jerked along, reaching the group of dignitaries with a deferential and ingratiating smile and clattered the shovels down before them.

When the shovels had been properly distributed to the largely uncalloused hands of the officials, the gold-plated one wrested from President Curtis by the chairman of the Reigning Board who after a whispered warning from Wyandotte of Agribusiness passed it along to Leo Lear, the eager dignitaries and the two uncomfortable farmers grouped themselves for the ceremony.

Since there was no ground near enough to the asphalt-surrounded complex to do a true groundbreaking, the photographers on hand were asked to photograph the group, some of whom were apparently unfamiliar with the operation of a shovel, from the knees up only. The university photographer alone did so, and in the local newspapers that bothered to print the photo as filler, the group seemed unaccountably poised to vandalize a parking lot. Leo Lear, in fact, actually drove the point of his shovel well into the asphalt and flipped out a large divot, an act that was carefully ignored by everyone there.

With the groundbreaking complete, the group turned to the enormous building behind them housing the chicken complex. An unceasing roar reverberated through its steel paneled sides. "As long as three football fields and as wide as two," the promotional literature described the structure, which contained in a central area at the front a large, plush administrative unit carefully sealed both hermetically and acoustically from the rest of the complex. Through the administrative unit, one could enter a change-room for floor laborers, who used a separate entrance, and the change-room in turn gave access to the containment floor itself. For the next part of the dedication ceremony, a pink satin ribbon was strung across the main doors, each end held nervously by a vice president. Just as President Curtis was about to begin his standard dedication speech, the delivery of which would alone have redeemed the event for him, Leo Lear with brutish indifference snapped the ribbon.

"I've got a plane to catch," he announced dismissively as he handed the foolishly large ceremonial scissors to President Curtis, who, swallowing hard, nodded with quick understanding before shoving the scissors to Vice president Swift..

For the ceremony's grand finale, the group tour of the containment floor itself, Wyandotte of Agribusiness became the man in charge. A founder and foremost proponent of large confined-feeding operations for the raising of food units and a winner of grants galore, confidence flooded through him and with a barely suppressed swagger he led the group grandly through the huge main doors and into the administrative area. They proceeded down the long aisle that separated two extensive sections of office cubicles, the work stations of a large staff of secretaries, accountants and technicians who kept up with the grant applications, implementations, and disbursement. All of them looked up admiringly from computer screens as the procession strode past and through the single door marked Change Room–Authorized Personnel Only.

"I know this is probably unnecessary," Wyandotte said, once the group had entered and the door closed behind them, "but since our workers have to wear these precautionary clothing, we've got to set a good example and do the same." Hanging by each locker was a yellow suit of some synthetic rubber-like material. "The suit proper should go on first, then the rubber boots, then the respirator, then the hood. If the boots are too small, let me know." A sudden increase in the already loud roar from behind the airtight doors leading to the floor of the complex made him raise his voice. "The suits and the rest you'll have to live with. And you should know," he added, prompted by President Curtis's nudge, "these are the same suits worn at the Transuranic Department in the Science Building before they're washed and transferred to the Center for Life Form Enhancement in Biology. They're then sent over here in a recycling initiative President Curtis has instituted that saves the University over three thousand dollars each year."

President Curtis took the rehearsed compliment impassively and began trying to fit the respirator over his great shock of wiry hair. He had long ago understood that there was neither plutonium nor unknown genetically altered pathogens facing the workers at the Poultry Complex, but just ordinary germs, viruses and fungi whose combating hardly required first-class protection. Besides, just as there were millions of chickens waiting to be raised in the Poultry Complex at Middle State and everywhere else, there were nearly the same number of potential green card or illegal immigrants who would willingly work in these animal hells in worn and contaminated protective gear, or even in no protective gear at all, depending on the level of poverty and oppression their families faced back home.

"I wouldn't have minded hard hats," President Curtis mumbled, his respirator terribly askew over his face, "but this I don't know. You all right, Leo?" he called down the row of increasingly unrecognizable figures.

Lear, whose yellow suit seemed tailored for him, paused before slipping his respirator on. "Let's just get this shit over with," he said without looking up. "I've got a plane to catch, remember. Which way do we go?" He slipped on the respirator, pulled the hood over it, and swaddled like some garish astronaut followed Wyandotte toward the double door to the Complex floor. The noise had grown even louder, and the Reigning Board members, the agribusiness officials, the Middle State contingent and the locals formed behind them and shuffled forward. Wyandotte rapped forcefully three times on one of the steel doors, waited until he heard an answering three and a loud click from the other side, then pulled it open.

"Right through here gentlemen," he said, but knew his already muffled voice from the respirator was positively obliterated by the roar that now blasted them.

The doors opened onto a raised platform with steps that led from each side five feet down to the floor of the facility. Six workers with leaf rakes as staffs had driven some two hundred chickens off the platform to make room for the dignitaries. Stretching from as far back through the dust and corrosive stench as could be seen, up to the foot of the just cleared steps where surging companies of chickens attacked from left, right and front against the rake-wielding workers, was a seething, cacophonous swirl of living things which were surely chickens but which could as easily have been maggots or the souls of the damned.

"Goddamn," Leo Lear choked from the rail around the platform, but said no more.

"Over one hundred fifty thousand units," Wyandotte knew he was shouting into his respirator but pretty much aware no one could hear him. He held up the first in a series of large, numbered flash cards he'd asked Vice President Swift to prepare for him and key to his remarks. He pointed to it and swept his arm out over the chaotic din. Unable to tell if the frozen attitudes of the dignitaries was in reaction to what lay below them or to incomprehension, he gestured widely again toward the uproar and churning moil on the floor, then pointed once more at the flash card, which he noticed with a start read: Six Weeks. He shook his head exaggeratedly at the group and rolled his eyes in self-deprecation, smiling to soften the censure, though aware his expression could not be seen. He searched clumsily through the cards until he found at number five the appropriate one, but the fringes of the group had begun moving uncertainly down the manure- coated steps to the facility's floor, the workers fending off most of the scraggly, maddened chickens who were desperate to retake the steps and platform, if only for a moment of space and rest before the great mass expanded to compress them back to their carefully calculated 0.53 square feet per unit. Even the railings around the platform and the tops of the many long, automated feeders and waterers placed throughout the facility had been factored into the calculation of the experimentally established minimum area per chicken-unit, below which, for some poorly understood biological imperative, the units simply refused to eat and died.

"Wait," Wyandotte called, "just a few more figures here."

But it was futile; no one could hear. Except for the few dignitaries who had ventured slightly down the steps, the rest were riveted by the ceaseless motion and roar from the floor. The greatest tumult was around the feeders and waterers, where the general pandemonium seemed intensified as the fight for food and water endlessly persisted. Chicken piled over chicken, were carried back and forth as on a sea, scratched and fought for a few pecks at the high-protein feed composed in part of the feathers and offal from the previous batch of units raised in the facility. Sudden great fights broke out in these areas, where sustenance was forgotten in a violence beyond reason. When a particular savagery spent itself, workers, who recently had begun to patrol only in parties of four for protection, moved toward the scene to gather the dozens of carcasses and fling them into the mobile death carts placed throughout the floor. Clouds of dust rose as from explosions and a stench like the aftermath of some great summer battlefield filled the floor and seemed even to seep through the cheap, steel-paneled walls.

Without rakes, the visiting dignitaries evoked no fear in the chickens, who by now in some number had evaded the armed workers and infiltrated to the steps, a few even to the platform. Two were trying to gain a roost on the separate shoulders of the shrieking Vice-chair of the Reigning Board, while two more charged between the columnar legs of President Curtis and flushed simultaneously up into his crotch. One squad had ignored the steps altogether and scaled the front of the platform where Wyandotte, given up on his presentation, was with initial unconcern kicking them with a veteran's aplomb back over the side until one, then three, then six attached themselves to his offending leg.

"Here," said Wyandotte, "here," shaking his leg and then, as three more began flogging up the other leg, bending to pull them away and fling them back to the floor. More of the crazed units who had reached the rail leapt with great cackles onto Wyandotte's inviting broad back and tore and pecked at it and one another in an exquisite frenzy.

"My god," he shouted, violently trying to dislodge those still attacking his legs, then straightening up only to dump most of the chickens on his back in a maddened mob among the dignitaries behind him on the platform. "We should probably," he said, as if in a dream where he knew no one could hear him, "move back to the administrative area and . . . ." But the lesser dignitaries, who through a sense of rank had hung back to give their betters the places of honor along the rails, were already pushing at the doors, which, to keep prying, unprepared visitors from viewing the filth and holocaust, had locked upon closing.

"Help!" one cried, "help!" as the others began frantically shoving from behind.

"Code Red," Wyandotte gasped, and then again, more weakly, "code red," and one of workers, assessing the situation, flung his rake aside, shouldered his way up the steps through the shrieking knot of dignitaries, and struck a large red knob to the side of the door, releasing a great klaxon horn that exploded and bore down like the trumpet of the last judgment. Wildly following the worker's retreat into the now undefended left flank of the visitors, a company of suicidal chickens scrambled and flogged into the crowd just as an ever-growing number cascaded over and through the railings.

"We should get out," Wyandotte whispered, and as the weight of chickens bore him down, he saw the doors, unlocked at the initiation of Code Red, burst outward and the yellow-suited, hysterical dignitaries burst out into the change room. Before a great whiteness settled over him, Wyandotte felt a strong grip and pull on his arm that lifted him out from under the torrent of chickens pouring over the platform and through the swung-back doors and saw Leo Lear, his perfectly fitting suit unblemished, shaking his head unperturbably at him. Lear jerked his thumb toward the doors.

"This ought to be good," he said, but Wyandotte, of course, could not hear.

By now the main body of dignitaries, escorted and pursued by hundreds of chickens, had reached in full rout the far end of the change room, where the single door impeded them only momentarily.

On the other side, a scattering of secretaries and technicians had begun to move cautiously into the center aisle and a few briskly toward the main doors to the outside. Most, however, in spite of the Jehovah voice of the klaxon deep within the building and the growing noise from the change room, simply looked up quizzically from their computers toward the change room door.

There were two great thuds against it, the first President Curtis, before it slammed back and the dignitaries hysterically burst through, chickens now beginning to outpace them, straight into the administrative area. For a split second the staff stood paralyzed in disbelief. Then they tore into the aisle, some falling, all screaming as the outpouring from the change room clawed, leapt and trampled over the fallen. With the main aisle momentarily clogged, the flood spread laterally along the back wall of the area until the space between it and the first row of cubicles was filled; then, as though at the shot of a starter's pistol, the great tide crashed over into the first row of cubicles, filled them, then cascaded over into the next and so onward toward the main door. Reams of memos, reports, letters, printouts of all types now were swept up into the rout, and the dignitaries and hundreds of chickens leapt and flogged from cubicle to cubicle like some high-hurdle race for the demented. Partitions collapsed, cables snapped, computers were smashed and the sputtering, useless shards dragged cracking and smoking along with the frenzy.

The main doors were mercifully large enough to accommodate the frantic mob and out they flowed, the dignitaries fighting to remove the suffocating hoods and respirators and escape from the main current of the flood. The chickens, inexhaustibly, flowed on. Helping Wyandotte steadily along through the shambles of the administrative unit and the unstaunchable flood, Leo Lear continued to shake his head in amusement.

"Hope you bastards have insurance," he said to Wyandotte, who still couldn't hear him.

In all, before the fire departments and then the National Guard arrived to halt their flow and seal the outer doors, over a hundred thousand chickens escaped. Most were unable to contend with the fresh air and ample range they found or to scratch up their own food, and, within a few hours of their freedom and not far from the complex, they expired. But not all. The most legendary survivor, several days later and

341

somehow avoiding an elaborate security system, leapt upon the live desk of a local television news set, whose commentators, neither of whom had ever seen a living chicken and whose reportage for the past week on the breakout had been slanted for rating purposes to provoke fear of feral chickens, fainted and caused the cancellation of that night's news, a news item that led the news the following night, complete with a televised tape clip of the chicken flying suddenly up to the desk, which caused the commentators, viewing it on their monitors, to faint again, once more canceling the broadcast. This might have gone on indefinitely had not the station's daily audience-survey showed that their viewers no longer cared about chicken stories and in fact were beginning to feel that the entire idea of raising chickens in Auschwitz-like conditions was a bad one. Quickly such an untenable belief was set right by the media, the Leo Lear Foundation for Truth, and Middle State's Office of Public Relations, who collectively showed that not only was confinement feeding the cutting edge of technology and therefore above criticism, but also that the grocery price of chicken would rise and that many family farms of families making over five million dollars a year would fail if the practice were stopped.

So the Great Chicken Breakout was apparently over. Yet some of the stalwart escapees managed to adapt, a few taken in and sheltered by families or individuals but most running wild, scattering and spreading ever outward from the Facility, to be seen darting through the woods by hunters at dawn, or perched on a school's playground swings, or strutting defiantly atop a Kentucky Fried Chicken marquee. Such sightings of the fugitives of the Great Breakout, whether individuals, little guerilla-like bands, or even a small domesticated flock here and there, kept its memory and spirit alive. But Lear's grant still went through. Lear, who jetted away over the chaos without a downward glance, got his tax break; President Curtis and Wyandotte got their cuts; and once the mass grave for the expired chickens had been dug, filled and covered, the Chickens Unlimited Poultry Complex had quickly been restocked with another one hundred thousand poultry units and things at Middle State returned almost to normal.

twenty-four
PRESIDENT CURTIS

For two weeks after the Great Poultry Breakout, President Curtis was plunged into the longest period of self-doubt and near-despair of his life. The humiliating affair had even received brief mention in the national press, which to his amazement failed to make clear both his total lack of responsibility in the matter and also the magnitude of its blow to his career prospects. Instead, the heartless ghouls of the media had treated the whole disaster as mere backwoods bungling and played it for laughs, one national network even having the gratuitous malignity to suggest that Middle State's already abasing nickname be changed from Roos to Roosters. Nor could President Curtis find a scapegoat to pin the debacle on. He would like to have issued Wyandotte a leaf rake and redefined him as Floor Worker, but having recognized and rewarded him only a couple of months previously for his excellence in research, he found demoting and humiliating the shaken poultry confinement expert difficult to justify. And unclear rumors that some contaminant from the Center for Life Form Enhancement was responsible for the feathered insurgency also led to a dead-end when the similarly recognized and rewarded Critson was the sole whipping boy tied to that stake. Leo Lear, who strode unconcerned from the catastrophe to his jet–how easily that great man could have had some underling take the fall. President Curtis could not, and his thirst for subordinate blood remained unslaked when a new threat appeared.

"He's from the *Journal*," Staull told him, Dean Wainwright nodding in slavish affirmation behind him as the two stood before President Curtis's desk. "He's their higher education reporter. Brumley's letter and your reply must finally have got their attention and they send this vulture down. He came to Wainwright here first, who sent him to me. As far as I know he hasn't seen Brumely or that whining kid yet, but he's been asking seniors at random about their being able to graduate on time. Junior White has found out that at least three are claiming to be in the same boat as that Warren. I imagine after he's talked to me he'll want to see you. We need to formulate an approach."

"Why do these things happen to me?" President Curtis moaned, unsoothed by every heat and vibrator unit of his chair and switching off their considerable power supply. "Why? Why? It's that damned Brumley. He convinced the kid there's a problem; he's kept the ball rolling. He wrote that damned letter that made us look bad and that I had to answer–*in writing*. The son of a bitch. Another faculty member. My god, why can't we have an on-line university or a virtual reality university–get rid of the faculty once and for all?"

He left his chair, moved aimlessly around his spacious office and stopped to stare morosely at his golf-ball collection. Not even the one in the plexiglass cube could comfort him, the one he had blasted out of the bunker onto the sixteenth green at the university golf course to within two feet of the hole while the Chairman of the Reigning Board and Leo Lear looked on. He turned back to the waiting Staull and Wainwright.

"So now we've got to handle the press. I suppose this is what you call a crisis, and the sixth rule of management theory is, when in crisis mode, discuss your options. So we might as well get discussing."

"I'm not sure, here," Vice president Staull ventured, but wouldn't the seventh rule be better? Circle the wagons and lie?"

"You take them in order, as they apply, Staull. First, we'll discuss our options."

"You'll notice," Dean Wainwright offered recklessly, "that rule seven might even be an option. I mean an option after we've gone over the true options under rule six. Then there might be options under rule seven. . . ." he trailed off under President Curtis's stare.

"As a first option," Vice president Staull said briskly, rescuing his underling, "we could modify letter Number 4, but in essence you've already used that in your reply that you had Vice president Dodson write in answer to Brumley's letter."

President Curtis stared glumly at his Persian carpet, whose intricate patterns seemed to mock him as though reflecting the tangle his life had become.

"Anything else?"

"Option Two, obviously, is keyed on letter Number Five. We admit an isolated and unfortunate problem and claim you are looking into it."

"I've got to admit there's a problem that we've caused?"

"Yes," Vice president Staull said, "but isolated, an anomaly. If we can word our press release obscurely enough, no one will understand we're admitting anything. Then we'll make your determination to solve things clear and forceful."

"Maybe," President Curtis said doubtfully. "I don't know. This taking blame—not that we are to blame—I don't care how round-about it's done, taking blame is not a safe career move."

"Granted," Vice president Staull said, "but I think we can make the whole thing sound like some—well, let's call it 'institutional weakness'. You know, nobody's fault, inevitable, an unforeseen, inherent problem in the system. That you're working hard to correct."

"Another option. Give me another one."

"Option Three is based on letter Number Eight—virtually the same as Option Two but here you appoint a task force to look into the matter."

"Now that's more like it. With that option I won't have to do anything, especially since I can appoint the task force and hand-pick the members. Hays the Emergency Preparedness Boy, he can go on it—he still hasn't found anything to do. And besides, this is definitely an emergency and he damned well can get us prepared for this one. And our limo driver—the Vice president of Shovels, the stupid, clumsy bastard—Swift, he can serve on it."

"Weebles," Vice president Staull threw out, "Stubby Weebles. Our Director of Signage."

"Huckston," Dean Wainwright presumed to add, this time unnoticed.

"Yes," President Curtis agreed, his mood lightening. There was a large pool of toads to draw on for this onerous and meaningless task force, and he was beginning to feel almost his old self.

"But there is one thing, sir," Staull offered carefully. "You'll have to chair the task force."

President Curtis stared at him, his jaw tightening.

"With the press breathing down your neck, we've got to show that you're truly concerned over the Too Few Courses problem and are actively involved in seeking a solution.

"I'd have to go to the meetings?"

"Yes, sir. I'm afraid so, sir."

"Next option."

"Sir," Dean Wainwright abjectly raised his hand.

"Yes?"

"How about the truth?"

"The truth?"

"Yes, sir. As Option Four."

"What, Wainwright," President Curtis said coldly to the near quivering dean, "do you call the truth?"

"Well, sir, in this case, I mean we admit that we're budgeting money everywhere but to hire adequate faculty and to pay the ones we've got a competitive salary or give them decent benefits. And as a result we don't have enough instructors to offer classes necessary for students to graduate in four years. Or I mean," he said desperately as President Curtis's face grew darker, "that there are more pressing budgetary areas than that of faculty expansion. It might be seen as an honorable and courageous admission that showed Middle State on the cutting-edge of academic honesty—excellence in academic honesty. Truth, Sir."

"Wainwright," Vice president Staull said warningly.

"Wainwright," President Curtis cut in with a heavy note of insincere patience. "Dean Wainwright. If you ever make it to an upper-management position, which I doubt you ever will—in fact," he said evenly, "you may not even stay at the level you're at—but if by some miracle you should rise, you need to learn that there are pressures at the top that make the truth difficult to ascertain. Sure I could take money from football and basketball, or worse, from discretionary funds and blow it on academics. But what would the Reigning Board say? What would the Roos Boosters say? They'd say, Curtis, you're not doing your job, and your job is balancing the demands of the diverse communities that make up the university. And they'd bring the balance back in place by throwing my ass off the scales, that's what they'd do. Then there's no telling who they'd get to replace me—probably some jock-sniffing maniac who would give money needed for the academic community to the athletic community. Truth is complex, Wainwright, a double-edged sword. Maybe as Option 15 truth is possible, but in general truth is out. You got that?"

"Yes, sir."

"So, as it now stands, we come up with the properly worded press release—by the way, where is Dodson? I don't have a Vice president for Public Relations for nothing—wait, is he in Public Relations or Public Information?"

"Public Relations, I think," Vice president Staull said. "Dodson is Public Relations, Gooch is Public Information."

"Okay, Public Relations, whatever. But Dodson could give you the low-down on the truth. Where is he, by the way?"

"He's in Munich."

"Munich?"

"Yes, sir. He's got a Special Improvement Leave to study at the Goebbels Archives."

"All right. So no Dodson. We'll have to implement Option Two without him. At least under that option I won't have to go to those useless Task Force meetings. Just make sure, Staull, that the press release has my admission of a problem so buried and coated over that ten lawyers couldn't pick it out. I don't want anyone to think I got a degree in Communications for nothing.

"Yes, sir. You can be sure I'll use every rhetorical dodge in the book. Since Dodson is unavailable I'll get that Calona motormouth to help out. A new faculty member, degree in something called rhetoric. He's in Flexner's office now, as Assistant to the Vice president."

President Curtis's smile was his first sincere one in days.

"Ah," he beamed, "another young faculty member who's found that"—his features twisted into a mask of amused, mocking contempt—"the *life of the mind* isn't all it's cracked up to be." He broke into a long, deep laugh, his first since the Chicken Breakout, that bent him double over his desk, finally gasping for breath while Staull and Wainwright joined in appreciatively

"Oh, god," Curtis managed finally, wiping his eyes, "the 'life of the mind'. All those profs I had in my undergrad days–grad school, too–they were working their asses off and not making any more than truck drivers. I told myself then, this 'life of the mind' baloney is not for me– I'm going into Education Management. Topped it off with a little Communications credential. Best moves I ever made."

Sitting back in his chair, President Curtis switched the heat and vibrators on low and looked pleasantly at his two apparently enthralled subordinates until Vice president Staull once again intruded upon his good mood.

"There's something else, sir. Brumley. We need to deal with Brumley."

"Yes," President Curtis leaned forward, scowling. "Brumley."

"Have you considered offering him a part-time administrative position to shut him up? Half his course load off and a five thousand dollar raise. We could ease him into place and then saddle him with more make-work than a camel. Send him overseas to some god-forsaken place. Several options here."

"That's a possibility. I've never seen a college teacher that five thousand more a year wouldn't make their knees buckle. But I don't want that son of a bitch to get anything–actually, I'd like to take five thousand off his miserable salary. No, I want him to hurt like he's made me hurt, like that chicken fiasco made me hurt. No, Staull, no mercy on him. We can start by seeing that his class schedule for next fall sends a message. And let's not forget his friends. That fat piece of garbage at Research Recognition and Reward Day–get him, too, and anyone else close to Brumley–there was some worm on the other side of that fat-ass. And does Brumley have a family? We could get them, too. Wait. What about connections? He doesn't have any rich or powerful relatives or friends, does he?"

"I doubt it, but I don't know."

"Put Junior White on it–Lear says we can use him until he's got him full time. Have White find out all he can on Brumley. And if he can't find out anything to our advantage, have him come up with something he can find out to our advantage. Get what I mean?"

"Yes, sir," Staull and Wainwright said together, Wainwright a little too loudly before choking into a submissive silence when both President Curtis and Vice president Staull turned to regard him.

"Wainwright," President Curtis said, "when I need you, I'll call you."

Brumley wasn't laughing. Neither was Greenman. Hobart was smiling, but it was a smile that Chairman Cole had once seen in a photo of an ax murderer. Teaching schedules for the next fall semester had come out, and each of the three had been assigned five classes, including three sections of freshman composition, the first such load strapped on a full-time faculty member in over ten years. Brumely's Monday-Wednesday-Friday schedule was for classes at 7:30 am and 4:30 pm and Tuesday and Thursdays at 8:00am and classes both nights from 6 to 9. His freshman classes were at 7:30 and 8:00 in the morning and one at night.

"We're overextended on upper-division courses, and a fall-off in full-time equivalencies in majors means there aren't enough literature or humanity classes to go around," an apologetic and nervous Chairman Cole reeled off to the unwavering stare of Hobart–Greenman and Brumley standing beside him.

"Horse shit," Hobart announced. "That's horse shit and you know it. We don't have *enough* upper-division courses; that's what started all this in the first place. Curtis get you to do this? Staull? Wainwright? I can see me getting shafted for Research Reward Day and curtailing Curtis's glory–curtail, to cut short, or maybe dog's ass, which I like better–but why Brumley? No, I know why in his case, but why Greenman?

"I want you to admit," Brumley stepped in, "that this has nothing to do with my teaching or anything else other than my not being a team player, right? Nothing in the evaluation policy or in the Faculty Handbook says kissing ass—excuse me, agreeing with all managerial decisions and acts or failures to act–is a requirement for raises or promotions, or fair teaching schedules."

"Well?" Hobart asked an even more uncomfortable Cole. Greenman, pale and trembling, remained quiet.

"We're overstaffed on upper-division courses," Cole began again, desperately, "and a fall-off in full-time. . . ."

"Merciful god," Hobart said, looking closely at Cole. "A man will do a lot for money, won't he? How much differential you get for being chairman? Five thousand dollars? And two courses off a semester?

And the immense prestige–you know the origin of *prestige*?–of being chairman. Is it worth it, Cole?" He wheeled mightily around and strode out. Greenman and Brumley remained behind.

"Did they tell you how long this would last, how many semesters we'd have this load?" Brumley asked.

"No," Cole finally said.

"Any penance they want us to do?"

"No."

"Cole, you've got to do something for Greenman. He has absolutely nothing to do with anything, other than sitting by Hobart at that miserable Research Recognition and Reward Day crap. Hobart can retire anytime. I'm done for; Curtis won't forget me. But you can at least help Greenman."

Cole nodded weakly, his eyes down.

"Thanks," Greenman said to Brumley as they walked away. "I'm sorry I'm such a coward. I wanted to say something, but I couldn't. I've always been that way."

"That's okay," Brumley said. "You've got a family to think about."

They shifted to one side of the hall to avoid a wooden pallet stacked with boxes empty now of the pipe fittings they had contained. The sprinkler system in Humanities Hall was now operable. The computer portals and hook-ups had also been installed. For awhile, it appeared, no more classes would be interrupted by authorized construction. The computers were in place and were now fully protected.

"If I really worried about my family, my kids," Greenman said, "I wouldn't be a part of all this. Not just Middle State. Everything. The whole show. Middle State is no different than the rest of the world. Maybe not as bad when you think about it."

"Then it's impossible to get away."

"Not if I were brave enough. And could get by on my own. You know–cut wood, grow food, do carpentry–that kind of thing. I'm not brave and I can't even grow a tomato. Or build a fire, even to get the charcoal going."

"Better teach your children well then."

"I don't have the courage to do that, either."

"Climb the smokestack? I could try," Brumley told a delighted

Warren in his office the next day. "Might have a little trouble getting up the ladder, but heights don't bother me. Old Cadoon, huh? I think I met him when I first came here; didn't know all about him for years afterwards. Hobart filled me in. I'd like to meet him, see what he's like."

Brumley said nothing about President Curtis's vendetta and his opening move with the schedules. *Not teaching the child to doubt*, he thought again, still unsure of the soundness of Blake's augury or even that he understood it. Too, he didn't want Warren to think he had risked his job for Warren's benefit, even such a job as it had become. No trumpets going before a good deed, Brumley thought.

"I think Mr. White will still park his truck behind the library, at least until he finishes his research. . . ."

"White? Junior White?"

"Yes, sir. He was on that signage committee with us."

"What research is Junior White doing, for god's sake?"

"I think it was about caring for dogs or training them."

"Those dope-finding dogs he so generously adopts?"

"I think so."

"Interesting. But yes, I'd like to meet Old Cadoon. Whenever it's convenient for you, and I mean that. I'll take the time. Always did want to go up those smokestacks."

In spite of the two sets of freshman composition themes he would need to return the following Friday, Brumley agreed to Warren's choice of that Wednesday night to climb the Center for Life Form Enhancement stack and meet old Cadoon. Why have principles about getting papers back quickly? The very last thing President Curtis and his henchmen were concerned with was when instructors returned their students' papers—why should he worry about it? Except he did. When a student, he knew how important it was to have them returned quickly. As for climbing the smokestacks, he doubted anyone would know or care about his doing so, and anyway he wasn't sure there was any rule against doing it in the first place. But rules were at times unwritten at Middle State and, when they were written, often applied retroactively. It might be well known to management that the smokestacks were frequently scaled and the carillons violated, but the practice would be tolerated until the wrong person was involved. Or, in his case, the right person. Then the crack-down would come.

But for tonight, the first truly spring night, clear, warm, promising an even warmer tomorrow and spring's full entrance with winter's door shut for good behind her—for this night Brumley felt rebellious, felt young. *Bliss it was. . . . .* But he felt no guilt and walked buoyantly behind Warren, carrying his end of the ladder until they reached the base of the smokestack and with surprising ease he went up the ladder and stepped onto the lowest stairstep, Warren not far behind him, panting more with excitement than exertion. Brumley could see he was eager for him to meet Old Cadoon and was proud to have arranged the meeting.

"You want me to go first?" Warren asked him.

"I don't think I'll stray off the path, but you've been here before. Sure, go ahead."

Warren had gone upwards and around only half the smokestack's circumference when he stopped and Brumley saw him bend down to feel the step in front of him. He motioned for Brumley to come up to him.

"This is his harness; you can see it hanging down. He ties it to one of the steps on this side where nobody can see it from below."

Warren had told him of Old Cadoon's inventive method of mounting to his aerie, and Brumley was once again impressed as they started back up.

"Hey," Brumley heard Warren say ahead of him, "you're here."

"Mr. Warren. Yes, I'm here. And I see you brought a companion. Is it. . . .Dr. Brumley, how are you. I believe we met briefly just before I left my employment at Middle State. Your first year here. Matt Cadoon. Good to meet you."

"Good to meet, or re-meet you."

"I hope it's worth the effort. Young Warren here and his friends don't seem to mind climbing up here, and I enjoy the isolation and view. But this isn't a location most people would choose for an informal get-together."

"I don't mind it at all," Brumley said, looking out over Middle State's campus to the dark countryside beyond. "Gives a new perspective on things. So this is where the Chairman of the Board's cousin plays the carillon tapes?"

"Yes, on the sound system just past us."

"Phony smokestack, phony carillon," Brumley observed.

"Excellent," Old Cadoon said smiling, "though both carillon and smokestack serve a purpose. Just a hidden one."

Warren was listening closely; Dr. Brumley and Old Cadoon were hitting it off well.

"Is it like the Artesian Fountain Theory you were talking about last time?" he asked.

"Lord, son," Old Cadoon said, "you don't forget much, do you? You've got a point, I suppose. Very little in this world is what it seems, especially not in human affairs. Would you agree, Dr. Brumley?"

"A lot isn't," Brumley said carefully. He and Old Cadoon, he felt, were generally of one mind–Hobart's stories and what little he had sensed in the past few minutes indicated their affinities–but he didn't want to give up what little independent critical judgment he had. "I suppose we are honest at times, at least as individuals. But there's something about institutions, at least after they get well established. Everything they do has a purpose in addition to the announced one."

"Then I suppose Middle State hasn't changed much" Old Cadoon said. "Still floating a teaspoon of piety on five gallons of self-interest in everything they do?"

"Pretty much so, I'm afraid."

"Growth still the Holy Grail?"

"Still the Holy Grail," Brumley affirmed. "Everything depends on it–money from the state mainly, which is finally what everything depends on. The more students, the more money. It doesn't matter what kind of students, though the administration likes to pretend it does. More budget money from the state, more money to the community, which pleases the Reigning Board, which means more money to Curtis which drives him to ever greater efforts to get more students of whatever kind–they'd empty the insane asylums and prisons to increase enrollment. Such is college, these days."

"Have you ever thought, Dr. Brumley, what 'college' meant when you were a student and what it means now."

"I could say the same," Brumley said smiling, "about 'life'."

"Very good," Old Cadoon nodded. "By my age you'll have further revisions to the term. Now Mr. Warren here may be mystified by all this bleak reflection," Old Cadoon said, turning to him. "Disillusioned, too. At your age you should climb this thing just to smoke a joint or the equivalent and then contemplate the sweetness and promise of the world. That's the only reason I would have at your age, if there had been joints back then. But things change; you come to see things as they are, or think you do. Perhaps what's needed is to have the scales fall from your eyes gradually and keep some hope, or the ability to recover hope, that things can be made better. But never, ever, say that it's all beyond redemption so I'll just stay out of the fight. You understand why, don't you?"

"Yes, sir. I think so."

"Good."

Brumley, one arm resting on the railing, turned and looked to the ground far below.

"You ever wonder if the examined life is worth living?" he said to Old Cadoon. "Not that you have much choice, if you have a certain kind of mind. But take the opposite extreme, the Chairman of the Reigning Board's cousin, for instance. They say once he puts in the carillon tape on Sunday he spends his time spitting over the side here, seeing how close he can come to the first splot he makes. He doesn't care, doesn't even know that the carillons are phony—he doesn't even know for sure what a carillon is, and doesn't care. The fact that he has the job only because of family connections doesn't mean a thing—he's never heard of nepotism. He climbs up a smokestack every Sunday, puts in a tape, spits over the side for thirty minutes, takes the tape out if he can remember to, climbs down and collects two-hundred dollars, tax free. He blows the money without a thought, lives without a thought, and is likely as happy as I'll ever be, probably more so. Is his life somehow not worth living? God, maybe I'm saying ignorance *is* bliss."

"It's ignoble bliss, though," Old Cadoon said. "I think."

"I think he's in some of my classes," Warren added irreverently.

"Really? You don't. . . ." Brumley began and then laughed when he saw Warren wasn't serious.

"No, not really. But I see what you're getting at," Warren said to

Old Cadoon, "about trying to see things the way they are. Is it like the Artesian Fountain Theory?"

"Mr. Warren, I can see you're determined to hear that theory expounded. You should understand I use the word theory loosely, satirically really–we need Dr. Hobart here to give us the etymology of *theory*. I suppose he's still at it, bless him–but whatever its origin, probably analogy is the better term. Dr. Brumley," he said, "would you like to hear it?"

"Sure," Brumley said. "I've got an analogy for Middle State myself."

"Good. We'll see how well they converge. My 'theory'," Old Cadoon began, "certainly applies to Middle State, but does also to all public universities and, *mutatis mutandis*, to private ones as well. And, incidentally, it elaborates on without appreciably modifying our remarks on Middle State's specious need for limitless growth–which is the need, as someone has said, of the cancer cell. And, it strikes me, of our economic system. But to my theory. All Middle State-type institutions are best understood as Artesian Fountains. Their source is in the state treasury, and unseen aquifers run from there to all public universities in the state. Each university is a fountain that spouts not water but money into the economy of the communities where they are located. Gravity is not the driving force, but pressure from local banks, politicos, businessmen and officials–that and the pumping of an ever-growing student population. Notice I'm not talking about the money students spend in the town where the school is located, for pizza and clothes and so on. That's considerable and important in the overall financial irrigation of the region. What I'm talking about is the operating budget of the university, something I can't imagine, Mr. Warren, you've ever given much thought to, to your eternal credit. The payroll money, for instance, pours into the pockets of Middle State's employees and out of them into the local coffers. Then there are university contracts for supplies and services that flood the accounts of local businesses with life-giving cash. Those who really control things know Middle State to be such a fountain, and believe me, they want it to be just that. But when being a fountain of money becomes the central purpose of the university, and in a sense it always was *a* purpose, then it's all over. John D. Rockefeller was once asked how much money does a man need?

Unable, of course, to imagine any other soul but his own shriveled one, his answer was, just a little bit more. That's how much any institution needs as well. So when attracting money is the central purpose, all corruption follows. You make up ways to attract money."

"Not bad," Brumley laughed. "I don't know how far you could take the comparison, but you're right–it surely fits with or complements the notion of growth being the Holy Grail. If you herd in every so-called student you can intimidate and mislead with visions of a failed life if they don't go to college to become a 'professional'–which is a clearly understood code for 'to make more money'–if you herd them all in, they'll eat up university resources by requiring remedial courses and they'll make teaching twice as difficult with classes conducted at a much lower level than they should be, which in turn bores and dispirits good, willing, interested students. In fact, the Artesian Fountain Theory fits in with my Two Realities Theory."

Warren and Old Cadoon waited expectantly.

"Middle State–and likely all similar such universities–operate under two realities. One is the Official Reality, the management-sponsored one. It claims their two-bit university is already a thumping success and is on the edge of Ivy League membership if only their Public Relations Office can whip up some more lies about it. Everything management utters for public consumption suggests that virtually all its students and instructors are committed to the life of the mind, that classes are small and well-taught by independent and unharassed full-time faculty who love their discipline and its material and who have ample time to prepare classes, grade their small amount of student work, do research of a high order and serve willingly on committees whose decisions are final. There's more to this Official Reality, but you get the idea."

"That's not the way it is," Warren said. "At least not the part about students."

"Nor, I'm sad to say," Old Cadoon added, "at least as I recall, the part about the faculty. And the other reality, Dr. Brumley?"

"It's the Real Reality. Many faculty who are uncaring, lazy, sometimes stupid, and whose dereliction doesn't matter. Students who haven't the mental ability to do college work or who haven't the slightest desire to do it–who aren't interested in learning in any formal sense, which, by the way, I do not criticize at all–more power to them if they follow their talents. There's also the administrative requirement for faculty members to do research while teaching twelve credit hours per semester, which means third-rate research and second-rate teaching, or vice versa. And management doesn't care. They have utter contempt for research, having done none themselves, and as for their teaching"–Brumley laughed in derision, and Old Cadoon knowingly joined in–"in the history of Middle State," he continued, "no administrator who came up from the faculty–and that's nearly all of them–ever voluntarily asked to return to full-time teaching. Not one. What does that tell you?"

"Why, very likely," Old Cadoon said wryly, "that there's a few long-suffering academicians who are willing to give up what they love more than anything–teaching and grading papers–for the heavy burdens of writing strategic plans and serving on committees and task forces and sending memos. And all so their more fortunate, if lower paid, colleagues in the classrooms can do their duties unencumbered with any concerns other than with their material and over their students. Teaching looks easy to those who have never done it," Old Cadoon observed to Warren, "but my experience, as a student long ago and less long ago as a teacher, was that the easier and more successful it appeared, the more work had gone into it. Even unsuccessful teaching takes effort. It's work. Many people do not like to work. They like to plan and have ideas about how other people can work."

"My roommate says it's all about kicking other people's behinds from a swivel chair," Warren ventured, bowdlerizing Plumb Bob's insight. "Maybe getting out of work and making others do it is part of his view."

"It's not part of it," Brumley observed. "It *is* it."

Brumley decided not to trot out Hobart's Medieval Church Theory though he felt Old Cadoon would approve and was certain Warren would enjoy it. But there was another theory, a much broader one he had mused on for several years without ever clearly defining.

"I've got one, or I'm working on it. Not for Middle State, or academia for that matter. It's sort of a general theory. The Three Lands Theory."

Warren and Old Cadoon waited.

"It's still pretty ill-formed. Maybe I'll work on it some and try it on you one of these days. I've thought about it for a pretty good while.

It's nothing important, just satisfying to me, what little I've thought through."

The three talked easily for awhile, Warren mainly listening. Brumley remembered the freshman themes he had to grade and that Warren likely had homework to do. It was getting time to say good-by to Old Cadoon and descend the smokestack, even if it was relatively early. He would go back to his office and began writing up the Three Lands Theory, for therapy if nothing else.

A light south wind reached them and the three fell silent in the warm spring night, Old Cadoon serene and resigned, Brumley outwardly calm but unsettled within, and Warren trying to assimilate and understand what he had heard. Below them, from an open office window in the Science Building, Junior White was keeping steady a parabolic reflector aimed at them with a high-quality microphone at its focus, the microphone attached to a computer that translated the conversation on the smokestack to bits of binary code that went directly to President Curtis's office where only a few seconds after it was spoken every word of the three was printed out for a careful review the next day. When the trio had gone down the smokestack steps and Brumley and Warren let old Cadoon with his harness climb down the ladder ahead of them before carrying the ladder back to Junior White's truck, Brumley returned to his office and, true to his intent, began to type on his Three Lands Theory. After three hours of reflection and revision, he had it.

The Three Lands Theory

There is first the land of the oldest of dreams—the Promised Land, Arcadia, the Golden Country, the Land of Milk and Honey. It is a gentle valley, broad, rich, green, well-watered, with meadows and tracts of woods along the stream and scattered about the floor and up the slopes. Here amity rules, with compassion and Eros the couriers of her edicts. Work here will not be labor, desire not bound with guilt. Thought will be free and sensuous, duty a pleasure, and the heroes those who taught love and peace.

Next is the Land of Commodification, a city on a plain,

where humans are one another's curse and bane, and where the powerful, under the black counterfeit of proffering milk and honey, deal out diversion, confusion and death. It is the land of King Calculation, of getting and spending, of insidious entertainment, of things enthroned, of noise and speed and no rest. Here live the preponderance of humankind, or rather, here they find themselves, cozened from birth, blinded by the lights, caught in a frantic, formless jig to a discord that never ends.

Finally there is the Rocky Land, the Land of the Barren Ridge. It lies between the Promised Land and the Land of Commodification, and while some of its inhabitants are born to it and some come voluntarily, all are Guardians of Arcadia who block and frustrate the promoters of commodification from colonizing and defiling that Promised Land. This land–the Promised one– those sentinels dream of it with breaking hearts that long for its shade and cool waters, and they hold the harsh uplands to watch over and protect that land of their dreams. That land, the land of milk and honey, is, of course, a dream. No one lives there. It may be that no one ever will. But the Guardians believe; they shape and preserve that land by the steadfastness of their vision, even as they stand alert on the dry ridge, beckoned to by the treacherous, glittering lights of commodification, tempting them to abandon their austere watch, to come down and join the fun.

Brumley was unaware that every stroke on his computer keyboard was transmitted also to President Curtis's office and stored on a computer to be read at the leisure of whomever President Curtis ordered to do so before they reported to him each day everything Brumley had written.

twenty-five
AIMEE BROODER

W arren knew he had passed the last two days in a swoon. He was acquainted with swoons from his reading, especially in the great literature written up through the nineteenth century, after which swoons had been replaced by inner-ear disturbances, drops in blood pressure, certain drugs, blackouts, temporary disorientation, synapses transmitter disorders and other up-to-date agents singly or in combinations. Drops in blood pressure, for instance, as well as certain drugs could cause blackouts, but then blackouts could cause lower blood pressure and lead to usage of certain drugs. Inner ear disturbances caused temporary disorientation, while frequent disorientation could bring about an inner-ear disturbance and even tumble the gyros of the middle ear. Trouble at the synapses were at times the problem behind everything, but certain drugs, drops in blood pressure and inner ear disturbances could shut down those neural transmitters or cause them to broadcast the wrong program. Warren preferred a swoon, and since he had a hunch that by next week his feet would be back on the ground, his head level and out of the clouds, and his entire self back in the usual inferno of desire without hope of fulfillment, he would for as long as it lasted absolutely revel in the moment of bliss that had so miraculously befallen him. Befallen. Inspired by Dr. Hobart, he had looked the word up after it came to him as fitting perfectly with swoon. And he was right to do so. A blissful swoon befallen. He grinned like a sap and knew it, and didn't care.

Two days ago, before their general science class began, he and Sola were talking of their encounter with Old Cadoon when Aimee Brooder, overhearing them, clearly began listening. Neither would have presumed to open a conservation with her, and, after continuing self-consciously for a moment, they awkwardly fell silent, relieved when the bell rang and Anderson began mangling the theory of evolution, about which, it seemed, there was much doubt since theoretically bumblebees couldn't fly and Noah's Ark had been found in a strata of rock only three thousand years old. Anyway, Anderson was obviously pleased to announce, evolution was just a theory and a theory is just an opinion, which, is no better than anyone else's—as everyone knows.

"As every stupid shit-head knows," Bolinger muttered, writhing in his seat.

"In a way, he proves Darwin's great insight," Bolinger proclaimed after class to Warren, who could see Aimee Brooder making her way toward them. "We live at the end of rationality in the darkest moment of human history, and he's the dimmest idiot that has flagellated the earth since the first protozoa. It's adaptation to the environment, survival of the unfitting, who is now the fittest."

"I heard you talking before class," Aimee said, appearing at Warren's side. Bolinger, after a nod to his miraculous advertising class partner and a quick assessment, drifted off.

"I thought Old Cadoon was just a story," Aimee said."

"No, he's real," Warren said and was unable to think of anything else to say.

"He lives on one of the smokestacks?" She laughed easily and Warren saw the unnaturally white teeth between lips whose resilient softness he felt could give ease on the clouds of paradise.

"No, he just goes up there. To enjoy the view. And think, he says. He's all right. Easy to get along with. He may be a legend, like Dr. Hobart says, but there's nothing weird about him—except that he climbs up a smokestack and contemplates the world."

I'm actually talking with her crossed his mind as they began walking toward Humanities Hall, and he took in, in quick sidelong glances, the dark eyes and the long, luxuriant dark-brown hair. And she was speaking back, evidently with interest. Except for Kimmee Deneen at the dorm party, she was closer to him longer than he had ever been to so beautiful a girl, other than on crowded elevators where their proximity even there could nearly overwhelm him.

He tried as they walked not to sensationalize Old Cadoon, but having no coveted material objects or high social position to offer such a creature as Aimee it was hard not to overstate his acquaintance with the legendary figure of Cadoon. He felt instinctively that something of note was required to lay at her feet: maybe tales of a mysterious adventure–or a kind of adventure–would do.

"Oh, no," he heard himself say to a question she had asked as though from a great distance and through a roaring in his ears–it was the gathering swoon falling full upon him–"I don't think you'd have any trouble climbing up there."

"Then," she said modestly–even, he thought, uncertainly, "could you take me up there to meet him?"

And before he could reply, she added:

"Any night would be okay. When your friend doesn't want to go."

For the rest of the day Warren was inwardly a peacock in full strut, tail feathers fanned in gorgeous display, turning, posing, warm and iridescent in the affirming sun. He hardly heard Dr. Brumley's lecture on Keats' knight-at-arms and felt only slight unease over how to break the news to Sola.

"You bastard," Sola said when Warren told him. "I don't believe it. She was in Queen Kanga's court at homecoming last year. She runs for Student Government shit–I think she was treasurer or secretary or something a couple of years ago. She's president of a goddamned sorority, for god's sake, drives a red Camaro, talks on a cell phone all the time. I'll bet she takes three showers a day. How do you do it? You lucky bastard."

"She just wants to meet Old Cadoon," Warren said as matter-of-factly as he could, not wishing to presume the slightest power of attraction.

He tried to shake off his swoon, telling himself repeatedly that Aimee, inspired by an overly-glamorized story and a need for something substantial in her life, merely wanted to meet Old Cadoon and that she needed Warren solely to fulfill her wish; and then her wish to meet Old Cadoon shifted to a desire to do so and that she needed him, Warren, to fulfill her desire and by god he would fulfill her and the swoon was upon him again, which he would struggle against to gain some perspective. But one perspective obliterated all the others, and in spite of suspecting that his true lot was likely the desert sands, life on the chain gang, or dying without having lived, he determined to act deliberately and to confront an essential fact of life, and since Anderson was giving a test over the biological segment of their General Science class on Friday and he'd then have some free time, he asked Aimee in their Wednesday class if Friday night was okay.

"I've got to work on my paper for Dr. Brumley's class tonight," he said apologetically, "and Thursday night study for Anderson's test. Friday's the earliest I can make it. I know that's party night, but he's likely to be up there then."

"You're going to study for Anderson's test?"

"Well, yes. I know it'll be simple-minded—they're all multiple choice or true-or-false—but there was a lot of material in the reading for this section. You. . .don't think you'll have any problem"?

Neither in Anderson's class nor in any of the several English classes they had attended together had Warren heard Aimee answer or ask a question or offer a comment of any kind, even though from her bright eyes and unfailing pertness he assumed she heard and registered every nuance of the material and lectures. Not even in Brumley's current British Literature class had she ever spoken, other than a slow, perfectly enunciated "here" to the roll call. A few weeks ago, while eyeing her after a quiz, he had an obtrusive realization that there was some variance between the content of the class and almost everything that Aimee had sprung from, was formed by, and apparently aspired to. He remembered looking at her beautiful profile and thinking with wonder what she felt about their readings. Turning slightly toward her, as though something on the other side of the room had caught his attention, he considered her face more fully and easily dismissed his disturbing thoughts, certain that this lissome, beautiful girl and the unbearable promise she bore lived in a world above the one she might mistakenly be thought to inhabit. Her silence in class, Warren felt sure, was owed to her awe at the insights and revelations of the great writers to whom they were being introduced—revelations of a vision exalted over the world of social status, willed ignorance and materialism that Aimee might once have been attached to but which now, as shown by her interest in Old Cadoon, she surely had renounced to rise with him, Warren, her heroic mentor, to a soft, enveloping cloud where for all eternity they would study with tender solicitude the core value of existence, several times a day.

"I know pretty well what will be on it," Aimee said. "I took pretty good notes."

Warren, who sat slightly behind and to the left of Aimee in Anderson's class, had often noticed that she filled her notebook largely with the Greek letters identifying her sorority and with another set of initials, both sketched in many variants with accurate perspective, ornate design and subtle shading, sometimes in color. Clearly, Warren realized, she had artistic talent, possibly unrecognized, which needed to be encouraged. And he had also seen that her returned tests and quizzes were nearly all B's. So she did well—almost certainly, Warren felt, through a quality she shared with him, a sure instinct of simply knowing what was important and remembering it.

The only problem, however, was that Half-life Anderson did not know what was important. His tests were filled with questions gleaned from the more trivial parts of their reading and the few lectures and class discussions they had when he was not taking them on field trips or demonstrating computer learning or conducting peer-group sessions or showing a movie. But since Aimee usually did almost as well on these tests as Warren, who studied diligently for them, he sensed in this fact not only her innate ability to know what was important in any area, but also a talent for reading personalities. In Anderson's case this meant perceiving his prejudices and unfounded beliefs and discerning how they would form his crippled notions of what was of consequence or interest in various scientific disciplines and what, therefore, would be on his tests. That she had ready access to stolen copies of his tests never entered Warren's mind.

"Anyway," she said brightly as they stopped before Warren turned to go in Humanities Hall, "Friday night is good. We won't have to worry about anything on Saturday."

Friday night just before dark a slow rain began, the first warm rain of the spring, and Warren was certain it was fate's way of once more drowning his just-kindled hopes. Add the prospect of her getting wet to its being only him she was meeting and he knew he would shortly be standing at the foot of the smokestack, an unmistakable fool carrying a ladder and wondering how he could hide his humiliation should anyone come along. But at eight o'clock, there at the base of the smokestack, Aimee in a hooded raincoat was waiting. Overhead the low clouds caught the bursts from the strobe lights and reflected them downward.

"I just got here," she said, a wisp of her dark hair clinging to her cheek. She looked up toward the carillon booth. "Do you think he's up there?"

"I don't know. It's been later than this when Sola and I were here. But if he's not here by nine-thirty or so, he's not coming."

"Where does he live?"

"In that general direction—over there," Warren pointed to the west toward a neighborhood of small houses built around thirty years ago. Many of them were now rented to groups of Middle State students, though most were still inhabited by townspeople and some faculty members, the latter mostly now retired, who had trickled into Middle State before the great enrollment explosion when salaries were even lower than at present, and who had managed by industry and thrift to purchase a house in that area. "I think he said he lived on Bonnie Brae, though he may have been kidding."

Only a few weeks before, they had read in Brumley's class some of Burns' poems and a few Highland ballads. Aimee nodded absently.

"I parked in the faculty lot," she said, motioning in the same direction. " Probably get another ticket, but I'm not walking any further in the rain than I have to. God," she said, looking up toward the carillon, "it's way up there."

The student parking area, utterly empty on Friday night, was roughly twenty yards beyond the faculty lot.

"They don't enforce any regulations on Friday night or weekends. Except for handicap parking," Warren explained, feeling himself about as interesting as a parking regulations pamphlet.

"You ready ?" He placed the ladder and moved as close to her as he dared.

"You don't have a raincoat," she said.

"This jacket will be okay. There's a roof over the carillon. . . ."

She stepped to him, opening her coat and was against him, her arms around him. It was more than he had imagined, and he had imagined much. They kissed twice, her breath quickening with his.

"We should go up," she said.

Warren held the ladder, instructed her to wait a few steps up the stairway until he had climbed up the ladder behind her and pulled it up. When he had done so, he went up to where she waited for him to kiss her again. The hood had fallen back from her head and with the rain sifting gently down on her luxuriant hair he put his hand freely and without fear on it, stroked it, kissed her face, her closed eyes, gently, and to the deepest satisfaction he had ever known, heard her sigh.

"We should keep going," she said and did not move and so he kissed her again and then again.

Please, Warren said to the spirit of Old Cadoon, *don't be there*.

They stopped twice more before reaching the carillon booth, which was empty.

"He isn't here."

"I'm glad," she said.

"Me, too."

Several cushions were stacked in one corner of the booth, carried there surely by Old Cadoon, since the Chairman of the Reigning Board's defective cousin spent his time there only in perfecting his spitting marksmanship. Warren arranged the cushions on the floor and, oblivious to Old Cadoon's unlikely appearance in the rain, turned to Aimee, who he saw in the weak throb of the reflected strobe lights was nearly undressed, taking her panties off in hallucinatory stations of motion though he supplied the graceful fall and stepping out.

"Take yours off, too," she said, almost pleading, and he did.

When he came back to himself, he was stroking down the curve of her waist, kissing her face. He opened his eyes to find her looking at him, smiling broadly.

"God, I needed that," she said, thrusting her hips against him and smiling again. Warren ceased moving his hand.

"I didn't bring anything, any tissue—you got a handkerchief? I can tell you didn't use a condom," and she pulled away from him. "Nope, it's running out, a lot. You must have been pretty horny."

"Yes," Warren said.

"Me, too. Carl has been gone all week and was busy the week before."

"Carl."

"Carl Colson. We're engaged, or practically engaged. He's a Pi."

"Oh."

"We're getting married when he gets settled. He and some buddies went to Nashville this week with Dr. Weebles to run in a marathon."

"Is that right?"

"He runs all the time," she said, pulling her panties back on in a series of nightmarish stages each frozen by the strobes. "I told him if he'd rather run than fuck it's too bad, but that's his business. Can you imagine what he'll be like next weekend? He's just *crazy* at sex;"–she shuddered against Warren–"he'll be out of his mind by Saturday. I can't hardly wait."

Warren was dressed as quickly as she was, and as he let the ladder down for her he said:

"I think I'll stay up here for a while. Old Cadoon may show up yet. You can get to your car okay, can't you?"

"Yes. God, it's running down my legs. Pretty good," and she pecked his cheek quickly and climbed down to the ground.

Warren hoisted the ladder up and mounted the steps back to the carillon booth. It was right there, he thought, looking at the cushions still arranged to make a narrow bed, and again he saw that perfect body, that face of dreams, jerked from pose to pose by the reflected light of the cold strobes. Now they lit the mocking scene of that memory, and Warren, suddenly aware of the rain seeping in his clothes and the keen chill, knew it was time to get back to the dorm.

"You know what I'd do?" Sola proclaimed, sprawled on Ho's bed. Along with Jeeks, Bolinger, Demumbers and Sheperd he had waited up for Warren's return, provided he did return. "I'd commission a T-shirt with her picture on the front and 'smokestack' underneath it. Either that or marry her."

They all waited for some comment from Warren, who now almost dry, had said nothing about his evening in spite of their obvious anticipation.

"She's the one I think she is, I'd marry her all right," Jeeks said evenly, his eyes half closed in lecherous contemplation.

"If there's one thing for sure in this world," Shepherd observed, "it's that Aimee Brooder is not going to marry you. Or me, or Sola or any of us. Except maybe Warren," he said expectantly.

Warren, who had picked up one of Ho's astronomy books and was leafing through it, ignored him.

"Well?" Sola said.

"Well what?"

"Goddamnit, how did it go, what happened? Give us a break."

"It's only right," Bolinger said. "We're up here making heartless love through a telescope or looking at playmate foldouts. Give us a little tale of hope from an alternate universe. Does the milk and honey really flow? Or is it just another hoax?"

"It's a hoax," Warren said, making sure to smile and shake his head in self-deprecation. Averse to boasting, he wanted badly to boast. He was even more averse to despair, his own or anyone's, so he let them believe that by normal male standards of success with women he had failed with Aimee. The greater failure, the despair below despair, he kept to himself. Not even the fact that he had—he now thought he had a word for it from his reading— *cuckolded* Carl Colson made any difference. In the world of Colson and Aimee, it didn't make any difference.

twenty-six
BOLINGER'S COMMERCIAL

"He's taking what?" a startled Shepherd said to Warren, who was on break from a paper on Ruskin.

"Introduction to Advertising. I thought everyone knew; he told me at the beginning of the semester."

"But why? Bolinger taking a class in advertising is like Jeeks taking a class in Relativity, or Colson one in Ethics. It's crazy."

"He said he wanted to know the enemy."

"And I'm getting to know him," Bolinger said, overhearing the conversation on his way back from the shower and stopping at Shepherd's door, bulging in his too small bathrobe with soap holder and towel in hand. "He's—or really they're—much more cunning than I thought. But the class, on the whole is. . . well, fascinating."

"What do you do in an advertising class?" Shepherd asked. "What's it like?"

"Eventually, as you might think, we'll advertise, do some advertising. So far we've only read 'visuals' Dr. Hokes posts on his web site each week. Everything is visuals; he doesn't believe in books. We didn't even have to buy the textbook. He scans each page of the readings and puts them on the web and then we read them on a computer in the labs. So no books. No quizzes, no tests, no papers. He's paired us up and every pair has to make a TV commercial as our course project. That's all we do, other than talk about the course readings—or visuals—which is where you find out how they do it."

"Are you still paired with Colson's girl?" Warren asked.

"Yes, your own Aimee. She's magnificent and treats me like the pariah Colson thinks I am. Actually, I think she'd treat me politely,

369

maybe even friendly, but he despises me so much he'd try to turn my dog against me, if I had a dog. Aimee seems to be his dog, so he has no trouble there."

Not quite his dog, Warren thought. His stray, maybe. But no, his dog, his pet.

"So you've got to do your class project with her and she treats you like shit?" Shepherd asked.

"Yes, but I ignore it for the privilege of sitting and talking with her and looking at her closely. I have no shame, obviously. It's the closest I'll ever get to such a woman, other than through the telescope, and I'm used to insults and ill-treatment. Plus, another benefit, I'm in control of the commercial, or almost. All she wants to do is star in it. The rest—making it—she cares nothing about except she insists Colson be in it, I'd guess because he's insisted to her. We're going to shoot it this Saturday, weather permitting as they say. It's going to be at the Wellness Center outdoor pool, the heated one, and if it hadn't been for Colson she might have laid me on the spot when I told her what her role was. To lie on a chaise lounge in a string bikini."

"What are you advertising, sex?" Shepherd asked as Jeeks and Hoh, the telescope stored for the night, drifted in, Demumbers right behind them.

"I'm not quite sure yet, keeping the old options open. Colson seems to have plans for it that he intends to effect through Aimee. I see him talking to his friends or to her, looking at me and smirking. He's so stupid he thinks I can't see he's up to something. Maybe he doesn't care that I can see."

Warren felt a rush of pity for Bolinger, knowing that behind the irony and stoic pretense Bolinger felt as keenly—maybe more keenly—the same cumulating despair as anyone would over the low hand the world was dealing him. It was one thing never to get a break; another to understand, as Bolinger did, the history and causes of not getting a break; the fact that the unworthy got breaks; and the reality that you did not, and why you did not, and that likely you never would. But still, so far, Bolinger had made his way.

"What about the prof?" Warren asked." Does he see you're doing all the work and she's doing nothing?"

"Oh, he doesn't care. I'm pretty sure he never looks at the commercials anyway. He can't keep his eyes off Aimee, plus he'd be glad to see me have to do it all. I ask him questions about advertising that make him uncomfortable."

"All right," Demumbers demanded when Bolinger seemed disinclined to say more. "What kind of questions?"

"The obvious ones," Bolinger said. "Like, how could anyone make a living by playing on the fears and anxieties of their fellow humans and lying to them?"

There was an awed silence.

"Bolinger, for god's sake, you didn't ask him that did you?" Shepherd finally said, laughing.

"Not all at once. I sort of led up to it. After we learned to run the camcorders and editing boards, we got into advertising methods and techniques, which is where I saw how much smarter they are than us. And Hokes teaches that stuff like a terrorist would teach bomb-making or hijacking, except he doesn't think he's hurting anybody. In fact, he thinks advertising does the world a favor. So I thought I'd raise some points about his so-called profession that no one else would raise."

"Bolinger," Warren said, "you can't keep doing that. He doesn't want to think about being wrong, or being in the wrong. You can't just keep up that approach forever. People make you pay when you show them up like that."

"I know. But what do you do? It's clear, isn't it, what advertising is and does? You play to greed and whatever else—materialism, status-seeking—by evoking fear and anxieties. And by lying. Anybody can see that."

Warren and Shepherd, without thinking much about it, felt something was crooked with advertising, but mainly they were like Hoh, Jeeks and the rest, to whom TV commercials were largely a contradictory mixture of annoyance and entertainment, not worthy of the slightest consideration.

"I don't get it,' Hoh said. "What do you mean, lying. And all that other stuff. They're just commercials. Some of them are pretty good."

"Yeah, the beer one, the 'tastes good, less filling' one," Jeeks said fondly.

"Oh, they're pretty good, all right," Bolinger heartily agreed.

"They're more than pretty good; they're works of genius–evil genius, as Churchill said of Hitler."

"'Evil genius'," Jeeks huffed. "Bolinger, what the hell do you mean. You heard Hoh. They're just commercials."

"All right," Bolinger said, suddenly serious. "Think. Take the soft drink commercials, all of them. Do you really believe that when you buy some tooth-rotting, non-nutritional soft drink the world turns to music and dancing and joy comes into your life?"

"But they don't say that," Demumbers protested.

"No, but they all show it, all of them suggest it, over and over. They can't outright lie, as Hokes is always saying, as though advertising is the most high-minded thing in the world. They can only sneak-lie, it's much worse. Hokes calls the method 'symbolic identification'–you associate your soft drink or whatever you're trying to sell with what you think people long for–wild abandon, love, status, whatever. You never *say* the soft drink will bring you those things–people could think about that and see what a load it is. But you *show* it, and then people won't think, they'll just feel. And according to Hokes, that's what advertisers want you to do: feel, not think. Or if you do think about all the dancing and music and unvaryingly beautiful people, you'll just say, 'how entertaining', or 'what an ass'. So you feel good about it and the next time you put your money in the machine and look at the selection, you'll punch the button for El Burpo Cola, and you'll never know why. And since most people refuse to believe they can be played for the fools they're being played for, the lies just go on and on. Or, as far as I can tell—and this may be the worst of all–people who are smart enough to know what's going on feel like the ad men's method is so commonplace, so established, that even talking about it is bad form or old-fashioned, so they keep quiet. And the lies just go on and on. It's like the way we live guaranteeing to end life but everyone ignoring it, remember that one? Everybody knows, nobody wants to admit it. In fact, the lies are part of the conspiracy."

"That's a bunch of shit," Jeeks said disgustedly.

"Their method or my elucidation?" Bolinger asked, amused.

"What?"

"Their method or. . .look, here's another example. Those jeep-like cars everybody is starting to buy–you know, four-wheel drives, boxy.

They're getting popular. You've seen the commercials—people churning them through a swamp or the desert or driving through the Grand Canyon or up Mount Everest. But Hokes read us an article that shows only ten percent of the people who drive them ever get off of pavement. So why do those commercials show what they do? Hokes says, *and he's proud of it*, that people who sit on their asses all day and are afraid for their miserable jobs and won't have an adventure until their funeral will see those commercials and feel that if they buy one of those things they'll be daring explorers and free as birds. He didn't say it exactly that way, but that's what he meant."

"Aw, come on," Demumbers said, "those things are neat. I'd like to have one."

"I would, too,' Bolinger concurred. "I'd like to have two or three. I'd like to have everything that's dangled in front of me. But I feel restraint is necessary to life. I asked Hokes, working up to my grand finale, if he didn't think one secret mission of all advertising is to make you think restraint isn't necessary."

"What did he say?" Warren asked.

"He said there are no limits and that we can be anything we want and have anything we want if we just try hard enough."

"Well. What did you say?"

"You'd have been proud of me. I kept my mouth shut. I've finally recognized that there's a degree of willed ignorance that's beyond correction. Hokes has reached that degree."

"Okay," Jeeks said, trying to figure it all out. "What would you do? I mean, how would you do a commercial, for a Coke or those SUV's?"

"Me? I wouldn't. For any amount, and you'd better believe you can get a big amount making them. But what can you say that's *truthful* about a soft drink that would make anybody choose—choose with thought, rationally—to buy it? That it tastes good? But you can't show how something tastes. I guess if I had to, I'd show somebody taking a drink and smiling and shaking their head in appreciation. But even then you'd start to slide. You'd choose only the best-looking people to do the drinking, with the flag behind them and other good-looking people of the opposite sex wanting to fondle their private parts because they're drinking the stuff. I don't know. One thing you couldn't do is just show a picture of a can and say how much high fructose corn syrup and empty calories and caffeine and carbonated water and dyes and chemical additives are in it." Bolinger reflected a moment. "I guess to make a soft drink commercial I'd show someone very average-looking sitting in their kitchen drinking a bottle or can. No music, no dancing, no leaping about—just sitting drinking a can. Then show them the next night, same thing. Then some time lapse or some technique—I've found out that with editing you can do anything–to show them drinking some every day, getting fatter, their teeth decaying, belching and their hair falling out from the chemo they had to undergo because they got cancer from the artificial additives. And the SUV's"–Bolinger was rolling–"I'd show some idiot in one grinding some peaceful landscape into rubble and then traffic-packed highways blasted through once-beautiful farmland and then a few bloody wrecks with mangled bodies and crying mothers and fathers and then cities with people choking and dying from smog and pollution and the globe warming and then oil wars breaking out because we've wasted it all getting 10 miles per gallon going nowhere for nothing."

He stopped.

"Bolinger," Warren laughed, "you'll never pass that course."

"Oh, I don't intend to," Bolinger said, lightly now. "I don't need to pass it to graduate. In the first place, I didn't take it to pass it; I took it to learn something, though not what they want me to learn. And anyway, who'd want to do anything but fail a course in advertising?"

"That's dumb," Jeeks muttered, who wanted to pass everything but didn't.

"Maybe it is," Bolinger agreed. "But look at it this way–I get to do close-ups with Aimee Brooder in a string bikini next Saturday. Pass or fail, learn or not, I'll get that much out of the class. Which reminds me," he said, securing the too-tight bathrobe as he rose to leave, "I've got to get started on our script. She'll have no lines, thank god, but I've got an interesting if ambiguous narrative planned. You're all welcome to come watch the shoot–free set passes to all. But you've got to keep behind the rope."

There were two ropes, one to keep Colson's crew on one side and the second to keep the dorm floor occupants on the other off the set and everyone's waving and mugging off camera. Bolinger had tried to authenticate his set, which consisted of a chaise lounge centered at the edge of the deep end of the pool, by somehow finding a pair of khaki jodhpurs, a pair of knee-high, lace-up leather boots and a megaphone. For his own part in the commercial, which would not be a full-length shot, he wore a conventional shirt and had borrowed one of Shepherds's brim caps that he turned around backwards when manning the camcorder. A few present recognized the parody, but once Aimee made her appearance and slipped out of her robe, none had eyes for Bolinger. Colson and his gang stood expectantly, Colson also in a bath robe, waiting to take the role Aimee was explaining to Bolinger.

"After you've filmed me, put the camera on the tripod so it shows us. Carl will dive in and swim up to us underwater and you come up here by me and stand and look out over the pool for him. Then he'll come up in front of us and we'll talk. You can put in the toothpaste stuff however you do it."

The commercial, Bolinger had announced, was for a fictional toothpaste, Ex-pozac.

Warren heard Aimee's instructions, as did everyone else. Before she began talking with Bolinger he had caught her eye. She had nodded, not at all distantly but clearly without interest or maybe much memory. What had she said about Colson's sexual prowess? The swoon, Warren felt, was likely gone for good, to be recalled only in the pain of its loss. He moved carefully back into the group but could not help glancing at her, often. On the other side, the Colson bunch didn't even bother to hide their glee as Colson dropped the robe off his lean shoulders and went to the side of the pool to stretch and bend, splashing water over his arms and sculpted chest to prepare for his dive and swim to the end. Something was up.

"All right," Bolinger called through the megaphone, "Quiet on the set. Lights"–there were no lights–"camera, action–roll'em. Or maybe it's roll'em, action, and so on.'

From its tripod he lifted the camcorder, hand-held for the opening shots, took a distant shot of Aimee, moved in, panned up and down her while she lay languidly, splendidly, in the black bikini, smiling and slightly craning and turning her head from side to side like some aspiring, untalented starlet trying for a part.

"Now, close-up. Longing, Aimee baby, longing," Bolinger

commanded, zooming in as Aimee half-closed her eyes, the sensual smile fading to a strained look of what she thought might constitute longing, never having experienced it for any length of time.

"Now, teeth," Bolinger called, "let's see those pearly whites," and she clicked back to the smile, raised her upper lip and thrust her face toward the camera, revealing a perfect, gleaming bone-white row of teeth that would have brought joy to an orthodontist.

"Okay," Bolinger continued to lumber around her, "sorrow now, sadness," and Aimee mugged a frown so synthetic that even Jeeks turned to hide a snicker.

"She should get an Oscar," Sola said.

"I'll give her Oscar," Jeeks leered, recovering.

"A little wiggle, some squirm," Bolinger commanded, writhing himself as if to prompt the eager Aimee, who did as directed, slowly, to perfection. Then, unprompted, as the camcorder quivered in Bolinger's hand, she raised one knee, the inside of her foot caressing her right leg, lowered it and slightly thrust her hips upward, the black triangle of the bikini swelling even more before she relaxed and then arched her slender back.

"Hold him, hold him," Warren said to Shepherd and Demumbers, who flanked a lathering Jeeks.

At that moment, Colson dove off the side and angled underwater toward the couple.

"Okay, now watch for him," Aimee said, leaning forward as Bolinger, obedient to her instructions, slipped the still-running camcorder properly onto its tripod, walked to the pool's edge by Aimee and looked gamely for the submerged Colson.

It was predictable. Scooting down, Aimee gripped each side of the lounge below her hips, braced, and with her perfect left leg launched Bolinger into the pool just as Colson rose like some pool god before the simpering nymph to gaze triumphantly at her as off camera his cohorts roared with laughter.

"Perfect," he said with a look usually given to an especially obedient Afghan dog. "I heard him hit all the way under water. Sounded just like a turd."

Bolinger, surfaced by this time and thrashing to the edge, laboriously began hauling himself out, one booted leg thrown up over the side and struggling vainly until Jeeks and Warren rushed under the rope to drag him soddenly onto the concrete. Water had filled the flared jodhpurs and poured out of the boots when he clumsily stood up, as Colson led a chorus of derision.

"You're a real winner, Bollie-boy," Colson sneered. "Lose about eighty pounds and you could be in show business," and he laughed even harder.

"Come on," Shepherd said to Bolinger as Aimee, to Colson's displeasure, offered a towel. "Let's get out of here."

"Let me get my work," Bolinger said, without a sign of humiliation or rancor or a look at Aimee. "This has got to be ready by next week. Be on campus TV. Should be a real laugh."

He carefully shouldered the tripod, camcorder still attached. Warren picked up the megaphone and with it dragged Shepherd's floating cap to the edge and retrieved it. All left together, Bolinger as cheerful as if all had gone as planned and the rest finding nothing to say.

"You going to watch it?" Sola asked Warren, again banished to the floor study lounge while Plumb Bob entertained an impetuous mid-day visitor.

"I don't want to see it again," Warren said. "It was bad enough live. Why see it again?"

Bolinger's commercial was to air in twenty minutes on the campus cable-TV station. Word of it had spread, and while most Middle State students were strangers to each other, the nature of the commercial and the casual cruelty of the pack promised a large audience for the showing of Bolinger's abasement. Many students were already gathered in central dorm study lounges and at the student center.

"We may not see it 'again'," Sola said.

"What do you mean?"

"Something's up. Bolinger's got this look. He's been working on the thing all week. When he got on the elevator this morning to take the tape to the station, he was humming. Does that sound like somebody who's about to show himself being humiliated?"

"Come to think of it," Warren said, beginning indistinctly to sense some possibilities, "he's been working on a drawing or diagram or something–a graphic he called it. He covered it up when I went down to his room the other day. Said it was for the commercial. I figured it was a bad picture of a toothbrush or teeth or something and didn't much think about it. I didn't want to make him feel any worse than I figured he did."

"Maybe it'll be a sign that says 'Colson is an Asshole', something like that."

"Maybe," Warren said. "But he can do better than. . .wait, wait a minute, listen, Shepherd said early this week he found this—you know how most everybody uses the bathroom stall next to the wall? Shepherd said he took the other one and there was a tape recorder propped on the toilet-paper roll with the mic hanging down just to the edge of the divider. He thought somebody had forgotten it or that Jeeks was up to something. Then it was gone that night. Bolinger had one in his room when I saw him working on that drawing—I'm sure of it."

"My god," Sola said wonderingly.

"We'd better go see this," Warren said, and the two made for the elevator and the ride down to Wilder Hall's main lounge.

Around thirty people were already there, the good seats apparently taken until Sola spotted Jeeks defiantly holding two chairs for them just in front of the large TV screen. In the ten minutes before the commercial was to air, while the station showed an instructive video on handicap accessibility and one on tolerance toward the disabled, another thirty students had eagerly packed into the lounge. On the screen, a formerly excluded quadriplegic student in a motorized wheelchair inched triumphantly up a hard-won ramp into the exercise room of the Wellness Center and The End appeared. The entire crowd fell expectantly silent.

"Did you put a tape recorder in the bathroom?" Warren whispered to Jeeks.

"A what? Hell, no. Did somebody?"

"Yes. I think we're about to find out who. By the way, where's Bolinger?"

"I think he's up in his room. Poor bastard."

At this moment the screen flashed on a message identifying the up-coming commercials as ones made by Dr. Marshall Hokes' 216 Introduction to Advertising class, most of which would be aired on the schedule to follow. The schedule then appeared; Eric Bolinger and

Aimee Brooder were identified as the producers of the first commercial, one for Ex-plozac.

"No," Warren said, disbelief rising as Jeeks looked over questioningly and Sola, a whimper of incredulity escaping him, began to rock back and forth in his chair.

"Is that what he called his toothpaste?" Jeeks asked.

Suddenly, on screen, Aimee in her black bikini was recumbent in full-color voluptuousness in the chaise lounge, the camera approaching, panning caressingly up the long legs, dwelling on the triangle of the black thong, up the flat smooth belly, past the swelling cupped breasts onto her beautiful face, where, instead of the languid smile, the painfully straining look of what Amiee meant for longing was smoothly edited in its place.

"Long to faht?" a formal, phony British voice-over, clearly Bolinger's, asked with distressed concern. "But sometimes get bottled up?" the voice continued as Aimee's face went back to expressionless and then an even deeper strain. "Then what you need is Ex-plozac!"

There was a cut to a huge, easel-mounted diagram of an almost cubistic human silhouette with a crude digestive system sketched in. Beside it, armed with a long wooden pointer, stood an Einstein-bewigged and-mustached figure in a white lab-coat, again unmistakably Bolinger, who struck the diagram forcefully with the pointer and announced in a thick, Teutonic accent:

"Two tablets uf Explozac twvice a day vill gurntee plunty uf expellble ghas, day and nicht. Nefer again vilt chew haf ze urch to purch but lack ze prezhure to splurch."

The diagram became animated with two tablets the size of pig-iron ingots dropping to the stomach, nosing into the intestines, all the while producing copious amounts of billowing gas while the pointer whacked at each stage of the process. The gas inflated down the intestinal canal to the anus where a momentary, pressure-building check was followed by an apparent relaxation of the final sphincter, the process repeated to produce successive discharges, shown as gaily-colored spumes puffing and rising from the ass like some festive smoke-signals. Then the British voice again:

"Yes, fahting is a gas with Ex-plozac. Ahsk your doctor about it."

Then Aimee was back on screen, her strained expression melding into a shot of her left knee rising to its apex, her hands gripping tightly the sides of the chaise lounge and her leg then extending as if for maximum clearance, followed by an enormous, sustained, reverberate fart, soaring recklessly a full octave to a gurgling hint of slurry at the end. Then a cut to her face, relaxing into the flashing smile of what now appeared triumphant relief. At this instant, Colson shot to the surface before her, raising himself half out of the water to regard the relieved and grateful beauty.

"I heard it underwater," Colson's not-quite-natural voice said. "Sounded like a eighty- pound turd. Perfect."

By this time Colson's voice could hardly be heard for the howls of laughter, but the screen switched back to Aimee, squirming like some delighted puppy under heavy praise, while unleashing a virtuoso series of ostensibly Ex-plozac-induced farts, breathtaking in their range of tone, pitch, volume and duration.

The screen faded momentarily, then Bolinger appeared as himself, a video tape in hand.

"Bonus commercial, for extra credit," Bolinger in a voice-over said, while with an antic simper Bolinger pointed to the tape. "Buy the tape of the Explozac commercial for only five dollars. See Eric Bolinger, 8th floor, Wilder Hall. All proceeds to go to him."

When Colson rushed raging from the stifled hilarity of his fraternity house to Wilder Hall to beat Bolinger to a pulp and then go on beating the pulp, he found the rest of the floor-mates had followed him grimly to Bolinger's room.

"Lay a finger on me," Bolinger said with maddening coolness, as if informing him of some legal nicety, "and I'll swear out a warrant for your arrest for assault, which won't look good on your grad school application. And I'll always have a witness with me."

Retreating madly back down the hall, Colson was hounded by numerous mock farts blown on palms, upper arms, and, from an unexpectedly talented Jeeks, an oboe blat with a cupped hand in the armpit. As the elevator descended, Colson's screams and roars of rage and his kicks and blows against the elevator's side could be heard until he reached ground floor.

From the sale of the tape Bolinger made over five-hundred dollars. Everyone on the 8th floor bought at least one copy, watching the saga alone and in groups many times. Especially replayed was the thunderous shower of farts that had been spliced together at the end, the more impressive of which were claimed by various residents and argued over for days.

twenty-seven
BRUMLEY

"This Brumley?" the rough, flat voice said over his home phone.
"Yes."

"Security. We need you to come to your office."

Before Brumley could even respond, let alone ask why he was needed, the line clicked and after a few seconds a dial tone came on. It had begun. He pulled out his campus directory, looked up Security's number and dialed it. He would at least make someone tell him what was going on.

"This is the Campus Security Office of Middle State University," a recording of the same rough, flat voice intoned. "Our office hours are 7:30 a.m. to 4:30 p.m. . . ."

Kaneesha, where was Kaneesha? Was she gone? Surely her sultry recording was not replaced after office hours by this unpleasant rasp. He listened to the voice recite the soulless menu, punching several numbers at the appropriate prompt only to get no answer at any of them. He tried to tell himself that perhaps there had been a break-in or a fire at his office, or maybe, even if it wasn't raining, a huge leak through Humanities Hall's porous roof which required his presence only to set things right and to assure him that officialdom was looking out for what was his and was there to help.

It was not likely. All day he had been vaguely aware that Chairman Cole had been called away from his office and that even Miss Pam, when he spoke with her, seemed withdrawn and looked at him with what he now interpreted as pity. Something clearly was going on. But why this unprecedented call to his house? Surely a firing or a notice of dismissal-for-cause was done with a registered letter, one meticulously drawn up by the university attorney and his staff, all the charges braced in iron bands to raise and tip the dumpster of his life's work into the legal-system garbage truck, landfill bound. Likely when he got to his office such a letter would be part of the package. His mind racing almost out of control, he thought of calling Hobart, who hearing what was up would have rushed to the office and no doubt caused such a scene that he, too, might be fired. Not that Hobart was exactly fireable. He would either mock and intimidate the dismissal into retraction or would happily quit. More than himself, Brumley thought, management would like to get rid of Hobart–not only unacceptably different but, behind the unkempt appearance and odd ways, truly sympathizing and concerned with students, despising and exposing cant and jargon, and willing to resist any official stupidity–almost as great a menace as Old Cadoon. Brumley, on the other hand, knew himself weak and afraid. Calling in Hobart as a witness or a comrade would only by contrast emphasize his own failings. That, he didn't need. His failings would be clear enough. He was as tongue-tied and unskilled at confrontation as most administrators were proficient at it. His only resolve in whatever was coming was not to grovel to retain a job increasingly hard to endure or even justify.

But what could he do if he lost his job? At his age, how could he make a living? Carving furniture by hand, that was pretty well out, as was baking bread or homesteading or running a corner grocery. He had no idea how any of these worthy tasks were done–who did any more? So absolute had been the break between direct living and the oblique, detached ways everyone now pursued that escape from the system–the combine, the monster–seemed inconceivable. No, those self-reliant callings were relics of a once-shared independence now largely displaced by such fabulous artifacts as systems managers, job-transition accelerators, merger facilitators, vice presidents of institutional effectiveness, and, to be overly fair and god help him, maybe even Professors of Humanities or even Humidities. But not, he felt, displaced for long. The old ways, after the near unimaginable and needless calamity of the Great Change, would be back.

But there was still his own place in all this. In such a post as Middle State, a rotten pillar in a soon-to-collapse edifice, how did one live, live right? If Hobart's analogy was valid, if modern institutes of higher learning were today's equivalents of the Medieval Church, then what was he? No more, he was afraid, than a waffling cleric, boldly calling for reform when among a few other sour malcontents, yet religiously attending all the empty rituals, mouthing the hollow chants, and obsequiously following all the leaden rules simply to retain his order's cap and gown and keep bread and cheese on the board. He briefly considered a shot of bourbon. No, better to face the summons as he was. Leaving a half-graded stack of freshman composition research papers on his table, he set out for his office.

As he crossed the street from the parking lot where Barnes endlessly fought for justice and the un-American way by taxing the rich and helping the poor, Brumley saw someone come out of Humanities Hall and start down the sidewalk toward him. It was Greenman, so preoccupied that he almost met Brumley before recognizing him.

"God, Brumley," Greenman said, and then was quiet.

"What are you doing here? You never come in at night."

"I . . .Cole called me up at home and wanted me to come in. Brumley, you won't believe this. They want me to go part time, or teach part time. They're starting a new program overseas. Africa. They want me to be a liason between Middle State and universities in Africa. It's unbelievable. In fact, it's insane. But it's for real, it's going to be done."

"My god," Brumley breathed. So Cole, at least, was up there waiting for him. The substance of Greenman's announcement, surreal and incredible, took a moment to register. "Africa? You don't know anything about Africa."

"Nothing," Greenman agreed. "I know nothing. Appleby's coming in from Capri for a week this summer and he's supposed to show me the ropes of the job. Then I'd start next fall."

"What are you supposed to do? What is the liaison for?"

"I'm supposed to–this is what Cole said–enhance cultural ties and negotiate an exchange program for Middle State faculty and students with"– he hesitated– "Uganda State University. So help me god, Brumley, they're not even insane, they're beyond insane." He took out a handkerchief and patted his face.

"Greenman?"

"What?"

"Are you going to take it?"

384

"I. . .I think so."

"How much?"

"What do you mean?" Greenman asked uneasily.

"How much more are they paying you?"

"Five thousand," he said, and then in a rush: "Brumley, I have to take it. Three kids, the oldest starts college in two years. You know what I make. You understand, don't you? I have to."

"Sure," Brumley said. "It's okay. I don't blame you. I'd do the same. But hold out for an enormous life insurance policy."

'Oh, god," Greenman laughed, and then came back to himself. "Maybe it won't be too bad. There's always some UN peacekeepers in the general area. And anyway, who'd have anything against a humanities teacher? I should be okay once I learn the ropes."

The ropes, Brumley thought, seeing them draped waiting around a stake, heaped about with gasoline-soaked tires.

"By the way," Greenman inquired, "what are you doing here? You didn't get a call, did you?"

"Yes," Brumley said, "I did. I think it's all over with me."

"But you've got tenure–they can't get rid of you."

"They can get rid of anybody."

"You should never have written those letters."

"I know."

"They never do any good."

"I know. I felt like I had to."

They stood uncomfortably for a moment.

"Well, I've got to get home," Greenman said. "My wife will want to hear the news."

"Sure," Brumley said. "Listen, Greenman, it's okay. You did what you had to. Good luck." He could not bring himself to offer congratulations.

"Thanks. Thanks a lot," Greenman said, and then, lowering his voice and glancing over his shoulder toward Humanities Hall: "I hope it goes all right with you. Tell the sorry sons of bitches where to get off." He squeezed Brumley's arm before heading for his car.

Brumley watched him go, then stood looking down the way where the nervous strobes of the twin smokestacks tirelessly proclaimed their ascendancy over Middle State. Before long, Old Cadoon would be unable to hoist himself up to their steps and defiantly mount to behold the darkened fields and the wonder of the stars. When Hobart was gone, and then himself–Hobart retired or fired, himself booted out probably tonight–who would remember Old Cadoon? One way or another, Warren and his rare friends who knew and evidently valued Old Cadoon would not be long for Middle State. Then, with even the young becoming evermore co-opted, there would truly be no one to recall with favor the venerable insurgent. Old Cadoon would become just some screwball, a misfit who didn't know which side his bread was buttered on.

Brumley for a change opted for the elevators, and when he rounded the corner a black-uniformed, barrel-chested campus cop barely turned his head to regard him as he punched the call button and stood waiting. The short sleeves of the cop's uniform shirt strained against the steroidal muscles of an upper arm as big as Brumley's thigh. He was chewing gum and on his thick belt hung a huge automatic pistol, a club, pouches of ammunition, a canister of pepper spray, handcuffs and a two-way radio. To Brumley's nod he had no response, and when the elevator came and Brumley entered, he walked in after him.

"You're out late tonight," Brumley heartily observed, to mask a paranoid idea that this storm trooper was there in some connection with him, to beat and torture not out of the question.

"Yeah," the trooper replied in a flat rasping voice, not looking at him and chewing slowly, steadily.

"I'm Brumley. Say, did you call me? At home a few minutes ago."

"No."

"I got a call from Security that I was needed in my office. Sounded like you."

The trooper said nothing. Brumley tried to find some detail on the inside of the elevator door to stare fixedly at and appear relaxed and unconcerned.

When the elevator doors opened at the usually-deserted eighth floor, another black-shirted trooper, shorter but otherwise identical to the first, stood waiting, chewing gum. Brumley, fighting down a near-panic, nodded to no effect at him. Should he demand to know what was going on? That would get the cards on the table, except he wasn't sure he wanted the cards on the table. The deck of aces up the sleeves of whoever was behind this could easily overwhelm the meager cards he held, which in fact were not cards at all. He had only the token that he had always done his job as directed by decency and common sense and some unwritten code of his discipline. He knew how feeble, how indefensible such an assertion would be, since his job, as he was too well aware, was officially defined by none of these.

Still trying to appear casually unaware, Brumley headed down the hall to the door for his suite, the two troopers not far behind him.

"Is anything wrong?" Brumley forced himself to ask as he stopped before the door.

"No," one finally said.

"Don't usually see you safety officers up here. First time, in fact."

"We're looking out for people's safety," one said, and Brumley laughed as though the remark was meant to amuse rather than taunt.

"How's Barnes doing?" Brumley said in spite of himself, nervously trying another human link to the uniformed gorillas.

The short one regarded him a moment, then turned to his fellow.

"Bad."

"Bad?"

"Yeah. Fired."

"Fired?" Brumley exclaimed. "Barnes? What happened, why?"

"Unfair ticketing."

"What is unfair ticketing?" Brumley asked, feigning ignorance, his heart sinking.

"It's ticketing unfairly. Computer caught him. Got that Kaneesha broad, too," he said with a harsh laugh. "Unfair ticket fixing, the dumb bitch. Tickets of poor kids."

The computer caught them. Barnes less than two months from having his pension vested, Kaneesha evidently in league with Barnes. Computers would eventually catch everyone, Brumley sensed, except those who controlled those who controlled the computers. No one would be safe. Robin Hood could steal once from the rich and be in the Tower before he could give to the poor; Washington would be penned and taken in Valley Forge, Zapata in the Sierra Madre; the Resistance of the future would hang from the lampposts of Paris without a bridge blown or a Panzer train derailed.

"You need some help?" the shorter one asked insolently as Brumley

387

fumbled to fit the key to his office, then the one to the building, in the suite door lock.

"No, I usually try two wrong ones before I get it right. They're all shaped alike," he said lightly, as though being bullied by two armed, black-shirted thugs was an everyday occurrence of no particular note.

When he finally got the right key and opened the door, the two troopers at least did not follow him through, and to his short-lived relief the door closed behind him. He walked across the white-striped green turf of the foyer and looked down the dark hall toward his office. The door was open and the light was on. There remained only to see the magnitude of what they'd do, and he walked down the hall and stopped in the doorway.

At Brumley's desk, President Curtis glanced up coolly from a single sheet of paper he had been reading. Chairman Cole, his back to Brumley, sat across the desk from President Curtis, a stack of Brumley's class notebooks on his lap. At the file cabinet, Dean Wainwright was pulling out a folder and hardly looked at Brumley, who for once this night felt himself do the right thing. He simply stood regarding them.

President Curtis went back to his reading, shaking his head in what appeared tired recognition that what he read was as contemptibly absurd as he had thought. Dean Wainwright angrily jammed the folder he was perusing back into the cabinet, extracted and opened another one and began to look through its contents. Only Chairman Cole seemed aware of Brumley's presence, almost turning his head to acknowledge him and then clearly unable to continue leafing through the notebooks. President Curtis, after the eternity of a full minute, looked slowly up at Brumley.

"Before you get any ideas that we've broken in your office and are going through your private papers,' he said, "get it straight that this is *our* office, not yours, and that you have no private papers here, only public ones."

"This is not your office," Brumley tried to begin, his throat constricted, heart racing, knowing already that in some official, utterly twisted way Curtis would be right.

"This is a state university," President Curtis went on, "and the state has put me in charge. So I'm in charge of this office. Being here I'm exercising my legitimate—my authorized—authority. You're lucky we even let you use this office, all the trouble you cause around here by showing what a great letter writer you are. And if you're starting to have some notions of turning your misplaced outrage into a lawsuit, forget it. You have no legal basis and if you try it anyway we'll out-lawyer you and the taxpayer will foot our bill. And if violence is crossing your mind, Troopers Hans and Ulrich down the hall would really like to get in on it."

"This is not your office," Brumley tried again. "And if it is, you can't just come in and read my files. This is America."

"It sure is," President Curtis agreed. "That's why, as I just pointed out, we've got to make sure it isn't your office we're breaking into and your files we're reading, but our office that we're inspecting to see that the criminal activities an informer will swear goes on in here are or are not happening."

"Criminal activities," Brumley shrieked. "What the hell are you talking about? There are no criminal activities going on in here. There never have been."

"Maybe not," Dean Wainwright interposed loftily, tossing a folder back in the file cabinet, "but that's what we can say we're here for, to find out—right, sir?" And without waiting for President Curtis's affirmative, went on. "Or, we can claim we simply wanted to support a valued faculty member by establishing he was not having sex with underage girls in this office, as rumor has it. Or that it's a cocaine distribution center. Or a meeting place for devil worshipers. There are several witnesses whose jobs depend on us who will swear to any of these, or anything else we want them to."

"What are you saying?" Brumley cried. "You goddamned pig, what are you saying? None of that is true."

"He's saying you're up the creek, Brumley," President Curtis took over. "Whether it's true or not doesn't matter. You only have to be charged with any of those heinous crimes Dean Fat-mouth here has now stupidly alerted you to and your ass is done for. No one walks away from even a rumor of screwing thirteen-year-old girls, let alone a charge of doing it. Conviction doesn't matter here, except for jail time. And devil worship is almost as bad as sex with underage girls, though not nearly as much fun. No, the media will jump on this, the public will eat it up. If you're charged, Brumley, convicted or not, in six months you'll be sleeping on cardboard in alleys. It's that simple. As for us, we've got enough dodges, covers and witnesses to counter anything you do. So just forget about suing us or attacking us or that this is America. You're through, and that's it."

"Don't forget the mug," Dean Wainwright, blurted, trying to recoup some lost favor and unable to contain himself. "Ratliff in the bookstore said two clerks reported you stole a mug. Or a book. Maybe it was a book about mugs, I don't know. And supplying alcohol on university property to that Warren kid's party, and saying in class that there was no god. And climbing up the smokestacks, against all university policies. Coming and going, troublemaker—we've got you coming and going."

The lies and accusations, more frightening in the range of information and the depth of surveillance they revealed than in the acts they reported or fabricated, left Brumley baffled and trembling.

"But what are you doing this for?" he asked wildly. "If you've got a legitimate reason to fire me, just do it. You don't have to convince me you're ruthless, unprincipled snakes; I know that. But you don't have any evidence against me. There isn't any. And if you suborn witnesses, remember that's a felony. Perjury is, too. I'll fight your corrupt asses and you'll lose. You don't have a thing on me, legitimate or not."

President Curtis looked unwaveringly at Brumley for a moment, then opened the center drawer in the desk Brumley up till now thought of as his own.

"Would you look at this," he said with mock sorrow, still staring steadily at Brumley and extracting from far back in the drawer a packet of photographs. He tossed them on the desk toward Brumley, who saw that the top one was of a slight, beautiful girl of around thirteen, naked and being penetrated by an older man whose face could not be seen but who was built much like Brumley. Cole, who could also see the photo, looked away.

"And what have we here?" Dean Wainwright said with feigned surprise, pulling from the back of the file cabinet drawer a clear plastic bag containing a white powder. "I wonder if it's coke?" he mused, taking out a generous pinch and snorting it violently into his left nostril. "Goddamn!" he cried, his eyes bulging. "I believe it *is*."

"You bastards," Brumley said, and then slowly, carefully, "you slimy, pig-fucking, lying sons of whores."

"Easy now," President Curtis said. "Remember Troopers Hans and Ulrich down the hall. And I'm sure you don't want to add slander to the charges we may bring against you, though that would be the least of your worries. Get too personal, I might trot out the devil-worshiper evidence. Or even worse, make this little tidbit public," and he gestured down at the page he had been reading. "*The Three Lands*," he announced with a sneer. "*The Golden Country. The Land of Commodification. The Watchers on the Ridge.* What a nice little picture. I suppose you're one of the watchers on the ridge, huh? A real hero who of course doesn't do anything but sit on his ass and write trouble-making letters or this useless garbage. Did your eyes fill with tears when you wrote about yourself? This would look good in every mailbox on campus, or maybe your wife and kids would like a copy, if you had a wife and kids. How about the Internet, would you like it published there, for all the world to laugh at?"

"Ah, I'm not sure you can put this on the Internet, sir," Chairman Cole spoke up for the first time. "That would violate university policy. In the Faculty Handbook. . . ."

President Curtis did not look at him.

"You hear that, Brumley? I can't let the world see what a fool you are because it's against university policy." He looked at a shrinking Cole. "*University policy*," he said with utter contempt. " *Faculty Handbook.* Worry about university policy and you'll never have an office much bigger than this bread-box. I'm in charge here, I call the shots, and if I want one policy today and another tomorrow, that's how it is. Maximum flexibility is the term. And if I want this do-gooder's tripe on the Internet, then it goes on the Internet."

"Publish it," Brumley said. "I'm not ashamed of it. And how did you get that? Steal it off my computer?"

"You can't get it straight, can you?" President Curtis said. "Have you forgotten already that this is not your office? Well, it's not your computer, either. In fact, nothing is yours that we can take away from you, and that's everything you've got, including this Three Lands garbage."

"No," Brumley said, "that's mine, it's the truth as I see it. You don't want it and for sure you could never have written it. About all you can do is write those garbled, self-serving memos and letters everyone laughs at."

President Curtis's face reddened and he glared with such animal ferocity that Brumley had to resist stepping back.

"The truth as you see it, " President Curtis said, with great effort regaining some composure. "Well, you see it wrong. This 'Land of Commodification' that you make sound so bad—that's the real promised land. Why do you think everyone lives there? Do you know why your valley of milk and honey is empty? It's because everyone who used to live there got the hell out as quick as they could get off their mule, drop their shovel, get in a car and hit the road. They didn't want to be in the peaceful valley; they wanted lights and action. You make that place sound good to cover the fact that you and all those, those—he glanced back at the page—those 'Watchers on the Ridge' are such losers. There's no place for you. You can't make it in the Land of Commodification and you say yourself the Promised Land doesn't exist. The Promised Land is just that—a promise. Like tenure or Social Security or a pension. Or university policy. It don't mean shit."

"No, you don't mean shit," Brumley said illogically, but the effect was immediate since President Curtis's face, which had lost some of its angry color once he began to pontificate, turned an even deeper red, his eyes bulging as much as Dean Wainwright's, who stood shuffling from one foot to the other, breathlessly following the exchange as he occasionally took another pinch from the plastic bag.

"That's enough, dumb-ass," President Curtis said, seeing the evidence disappear and diverting his rage to the wild-eyed dean. "Save a little for the workings of justice." He turned back to Brumley. "Brumley, and I'm telling you straight, if I don't have your resignation on my desk—my real desk, not this one that I'd be ashamed to be caught sitting behind—if it's not on my desk by noon tomorrow, I won't be responsible for what happens."

When Brumley burst through the office suite door, Troopers Hans and Ulrich, leaning against the wall and chewing gum, stonily followed him with their eyes as he strode past them and down the hall. After he had turned the corner to the elevators, behind him he heard a clipped remark and a quick laugh of derision. Trembling, he punched the button and waited for the ride down.

twenty-eight
FIRE

Warren was dreaming of Kimee Deneen. He was walking with her down a narrow wooded trail above a rhododendron-shrouded stream, sandstone cliffs above them. Mist rose from the unseen water and the green rhododendron and then upwards through the tall, straight-trunk trees, their crowns soaring toward the morning sun whose slanting beams the mist revealed. The small sound of the hidden stream carried to them above the rhododendron, and the songs of birds came from along the stream, from the trees, from all around. They had stepped out on a small point of rock that stood half-way between the stream below and the cliffs above and stood still before the enclosed and secret world they had come to. She looked at him. *I want you to have all this* she said, and it meant the beauty and the shelter of the cove and them beholding it. And then he knew, with a swelling in his breast that might fill and redeem the universe, that she meant also herself and with passion and grace and hope was offering herself to him.

But a bell began to ring and he saw her moving inexplicably from him, back up the trail, summoned, apologizing—it was a phone ringing shrilly, calling her to some much more compelling, much more busy life, and she was drawing away, her eyes sad but helpless, lapsing into a world beyond the green glen, a world where he could not and would not go.

The smell of smoke came to him before the jolting clamor of the fire alarm registered itself, and he was instantly out of the bed and to the door before the ideas of *fire* and *get out* had even formed. The knob was cool and he wrenched open the door only to be hit by a blast of smoke and heat. Instinctively and through an almost dream-like memory of some fire safety talk he had heard as a child, he fell to the floor and found the air slightly more breathable and scrambled out and away from the orange brightness that billowed down the hall just to his right. Yells chorused with the insistent alarm from before and behind him; a door opened as he passed it and someone spilled out and over him and they fought frantically for a moment to free themselves from each other. A few feet further on he scrambled over the twitching legs of a stretched-out body and in his panic thought of helping whoever it was toward the stairwell even as he was driven on by the overwhelming urge to get away from the flames, to get out. At the stairwell door someone had gone through just ahead of him and he pushed through as two others, one bellowing in fear, tumbled through behind him and all lay gasping on the landing. The air in the stairwell was clearer, the flames not visible.

"He's back there," the one bellowing managed. "He's still back there."

Warren felt the door being pushed violently open and someone dragging someone else fell coughing and retching backwards onto the landing and among those sprawled there. It was Jeeks pulling Bolinger, whose unconscious form blocked the door until they all rolled him through, but not before more heat and smoke blasted into the stairwell and they heard the flames. Shouting, part carrying and dragging Bolinger, they descended the pitch-dark stairs. None of the emergency lights had come on and two floors down, where the air was virtually fresh, Jeeks lit his cigarette lighter and frantically tore one of the battery-operated emergency lanterns off the wall. There was no on-off button, just an electronic device that apparently didn't work, and Jeeks dropped the light and returned to Bolinger. "Get under his head and raise him up there; he'll hit his head," Sola said, and they paused a moment. It was coming to them that the fire was only on their floor, and by then those living on floors they had passed were beginning to press into the stairwell. Someone had a flashlight.

"Where is it? Is there a fire? I smell smoke."

"It's on the top floor," Warren yelled. "Look out, we've got a guy hurt. Let us get him down."

Those entering the stairwell behind them had not seen the flames and slowed down, though now the group carrying Bolinger were hindered by those from floors below jamming the stairwell. But there was no panic and they moved down steadily. Bolinger suddenly began to jerk, then gasp and cough heavily.

"You're okay," Jeeks said. "We're about out. He's okay."

"It's all right," Warren added, gasping himself. He and Sola and Shepherd had borne most of Bolinger's weight and were staggering; Jeeks and Hoh were not much better. They navigated the last turn, others helping them now, and went through the emergency door and out into the night air. Sirens could be heard in the distance, growing nearer, and Warren felt time slip and for a moment himself numbly back in his first visit to Middle State and the sirens calling to the Transuranic hot side that belated and impotent help was coming. In a near-dream he helped lay Bolinger, still twitching, in the grass beside the sidewalk. Someone from a lower floor had illogically carried down a pillow and offered it. Warren, who could now see that Bolinger's arms and face were burned, raised his head and slipped the pillow under it. Bolinger, unconscious, continued to cough and jerk.

The fire trucks arrived, then ambulances, and as someone began checking Bolinger, Warren became aware of a milling but largely silent, shocked crowd in the parking lot. He looked up to see smoke pouring out of the windows on their floor and realized, as in a nightmare familiar to all, that he was standing in public, somehow unnoticed, in his undershorts. Then he saw that a large number of others who had evacuated the building were in the same nightmare, and he moved shakily away from the paramedics now surrounding Bolinger and collapsed beside Sola and Jeeks. Shepherd lay further on, and Hoh, hands on his knees, was vomiting beside the dorm. As a paramedic offered Warren an oxygen mask, he saw Bolinger, strapped on a stretcher and tubes running into him, being slid into an ambulance.

"Is he okay?" he managed to ask the paramedic, a small, intense woman who placed the clear mask over his mouth and nose and stretched the strap over his head.

"I think he'll be okay," she said. "You just breathe," and she moved, an efficient angel, to minister to a collapsed Hoh.

The next afternoon Warren sat with most of the other dorm floor residents around a large cafeteria table. Jeeks was occasionally still coughing, as was Mo, whose room was past Bolinger's toward the floor study lounge and who, along with Demumbers, had to crawl through the smoke-filled lounge to the other stairwell. All morning they had milled around the dorm's main lounge, trying to find out what they could as a fire marshal interviewed them one by one to find out what he could. Now they were waiting for Plumb Bob, who had been out visiting the previous night and had not heard of the fire until the next morning when he got the story from Warren and the rest. He had gone immediately to the local hospital, where he knew two nurses well, to find what he could of Bolinger's condition.

"They said he'd be okay," Warren reassured everyone again. "That medic did. It's going to be all right."

"He didn't look too good to me," Hoh said.

"I guess not," Jeeks said. "I don't know how long he was trapped in his room before he got out. He had to run through the fire. It was all in front of his door. When Hoh opened ours, I saw him kind of fall past. He didn't get far, but so much was going on it's kind of hazy."

"And you didn't go out with Hoh?" Sola asked. They had heard Jeeks' story, and everyone else's, but wanted to hear them all again.

"When Hoh went out, I shut the door. Crazy, but the fire was right there. Then I got it together, or think I did—the smoke under the door was bad—and I opened it and got out and down the hall. Fell over Bolinger. He was sort of propped against the wall. Still breathing that smoke. I got hold of him and pulled him along."

"He fell just in front of me when I got out," Hoh added his part. "I didn't know he was hurt. I don't know if I'd have stopped anyway. The fire was going."

"I went past him," Warren admitted. "I didn't do anything."

"Me either," Sola said.

Shepherd, whose room was next to the stairwell, looked at Jeeks.

"I didn't go past him, but I'd have gone on, too. Jeeks, you're a hero."

"Oh, yeah. More like I got no sense. The smoke affected my brain."

"The fire marshal said the ceiling tile was probably where the smoke came from," Warren said. "I thought that stuff was fireproof."

"Fireproof," Sola said, "not smolder-proof."

"When is it Plumb Bob will be back?" Mo asked.

"He didn't say. He's been gone long enough," Warren told him.

"The fire marshal talk to everybody?" Sola asked.

"He asked me about fifty questions," Warren said, and everyone else indicated the same. "I couldn't answer most of them."

"I told him if he had a fire breathing up his ass he wouldn't have stopped to take notes," Jeeks observed. "He wanted to know if I had 'detected the odor of a flammable'. I said, hell yes, I was swimming through it. Then if I saw where the fire was. Yeah, I told him. Behind me."

"He meant gasoline or something. With the flammable thing. They think it was set."

"Think, hell," Jeeks said. "The fire was all in front of Bolinger's door."

"It was," both Mo and Demumbers agreed, and Mo went on: "If it was not by our door or by Jeeks and Hoh's door, then it started in front of Bolinger's door."

"I wonder if we can salvage anything," Sola said. "This is all I've got to wear"–he indicated what he had on. "I'm willing to go a few days, but after that I don't know. I'd at least like to have something to wear to graduation."

"You're lucky you're graduating," Hoh said, who like Warren and Shepherd had been unable to get the courses he needed and faced at least another semester at Middle State. Unlike Warren and Shepherd, his family could afford the extra costs. "Maybe if we don't get anything, you can paint your legs black and with the gown on nobody will ever know you're naked underneath."

"I may have to," Sola pointed out. "Fire marshal said there was just smoke damage and minor water damage except for the rooms next to Bolinger's."

"Wouldn't you know," Hoh said, whose room was evidently in the major damage category. "Clothes, books. Probably the scope's gone, too."

"Surely we'll get reimbursed for our stuff, won't we?" Sola continued to ask. "I mean, there's insurance."

"There weren't any sprinklers or emergency lights," Warren pointed out. "What makes you think there would be any insurance?"

"I didn't hear anything about reimbursement this morning,"

Demumbers said. "Volker—is that his name, the guy that's head of dorms?—he came up to Jeeks and me trying to find out what we'd lost and needed until someone in a suit saw him talking to us and called him away."

"That suit didn't want him talking to us," Jeeks said.

"Who didn't want him talking to you?" Plumb Bob, who had come in unnoticed, asked Jeeks.

"The suit," Jeeks said, and all began asking about Bolinger.

"Stable, he's stable. The burns aren't real serious and his lungs will be okay." And then the only shadow they ever saw on Plumb Bob's chiseled face passed over it. "But it's not good. He's still out of it. His reflexes or something are bad."

No one spoke.

"He has a damaged brain?" Mo asked tentatively.

"They think so."

"Is. . . ." Warren began, but was unable to go further.

"Is it permanent?" Sola managed.

"I don't know," Plumb Bob said. "I couldn't get a straight answer. He's still in a coma. I guess it's a coma—unconscious, Sharon said—same thing."

"But he could come out of it. People do all the time."

"Yeah, he could come out of it."

"Will he still be Bolinger if he does?" Jeeks' question cut through the clamor.

"I don't know," Plumb Bob said. "Nobody knows. There's nothing to do but wait. Now, tell me what were you talking about when I came up—who's not talking?"

"We haven't heard about the stuff in the rooms, if we get our clothes replaced, books," Warren said. "I didn't think to ask. Or I did but I thought they'd say something. They never did."

Many of Middle State's top brass had been at Wilder Hall that morning, though none of the dorm floor occupants recognized any of them. Vice president Dodson of Public Information was on the spot, assessing how many buckets of whitewash might be needed to cover the damage; Vice president Timmons of Student Affairs was there, since students were involved and the word student was in his title; Vice president Gooch of Public Relations came to see that Public Information didn't get all of whatever administrative advantages might accrue; the dapper Vice president Flexner of Recruitment and Retainment was not there but had sent his assistant, the rattle-mouth Calona of Rhetoric, with a packet of scholarships should any be needed and to help Vice president Dodson of Public Information with whatever glossing process might be required; the sheepishly unprepared Vice president Hays of Emergency Preparedness slunk about; Vice president Staull of Academic Affairs was there for visibility's sake; and there were several assistants and various directors present. All were there, all were visible, even prominent, talking seriously among themselves and pointing and generally interfering with the firemen and fire marshal's crew. Even President Curtis had shown up for a moment but had bolted when word of a just-arriving television crew reached him. Television time, usually President Curtis's highest desideratum, could fatally link him with this embarrassing incident and complete the poisoning of his career that began with the Great Chicken Breakout and threatened to be further contaminated by the Too Few Courses distraction.

"I wouldn't make any statements right away," Administrative assistant Larson had told him with real warning in her voice. "We're pretty well covered by Sovereign Immunity, but you never know. A good tort lawyer might find a loophole."

"Loophole?" President Curtis exclaimed. "That Sovereign Immunity was supposed to be loophole-proof. And anyway, loopholes are for us. Little people aren't supposed to find loopholes."

But he knew Larson was right, and after he had ducked the television crew the rest of the administrators had refused comment until the facts of the matter were known.

"Till the facts were known." Plumb Bob said with a disgust unusual for him. "Did anybody say the main fact is that Bolinger's got brain damage and they didn't have a sprinkler system? It's a good thing I wasn't there this morning."

"The fire marshal suspects somebody set the fire," Sola told him.

"Think, hell," Jeeks snorted. "I told you, the fire was in front of Bolinger's door. At least it started there."

"Well," Plumb Bob said, smiling grimly, "there's a fact that ought to relax some assholes."

He looked significantly at the others, who looked blankly back.

"Don't you get it?"

None of them did.

"It gives the big boys a way to wiggle off the hook. There'll be something to blame other than their own negligence. I've seen it all before; the military's got it down to an art, though at least in the service if you're in barracks without sprinklers somebody walks fire patrol all night. On the other hand, you'd better believe we'll get paid for what we've lost. In fact, I'm going to Curtis's office as soon as I eat, and I guarantee you before dark we'll be in the best motel rooms in town with a little walking-around money to boot. Books and clothes don't cost much. To keep us happy they'll give us twice what we lost is worth if we squall loud enough."

"You mean sue them?" Sola asked, shocked.

"No, just be loud enough. Visible enough. Usually they like visibility; on this they won't. Anyway, you can't sue them," Plumb Bob said. "They had a law passed that says you can't sue them. I tried to get this girl I knew to file a suit–a medical records thing. But you can't. So forget that. Anyway, there's no need to for us to sue–just act like you'll never stop bad-mouthing Middle State if you don't get paid and love it if you do, and they'll come across. What they want more than anything is to kick your ass from a swivel chair and for you to love them."

"But what about Bolinger?" Warren asked.

Plumb Bob thought a minute.

"Hard to say. Curtis might be decent, go to see him, to talk to his folks. Maybe even apologize for no sprinklers–you hear they're saying the ceiling tile is where all the bad smoke came from. If there had been sprinklers there wouldn't have been any smoke. So maybe they could even pay Bolinger's folks for whatever they're out–hospital, medicine, whatever. But I don't know. Maybe there's some loophole in the no-sue law, and if somebody finds it and sues and Curtis and his bunch have apologized or even looked sorry, then that would mean they admitted being responsible and would have to pay big. Or the university pay big. Probably it's like with corporations. Corporate higher-ups never pay; I learned that much when I was a Management major. When one of them screws up, shareholders, employees, the little people–especially the little people–they pay, not the big boys. I imagine it's the same for schools when the president screws up. The taxpayer pays. The Bolingers pay."

"What I think," Warren said, "is that if they apologize or pay for Bolinger's being in the hospital it would mean they admit they were in the wrong, and they don't believe they're ever wrong."

"Probably," Plumb Bob said without enthusiasm. "You're catching on. No, Bolinger won't be getting any flowers. Not even a get-well card."

"Wait," Sola said, trying to puzzle it out. "Won't they look awful bad if that gets around–that they don't really care about Bolinger?"

"Who'll remember it besides Bolinger's folks? And they're not rich or powerful, so it won't matter whether they remember or not."

"We'll remember it," Warren said quietly. "I've got some profs who'll remember it."

"Remembering is easy," Plumb Bob said. "Making sure nobody forgets, that's what's hard. So don't count on the profs. Us either. Look, it's like this. Curtis and his bunch can take cover behind whoever set the fire and count on nobody flushing them out or even remembering their part. Believe me, they're circling the wagons and considering their options now–they've all read the Rules for Successful Management. In a few years they'll go on to bigger jobs or a fat retirement. Bolinger's folks will have to take care of Bolinger on their own, until he dies, or they do." He stood up and looked at them with an authority they had never seen him show. "If he's in the shape I think he's in, we better hope he dies soon."

They watched him go toward the back of the food line, nodding with unusual brusqueness to greetings left and right.

"Want to go over to Curtis's office?" Sola asked the table.

"Yes," Warren said.

"The rest of you?"

"I don't know," Hoh said. "I'll wait and see what Plumb Bob gets done."

"They'd deport me to Morocco," Mo said. "I cause no trouble."

"Jeeks?"

"Naw. That's not for me. I didn't have much that was worth anything anyway. They can give me what they want and I'm gone. Maybe I'll join the Marines, like Cantrell. At least if they kill you in the Marines you expect it."

"Don't do it," Warren said.

"Probably won't," Jeeks said.

"Who do you think set it?" Shepherd asked him cautiously.

"Hell, you know who did it. Colson did if anybody did."

"Should we tell anybody about him and Bolinger? The commercial and all?"

"I already did," Jeeks said. "I hope they give him the chair."

Colson got the chair, all right, along with Aimee Brooder, the two sitting proudly ten days later in their cushioned seats flanking President Curtis at the outdoor commencement as the Outstanding Male and Female graduates.

twenty-nine
OUTDOOR CEREMONIES

Up until a few years earlier, graduation ceremonies at Middle State had been wisely held in the air-conditioned basketball arena.

"We should hold graduation ceremonies outside," President Curtis had announced one day to a dismayed Vice president Staull, who, until the subsequent, predictable appointment of a Vice president of Ceremonies and Observances, was in charge of the event. Since mid-May could be uncomfortably warm and rain was always a possibility that time of year, Vice president Staull saw President Curtis's idea for the idiocy it was.

"That would be an excellent idea," he said with enthusiasm, while the need for a large, temporary, raised and sheltered stand for the officials and dignitaries, along with hundreds of extra chairs for the relatives and friends of the students loomed before him. "I wonder if we can count on the weather cooperating?"

"Of course we can," President Curtis said. "It will be May; that's springtime–what is so rare as a day in May? April is the cruelest month, Staull, not May," he continued, looking closely to see if Staull appreciated his broad cultural knowledge. "Anyway, look at this," and he displayed the cover of the latest issue of the *Journal of State University Presidents* for Staull's admiration. It depicted the outdoor graduation of a prominent western college, a large city in the arid valley below it and in the distance mountain peaks against a cloud-free sky whose sun heartened and warmed the large assemblage gathered for the event.

"That's very impressive, sir," Staull said without conviction. "But they can count on good weather out there. After all, they're in a desert."

"A desert? Get off my ass, Staull. Where do you get that idea? Look at those people. Look at the size of that water fountain, that city. That's a golf course over near the mountains or I don't know a sand trap from a sand dune. If they've got a golf course, they've got to worry about the weather just like everybody else. If they're gutsy enough to have an outdoor graduation, there's no reason we can't have one, too."

President Curtis liked the thought of a light spring breeze ruffling his silk academic gown and a beam of sunlight lancing down to illuminate him as he made his speech to the graduating class, and he liked even more the thought of becoming the president of a large, prominent western university that paid its CEO a princely salary and bankrolled his membership in an exclusive country club with year-round golf outings and tee-times of his choice. Holding Middle State's graduation ceremonies outside could be the first real step toward having his educational leadership abilities recognized in a truly career-enhancing way, and he made an immediate executive decision to put Middle State on the map the next year with the first open-air graduation exercise in the state.

The great peal of thunder that accompanied the opening strains of *Pomp and Circumstance* the next spring heralded a storm of such ferocity and duration that the scattered graduates two weeks later received their warped and mildewed diplomas by mail. But in spite of the many outraged letters from disappointed parents, President Curtis could not abandon his vision, and the next year the ceremonies were held, this time in a record heat and merciless sun that resulted in five cases of heat exhaustion in the unshaded crowd, ten in the heavily robed and mortorboarded students and an equal number in the faculty, one of whom, Meyers, appropriately of Abnormal Psychology, went mad and caused an incident that until the Great Chicken Breakout had no equal in tarnishing President Curtis's career prospects. Thereafter, his luck with the weather on graduation day had held, and for this year's ceremonies the radars, thermometers, barometers, and computer models of the National Weather Bureau assured near-perfect conditions.

They could never be perfect enough to reconcile Brumley to what he knew should be a culminating day of attainment for Middle State's seniors, one that he should share with wholehearted celebration and a sense of his own part in their accomplishments. But in truth, graduation day was a torture for him and, he suspected, for more of his colleagues than would ever admit it. Attendance at the ceremonies was not quite required of the faculty, mainly because, for various reasons, enough showed up to make mandatory attendance unnecessary. Some came–many, in fact–for the self-importance of wearing the academic costume of mortarboard cap, velvet-trimmed gown and colorful hood, much as Junior White delighted in donning the hot-side garb. They showed up largely to feel, for once in the year, some sense of distinction and worth. Others of the faculty, hoping with their zestful presence to catch the eye of a superior, came as a matter of course. Had they thought their career prospects would be advanced, Brumley felt certain they would have attended an administratively sanctioned demolition derby, or flea circus, or lynching.

Brumley attended because he thought he should, but each year with a hope that was inevitably betrayed. The situation was much like the opening of every fall semester, when, with a three-week break following summer school behind him, he came somewhat refreshed to the new term, invigorated by the prospects of engaging himself anew with the material of his discipline–easily the most inexhaustible and engaging of all studies–and excited by the young and presumably eager faces in each class. His enthusiasm barely survived the first set of flat, indifferent papers. Graduation day exercises had that same initial air of potential, quickly exhausted once the speeches began. Vice president Staull gave the introductory remarks, followed by a prayer from a local preacher that Brumley and a few other faculty members defiantly refused to bow their heads for. This year, the awarding of an honorary doctorate to Leo Lear would follow; then the Outstanding Male and Female Seniors each would speak. Up until three years ago, all had been capped off with remarks by a visiting speaker, when Grafftee, a famous Middle State graduate and benefactor, the founder of Barely Legal Accounting with diversification into adult entertainment, had staggered drunkenly to the podium for a few disconnected comments before being led away to the great merriment of the students and most of the faculty, including Brumley. Since then, President Curtis had concluded the oratory with remarks that yearly grew more shallow and clogged with cliché.

After the speeches came the interminable awarding of diplomas, a ritual that brought Brumley an unsettling mixture of satisfaction and despair. As the graduates filed past President Curtis to be given his or her certificate, for each that Brumley recognized and knew as actually having been educated, there was another that he recalled being as impervious and resistant to ideas and thought as a glazed brick to water. Some he had taught as freshmen and not seen since, whose presence in the line made him start in dismay that a person of such indifferent and limited ability in academic matters had lasted even a year in college, let alone become a graduate. Increasing his disquiet at hearing those names called was his own uncertainty at his judgments of these students. Who was to say that the least promising members of his freshman composition class were such only because he, Brumley, taught them poorly and that after suffering through the horrors of his class they had found themselves and gone on to successful or at least passable academic careers in Organizational Communication or Home Economics or Social Work or Educational Leadership.

But behind all his equivocation about graduation day was the great question: what did he serve? Was Middle State a benign modern institution that fulfilled its social duties well and even educated at least some of its students to know themselves, to look critically at the assumptions of their society, and to have some knowledge of history, the arts and sciences? Or was it largely a reflection of all that was wrong with the larger society—a roiling vat of careerism and money-grubbing, worthy ideals long evaporated, masking its stench as it grew more rotten with the perfidious perfumes of image building and public relations? Was its function now to educate, or to prosper by encouraging ignorance, not least about itself? If to educate, Brumley felt, it was only peripheral and occasional, and largely by accident. But he wasn't sure.

His ambivalence toward graduation day did not resolve itself as unequivocally as did that of Meyers of Abnormal Psychology, a slight, mild-mannered man of middle years whose decades of study in his field failed to shield him three years ago against the deranging sun that broiled for an hour on the flat, black top of his thin mortarboard. Meyers, spotting through his growing delirium an especially thick-witted and insouciant Physical Exercise and Leisure major in the graduation line about to receive his diploma and be loosed upon the world, felt something ignite and sped raving down the aisle to hurl his frail body in a textbook open-field tackle against the surprised hulk and send him crashing out of line, suspending for a moment the entire procession.

Brumley, who had often felt a similar impulse, was shocked by Meyers' howls of warning and despair as he was carried struggling out by two muscled security associates. But if Meyers' desperate act was shocking, it was also diverting, and its underlying significance was not lost on other faculty members than Brumley, who had wished for some spectacle as enlightening if less traumatic at every commencement since.

"Did Meyers ever get out of the nut house?" Hobart asked as he, Greenman and Norens sat in full academic regalia in the coffee lounge twenty minutes before graduation exercises were to begin. "Looks like a lunatic with a PhD in Lunacy would cure quicker than your ordinary bedlamite—that's bedlamite, from Bethehem, the hospital. . . ."

"We know that one," Norens broke in. "Christ, Hobart, show a little more sensitivity."

"The holy waters of euphemism," Hobart said gaily, "never exorcised a single demon. But you're right. I am a bit hard on our colleague Meyers. Seriously, how is he, anybody know?"

"Walking the streets," Greenman said. "He doesn't live too far from me. Medicated to the eyeballs; walks twice a day. Between him and Stub Weebles you could set your clock. Weebles runs by at seven and four; Meyers walks by at nine and three."

"I hear Weebles has gone into management," Brumley noted. "Head of Signage."

"Head of Signage," Hobart considered slowly. "What an anatomical, mucous-filled vision that evokes. Speaking of management, Brumley, have you heard anything about your case?"

"Nothing. You were probably right. It was all a bluff."

Brumley had simply ignored President Curtis's demand for his resignation and, not quite to his surprise, had received no further commands or threats.

"I thought so. You're like a blowfish to those sharks. Helpless little minnows, they'll prey on them. You've got too many spines, stick in their craws—that's from *crage*, Middle Dutch, throat, by which they don't have you."

"No," Greenman observed sadly, "but they've got me by mine. Curtis has probably forgotten about me, but somewhere his fate for me is in the system. I've got until four this afternoon to accept or refuse the Directorship of Congo Basin African Studies Abroad."

The others were quiet. Greenman's dilemma was agony enough to him without any well-meaning advice on their part.

"How much longer until the festivities begin?" Hobart asked. He was finishing off a large, cherry preserve-filled croissant with a huge glass of milk as a chaser. His gown, stained with a spilled beer he had rushed to without disrobing after the scorching graduation day when Meyers snapped was now speckled with flakes of pastry and one bright red streak of artificially colored cherry syrup, which actually complemented the crimson touches in his doctoral hood. His motarboard tassel, Brumley noticed, was gummed with what appeared to be dried salsa. No one's academic garb at Middle State approached Hobart's in its misrepresentation, though it was assembled without any attempt at duplicity. Most of the administrators who attended graduation and some of the faculty spent large sums on special-order gowns of peacock colors and on the hoods of even greater splendor that draped round their necks and hung down their backs. Their mortarboard caps were sometimes berets or porkpies; one daring and up-to-date assistant professor had even worn backwards a baseball cap, complete with tassel. Any year now, as a bold show of support for cultural diversity, Brumley expected a sombrero or burnoose.

Hobart's outfit, however, was not distinguished by its ostentation or even its spuriousness–in contrast, for instance, with that of the inebriated bookkeeper-pornographer Grafftee of Barely Legal, who on the day of his momentary disgrace had worn a chartreuse gown and scarlet hood ordered for him by President Curtis and proclaiming him a Doctor of Philosophy in Particle Physics from the University of Heidelberg. Instead, Hobart's outfit owed its misinforming uniqueness to its gradual assemblage over the years. Initially, he had worn the simple Bachelor of Arts gown and cap in which he had accepted his baccalaureate, along with the doctoral hood he had later worn when presented with his PhD. He had made use of the gown until it could no longer contain his mature bulk, then had purchased the Masters gown of a retiring spinster of considerable girth and worn it until its dangling sleeves became so encrusted with orts and food stains that it had to be thrown out. He then was given another retiring colleague's doctoral gown; then, his own hood long ago relegated to use as a shop rag, yet another colleague's hood. One of a series of tassels that hung from a tie rack with his three ties completed his wardrobe. This year, Hobart would attend graduation as a Professor of Economics with a doctoral degree in Civil Engineering from Vassar.

"Have you seen the paper?" Norens asked significantly.

The year's final issue of the *Middle State News* traditionally came out the day before graduation.

"What?" Brumley asked.

"Well, let's just see," Hobart rumbled, producing a copy from beneath his gown–reading material for the ceremonies. "I did see a few items that caught my eye. First, there's our dear president's first public comment on the fire. Then. . . ."

"So he's conferred long enough with the university attorneys and public relations department to issue a statement."

"Not a statement. A rant. Against the murderous arsonist who cravenly took the life of an innocent Middle State student."

"No mention of the absence of sprinklers?"

Hobart pretended to scan the article carefully.

"By golly, there doesn't appear to be a single word about the sprinklers, or the lack thereof. I can't believe it. He must have clean forgotten about that little detail."

"They had on the news the other night that our budget request to the legislature last session had retrofitting the dorms with sprinklers twelfth on a wish-list where usually only the first four items are funded. It was behind a new rock-climbing wing to the Wellness Center and a university jet, among other things," Greenman said dryly.

"Ah," Hobart sighed, "a university jet. A jumbo for the football team and to carry the summer junketeers abroad? Or a sleek corporate model, fit only for Curtis and his sycophants? I don't believe our newspaper here even mentions the subject. But there is more. The Outstanding Male and Female Seniors have been named. Want to know who?"

"No," Norens said, "not really. Actually, yes, but once I do I'll wish I didn't."

"Our outstanding female senior," Hobart announced, "is the ever-glamorous Aimee Brooder–I see Brumley is aware of her attainments; you too, Norens. And our superlative male is none other than the entirely detestable Carl Colson."

"No," Brumley groaned. "Colson? Brooder? Great god, how do they pick these things? Colson is the, the. . . ." He sputtered to an impotent silence.

"Think of their progeny," Greenman said. "They're coming in twenty years. Maybe I'll be lucky and be in Africa when they get here. Or dead," he reflected gloomily.

"Aimee Brooder," Norens said with uncharacteristic intensity, "is the most studiously ignorant human I have ever had in class. I'm sorry, but it's true."

"But she has," Hobart gleefully read from the paper, "a 3.4 grade-point average–that's about a B+, isn't it? Colson had a 3.2. Apparently they were greater scholars than anyone thought."

"They're cheats," Norens continued, and Brumley agreed. "At least Brooder is, though god help me, she got a B- in my American lit class."

"Well?" Greenman asked when Norens didn't continue.

"She seemed bright and alert; never said anything, but I thought she took notes religiously. One day during a quiz I walked down her row. She had her open notebook on an empty desk behind her. It was filled with intricate doodles, under the heading 'Henry James'. After the quiz I asked her what was the title of the James novel we'd been discussing for the past two days. She had a copy of it in her pile of books. *What Masie Knew.* She didn't know–the title, let alone what Masie knew. . ."

"I could never figure that out either," Hobart admitted.

"She had no idea. From her demeanor in class, her tests, you'd think she was fairly sharp and involved. How she did well I don't know, though I have my suspicions. She was embarrassed and shocked when I asked her the title. Offended, too, though she kept that barbie-doll smile."

"She'd learned to play the game," Greenman said. "It wasn't right for you to make the game real."

"Colson's worse," Brumley said. "He was in my humanities class last fall. A shameless, calculating hypocrite. Bolinger"–a pang shot through him–"made a fool out of him one meeting. It was wonderful. Exposed the arrogant little twerp for what he was."

"But he's the Outstanding Male Senior," Hobart pointed out regretfully. "And Bolinger's a vegetable. There's a story about Bolinger in here, too. Really about the fire, but a paragraph about his condition.

Not a goddamned word about what a student–what a person–he was. And Brooder and Colson are our outstanding seniors. If you ever had any doubts about how to value these honorable and august ceremonies that we need to get our dilatory asses down to, they should now be dispelled."

"Looks like a witches and warlocks convention," Greenman muttered as the four exited Humanities Hall. A number of robed and similarly tardy faculty members were hurrying singly and in groups into the quadrangle to join the majority of their colleagues already seated. The crowd this year seemed larger than usual to Brumley, perhaps because of the weather. High, but as all the instruments agreed, so far rain-free clouds screened the sun, which coupled with a light wind assured the ceremonies would pass with no heat-induced medical problems. At one end of the quadrangle, the raised and shaded temporary dais that unmistakably grew larger every year held the administrators and dignitaries, along with the two Outstanding Seniors. Directly in front of the dais and stretching back for a considerable distance were the soon-to-be-filled seats for the graduating class, its members now lined up behind the library for their procession into the quadrangle. In a horseshoe-shape around their presently empty chairs sat hundreds of proud and expectant relatives and friends of the graduates, with the faculty seated together half-way down one side. A slight upward slope there gave them an elevated view of the proceedings, one that Brumley would as soon not had since he could not help but attend to the ceremony and crowd. Had only the mortarboard in front of him been visible, he could have given full attention to the abandoned detective novel he had picked up in the coffee lounge.

"Who's that with Huckston?" Norens asked cautiously as they found four empty seats together.

Looking down the way, Brumley was pained but not surprised to see Huckston talking confidently with Bohannon of Theater and Davis of English, both of whom appeared absorbed in whatever line he was feeding them.

"It's Bohannon," he said to Norens. "I hear he's broken up with the woman he was living with."

"She dumped him," Norens said. "Didn't you know? He came home after a weekend retreat with his class and found the house stripped down to the nails. She did leave him some of his clothes and his books but cleaned out their joint bank account. As far as I know, he has no idea where she went."

"Justice," Hobart observed. "At times there is such a thing."

But not, Brumley thought, if Huckston gets Bohannon, which he almost certainly would. He looked over at the pair. Not even the shapeless academic gown could smother one last vision of Bohannon's graceful body, the seven veils one by one floating away. Huckston, self-assured and relaxed, a lock of his lightened hair straying artistically from beneath his motarboard, talked on. Probably displaying his sensitive concern over bathroom signage, alternating for Davis's sake with a few penetrating remarks on *Columbo*.

"Speaking of our esteemed colleague Huckston," Hobart said, "I see he's been elevated into the administration."

He handed his copy of the newspaper past Norens to Brumley; Greenman, on Brumley's left, leaned forward to read it with the rest. News of Huckston's preferment into administration was in a feature titled "New Faces in New Places" that appeared in each year's final edition of the *Middle State News* and contained notice of promotions and transfers within Middle State bestowed by management on the faithful, the news withheld from the rest of the university until the end of the term when the faculty was ready to disperse prior to summer school. It also revealed which Middle State administrators were going to glory in new and distant venues.

"Huckston will be Assistant to the Vice president for Public Relations," Brumley read aloud. "That about caps it. A hack comes home."

"What will he do?" Greenman asked.

"Inflate the trivial," Hobart considered thoughtfully. "Lie."

"You think they'll get any work out of him?"

"Much activity. No work."

"Check this out—Eigleman is now Vice president of Computer Application Enhancement. I hope they've got him a padded office and a good supply of Thorazine."

"Look," Norens pointed out, reading further down the column. "Vice president Hays is moving on."

"What?" Hobart said. "Where to?"

"Good lord," Norens exclaimed, "he's been hired by NASA. As 'Assistant Manager of Earth Orbital Sub-planetary Object Preparedness'."

"Can it be. . . ," Greenman began in wonder.

"Yep," Brumley said with grim satisfaction. "Assistant Manager of Asteroid Preparedness. For NASA. A winner at last."

"But NASA?" Norens exclaimed. "All those scientists and technicians? He doesn't know an asteroid from a hemorrhoid. He won't last a week."

"He's not there as a scientist or technician," Hobart observed archly. "He's there as manager. He'll do well. Are you paying attention, here, Brumley? NASA? The rockets' red glare? Shuttles bursting in overly-humid air? Your day may yet come. The offer may be in the mail."

At this moment the student ensemble's opening notes of *Pomp and Circumstance* pealed out and the four settled back in their seats, Hobart retrieving his copy of the student newspaper and, spreading it widely, continuing to read. Brumley, glancing up from the printed graduation program handed to all on entering the quadrangle, took in the large scene around him as the head of the procession of graduating seniors entered the quadrangle, marched down the aisle that separated the two sections of their assigned seats, and began peeling off to their places. Occasionally he identified a student, but not often. Most appeared self-consciously proud, as they should, he thought. It was their day. However ill-educated, whatever slackers, cheats, barbarians and dedicated anti-intellectuals walked with the honest and hard-working, all assumed the mantle of accomplishment, and, in spite of what he knew, Brumley wished them well, all of them.

Almost all of them. He scanned the program to get some feel for the ceremony to come, then looked to the raised dais packed with robed and capped figures and saw, seated on each side of President Curtis–who was leaning forward to talk down the row to the Chairman of the Reigning Board–Aimee Brooder and the odious Colson, smug and expectant, awaiting the moment they could rise and flaunt their undeserved, hollow honor for the envy of their lesser fellow graduates. Brumley imagined with dread their coming speeches, which could not greatly differ, he felt, from those of the Outstanding Seniors of past years—predictable platitudes or flutey, grandiloquent paeans to their own self-importance thinly disguised as applying to all in the class. None had ever shown a familiarity with any academic or even vocational subject they might have studied, a familiarity that would have moved a large number of faculty, himself certainly among them, to feel not all had been in vain. Surely this time would be no different, and for once he hoped Colson, because he had none, would refrain from showing his learning. A few remarks from him on the Road of Life, the Distant Future, and then a Fond Farewell would lead well into President Curtis's hackneyed Land of Dullness.

To the right of Aimee Brooder was the empty chair of Leo Lear, whose honorary Doctorate of Commerce was to be awarded in absentia, the honorable Dr. Lear having to cancel his appearance due to an urgent meeting to consummate the largest merger in the history of merging, one that would issue in Lear's becoming CEO of Food, Clothing, Shelter and Commodities Unlimited, a global conglomerate of unprecedented scale. Accepting the degree in Lear's absence, and occupying the seat next to Lear's empty chair, sat to Brumley's astonishment and disbelief an academically caparisoned Junior White, delighted by his garb and leering at an enthralled Aimee while with a hardly discernible motion of his head he roguishly twirled his mortarboard tassel with the easy skill of a Las Vegas stripper.

Past Junior White and also on the other side of President Curtis the members of the Reigning Board sat, along with the winners of the Benefactors Club's contribution contest for that year, including the incredibly wealthy alumnus Chinny, who had invented the concept of Organic Gasoline. In the second row were various town and area officials and officers of the athletic Booster Club. Then came the ranks of Middle State vice presidents, twelve out of a total of how many Brumley could only speculate—there seemed to be a new one added monthly, though the apparent growth could be somewhat less given the transfers of individuals within the ranks and the changes in titles that various divisions and areas periodically underwent. Recently, after some accounting irregularities were uncovered in his area, the Vice president for Finance and Administration had been reassigned as Vice president of Administrative Services; and not too long before that, the Vice president for Assessment and Evaluation had been re-titled as Vice president of

Institutional Giving and Trust Fund Establishment. And earlier in the spring, a new one had been proclaimed: Vice president of Enrollment Management. From the opaque soup of the official announcement, Brumley had spooned out the true duties of whatever creature would hold the position. He, or she, would admit to Middle State those who would maximize profits, whether in the form of tuition, grants, state scholarships, future endowments or gifts from grateful, affluent parents. There was no end to it, Brumley thought. In the years since he had come to Middle State, management personnel had gone from a small percentage of overall employees to now outnumbering teachers, a fact, he felt sure, that instead of being acknowledged as a clear and scandalous disgrace would be fatuously defended by Curtis and all his lackeys. Likely, he thought, a new Vice presidency of Administrative Interpretation and Rationalization would be formed and generously funded to counter the preposterous and insidious idea that work was more essential than managing work and workers more necessary than managers.

On the far flanks of the President's row sat several Middle State directors and deans of Middle State's colleges, Wainwright among them. Departmental chairpersons occupied the next row, and in the several rows behind them, this year for the first time, were the superintendents of school systems and the principals of high schools within a radius of one hundred miles of Middle State. Their attendance had been cinched by the only idea of worth ever to come to Vice president Swift of Logistics and Hospitality, one that guaranteed his job in perpetuity. He had lured these leaders of secondary education, who might be expected to direct their students to come to Middle State, by providing for them after the graduation ceremonies a taxpayer-funded luncheon at the sumptuous Alumni Club, featuring a rich and varied menu from king crab to catfish and from filet mignon to hamburger. A free, well-stocked bar was also available, and the plush sleeping accommodations at the Club were thrown open to those unable to drive after the event.

It was all in place, Brumley saw, as the stir of music continued. The last graduates were now entering the quadrangle. The high clouds appeared to be thickening, veiling the sun even more, and, Brumley, almost laughing, thought again of the heat-maddened Meyers, gown billowing around his slight form, bounding through the throng to level

415

the blank, unsuspecting dolt, ten steps from being certified a college graduate. Meyers' act had been for nothing. The graduation line had hardly paused, and before Meyers' shouts of warning died away as he was carried to the waiting ambulance, the target of his desperate act was sheepishly receiving his sheepskin from a sympathizing President Curtis as the audience applauded his resilience and determination. Brumley suddenly thought of Bolinger and saw again that hand flash through the fog of some dreary class to signal that a mind, brave and alive, was ready to ride. Warren was sitting on one side of Bolinger in amused admiration, while Kimee Deneen, radiant and warm, listened attentively from the other. But Bolinger would receive no diploma, not today or any day. Nor would Warren be in line, though he said he would attend to see his friends graduate. There it was. Aimee Brooder and Colson the Outstanding Seniors, while Warren and Bolinger, both of whom demanded to know, were denied the procession, Bolinger denied forever.

Brumley came back to the present, the strains of *Pomp and Circumstance* dying away and a stir of both resignation and anticipation moving through the crowd. Even those unacquainted with such proceedings—many of the graduates were the first in their family ever to attend college—sensed that their moment of pride would be only a moment in a long, numbing and unavoidable ceremony. For Brumley, who wondered if he could feel pride in any graduate, only the boredom loomed ahead. As Vice president Staull moved to the podium to open the event, Brumley extracted his borrowed detective novel from beneath his gown, knowing that in spite of how much murder and complexity it contained he could not keep himself from listening to most of the coming speeches. Staull, however, was clearly under instructions to limit himself solely to welcoming all in attendance, pointing toward the general course of the proceedings and then introducing the preacher—no more. Brumley opened his book. To his horror, he saw that it had been assigned in one of Colona's rhetoric courses and had been heavily underlined, apparently at random and almost completely. He began trying to read.

thirty
GRADUATION

Across the way from the faculty section, Warren sat with Kimee Deneen, both largely silent as the crowd had grown around them and the graduates filed in. He had come to realize that increasingly he could be near Kimee Deneen without a sense of dumb wonderment or panic.

"Are you coming back next semester?" Kimee Deneen finally asked.

"I don't know. Maybe."

"Have you seen Bolinger?"

"Last weekend. At his house. We rolled his chair outside–me, Sola, Jeeks, Hoh, all of us. Even Plumb Bob. He seems to like being out, I think he does. Mostly ,though, he just sits there."

"Oh god."

Warren nodded.

"His folks. When we were about to leave his mother had us get together for a picture, and then to have some cake she'd made, and then his dad wanted to show us around the yard and then look at some of Bolinger's old papers and high-school class projects. It was like if we left, Bolinger wouldn't have anything. We're going back tomorrow, mainly for them. Bolinger doesn't know it's us."

Warren knew their visits would grow less frequent with ever fewer of the group coming each time. With summer break and some of the dorm floor members graduating, such would be inevitable. But that aside, Bolinger would gradually be forgotten, except by his parents who, Warren could see, would always love him. But he, Warren, by god he would visit regularly, or would write if he couldn't. What if it were your parents and nobody came to see you?

"About coming back here," he said, "probably I won't. I don't know what I'd do if I graduated."

"You should come back," Kimee Deneen said. "You're smart. You are."

"Thanks," Warren said, comforted in spite of himself for the first time since knowing Bolinger's condition was permanent. "But I'm not too smart. If I was I could figure out something to do. I mean, something worth doing. I'm not sure there is anything."

"You know there is," Kimee Deneen said. "You could be a teacher. Or anything–a doctor or a nurse–really, guys are nurses now. Or a carpenter."

"I think I'll be a revolutionary," Warren said, smiling now under her concern. "Except that never seems to work. Maybe I'll go into advertising."

"Like Bolinger's commercial?"

"Yes. The guerilla ad man. Like Bolinger."

They were quiet a moment, watching the graduates coming in.

"Have you seen Dr. Brumley?" Warren asked.

"No, have you?"

"Last week. He said he might not be here next year; the president has it in for him. It was those letters he wrote for me. I'm not much luck for anybody lately."

"It's not your fault if he's in trouble for trying to help you. You deserved help."

"Maybe."

"Why is he in trouble anyway? Can't you write a letter? It's a free country."

"Not really."

"Besides, he's a good teacher. He cares about what he teaches. I like him."

They surveyed the crowd, Warren scanning the faculty across the way to see if Brumley had come.

"Look, there's Colson, by President Curtis," Kimmee Deneen said, looking toward the dais.

"I saw him."

"Aimee Brooder's on the other side."

"Yes," Warren said.

"They'll both make speeches."

"That goddamned Colson."

"What?"

"He set the fire. I know he did."

"Do you have proof or something?"

"He did it. If you'd seen him when he came up to get Bolinger over the commercial, you'd know. He'd have killed him then if the rest of us hadn't been there. Believe me, he did it. Now he's Outstanding Senior. Stupid and cruel bastard. He won't have a problem finding something to do. And he's graduating on time."

"It's not your fault. That you're not."

"I know. But if Colson had been in my place, he'd have graduated. He'd have taken five directed studies courses or managed to get the courses he needed approved with only three people in them or had some other courses substituted for the required ones. He'd have found a way. Middle State was made for him. He wouldn't be Outstanding Senior if it wasn't. Same for Aimee, in another way. She's a body–I mean," he said quickly clarifying himself, "she's just here, whether she learned or even heard anything in class. She counted in the enrollment figures."

As the student ensemble came to the end of *Pomp and Circumstance*, Warren and Kimee Deneen turned to watch Vice president Staull welcome all in attendance before calling on the preacher. There would be more before the Outstanding Seniors spoke, and more afterwards. It was Colson Warren was waiting for.

Brumley did not bow his head or even remove his mortarboard as the local preacher, certain he was in a den of secular relativism and heretical religious diversity, boldly took the martyr's stance and prayed an unabashedly Christian prayer with many references to Jesus before taking his comfortable seat. Vice president Staull next introduced President Curtis, who secretly felt that after such a prayer the Lord surely would part the lowering clouds and ray down a beam of sunlight upon him as he stepped to the podium. When none appeared, after a brief stern survey of his audience, he began.

"Graduates of Middle State; parents, friends and relatives; honored guests, I welcome you to this signal day in the lives of those sitting out here before me after four years of toil and application. Before we recognize two of them—representative, we hope, of them all—we wish first, by the direction and with the approval of Middle State University's Reigning Board, to honor one of Middle State's great supporters and benefactors, Mr. Leo Lear, with an honorary Doctorate of Management."

Taking his cue, Vice president Staull arose from his seat and carrying a resplendent hood came to stand by President Curtis.

"Even as I speak," President Curtis said wistfully, " Mr. Lear is on his way to China in his own jet, speeding to finalize a trade deal and merger that will result in benefits to the entire world. Accepting this honor in his absence is his representative, Augustus White, Jr."

Junior White, alert and waiting, stood eagerly and with his mortarboard cocked rakishly, stepped to the podium, grinning proudly at the audience and accepting with unrestrained delight the showy, many-hued hood draped over his head by President Curtis, who had to call him back from his strutting return to his seat to receive the actual certificate conferring Lear's honorary degree, the only degree of any kind Lear had ever been awarded.

"Now," President Curtis resumed, "as is fitting, we wish to recognize this year's two Outstanding Seniors. Indeed, all of our graduates are outstanding. . . ."

"Right!" Hobart agreed emphatically from past Norens. "Thirty-seven percent are graduating cum laude, eight percent summa. They're brilliant, absolutely brilliant."

". . . .and we salute them all," President Curtis continued. "Chosen as Outstanding Female Senior this year is Aimee Brooder. Graduating with honors and a 3.4 grade point average, Aimee is not only an outstanding student but participated in many extra-curricular events, programs and activities, far too many to mention. . . ."

In spite of himself, Warren across the way saw the beautiful body caught again in the reflected light from the strobes. One extra-curricular activity she didn't get credit for, he thought.

". . .far too many to mention if we're ever to get these diplomas out before dark. Without further to-do, I present you with this year's Outstanding Female Senior, Aimee Brooder."

Aimee arose and moved to the podium, standing quietly for a

moment to see that the text of her speech was being clearly projected on the teleprompters President Curtis had installed for her and Colson, though for his speech he had ordered they be turned off. Aimee's appearance was tarnished only slightly by the clear indication that being admired by over three thousand strangers was the high point of her life. She looked out at the assembly, smiled and tossed her magnificent hair, and began her speech.

"Three years and eleven months ago, when I first came to Middle State for my Summer Orientation visit–or Summer O we like to call it–I did not know what college life would be like. I was from a small town, and while I was active in many aspects of high-school life, I did not know what to expect in the much larger and more demanding world of higher education. Today, I would like to think back briefly on what I, and most of we graduates today, were those many years ago when we first arrived here, and what we have become while at Middle State. Think along with me.

"Summer O–what an exciting time! Groups of we freshmen were introduced to seniors who were to guide us around campus. I remember Greg, our crew's guide, who later was to take me to my first fraternity event, leading us from the Student Center to see the many sights around campus. We passed several artists specially invited by President Curtis for the occasion with their little painting stands and paint board things with a hole in them, painting beautiful pictures of trees and buildings. I knew then that I was in another world from that of my early days. We then went to see the Faculty Softball Game, where I realized that college teachers were not just serious thinker-types but could be ordinary people like everybody else–though some of them, we found out, knew all kind of things we had never heard of. Then we saw the different science laboratories and visited all the other buildings. It was all new to me, and I felt I was in a new and wonderful world, one that would make me into a different person than I had been."

From the graduates' section Brumley heard a garbled voice call out something about a TV-commercial star. Aimee, whether she heard it or not, went on, smiling, unperturbed.

"Then came the start of classes! My first ones were a shock, and I feel they were to all of us. Unlike high school, where you had to go to every class every day, in college you don't, and if you're not careful, it's easy to just not go to class when you don't want to and fall behind before you know it. I struggled that first semester because there was so much to do—rush and dating and parties and all the things that take us away from our true goal of getting a degree. But gradually we all found out how to fit our studies in with our social lives, and while I was not a perfect student I did manage to graduate with honors. I have many of my teachers here at Middle State to thank for that.

"Today we come to an end of our stay at Middle State. But I will never forget the good times I had here. Middle State has made me what I am. My dream continues. I now hope to earn a law degree and then go into public relations, specializing in crisis management. That dream is well on its way to being a reality, but it couldn't have been without you, my instructors and many friends who make up in part this university, which is the third best value among institutions that award the Master's degree of all upper mid-south and lower mid-west former teacher colleges as rated by a prominent news magazine—Middle State University."

There was warm applause from the larger crowd and from the dais, less from the graduates, much less from the faculty, many of whom were very still. Hobart chuckled loudly. Brumley sat in shock. Before this stunningly beautiful, self-assured young woman he and many of his colleagues had spread the hard glories of Western thought, none of which had made the slightest impression upon, had even penetrated whatever assumptions—or was it instincts?—that shielded her like tungsten. What had gone on behind that face, a rival even to Kimee Deneen, when in his British literature class they had discussed—who?—*every writer* he had assigned? Not one, not a single work of a single one of those visionary men and women of the last two hundred years showed anything but pity or contempt or fear for all that Aimee aspired to be or be a part of. And none of their compassion or fear or scorn had evidently even registered with her, not Blake, not Shelley, not Arnold, Dickens, Woolf, Orwell. She had majored in literature, and yet the material had evidently been of no more significance to her than a series of pointlessly random numbers. When their works had been discussed in his class—and American lit was even more condemning— *what had gone on in her mind*? And then her dream. To be a public relations hireling, specializing in "crisis management." Did she hear the trumpet of such a calling at Middle

State, a calling to serve the masters by covering up their crimes? Was this a result of her education?

Before he could assimilate the full, vertiginous horror of it all, President Curtis, still applauding, had retaken the podium.

"Thank you, Aimee. I believe we can all see why you were named an Outstanding Senior. If Mr. Lear were here today, I believe you would have your future assured. He's always on the lookout for personnel who show such promise and who can work well under him to help his firm grow. But you don't get all the honors today. We have the other Outstanding Senior yet to go, and without taking any more time—at least until it's my turn—I'd like to introduce as our Outstanding Male Senior, Mr. Carl Colson. Carl, step up here." And he shook Colson's hand and patted him warmly on the shoulder as they passed.

This, thought Brumley, his spirits sinking even further, should *really* be something. Colson positioned himself at the podium and looked out confidently at the hushed crowd.

At that moment, the sound of a perfectly timed, jeering fart cracked from the seated graduates in front of him, followed by the heroic stifling among the students, and many of the faculty who were in the know, of a mighty, collective laugh, a jumbled noise that grew and endured for some seconds and that left Colson, his face reddening with anger, briefly unable to go on. As the disturbance gradually faded, with only an occasional hysterical relapse from a student here and there, Colson swallowed his rage, gathered himself, focused on the teleprompters, and began.

"President Curtis, members of the Reigning Board, and honored guests—I would like to be adult for a moment and thank. . ."

A quick, high-pitched fart of indignant protest shrilled from further back in the student ranks and Brumley, struggling like most of the faculty and students to retain some sense of decorum, could barely keep from pitching forward onto the grass, doubled with laughter and clutching his sides until he had to be borne away. With considerable effort he managed to restrain himself again, grateful for the quivering gowns and jouncing tassels around him that showed he was not alone in his deliciously juvenile response. To his grudging admiration, he saw Colson, almost shaking with fury, collect himself and begin again, this time without the sarcasm.

"As I say, I would like first to thank those who have named me Outstanding Senior. There are many others, some of who are tragically not with us today, who might have been considered worthy of the honor. To be chosen over them is a recognition I will always cherish. This morning I would like to turn to some knowledge that I and all of the seniors here learned while at Middle State to underscore a crucial piece of advice in living."

What? Brumley thought. Was Colson about to do what no Outstanding Senior had ever done and display a familiarity with something he had learned while a student? Across the crowd, Warren, too, came alert. It did not seem possible.

"We all know," Colson continued, "that we should strive to make this world a better place in which to live in. And there is no better way to make the world a better place to live in than through teamwork. And there are two figures from history—two famous figures—who can show us how important teamwork can be. The first is Socrates, the great Greek writer. Now Socrates, as we know, had been told by Delphic Oracle, one of the Greek gods—in those dark ages people thought there was more than one god—that he was the smartest man in Greece. Of course, he wanted to live up to being ranked number one, so to keep current he went around to people in different career fields and tried to learn what they knew. Finally he thought he had learned enough and went into philosophy and became one of the most popular philosophers the world has ever known, even if his life style was a little weird. Nevertheless, he is, as we all know, still widely read today."

Brumley sat in disbelief. Should he surrender now to a different kind of hilarity? Or should he heed the same admonitory voice that Meyers did and race along the aisle, leap to the podium, wrestle Colson down into the dirt? Since he graded all tests without looking at the student's name on the booklet cover, Brumley never knew who had written the demoralizing answer to his question on the *Apology*. Now it was clear. Colson, of course, who had also ignored Brumley's lengthy, careful note pointing out all his answer's misconceptions and distortions. He looked around him to see the reaction of his colleagues to Colson's imbecilic babble. To his right, Norens sat wide-eyed, while Hobart, to the disgust of Huckston and Davis down the way, now laughed openly. Mulholland of Psychology sat with one hand shading his eyes, shaking his head, and Talbot of Biology whispered animatedly to a vigorously agreeing Conners of Chemistry. Stephens, absorbed in editing what was likely his Rats in Literature study, was paying no attention to any of the proceedings. Sitting together, as befitted a research clique of such recognized superiority, Wyandotte, Mill, Critson and Jenkins seemed mildly annoyed and puzzled at the disrespect shown by some of their fellow faculty members toward this fine address by an award-winning graduate.

"But Socrates could never have accomplished all he did on his own," Colson went on. "It took teamwork. All of those people Socrates learned from did their part, and Socrates knew it. His going to them for knowledge and advice, even though he was the smartest man around, is an example of how we should live today. Everyone should work together as a team to make this a better world.

"Now another great figure who believed in teamwork was Machiavelli, another great writer. Machiavelli came from Italy, which is not far from Greece, and wrote a book called *The Prince*, which was like an instructional manual that gave good advice to those who wanted to be successful in the field of leadership. He was fair, like a real team player, and when he gave advice to those future leaders who wanted to know how to act in a given situation, he always gave them a choice before he told them what to do. For instance, he said that a leader could be liberal and give out grants and welfare, or he could refuse to tax and spend and instead let the market take care of people. Machiavelli said it was best to let the market take care of things. Even though he wrote this many years ago, his advice is still good today, because last year in my Managerial Economics class Dr. Leo Lear, who was just honored today, spoke as a guest lecturer on just this point that we don't need the government taking our hard-earned dollars and spending them on needless projects or on those who won't work.

"But mainly Machiavelli stressed teamwork. For example, he said that to have a strong country—which means everyone should work together as a team—the leader should not be doing everyone favors but should enforce the laws that everyone has to obey. When he is seen as a strong leader, everyone else will be strong. In other words, he is like the president of student government or the captain of a football team: when he or she is strong, the whole organization is strong, and teamwork is again seen as important."

Brumley was incredulous. Colson was not even making sense within his own inconceivably garbled misreading and misapplication of *The Prince*. He looked again around him. The dismayed were now aghast, the accordant still enthralled.

"But Machiavelli believed in more than teamwork in his country and his government," Colson careened on. "He believed also in teamwork when it came to God. He thought that more than anything a leader should show he was religious and should be like his subordinates and go to church regularly and pray, not just in church, either, but even on the street corner if the need to pray hits him."

Hobart's agonized groan could be heard well out into the student section, some of whose occupants, to Brumley's immense gratitude, seemed as appalled at Colson's fatuous perversions as Hobart was. Even the preacher on the dais appeared uneasy. Oblivious, Colson went on.

"A whole country—or organization of any kind—under proper leadership and working as a team can accomplish anything. The sky's the limit. Let me give you one last example from our own time—this one a little sad—that shows how important teamwork can be in everyday life and what it can do.

"As most of you know, a little over a week ago a tragic fire at Wilder Hall here at Middle State left Eric Bolinger, who would have graduated here today, with brain damage. None of us who stood watching that fire that night will ever forget the emotions we felt. The thought of Eric trapped in his room was too horrible to think about, but today we must think about it if he was not to have suffered brain damage in vain. That night as the inferno raged, several of us in the crowd discussed breaking through the police lines to help Eric."—Colson paused to allow the import of his nascent heroism to sink in— "But cooler heads held us back. These cooler heads were team players. They knew that if they let anyone return to that raging inferno, not only Bolinger would have suffered brain damage, or even been killed. Those people saved lives. We should honor them just as we do Machiavelli. In life in general, teamwork, with good leaders, can make for a better world."

Only a coordinated, audience-wide breaking of wind could redeem this, Brumley thought, while at the same time he sensed something was wrong, some strange inconsistency that he couldn't quite grasp was buried in Colson's narrative of transparent self-praise. But someone else did. From across the way, came a clear shout:

"How'd you know he was trapped in his room?"

Of course, Brumley thought–that's it. He looked across the sea of mortarboards toward the point indicated by the turned heads and craned necks but could not identify the source of the challenge. Colson faltered only a moment before remounting his hack.

"In closing, I would like to thank Middle State for all it has done for me. When I came here five years ago, I was young and not interested in the great questions or in helping make our world a better place in which to live in. Today, like Aimee said–or does–I have a dream, and with further education, I hope to have it come true. Next fall, after I have traveled abroad this summer in Middle State's Graduates Abroad program, I intend to pursue an advanced degree in Educational Leadership. My dream is to someday help others to have the same quality education that I have had here. I hope that my dream–like the dreams all of us have–will come true. Working together as a team, we can see that they do. Thank you."

Before the obligatory applause could begin, from the same area as the shouted question, a loud boo hooted out, joined by another in a higher register. Brumley looked again and this time saw Warren and Kimee Deneen standing, their hands cupped around their mouths, hooting and yelling at the now discomposed Colson. "How'd you know, Colson–how'd you know?" rang out over the bewildered and embarrassed crowd.

As he passed Colson on the way to regaining the podium, President Curtis briefly reassured his Outstanding Senior, then angrily signaled to someone behind the seated audience where Warren and Kimee Deneen still stood, booing and shouting. Suddenly Trooper Ulric and another campus cop were making their way toward the pair, and reaching the row where they sat, motioned for the two, who ignored them, to come along. From the podium, barely controlling himself, President Curtis announced:

"It looks like we have some radicals who disagree with the idea of teamwork. While they are escorted out,"–looking at Trooper Ulric he jerked his head toward the periphery of the quadrangle–"I think we should give Carl here another round of applause to show that we are behind him—as a team."

There was a solid wall of applause as Trooper Ulric moved menacingly down the row, where to Brumley's relief he saw Warren, who had sat back down, rise and with Kimee Deneen following him walk unresistingly out ahead of the muscular trooper, who followed expressionlessly, chewing with his ponderous jaws the dab of gum he was apparently never without. The sight of the defenseless and unresisting pair escorted by the black-uniformed goon curtailed most of the applause, and Brumley was sure he even heard booing from around him as the disruptive pair was removed. As they disappeared behind the crowd he swung his gaze back to President Curtis at the podium. He could hate that man—a man who he had seen first hand would stop at nothing to assure his privileged position, or maybe just to preserve his ever-precarious sense of superiority. It didn't matter. Curtis would lie, threaten, frame, likely hire a murder—too chickenshit to do the deed himself—and all to be head of a place like Middle State! Or some other, similar place, it didn't matter what or where. In some incomprehensible way he was even proof against his own paltry ambition, his heartlessness, his bungling. Only someone more base than he was could ever displace him.

From behind the podium, President Curtis watched Warren and Kimee Deneen being escorted out, a thrill of fear spangling through him as he recognized Warren—and with a luscious beauty, too, the undeserving little bastard—as the troublemaker behind the whole Too Few Courses crisis, a mere student who on principle wouldn't let his bread be buttered, and he thought of circumspectly approaching Troopers Ulric or Hans about simply disappearing the bothersome malcontent. Obviously Warren was the kind that wouldn't scare; he was like that Brumley, a real troublemaker who hadn't even resigned when faced with overwhelming evidence of his perversions and crimes that Curtis was too fearful of being exposed as manufacturing to use in preferring charges against him. Warren might be as hard to intimidate as Brumley; in fact, President Curtis remembered, they were in league with one another, Brumley wrote letters detailing the injustice done Warren and others, letters that threatened the smooth running of Middle State and Curtis's own comfort. It was a conspiracy, he felt sure. Maybe he could get the troopers to disappear Brumley in the bargain, Brumley and that fat, unkempt friend of his—all his friends for that matter. With effort, President Curtis forced himself back to the moment. He recalled that he was still president, still commanded the podium, still stood sternly watching the fledgling co-conspirator being dismissed at his orders from the assembly. Why be concerned? They might never be back. Brumley might yet cave in and offer his resignation from fear of disgrace. Indeed, why worry? He took a deep breath, raised his head, and in his mind quickly ran over the opening sentence of his speech. The teleprompters had been switched off. He was on his own. He was ready.

"Just a little disruption. Free speech is the hallmark of a university, as they say. But now, ladies and gentlemen, friends and families of our graduating seniors, and honored guests. I want to welcome you today to the meaningful part of Middle State's outdoor spring commencement ceremonies, ceremonies that seem, if you consider their appellation carefully, to be terribly misnamed. For today signals the completion, the end, of most of our graduates' education, while the word commencement means, not an ending, but a beginning!"

"Commencement. Homophonous with co-mincement," Hobart said informatively. "The utterance of commonplaces with affected eloquence."

"And truly today does mark such a beginning," President Curtis triumphantly deduced, "a beginning of a new life for our graduates here arraigned before us. It will be life in a world much different from that of only a few years ago, and indeed, change, more and more rapid change, is the sign of our times. As an example, consider that only a few years ago computers were distant mysteries to us, often the subject of stories and movies where they were presented as threats to take over the world and control human lives. Today, we know how foolish that notion is, and many of our graduates not only own one and spend large parts of their day in front of it, but plan lives designing or programming or selling them, or of using them in various ways in their careers. Here at Middle State we have gone to great lengths to see that all our students are literate in computer usage and can use the many resources computers make available to us, not just in the schools and workplace but in the privacy of our own homes. Like television, computers have proved to be a great technical innovation and tool for learning that will change the face of the world, and I am proud to say that Middle State is on the cutting edge of this triumph.

Brumley sighed. There was no hope. His eyes down, slowly he stood, then looked up sadly out over the crowd. He turned around toward his seat. Carefully, he removed his mortarboard and smoothed his hair.

"And it is not only in computers that we have seen great changes in our time, but also in. . . ."

President Curtis fell silent. His silence lengthened. There was no apparent reason for it, no interrupting catcalls, no insulting hand-held sign, no faux farts. Nor did he see Brumley. The audience, which was somnolently drifting along with his well-modulated tones, began slowly to tense with unease.

He had lost his place, had forgotten the next great change he intended to ring down. Knowing how impressive it was to rise before an audience and appear to speak extemporaneously and without even notes, President Curtis always memorized his speeches and practiced giving them exhaustively until his delivery sounded impromptu, as if he were accessing a great throng of thoughts and ideas, ordering them, then easily marching them out. But there was a problem. If he lost his place, he was screwed, and he had lost his place. The more desperately he sought for the track that would lead him back to his train of thought, the further the train hooted into the tunnel and the darkness grew.

The silence extended a puzzling five, a disturbing ten seconds, while Brumley, wondering if the silence was directed at him but no longer caring enough even to look around, deliberately placed his mortarboard on his chair, straightened up, and began unhooking his hood from his gown. At the podium, the tunnel finally opened up and President Curtis caught his train and resumed his journey. He made no sign anything had been amiss.

"--Science. There have been many scientific advances in our time that would seem miracles to our forefathers and foremothers. Atomic power, to take but one example, while it has its well-meaning but misguided critics, has given us energy to light our cities and rural areas, to air-condition our homes and places of business and work, and to run the many modern, labor-saving appliances that brighten our lives."

"Who wrote this for him, General Electric?" Hobart asked casually, his voice carrying over most of the faculty section. He was watching

Brumley—as were many—who now slowly removed his hood and began folding it neatly.

"At Middle State," President Curtis continued, "we are proud that our Transuranic Department is a part of this great thrust and is doing its part to see that even the waste products of atomic energy are recycled, for the good of the ecology. Thus is nature tamed while at the same time it is enhanced, something unimaginable to past generations."

Brumley now unzipped his gown and sorrowfully stepped out of it, then folded it, with care.

"Take it off," Hobart said in rhythmic delight, but in an undertone, "take it all off."

"Biology, too," President Curtis went on, "has seen many marvelous advances in just a few short years. From the discovery of DNA, which I'm sure you all have heard about on television, has come a multitude of benefits as scientists have realized how life forms can be genetically improved for the betterment of mankind—and perfectly safely, I might add."

Brumley lay the folded gown on top of the hood and turned to look at the podium. He had missed nothing Curtis had said, not one stale witless word. Shaking his head sadly, he excused himself to an unnecessarily alarmed Greenman, and moved past him. Norens and Hobart watched him go.

"Excuse me, excuse me," he continued to say quietly as he edged on down the row, the startled, apprehensive faces relieved—and a few disappointed—to see that nothing disruptive seemed imminent. President Curtis, slicing along on the cutting edge of popular assumption and ignorance, vaguely noticed someone walking out on his eloquence, but continued.

"This genetic modification, joined with breakthroughs in agriculture, has resulted in high production meat and egg yielding units that can be raised in mass, and in vegetables—tomatoes, for instance–that can be shipped for thousands of miles, even across oceans, then be stored for weeks and still taste just like they did when they were picked. In these areas, too, Middle State is doing all it can to see that these scientific endeavors are encouraged and supported in order to wipe out hunger around the world. Our Center for Life Form Enhancement and our Leo Lear Chickens Unlimited Poultry Complex are successful and growing enterprises that have the support of our business leaders throughout the country. Famine and starvation, two of nature's greatest disasters, are well on their way to being vanquished, and Middle State is on the forefront of their rout."

The sweep of his metaphor filled President Curtis with pride, and pausing to let the audience fully assimilate his eloquence he suddenly recognized the figure slowly making its way through the faculty section toward a side aisle and then unconcernedly passing along it away from the assembly. It was Brumley, Brumley, walking nonchalantly, insolently out on this stirring speech, on this solemn ceremony, a thankless troublemaker who didn't know which side his bread was buttered on–walking out when he knew of, had even seen, the undetectably falsified photographs that could be used to send him to prison for having sex with a thirteen-year-old girl. President Curtis's mighty confidence sagged, his mind faded out for a moment, and again he lost his place.

"Finally," he managed, "the two talks–speeches, the fine words from our two Outstanding Graduates, or Seniors, of a moment ago–."

When he did speak impromptu, President Curtis usually botched the job, and this time he was fortunate to recover his place without another seemingly aphasic gap in his delivery.

"Workers, workforce, yes–these two outstanding talks, most important of all they remind us of the workforce necessary for the world of change that is everywhere around us. It is a workforce whose members live in a shining Land of Commodification and who must be ready to be retrained in our educational system at a moment's notice to meet the challenges of the ever-shifting job market that science and innovation create. It is a work force that must be mobile, that must be ready to relocate from place to place, for unlike the past, when people often lived their entire lives in just one place and held one job, today the average person moves eight times during their lives and holds four jobs. So today we must be ready to pack up and move out to new horizons, to the Golden Country, the Promised Land, as the job market dictates. Take Miss Brooder, here," he said, turning in a dangerous deviation from his speech to beam at a quickly alert Aimee. "She may be in public relations for a firm on the East Coast for awhile, and then find herself in a year or two on the West Coast, controlling a crisis there."

He again lost his place, but instead of turning back to the crowd he continued to gaze with a broad smile at the exquisite face of Aimee, desperately seeking the path back to his speech and unaware he appeared more and more to be lecherously transfixed by the juicy piece and unable to tear himself away. An amused and appreciative murmur from the student section and some uncomfortable shifting along the row of Reigning Board members brought home the impropriety of his stare at the same time it shocked him back to his lost place.

"Yes, Aimee will undoubtedly move around," he said, as the chairman of the Reigning Board winced and frowned and Hobart's laugh of sheer delight joined the heightened buzz from the students. "And so will most of our other graduates. And all will need to be professionals, which is what coming to Middle State has prepared them for. They will need leadership abilities, and all will have them, for their time at Middle State has trained them all to be leaders. The administration and faculty here are like Watchers on a Ridge, guiding our students below us to the right paths of accomplishment and self-realization. Soon, even more Middle State students will be guided yearly as next term our new pilot program of shortened class periods begins."

Having now reached the edge of the seated crowd but still within hearing of President Curtis's amplified voice, Brumley stopped for a moment, incredulous, and then moved on.

"So with science giving us the tools, and training giving us the managers and work force to use these tools, we may be sure that a bright future awaits us, one where Mother Nature serves us predictably and well, and human suffering, even discomfort, will be no more. And now, ladies and gentlemen, without further to-do, I give you the work force of this new world, the Middle State graduating class, who will now receive their diplomas."

Vice president Staull and the Vice president for Registration moved forward to stand by the tables stacked with diplomas, while President Curtis remained for a moment at the podium to bask in the polite, obligatory applause. It was then that the first impertinent drops of a slowly escalating, eventually steady and soaking rain tapped playfully on his stylish, silk mortarboard.

Skirting the crowd and hoping to intercept Warren and Kimee Deneen, the thought of President Curtis's speech almost crushing him with despair, Brumley lifted up his face and felt the drops with a satisfaction approaching joy.

thirty-one
RECESSIONAL

Walking slowly, Brumley reached the head of Gingko Walk. The light rain had become steady, its soft fall muting behind him the graduates' names being called in alphabetical order by Vice president Staull as each graduating senior had his or her ten seconds of recognition. They were through the G's. Six hundred and forty-eight of them, the program had said, almost two hours to herd them all through. Far down the way, beneath the now-closed library's portico, he saw Warren and Kimee Deneen talking. Before they saw him, Kimee Deneen walked away, Warren lifting his hand in farewell and watching her go in the rain. Brumley stopped, the rain unnoticed falling on him, and remembered her distracting, youthful beauty in his humanities class, then thought fleetingly of Kaneesha, then of Norens back at the ceremonies, the rain sifting down on her. Warren, he hoped, maybe he would have some luck. He was modest, kind-hearted, non-conforming– ambitious to make a living, not a killing. It would take luck.

He saw Warren turn away from the receding form of Kimee Deneen, then move back to stand under the portico. Brumley, too, watched the distant figure of Kimee Deneen until she disappeared behind a row of blooming shrubs; then Warren caught sight of him and waved, waiting while Brumley passed under the interwoven, sheltering arbor of the gingko trees, branches now beautiful with their fan-like leaves, their wasted, rotting fruits still months away. In their native place, Brumley thought, the trees fit all year-round; on ill-chosen ground they were largely a nuisance.

"Hey," Warren said. "Did you leave early?"

"Not early enough."

"Did you see what happened—with me and Kimee Deneen?" he asked, a little uneasily.

"Yes. Good for you. I heard you, too. Anyone got any proof against Colson?"

"I don't know, but you heard what he said. How'd he know Bolinger was trapped unless he knew where the fire was, and how would he know that unless he set it? Isn't that enough? He said it in front of three thousand people."

Youth, Brumley thought. They actually believed a clear indication of being a criminal meant something.

"I don't know," Brumley said carefully, again about to teach the youth to doubt. "He could say he was speaking retrospectively, that he was afraid someone might be trapped and later found out it was Bolinger. Then projected that back on his memory. After hearing that speech, would anyone doubt a little confusion there?"

"But he hated Bolinger. He hated him. We all saw him, he wanted to kill him. And the fire was set in front of Bolinger's door."

"I'm not sure motive is enough to get him. Even along with a slip like he made, even in front of three thousand people. Besides, even if the details of the fire haven't been made public, Curtis would probably swear he told Colson all about them. But you still did good to put it to him like you did," Brumley quietly added. "It'll make him sweat."

"I don't know. President Curtis didn't seem to catch it. He threw us out and patted Colson on the back. I saw him."

"President Curtis," Brumley began, then paused. Why keep it up? President Curtis, he wanted to say, is Colson matured—even more arrogant and self-aggrandizing, but also more adroit at hiding it.

"President Curtis," he said," you're right, he probably is on Colson's side."

"But somebody ought to do something about Bolinger. You can't just murder somebody, or try to. It would have been better," Warren said, his voice breaking, "if it had killed him."

Brumley looked out and up at the two smokestacks, their incessant warnings pulsing through the rain. "Yes," he said, "it would have been better."

"It's not right."

"I know."

"So there's nothing we can do, I can do."

Not, Brumley thought, if you want to lead a life that's easy, pleasant and decorous. If you do, then how soothing to realize nothing can be done. What a relief mock despair can be, how disburdening of commitment, how sanctioning of apathy with a clear conscience.

"There's plenty you can do," he said. "You could press the police or fire marshal or whoever might be looking into it—go to a newspaper. You could do that, tell them what you know."

"Jeeks—he's on our floor—he already told the fire marshal about Colson coming by to get Bolinger for the commercial."

"That's good; maybe if you contacted the marshal and told him independent of your friend—and had others tell him. Keep on him, or them. Bolinger's parents might do the same, though I imagine they have enough to occupy them."

"I can do that. I will."

"Maybe do your own asking around. Has anyone tried to find out what Colson did, where he was that night? Or at least before the fire?"

"An alibi," Warren said, "does he have one?"

"He probably does," Brumley said, "but you might look into it." He was certain Colson would have an alibi placing him on the moon, or probably in church, when the fire was set. "But don't bet things will come out right. All you can do is try. Anyway, you're already doing something—you've done something—even if there's never any justice for Bolinger."

"What do you mean?"

"You've stood up to Colson, the little shit," Brumley said, more vehemently than he intended. "You called him what he is in public. In considerable public. You let him know you weren't afraid, that somebody was on to him. He'll never get over it, not completely. The Colsons of the world only make it because everyone else is too decent to call their bluffs. When you and Kimee Deneen—maybe especially Kimee Deneen—were willing to stand up in front of a crowd and disrupt a solemn, official event to tell the truth, you were doing more than you know. Even if you were afraid."

"I'm still afraid. It was graduation."

"I know," Brumley said. "Ceremonies. The Colsons—and the Curtises—they count on ceremony, propriety, decorum to keep you quiet.

437

That phony fart somebody made when Colson started his 'speech'–
nothing is more terrifying to power than that. Do you understand? A
few well-timed farts at Nuremberg and Hitler would have ended his
days in a nut house. I exaggerate, but you get my drift."

"Yes," Warren said, smiling. "I think it was Sola, the first one–he's
a friend, on my floor."

"That's good. The more the merrier. The point is, never let the
Colsons and the Curtises rest. If you ever say there's no use in opposing
them, that it's not worth upsetting yourself to do so, then you deserve
them and you make it likely they'll endure and prosper. And make
things miserable, as long as things last."

He looked again at the mighty towers through the mild spring rain.
In the distance, muffled, Vice president Staull was still calling names.

"Which may not be very long." he said. "I should have done more
myself."

"You've done a lot," Warren said. "You tried to help me. Really it
helped everybody to show they didn't have enough courses for people
to graduate on time. Showing how things really are–you've got to do
that. If you don't, it'll be like Bolinger said, that we're ending life and
we know it, but at the same time we refuse to know it. I think you did
plenty."

"Maybe," Brumley said. He couldn't tell Warren the consequences
of his evidently failed attempts. In fact, he wasn't sure what the
consequences were. That he had been threatened, that he had been set
up for disgrace or even prison, that there was apparently nothing Curtis
and his gang wouldn't do or condone to keep their power—those things
he didn't want to reveal. But if he encouraged Warren to resist injustice,
shouldn't he tell him there was a price?

"You know I may not be here next year," he began.

Warren looked at him, slightly embarrassed.

"I'm not sure yet. Curtis very much wants me gone. I'm not sure I
don't want to go. If I thought things were better anyplace else, I would
go. Maybe," he said wryly, "I need to be retrained or redefined. You didn't
hear Curtis's speech. Big on work-force mobility, relocating, retraining.
What a world he advocates. Everybody a lost nomad, corporate chattel–
allegiance to a paycheck. But we'll all be happy because science will
eliminate hunger for those who can afford food and will give us gadgets

and big houses to take our minds off our minds. And there's a Curtis everywhere, at the head of every Middle State in the country. It's hard to get away."

Warren was quiet. He didn't mean to pry. No one wants to hear a person talk about losing a job or failed choices. And Brumley was a professor; he was a mere student. A professor, or any adult, talking to a student about losing his job wasn't how it was supposed to be. Even worse, try as he would to think otherwise, Warren felt himself the cause of Brumley's problem.

"You ought to keep teaching," he said sincerely. "Kimee Deneen said you were good. Everybody does. You were committed."

"Thanks, thanks a lot. I appreciate that. But anymore you can't teach outside the system. That was over with Plato, or Socrates. . . ."

"The great Greek writer?" Warren quipped, and Brumley laughed with him.

"Yes, ranked number one. Have you ever heard such stupidity? I thought Aimee Brooder's speech was bad. Colson's was worse. Machiavelli, the team player. I couldn't have been much of a teacher if their speeches are any indication of what they got from my class."

"No," Warren said. "There are some people who don't get anything out of any class. Either they're not able to or they don't want to. It's not your place to get them to care, not in college—maybe not anywhere. Why is it that no one expects everybody to be great at sports or even care about them? It's no different with school, with doing good at school or liking to study, not really."

"You're right, but there's an enormous establishment that depends on convincing everyone that there is a difference, that differences in physical abilities are obvious but everybody's mental abilities are about the same. It's the racket, the combine. And like I say, you can't teach outside it."

"Why can't you?"

"Well," Brumley said, and stopped.

"I don't see why you can't," Warren said.

"First, you've got to eat."

"You could work at something else part time. If you don't buy gadgets, you could make it."

"Even if I could live by my ideals, which I see are coming back to haunt me," Brumley said, smiling at Warren, "who'd come to learn? I couldn't give official credit or a degree. To teach, you've got to have students."

"But you might get them. Maybe good ones."

"If I had a Nobel Prize, I might attract some," Brumley said. But I don't. And what about facilities?"

"You wouldn't need much. You wouldn't have to have computers. Einstein didn't have one. He did a lot better than the ones who do."

"You know," Brumley said, catching the spirit, "you've got a point. You don't need a modern building with central heat and air and projection screens and cable TV. A barn might do. A barn and some chairs or even bales of hay, and some chalk and, and a slate—no, wait, there ought to be plenty of blackboards around that computers have displaced. I could go high-tech and get a blackboard. Socrates didn't have a blackboard, did he; he didn't even have chalk. Just a free mind and willing students. But we'd need a faculty. I'm not the wisest man in Greece so I'd need some help in other fields. There might even be some at Middle State—Talbot could teach biology, Conners chemistry; there're others, I'm sure there are. Maybe we could even find a barn beside a sacred grove, how would that be?"

"Sounds good to me," Waren laughed. "When do I sign up?"

"The only problem, though, is what you'd do once you'd learned all you could there. You wouldn't have a certificate. How would you live? What kind of job would you get?"

"I'd get a job I could live with. That's why I'd go in the first place. Isn't that what an education is for? Not just to get you a job, but to show you what jobs are worth having. And to consider what kind of life is worth living. Anyway, I'm not sure what I'd do if I graduated from Middle State, or what I'd want to do. I don't want to spend my life doing something that I finally can just barely stand, or that I can't stand myself for doing."

"Yes," Brumley said. "Anymore you're lucky to be able to do something you even like doing. I thought at first I was the luckiest person imaginable; I was going to teach what I'd always loved. But then there was the racket. One way or another I had to get involved with it. But there's always the barn and a piece of chalk, isn't there? If I had the nerve."

They were silent for a moment, the rain softly falling and the names of the graduates, now to the W's, coming to an end.

"Listen," he said, "go back to Middle State and graduate. You're free. You'll be above them. Life is a compromise—Socrates never said that, but it is. It's the degree of compromise that matters, though everybody who thinks about it believes they didn't give in much, at least not where it was important. You won't give in where it matters, that I'm sure of. But you don't have to listen to me; you know best what to do about going back and graduating. I shouldn't advise you on something so important."

"At least you're advising me," Warren said. "Most of the time my advisor wasn't even in his office—he was in Spain or somewhere."

They both smiled at that. Brumley looked out at the rain, still coming down steadily. By now every academic gown from the thin, rented ones of the seniors to the thickest most ornate robes of the administrators would be soaked through, and the calling out of student names, now to Young, still went on. Even on the dais the administrators and dignitaries must have been uneasy, watching the graduates and their friends and relatives' growing discomfort while they sat dry and sheltered. When the world was right, the students and guests would have a roof, the administrators taking their chances with the weather, along with the faculty, who had to in any event. Down the way, construction was well along on the rock-climbing wing of the Wellness Center. The smokestacks stood ascendant. He thought of Old Cadoon.

"Any plans for the summer?" he asked Warren.

"Work. Laying brick. A friend of my dad's a contractor."

"I can't lay them, but I could carry them. Pay OK?"

"Pretty good."

"Could a man live on it—if he didn't buy gadgets?"

"Sure."

"I may need a job," Brumley said, and down the way a great cheer of pride and relief broke out as the student ensemble struck up the Recessional. Graduation ceremonies at Middle State were over. School was out.